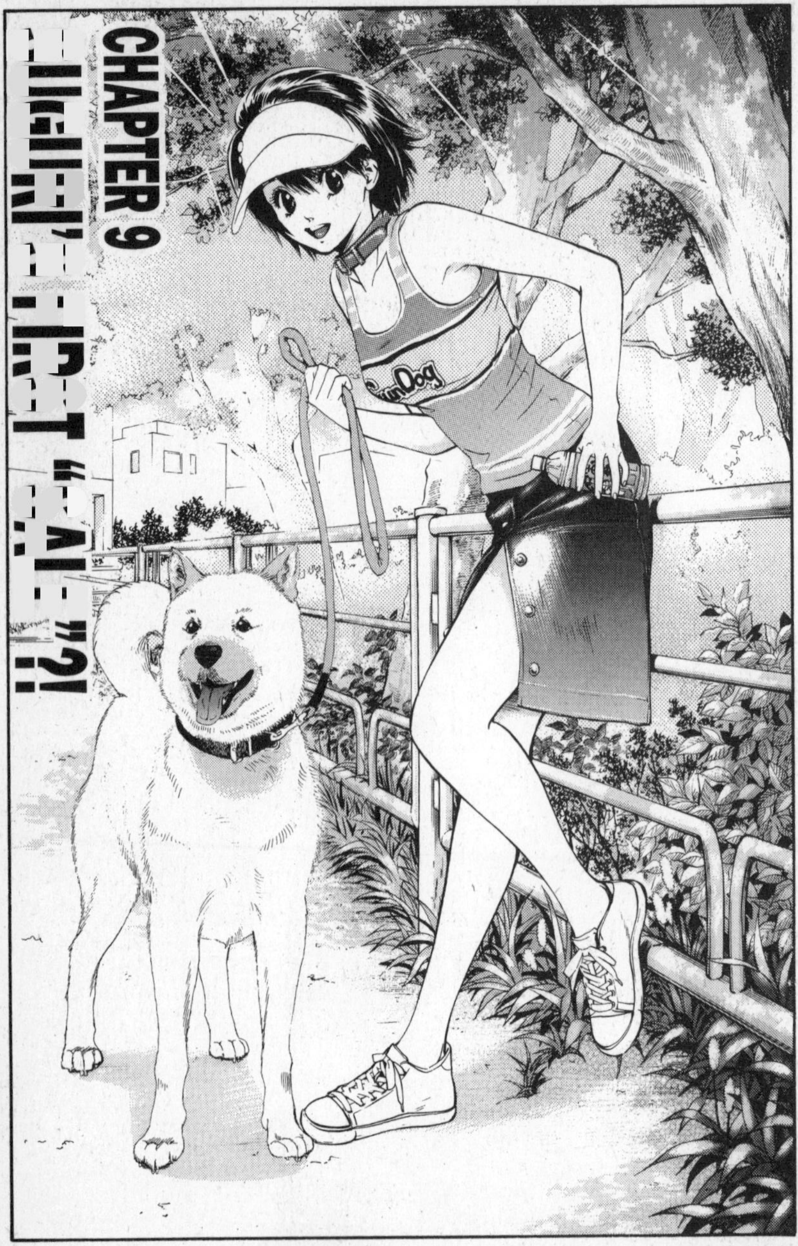
CHAPTER 9

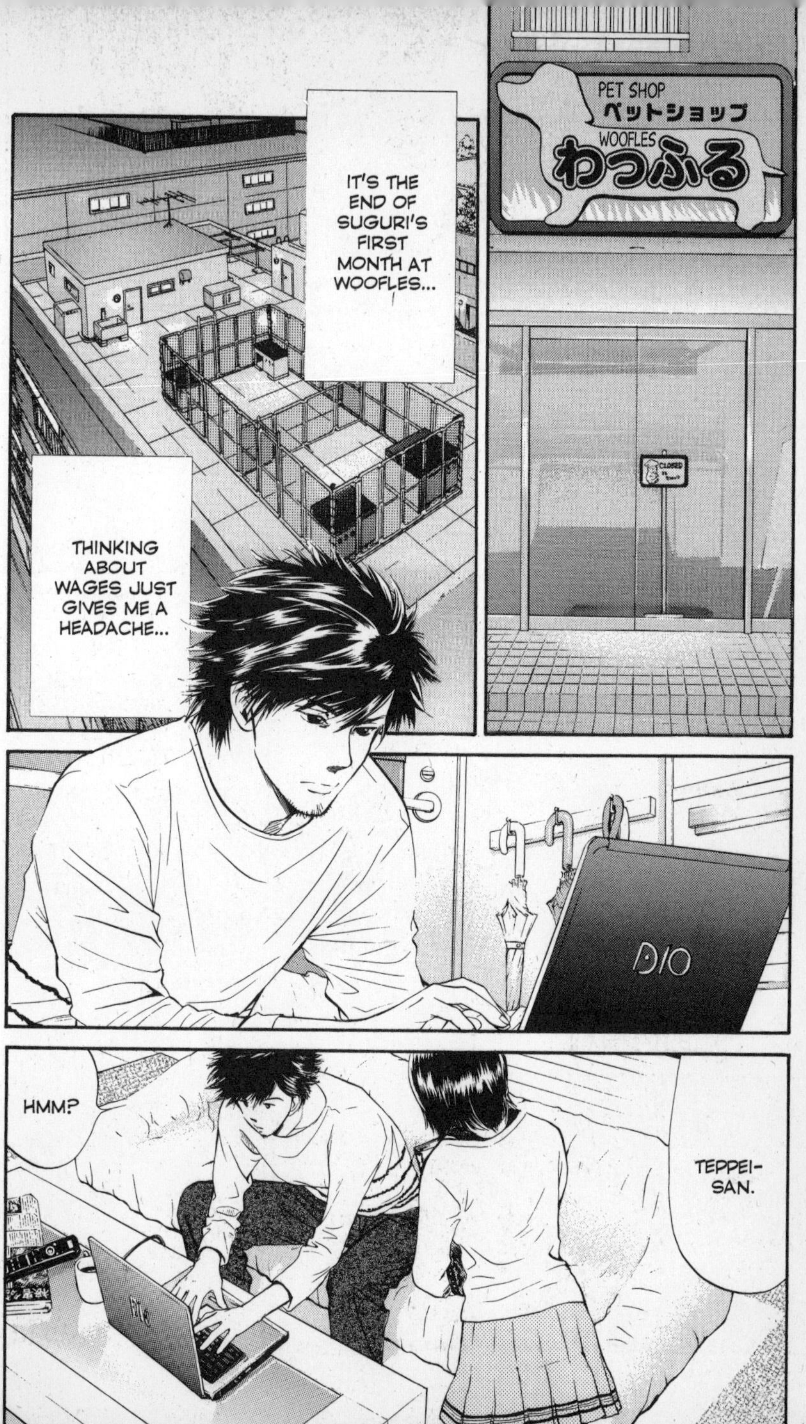
PET SHOP
ペットショップ
WOOFLES
わっふる
IT'S THE END OF SUGURI'S FIRST MONTH AT WOOFLES...
THINKING ABOUT WAGES JUST GIVES ME A HEADACHE...
DIO
TEPPEI-SAN.
HMM?

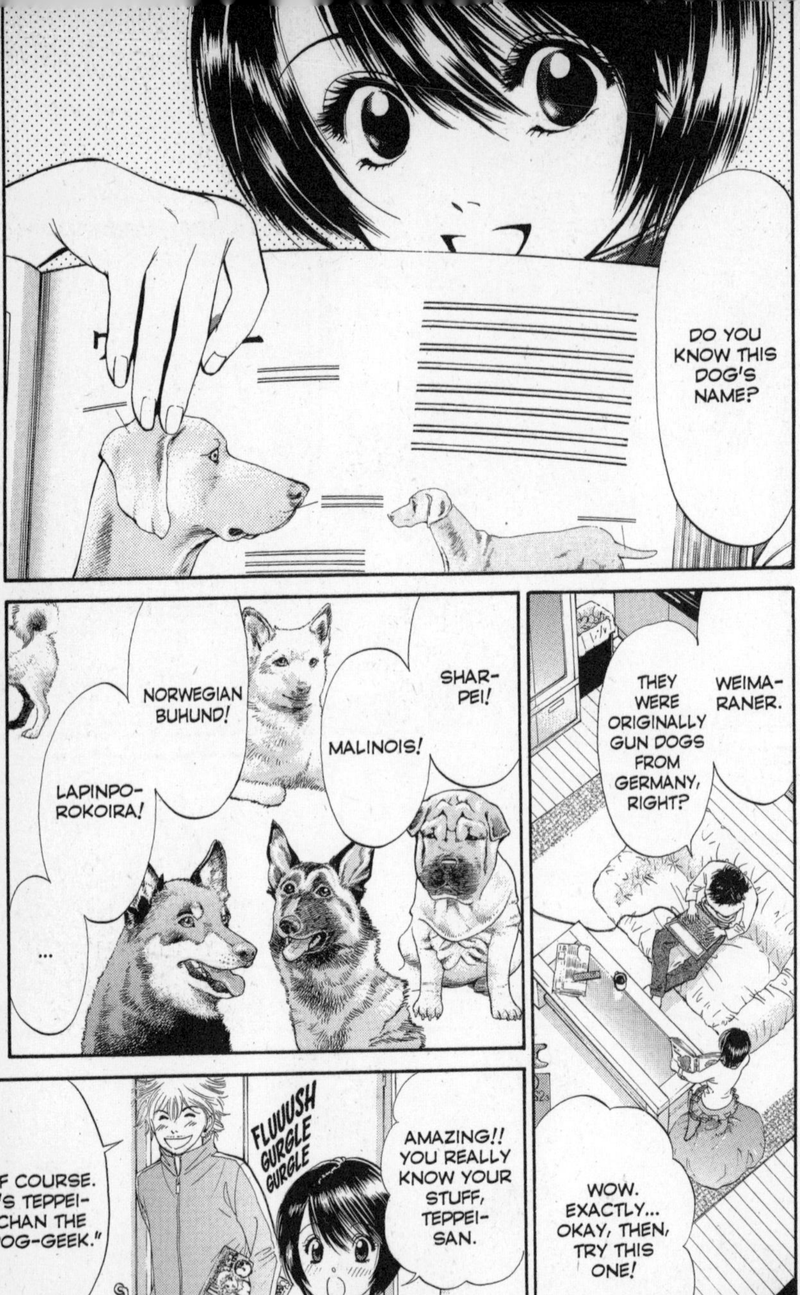
DO YOU KNOW THIS DOG'S NAME?
WEIMA-RANER.
THEY WERE ORIGINALLY GUN DOGS FROM GERMANY, RIGHT?
WOW. EXACTLY... OKAY, THEN, TRY THIS ONE!
SHAR-PEI!
MALINOIS!
NORWEGIAN BUHUND!
LAPINPO-ROKOIRA!
...
AMAZING!! YOU REALLY KNOW YOUR STUFF, TEPPEI-SAN.
FLUUUSH GURGLE GURGLE
OF COURSE. IT'S TEPPEI-CHAN THE "DOG-GEEK."

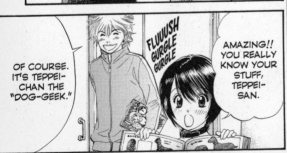

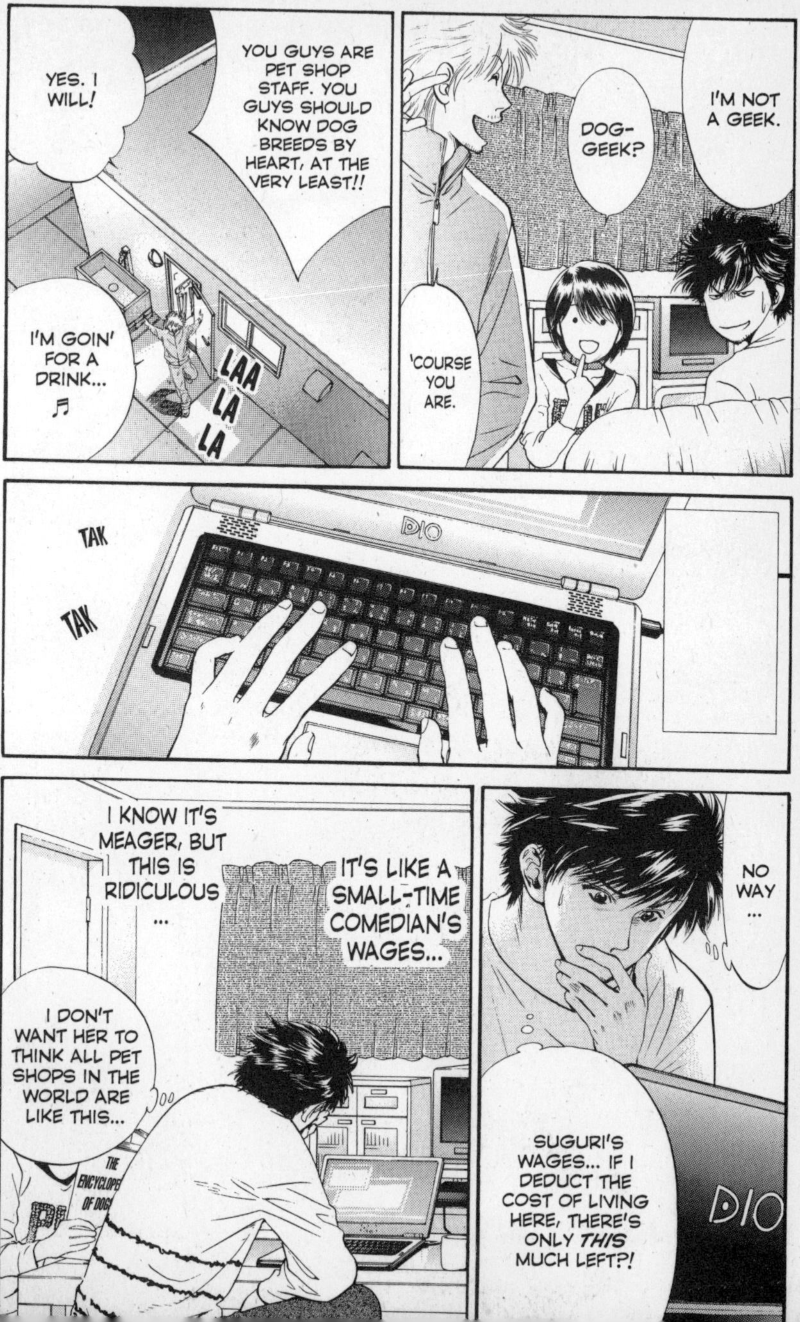
I'M NOT A GEEK.
DOG-GEEK?
'COURSE YOU ARE.
YOU GUYS ARE PET SHOP STAFF. YOU GUYS SHOULD KNOW DOG BREEDS BY HEART, AT THE VERY LEAST!!
YES. I WILL!
I'M GOIN' FOR A DRINK... ♬
LAA LA LA
DIO
TAK
TAK
NO WAY ...
SUGURI'S WAGES... IF I DEDUCT THE COST OF LIVING HERE, THERE'S ONLY *THIS* MUCH LEFT?!
DIO
IT'S LIKE A SMALL-TIME COMEDIAN'S WAGES...
I KNOW IT'S MEAGER, BUT THIS IS RIDICULOUS ...
I DON'T WANT HER TO THINK ALL PET SHOPS IN THE WORLD ARE LIKE THIS...

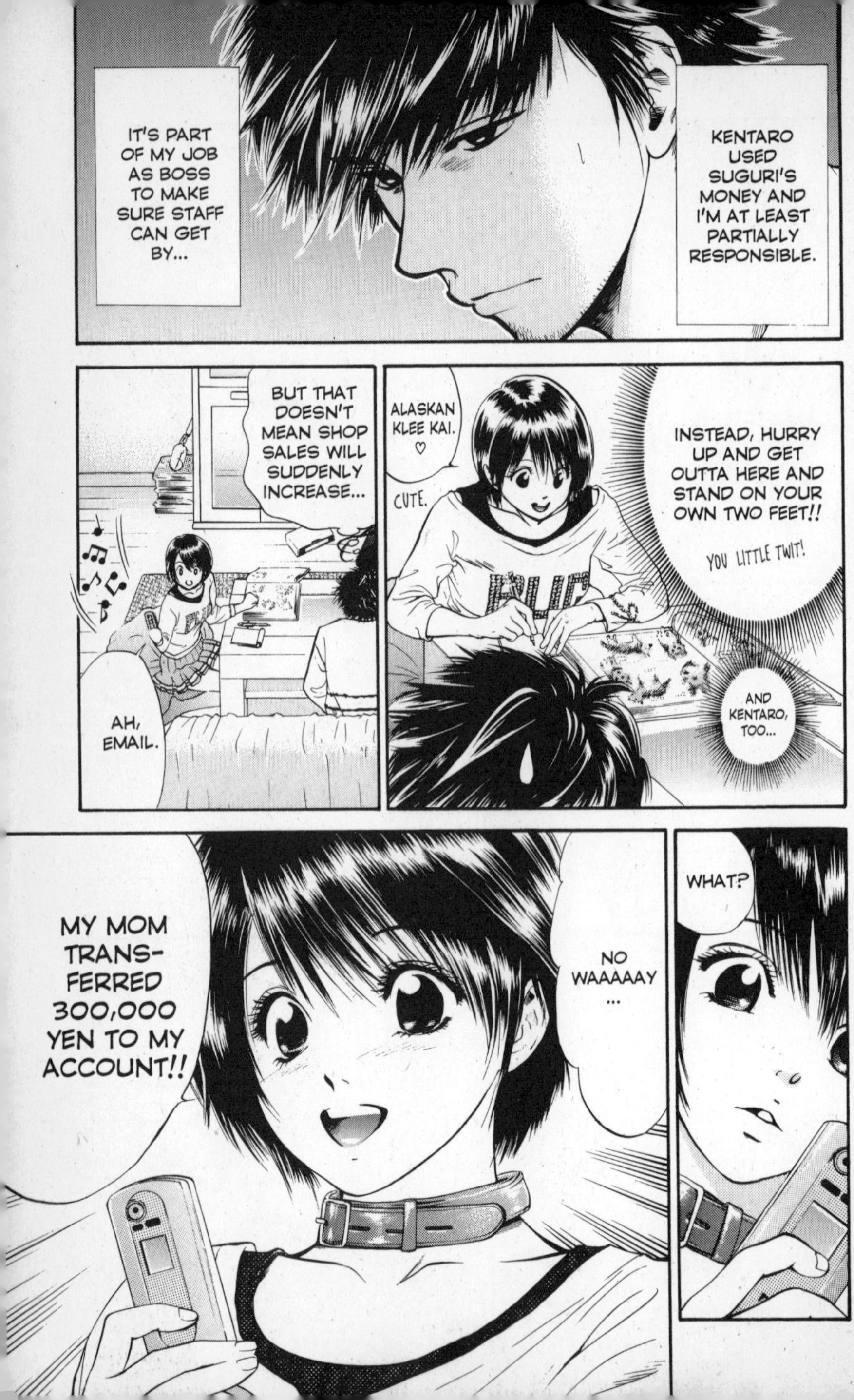
KENTARO USED SUGURI'S MONEY AND I'M AT LEAST PARTIALLY RESPONSIBLE.
IT'S PART OF MY JOB AS BOSS TO MAKE SURE STAFF CAN GET BY...
INSTEAD, HURRY UP AND GET OUTTA HERE AND STAND ON YOUR OWN TWO FEET!!
YOU LITTLE TWIT!
AND KENTARO, TOO...
ALASKAN KLEE KAI. ♡
CUTE.
BUT THAT DOESN'T MEAN SHOP SALES WILL SUDDENLY INCREASE...
AH, EMAIL.
WHAT?
NO WAAAAAY...
MY MOM TRANS-FERRED 300,000 YEN TO MY ACCOUNT!!

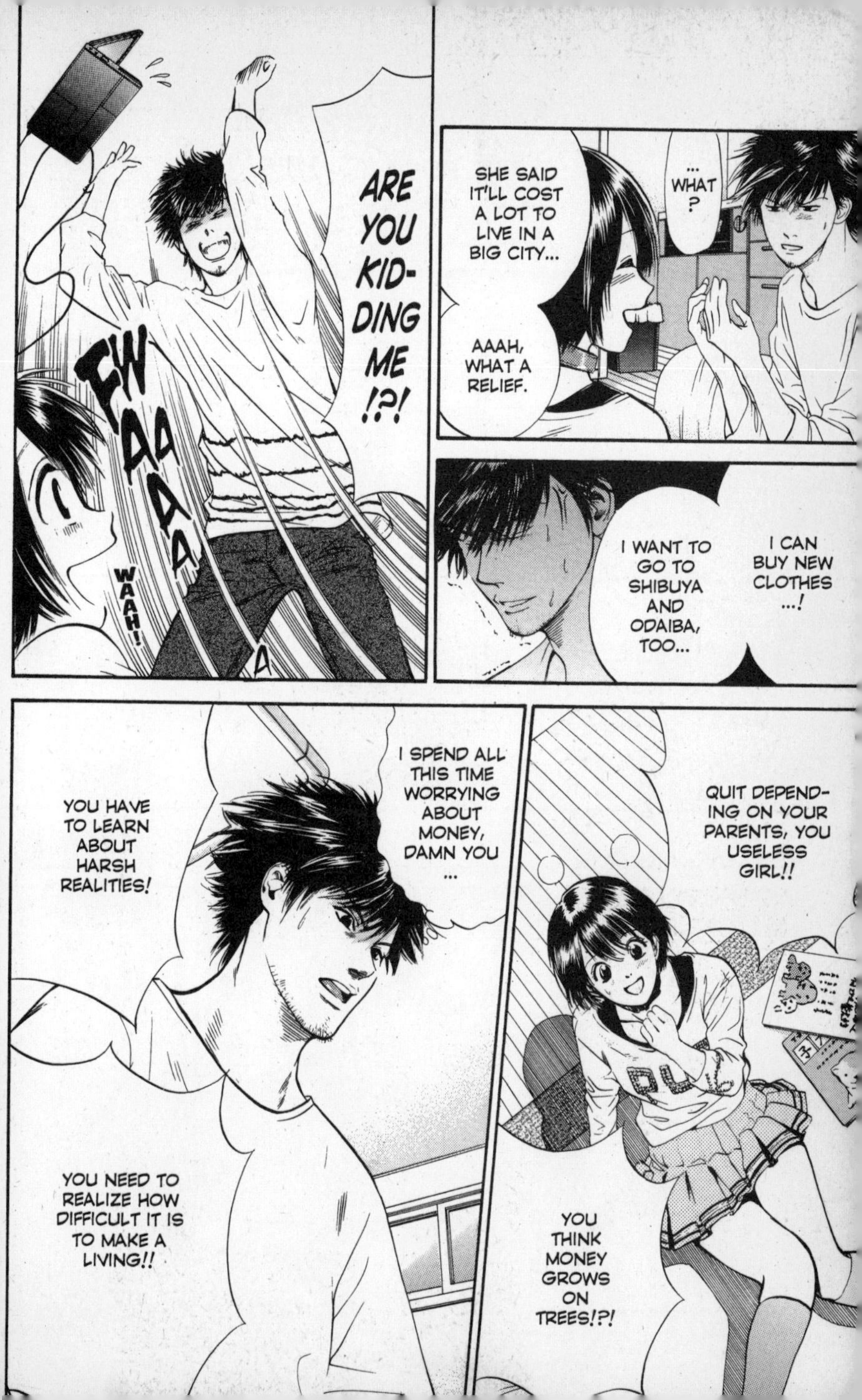
... WHAT ?
SHE SAID IT'LL COST A LOT TO LIVE IN A BIG CITY...
AAAH, WHAT A RELIEF.
I CAN BUY NEW CLOTHES ...!
I WANT TO GO TO SHIBUYA AND ODAIBA, TOO...
ARE YOU KID-DING ME !?!
FWAAAAAA
WAAAH!
QUIT DEPEND-ING ON YOUR PARENTS, YOU USELESS GIRL!!
YOU THINK MONEY GROWS ON TREES!?!
I SPEND ALL THIS TIME WORRYING ABOUT MONEY, DAMN YOU ...
YOU HAVE TO LEARN ABOUT HARSH REALITIES!
YOU NEED TO REALIZE HOW DIFFICULT IT IS TO MAKE A LIVING!!

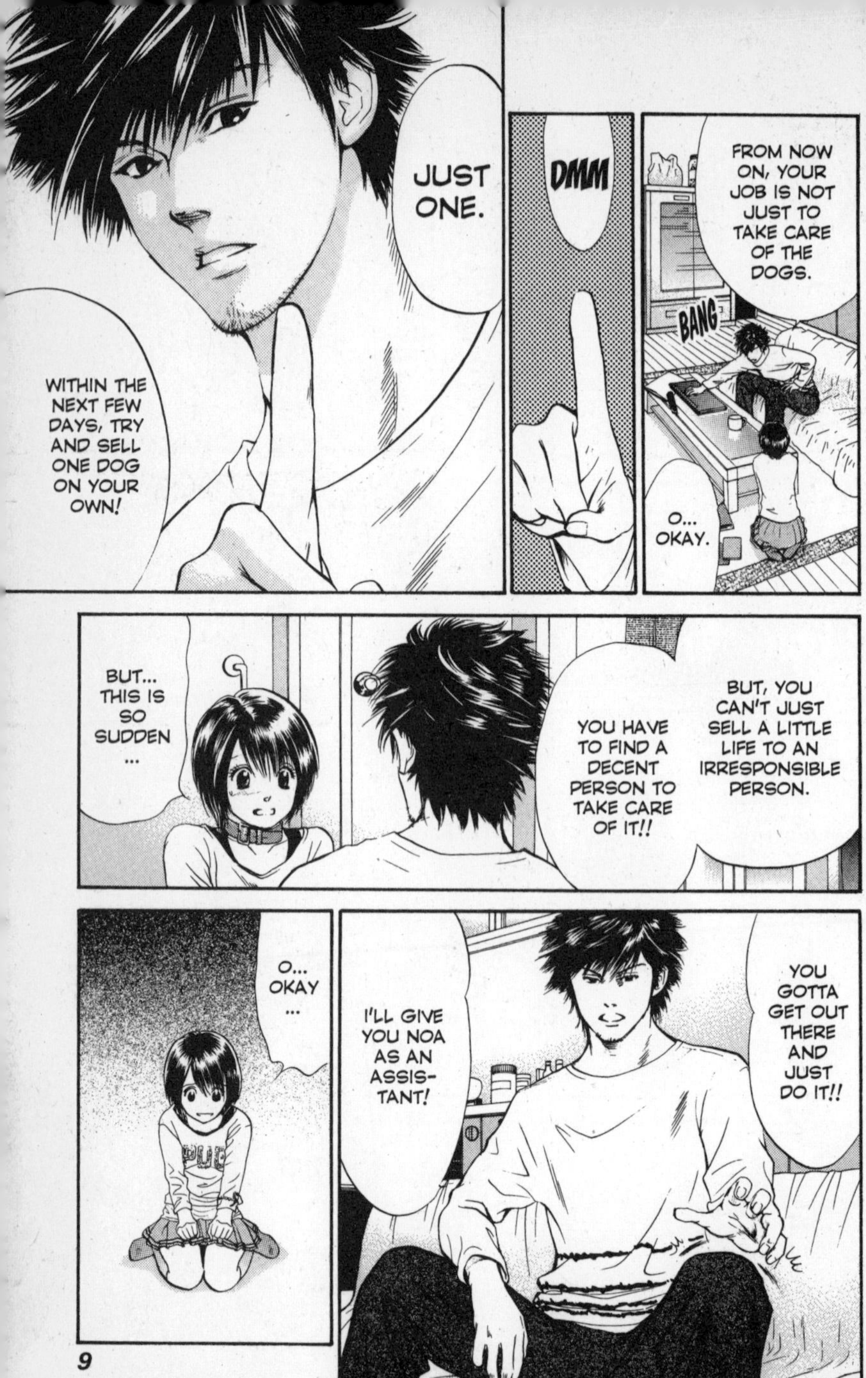
FROM NOW ON, YOUR JOB IS NOT JUST TO TAKE CARE OF THE DOGS.
BANG
O... OKAY.
DMM
JUST ONE.
WITHIN THE NEXT FEW DAYS, TRY AND SELL ONE DOG ON YOUR OWN!
BUT, YOU CAN'T JUST SELL A LITTLE LIFE TO AN IRRESPONSIBLE PERSON.
YOU HAVE TO FIND A DECENT PERSON TO TAKE CARE OF IT!!
BUT... THIS IS SO SUDDEN ...
YOU GOTTA GET OUT THERE AND JUST DO IT!!
I'LL GIVE YOU NOA AS AN ASSIS-TANT!
O... OKAY ...

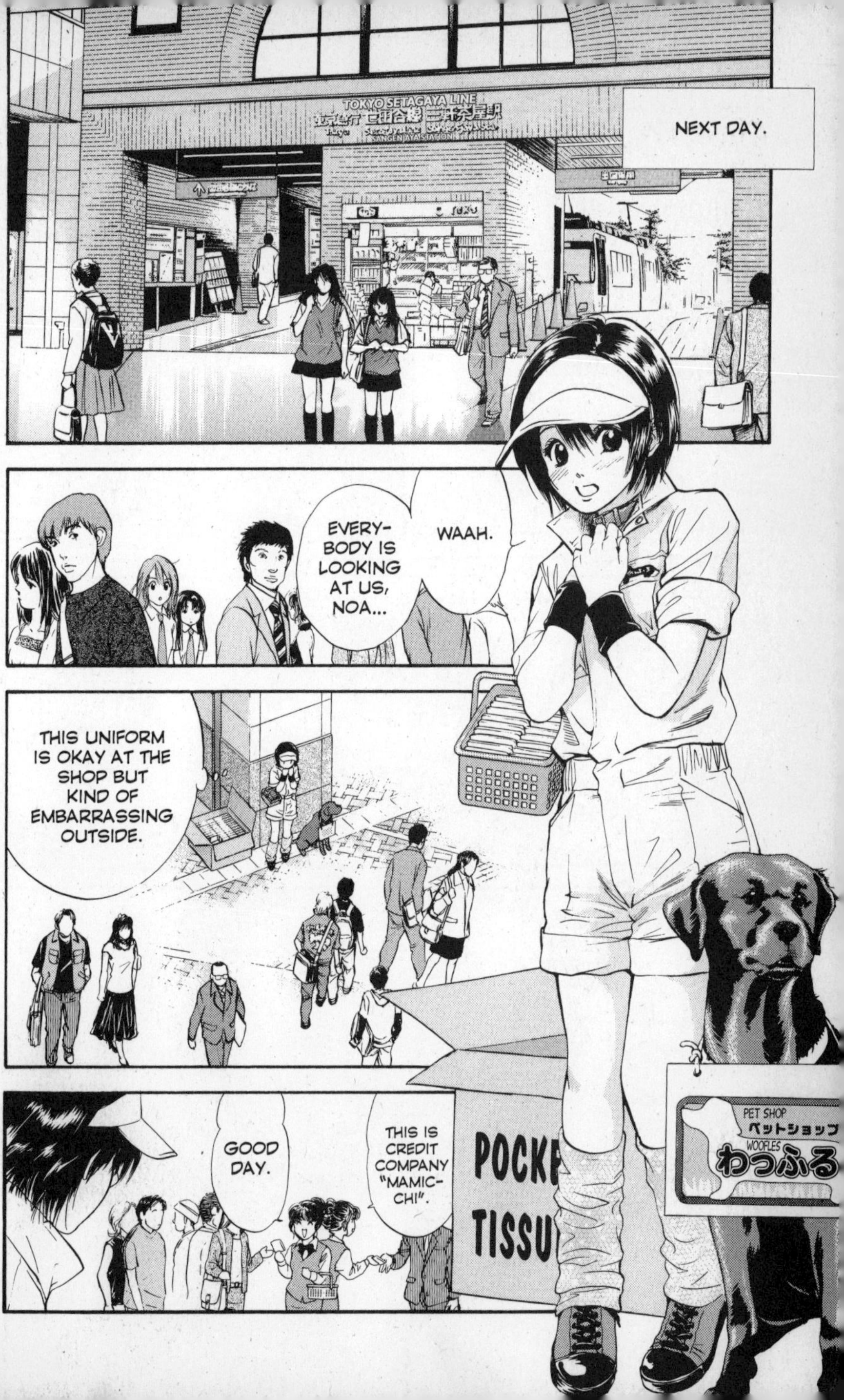
TOKYO SETAGAYA LINE
SANGEN JAYA STATION
NEXT DAY.
WAAH.
EVERY-BODY IS LOOKING AT US, NOA...
THIS UNIFORM IS OKAY AT THE SHOP BUT KIND OF EMBARRASSING OUTSIDE.
PET SHOP
ペットショッフ
WOOFLES
わっふる
POCKE
TISSU
THIS IS CREDIT COMPANY "MAMIC-CHI".
GOOD DAY.

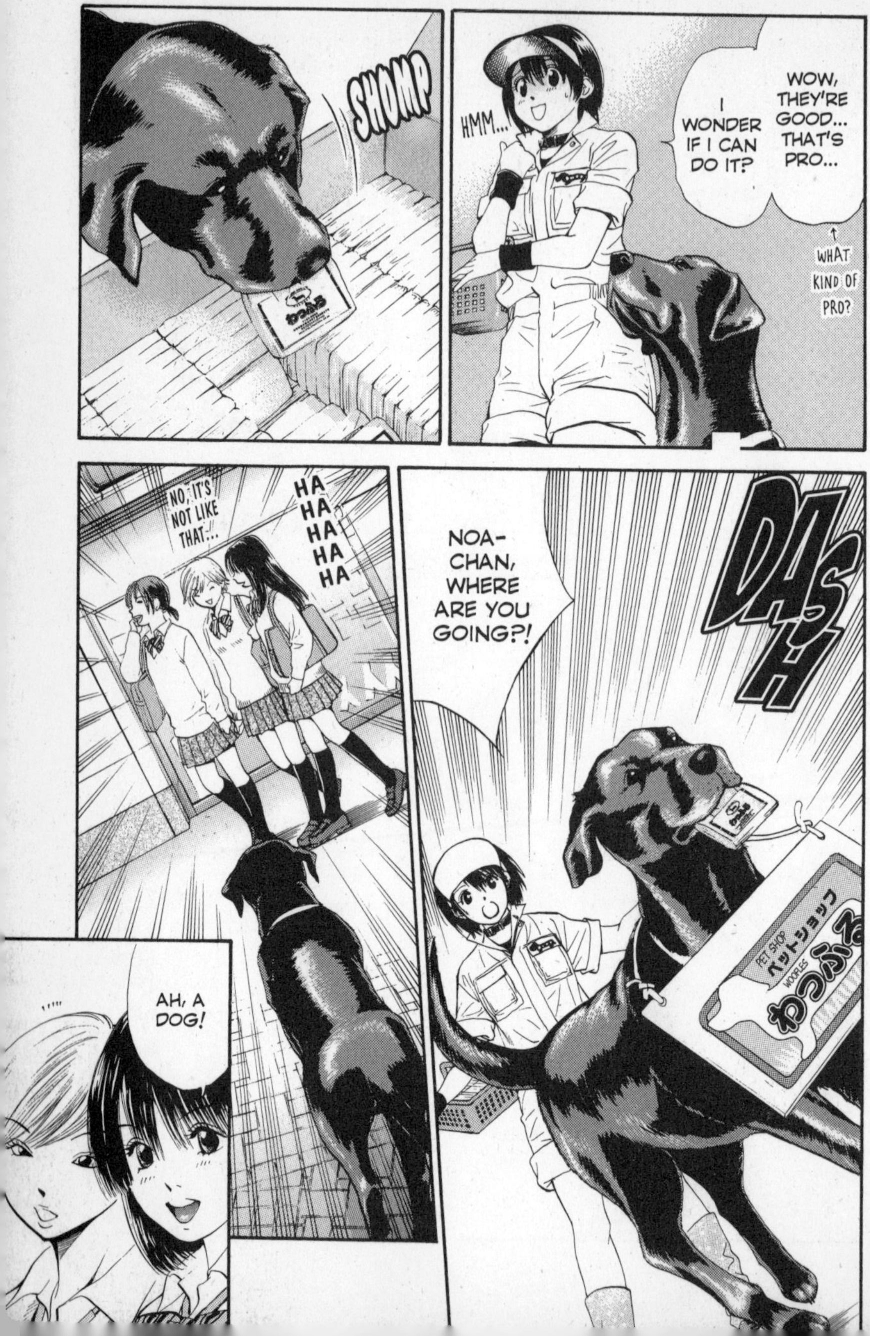
WOW, THEY'RE GOOD... THAT'S PRO...
I WONDER IF I CAN DO IT?
HMM...
WHAT KIND OF PRO?
SHOMP
DASH
NOA-CHAN, WHERE ARE YOU GOING?!
PET SHOP
ペットショップ
WOOFLES
わっふる
HA HA HA HA HA
NO, IT'S NOT LIKE THAT...
AH, A DOG!

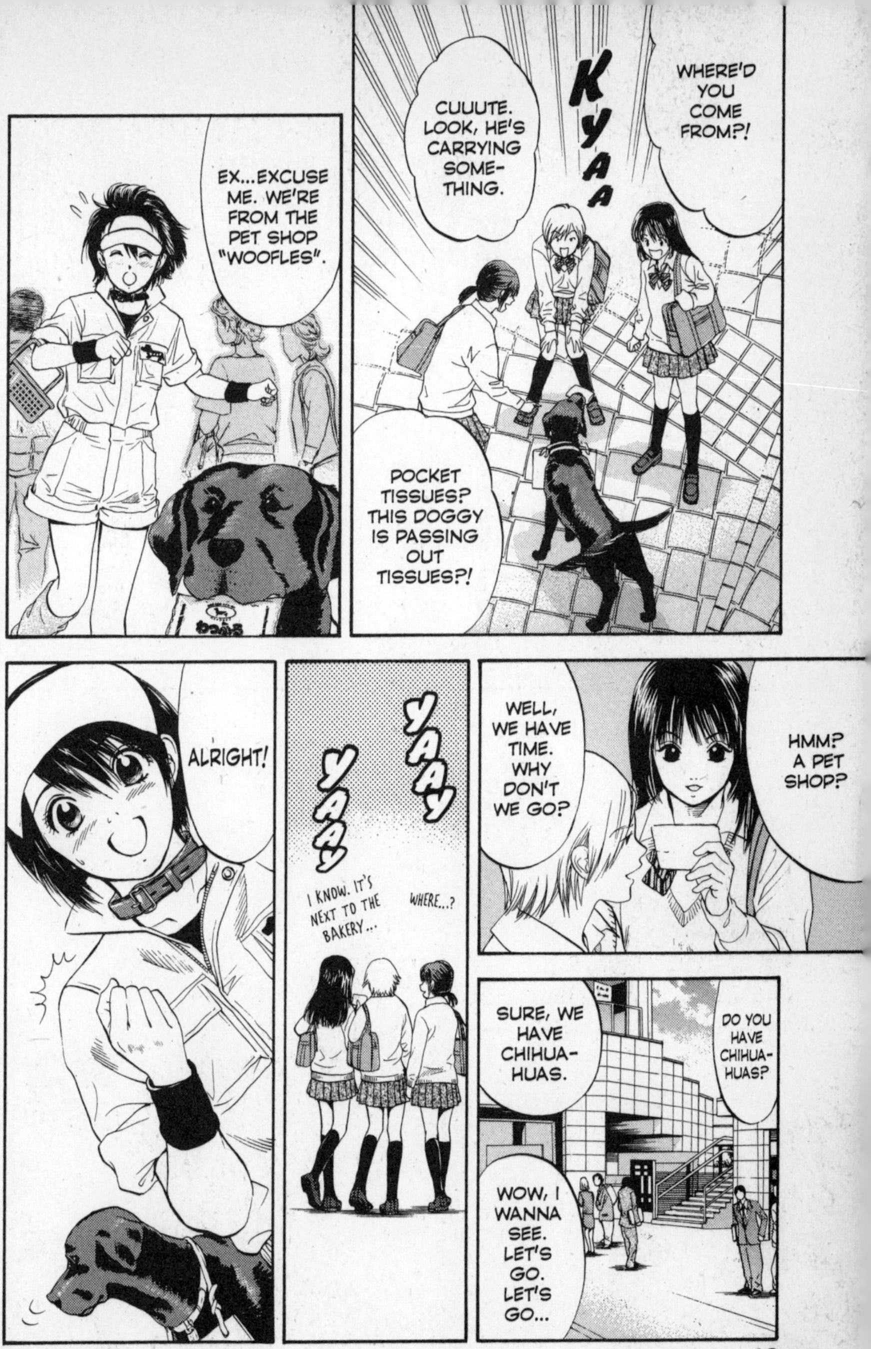
WHERE'D YOU COME FROM?!
KYAAA
CUUUTE. LOOK, HE'S CARRYING SOME-THING.
POCKET TISSUES? THIS DOGGY IS PASSING OUT TISSUES?!
EX...EXCUSE ME. WE'RE FROM THE PET SHOP "WOOFLES".
HMM? A PET SHOP?
WELL, WE HAVE TIME. WHY DON'T WE GO?
DO YOU HAVE CHIHUA-HUAS?
SURE, WE HAVE CHIHUA-HUAS.
WOW, I WANNA SEE. LET'S GO. LET'S GO...
YAAAY
YAAAY
WHERE...?
I KNOW. IT'S NEXT TO THE BAKERY...
ALRIGHT!

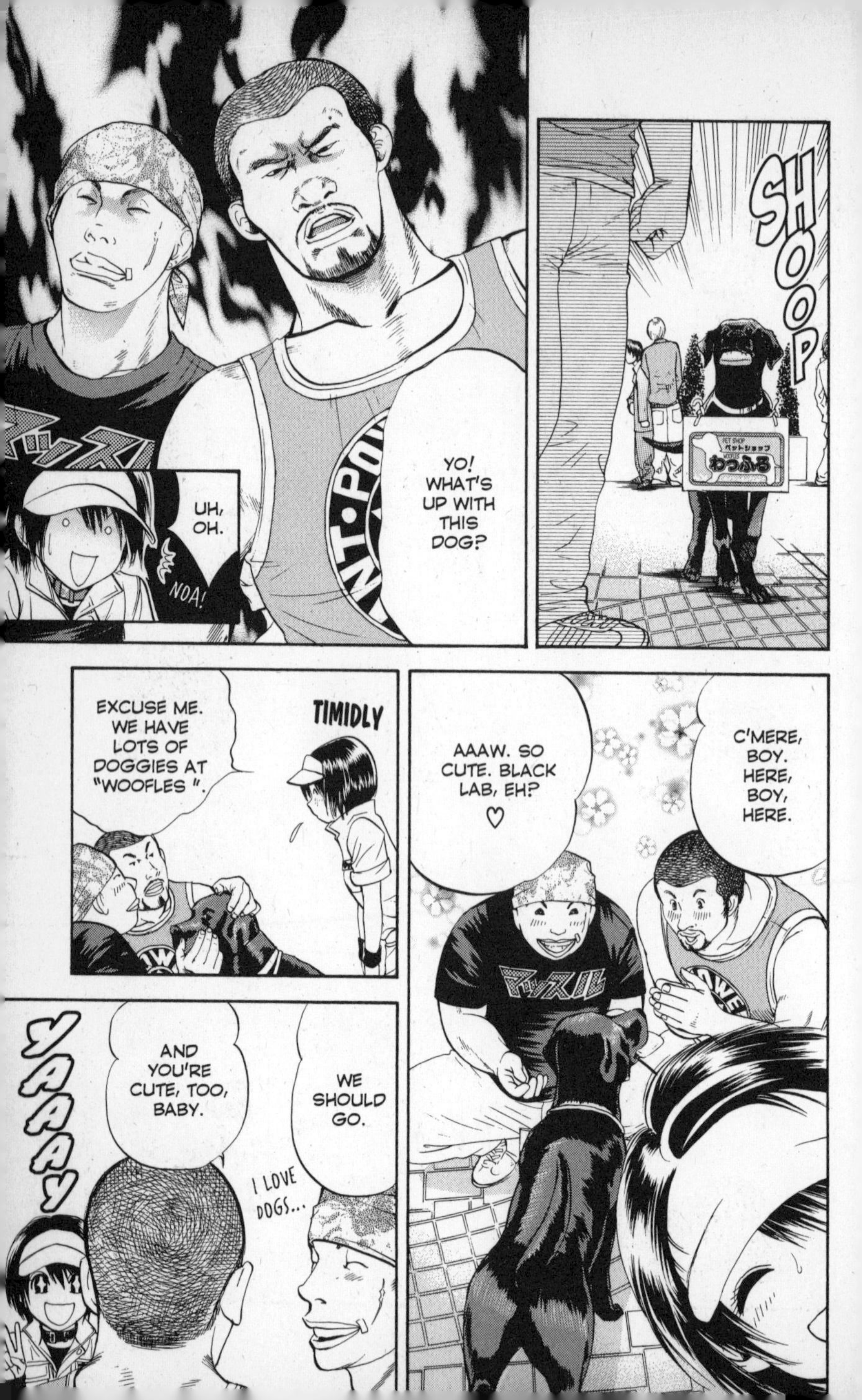
SHOOP
PET SHOP ペットショップ わつふる
YO! WHAT'S UP WITH THIS DOG?
UH, OH.
NOA!
C'MERE, BOY. HERE, BOY, HERE.
AAAW. SO CUTE. BLACK LAB, EH? ♡
EXCUSE ME. WE HAVE LOTS OF DOGGIES AT "WOOFLES".
TIMIDLY
WE SHOULD GO.
AND YOU'RE CUTE, TOO, BABY.
I LOVE DOGS...
YAAAAY

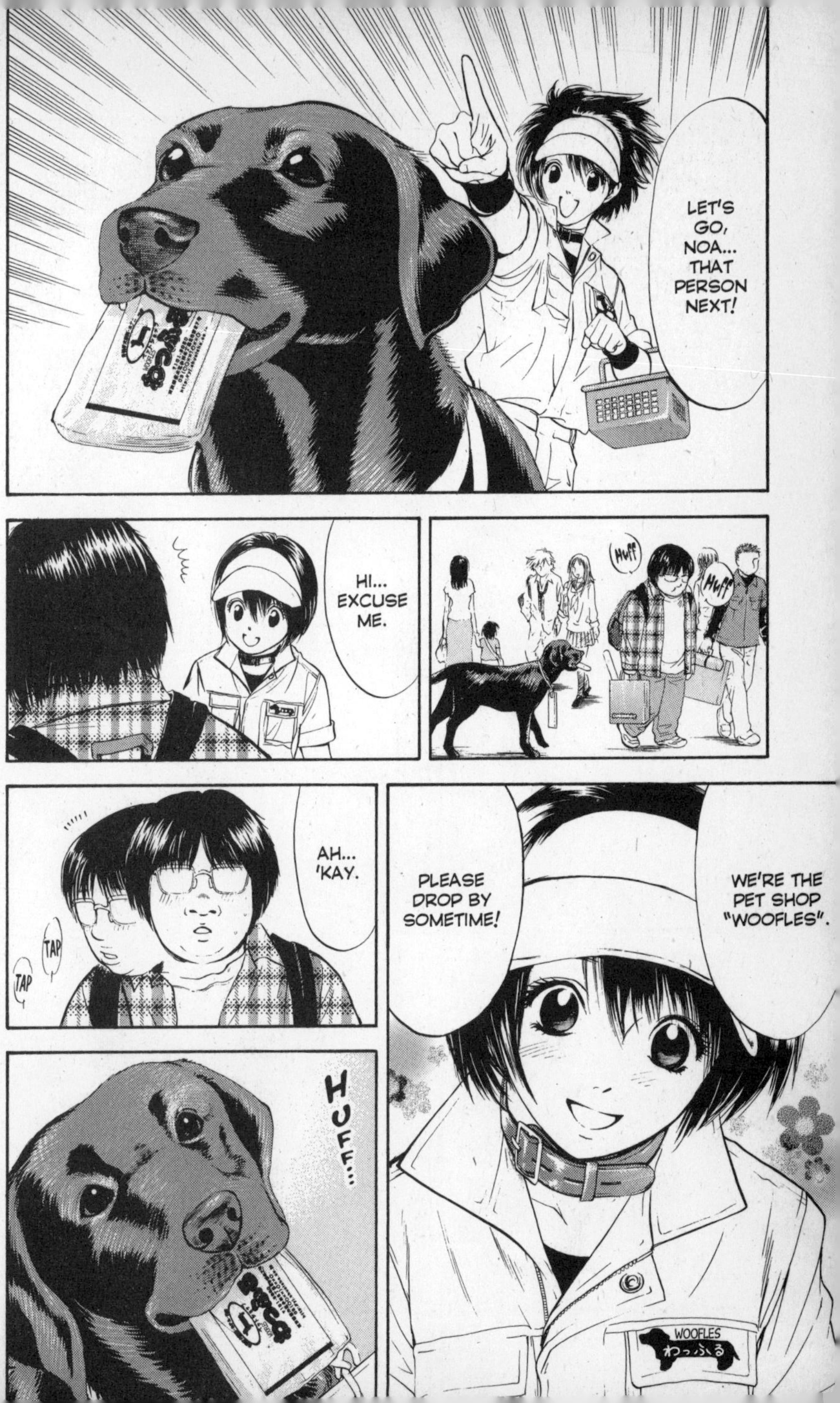
LET'S GO, NOA... THAT PERSON NEXT!
HUFF
HUFF
HI... EXCUSE ME.
WE'RE THE PET SHOP "WOOFLES".
PLEASE DROP BY SOMETIME!
WOOFLES
わっふる
AH... 'KAY.
TAP
TAP
HUFF...

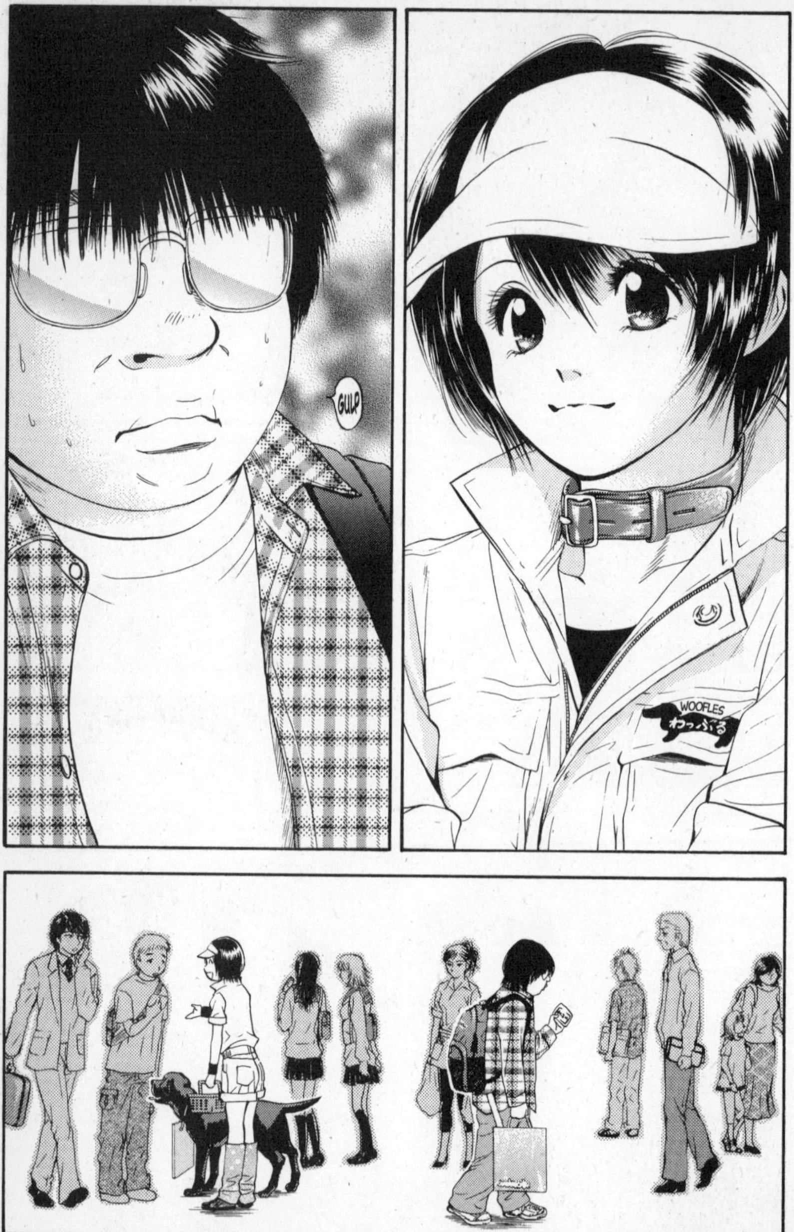
WOOFLES
わっぷる
GULP

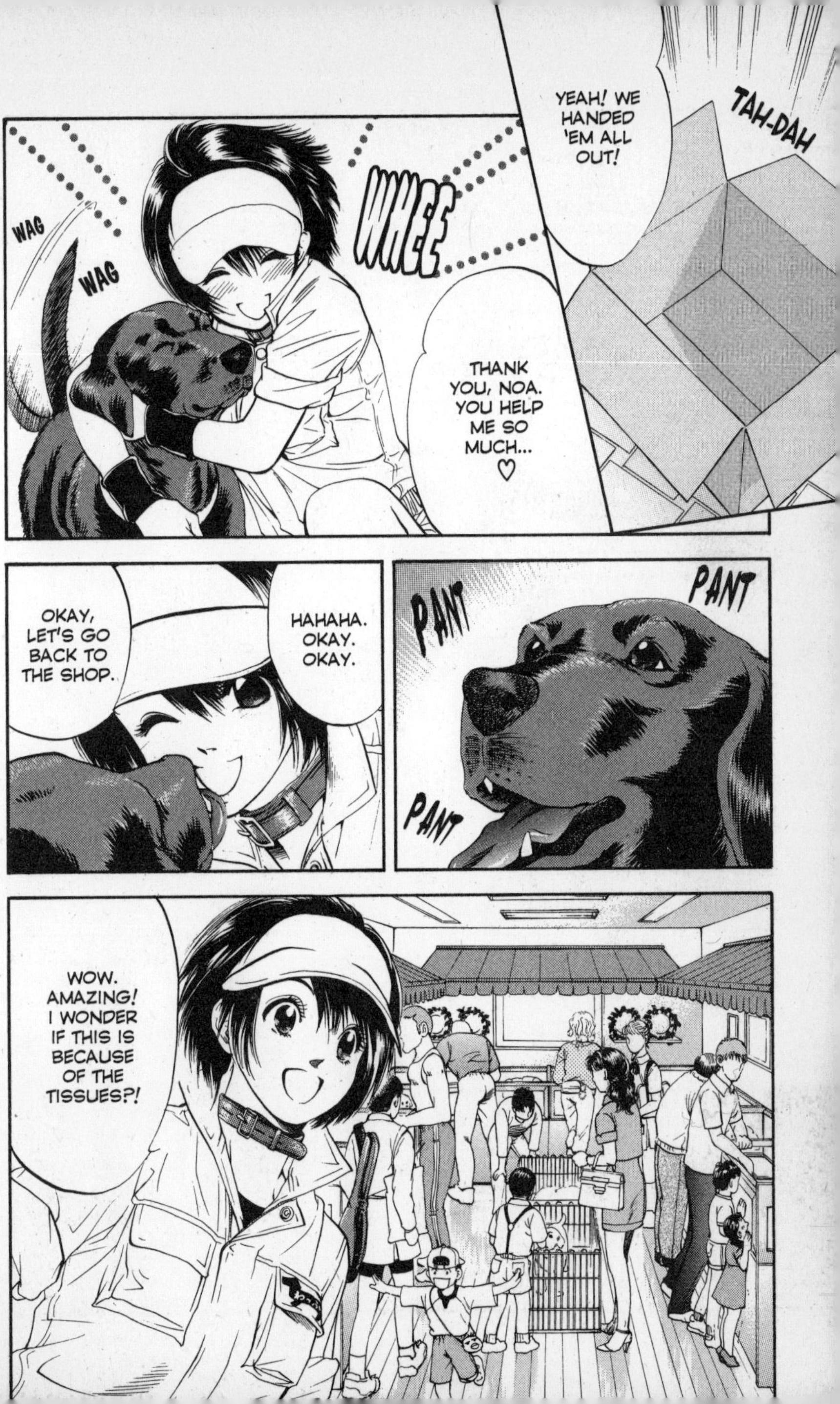
TAH-DAH
YEAH! WE HANDED 'EM ALL OUT!
WHEE
WAG
WAG
THANK YOU, NOA. YOU HELP ME SO MUCH...♡
PANT
PANT
PANT
HAHAHA. OKAY. OKAY.
OKAY, LET'S GO BACK TO THE SHOP.
WOW. AMAZING! I WONDER IF THIS IS BECAUSE OF THE TISSUES?!

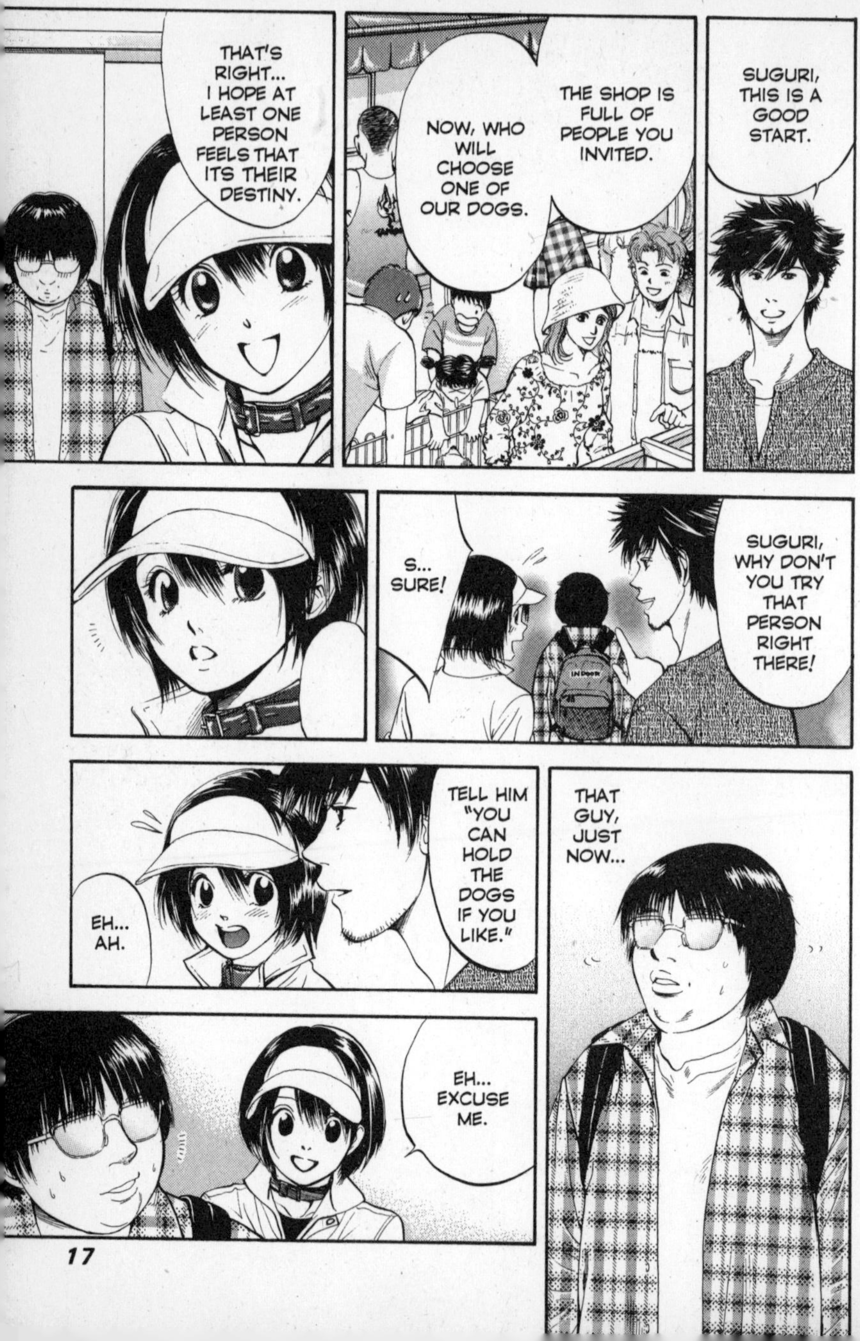
SUGURI, THIS IS A GOOD START.
THE SHOP IS FULL OF PEOPLE YOU INVITED.
NOW, WHO WILL CHOOSE ONE OF OUR DOGS.
THAT'S RIGHT... I HOPE AT LEAST ONE PERSON FEELS THAT ITS THEIR DESTINY.
SUGURI, WHY DON'T YOU TRY THAT PERSON RIGHT THERE!
S... SURE!
THAT GUY, JUST NOW...
TELL HIM "YOU CAN HOLD THE DOGS IF YOU LIKE."
EH... AH.
EH... EXCUSE ME.

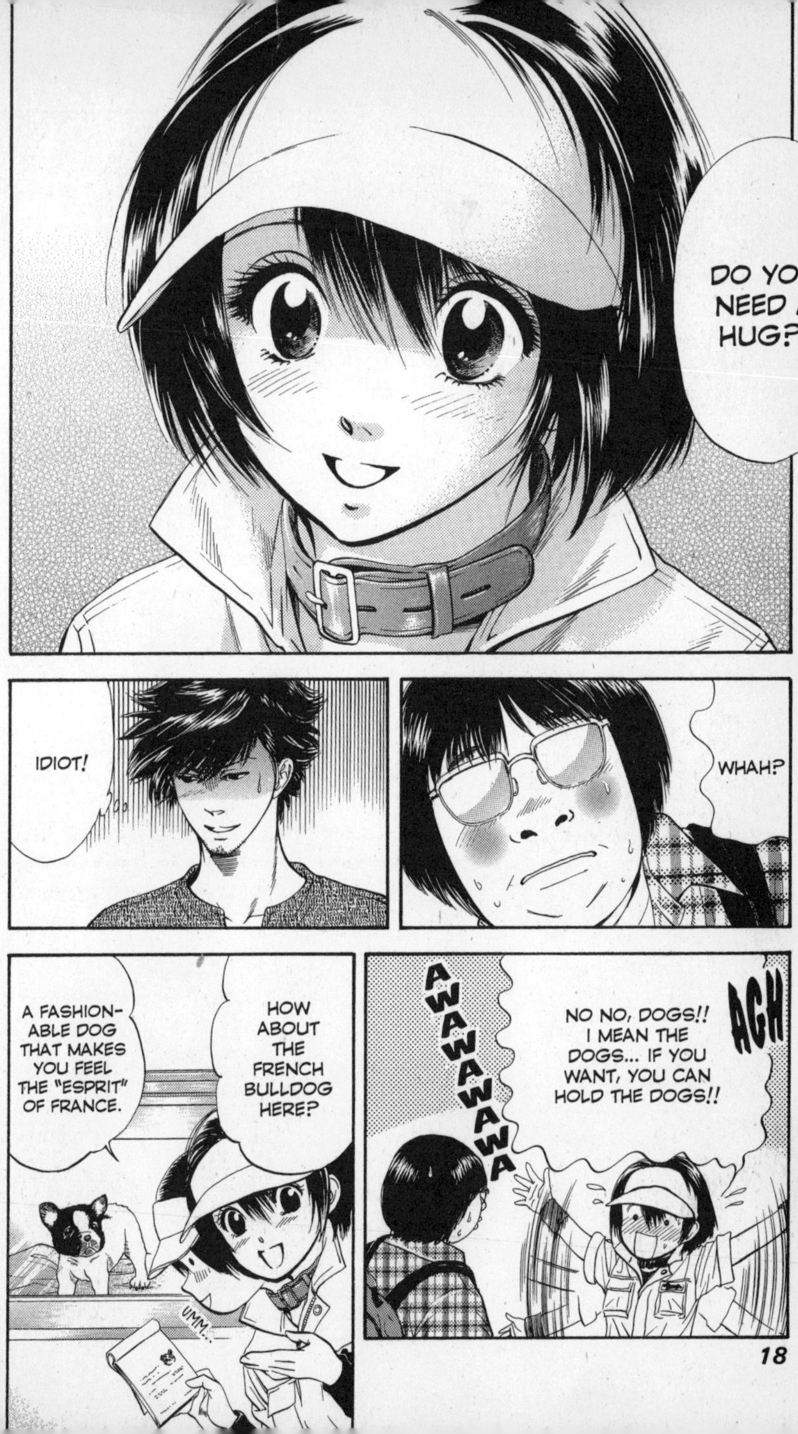
DO YOU NEED A HUG?!
WHAH?
IDIOT!
ACH
NO NO, DOGS!! I MEAN THE DOGS... IF YOU WANT, YOU CAN HOLD THE DOGS!!
AWAWAWAWAWA
HOW ABOUT THE FRENCH BULLDOG HERE?
A FASHION-ABLE DOG THAT MAKES YOU FEEL THE "ESPRIT" OF FRANCE.
UMM...

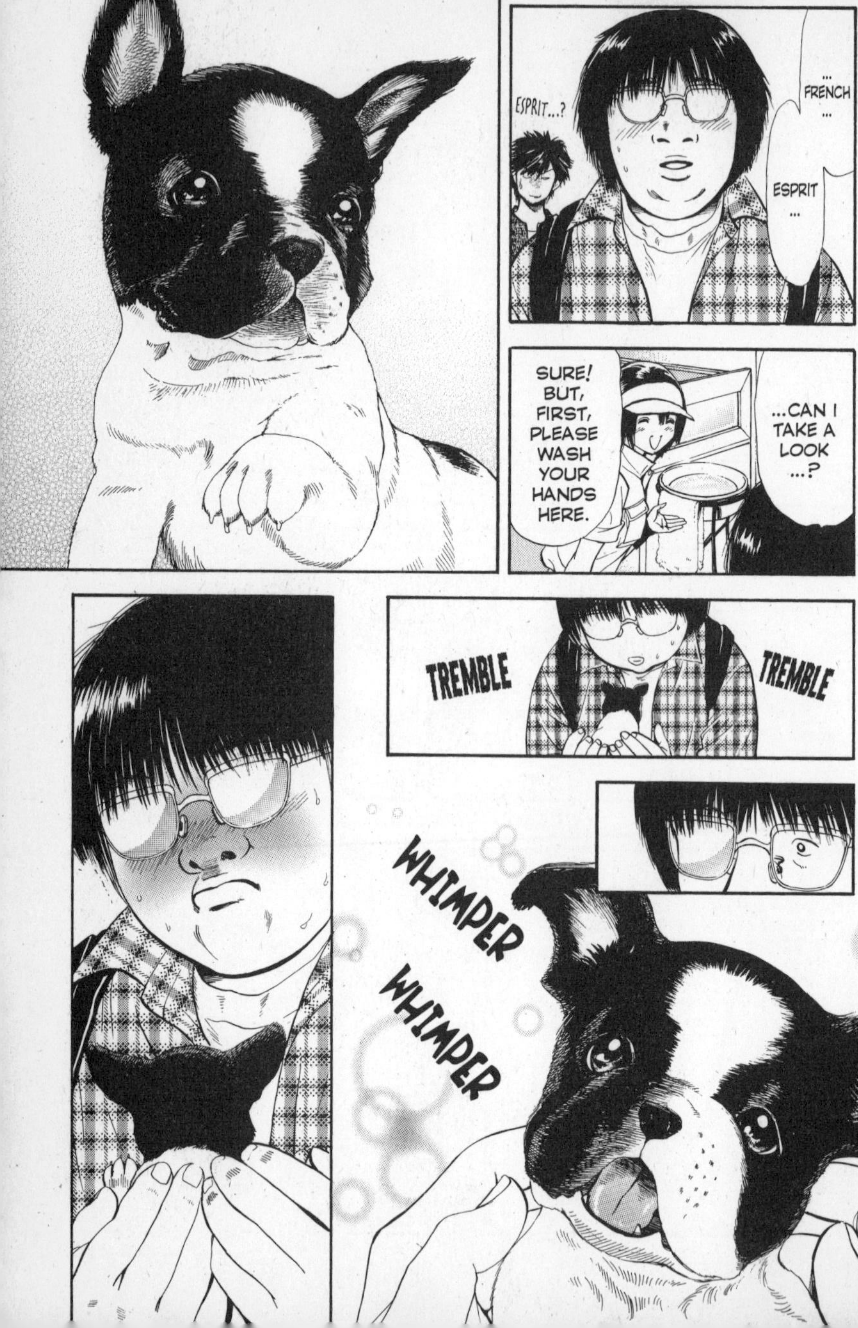
... FRENCH ... ESPRIT ...
ESPRIT...?
...CAN I TAKE A LOOK ...?
SURE! BUT, FIRST, PLEASE WASH YOUR HANDS HERE.
TREMBLE
TREMBLE
WHIMPER
WHIMPER

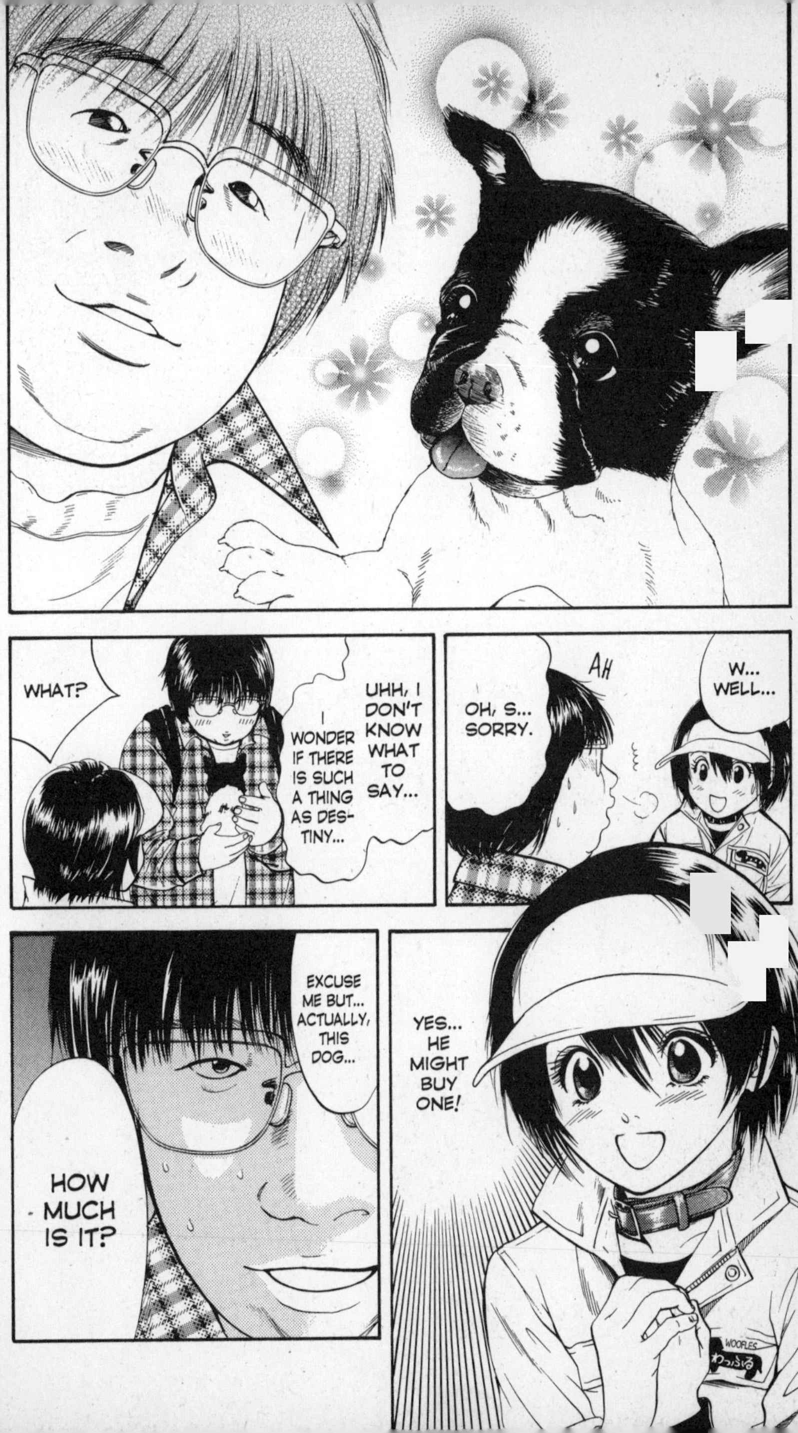
W... WELL...
AH
OH, S... SORRY.
UHH, I DON'T KNOW WHAT TO SAY...
I WONDER IF THERE IS SUCH A THING AS DES-TINY...
WHAT?
YES... HE MIGHT BUY ONE!
WOOFLES
わっふる
EXCUSE ME BUT... ACTUALLY, THIS DOG...
HOW MUCH IS IT?

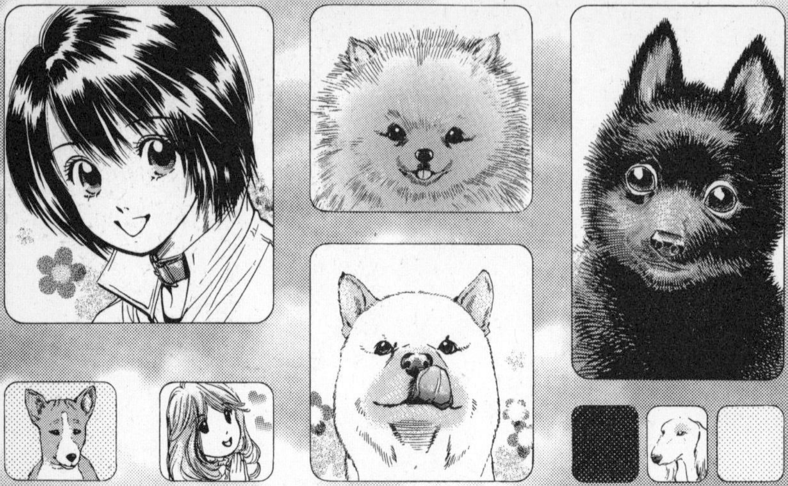

CHAPTER 10
AN IDOL JUST FOR ME

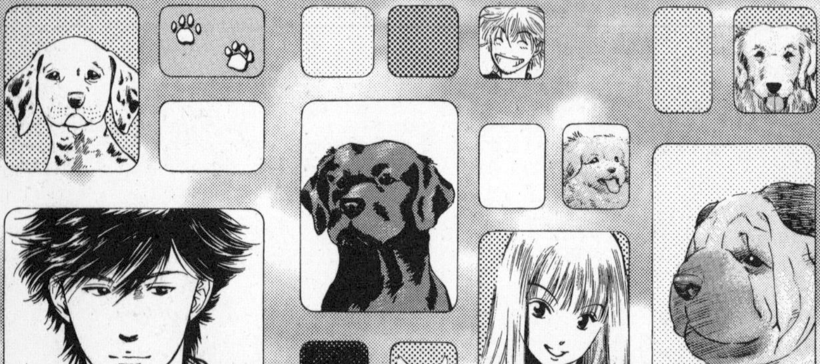

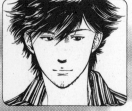

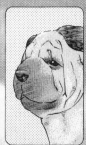

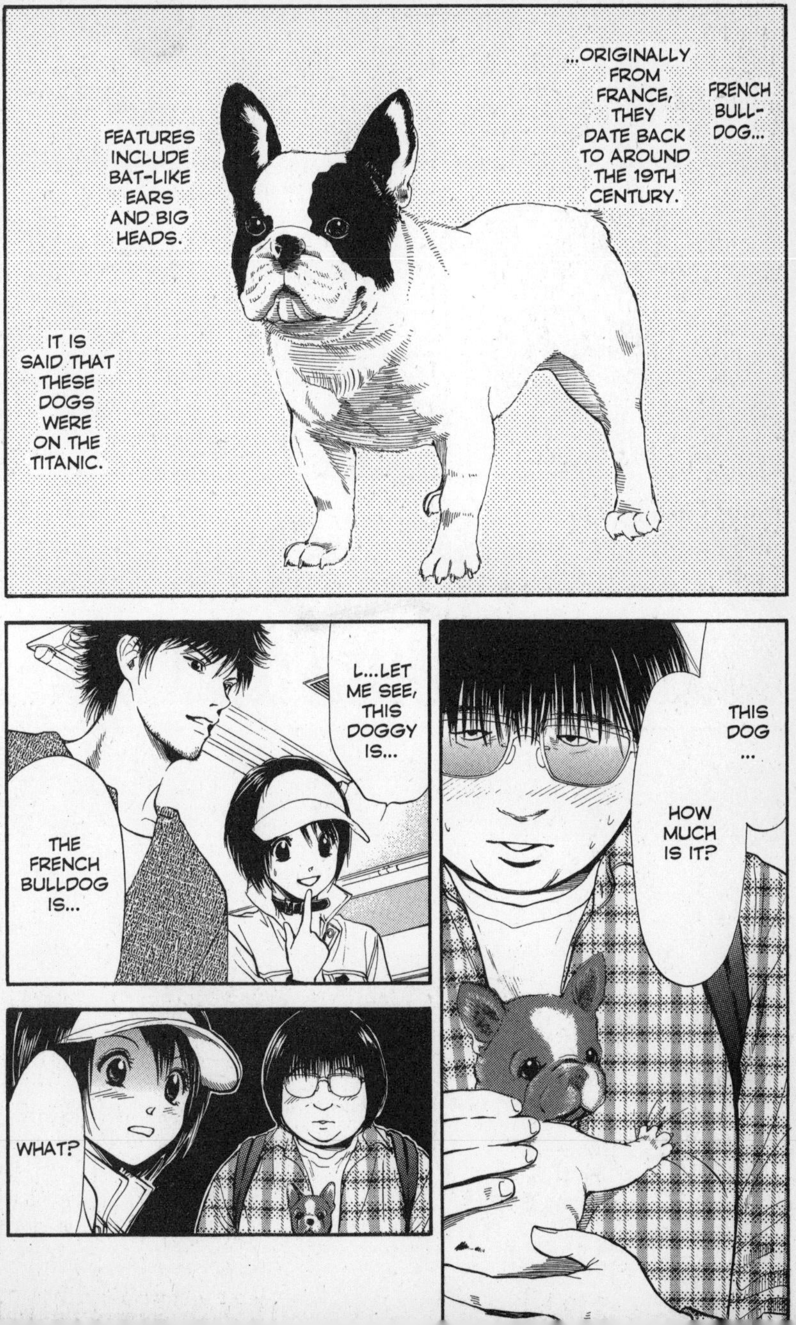
FRENCH BULL-DOG...
...ORIGINALLY FROM FRANCE, THEY DATE BACK TO AROUND THE 19TH CENTURY.
FEATURES INCLUDE BAT-LIKE EARS AND BIG HEADS.
IT IS SAID THAT THESE DOGS WERE ON THE TITANIC.
THIS DOG ...
HOW MUCH IS IT?
L...LET ME SEE, THIS DOGGY IS...
THE FRENCH BULLDOG IS...
WHAT?

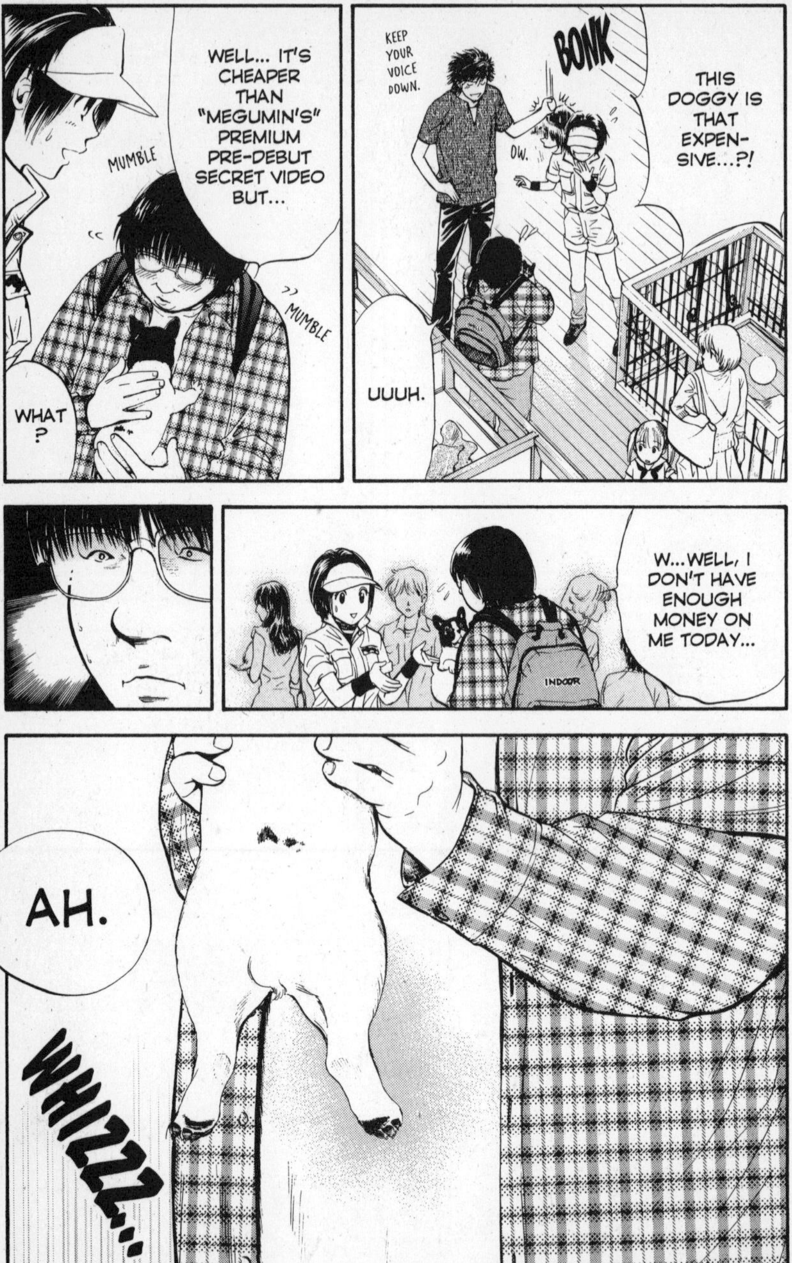
THIS DOGGY IS THAT EXPEN-SIVE...?!
BONK
KEEP YOUR VOICE DOWN.
OW.
UUUH.
WELL... IT'S CHEAPER THAN "MEGUMIN'S" PREMIUM PRE-DEBUT SECRET VIDEO BUT...
MUMBLE
MUMBLE
WHAT?
W...WELL, I DON'T HAVE ENOUGH MONEY ON ME TODAY...
INDOOR
AH.
WHIZZZ...

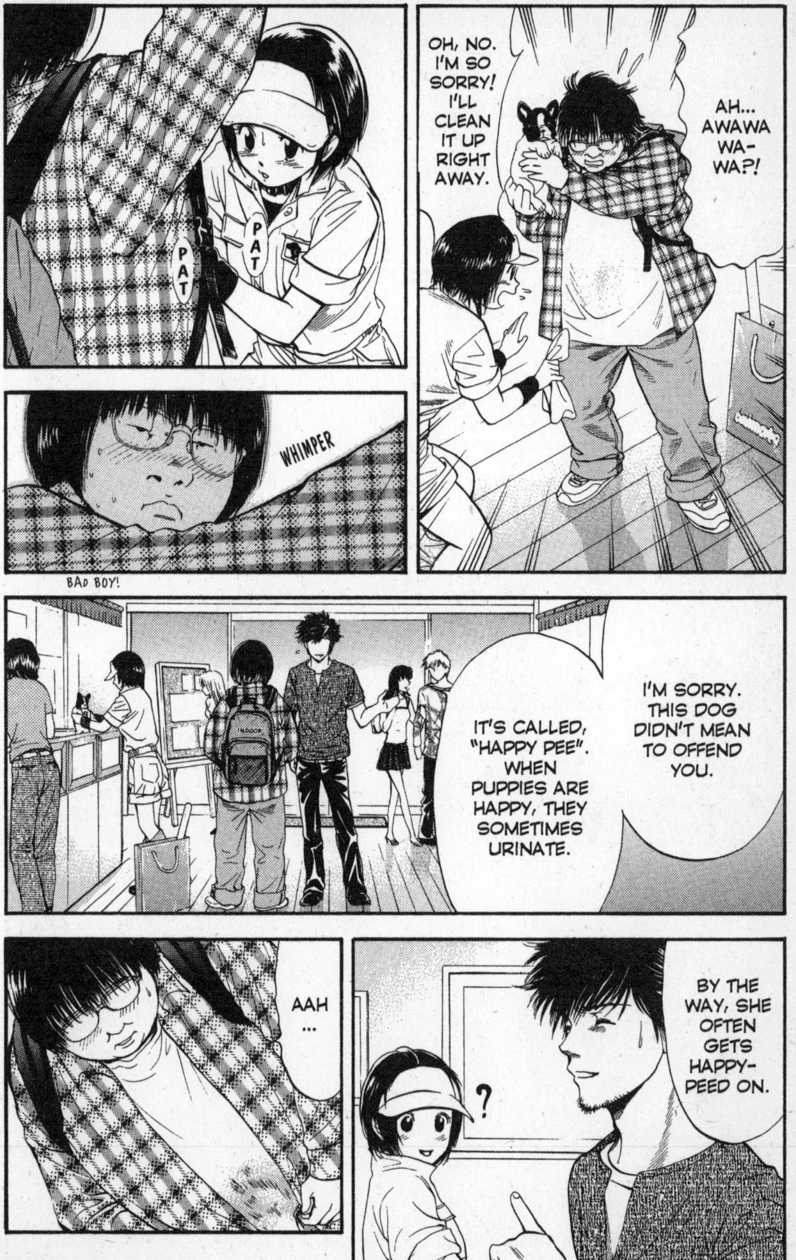
AH... AWAWA WA-WA?!
OH, NO. I'M SO SORRY! I'LL CLEAN IT UP RIGHT AWAY.
PAT
PAT
WHIMPER
BAD BOY!
I'M SORRY. THIS DOG DIDN'T MEAN TO OFFEND YOU.
IT'S CALLED, "HAPPY PEE". WHEN PUPPIES ARE HAPPY, THEY SOMETIMES URINATE.
BY THE WAY, SHE OFTEN GETS HAPPY-PEED ON.
?
AAH ...

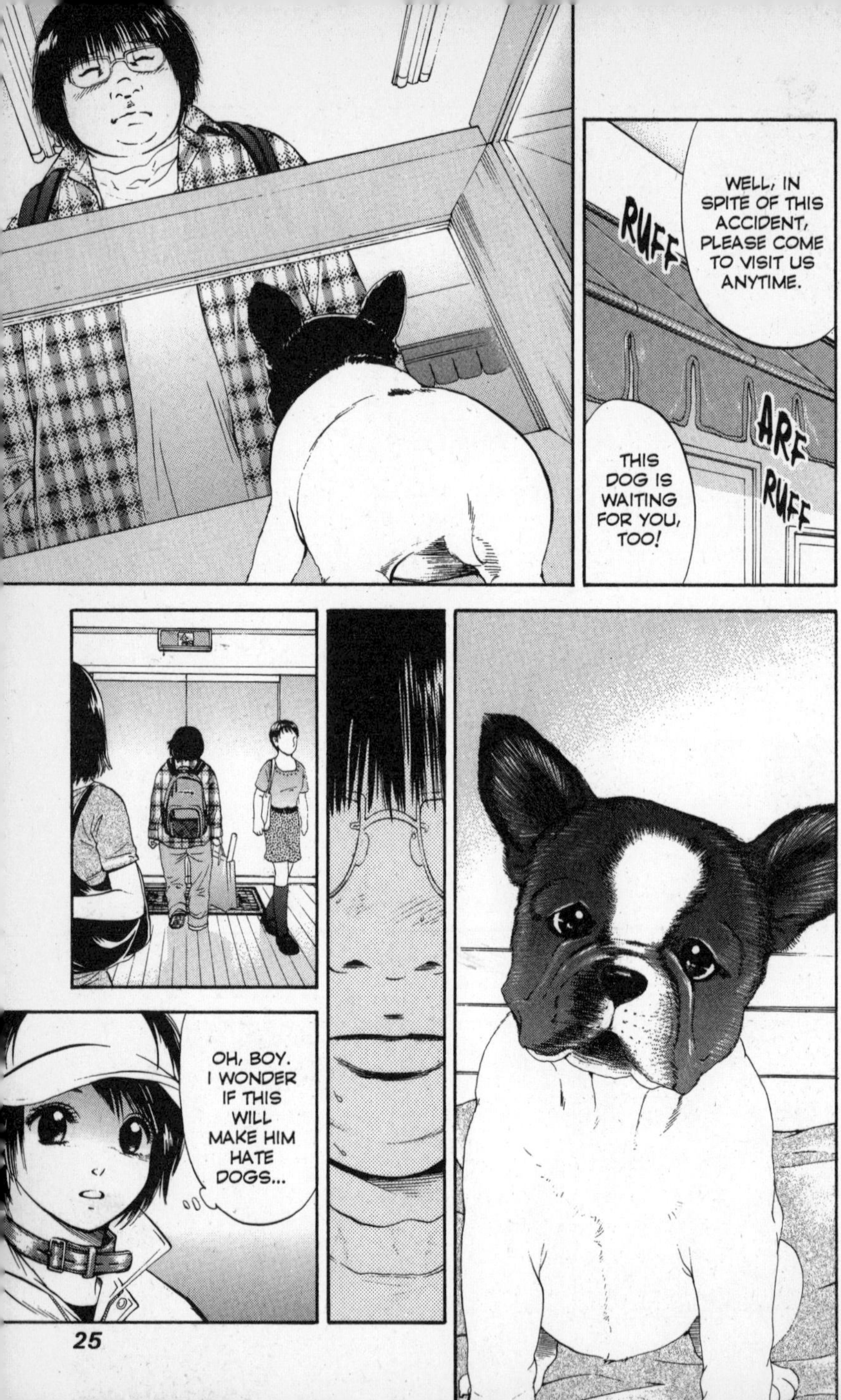
WELL, IN SPITE OF THIS ACCIDENT, PLEASE COME TO VISIT US ANYTIME.
RUFF
ARF RUFF
THIS DOG IS WAITING FOR YOU, TOO!
OH, BOY. I WONDER IF THIS WILL MAKE HIM HATE DOGS...

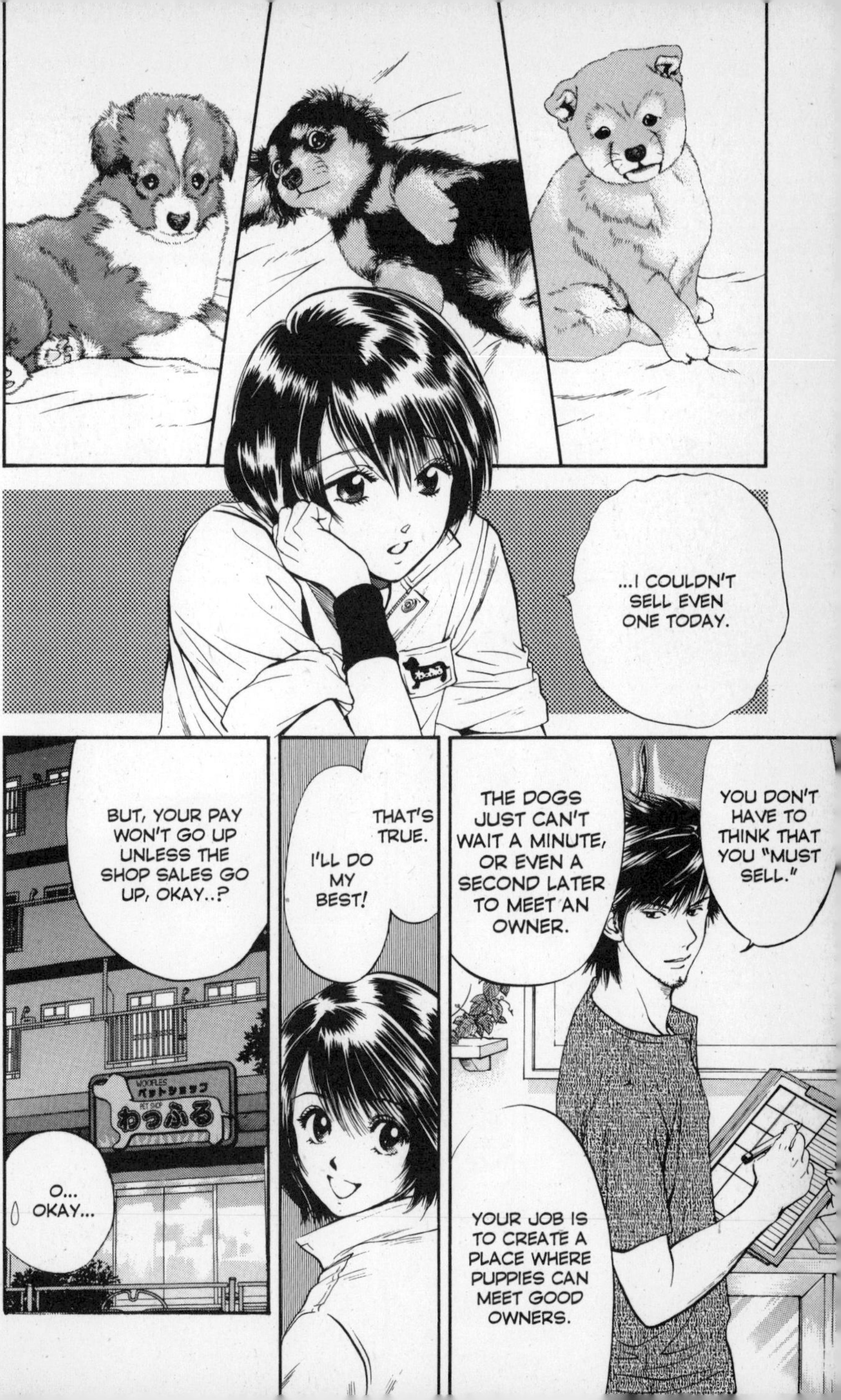
...I COULDN'T SELL EVEN ONE TODAY.
YOU DON'T HAVE TO THINK THAT YOU "MUST SELL."
THE DOGS JUST CAN'T WAIT A MINUTE, OR EVEN A SECOND LATER TO MEET AN OWNER.
YOUR JOB IS TO CREATE A PLACE WHERE PUPPIES CAN MEET GOOD OWNERS.
THAT'S TRUE.
I'LL DO MY BEST!
BUT, YOUR PAY WON'T GO UP UNLESS THE SHOP SALES GO UP, OKAY..?
WOOFLES
ペットショップ
PET SHOP
わっふる
O... OKAY...

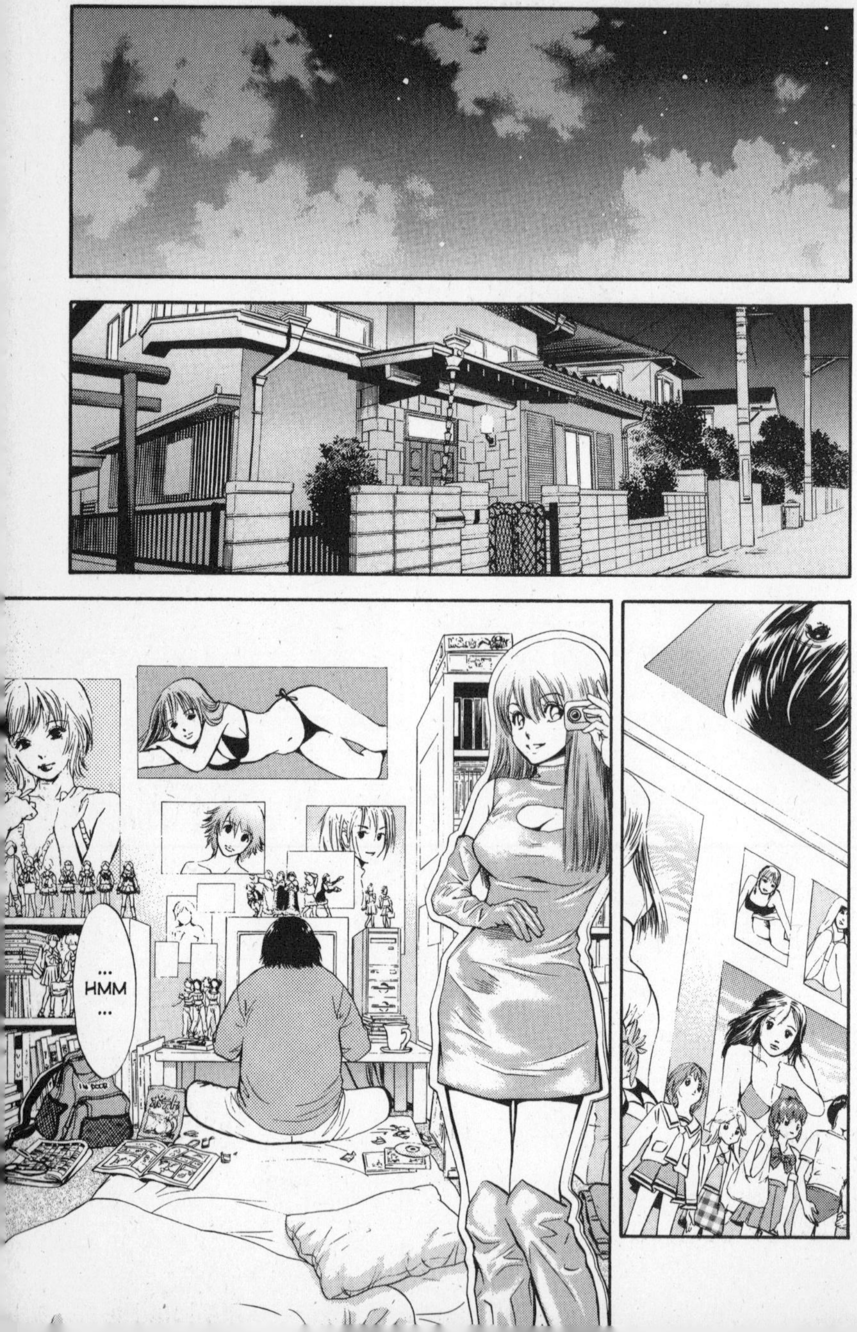
... HMM ...

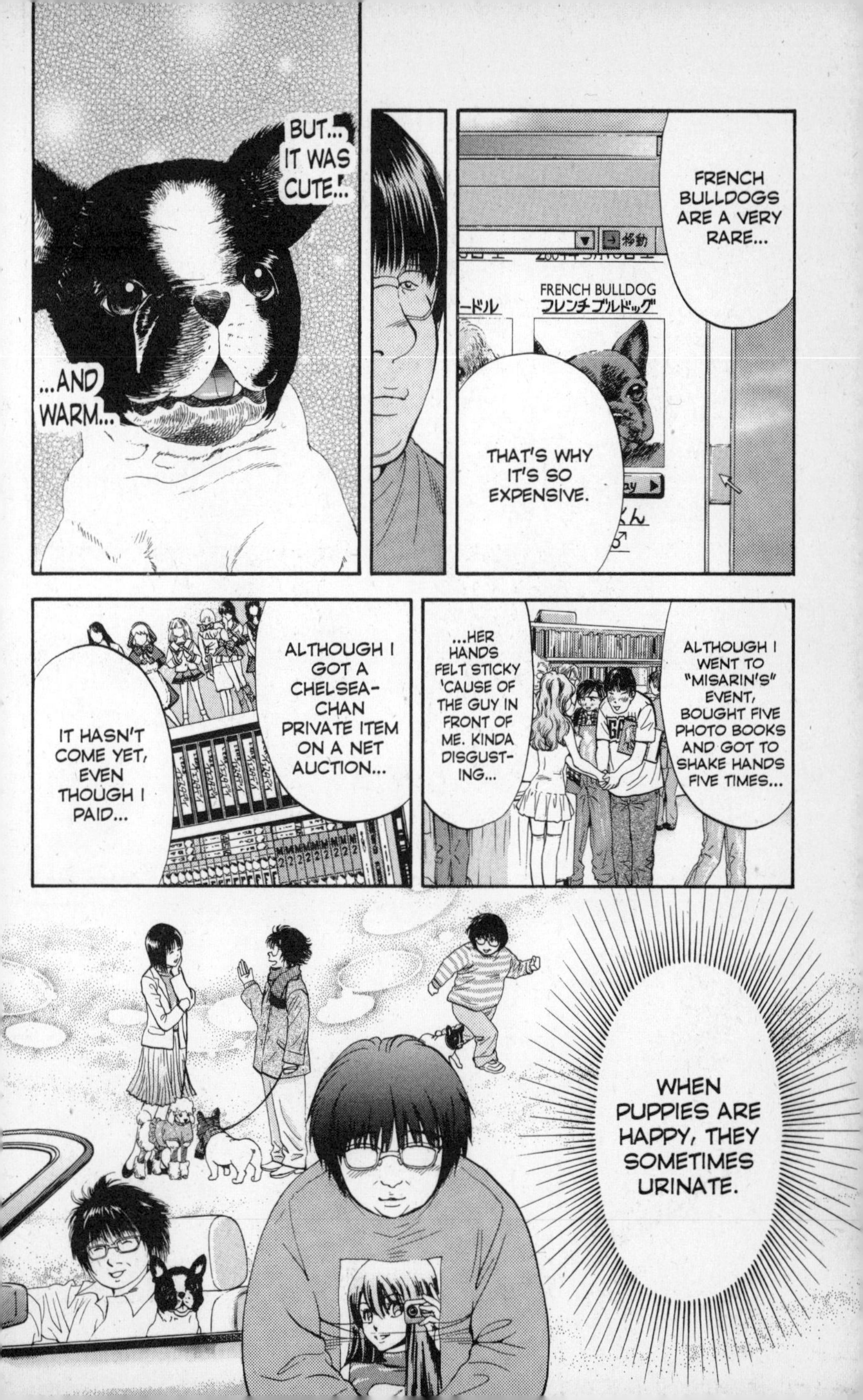
FRENCH BULLDOGS ARE A VERY RARE...
移動
FRENCH BULLDOG
フレンチブルドッグ
THAT'S WHY IT'S SO EXPENSIVE.
BUT... IT WAS CUTE...
...AND WARM...
ALTHOUGH I WENT TO "MISARIN'S" EVENT, BOUGHT FIVE PHOTO BOOKS AND GOT TO SHAKE HANDS FIVE TIMES...
...HER HANDS FELT STICKY 'CAUSE OF THE GUY IN FRONT OF ME. KINDA DISGUSTING...
ALTHOUGH I GOT A CHELSEA-CHAN PRIVATE ITEM ON A NET AUCTION...
IT HASN'T COME YET, EVEN THOUGH I PAID...
WHEN PUPPIES ARE HAPPY, THEY SOMETIMES URINATE.

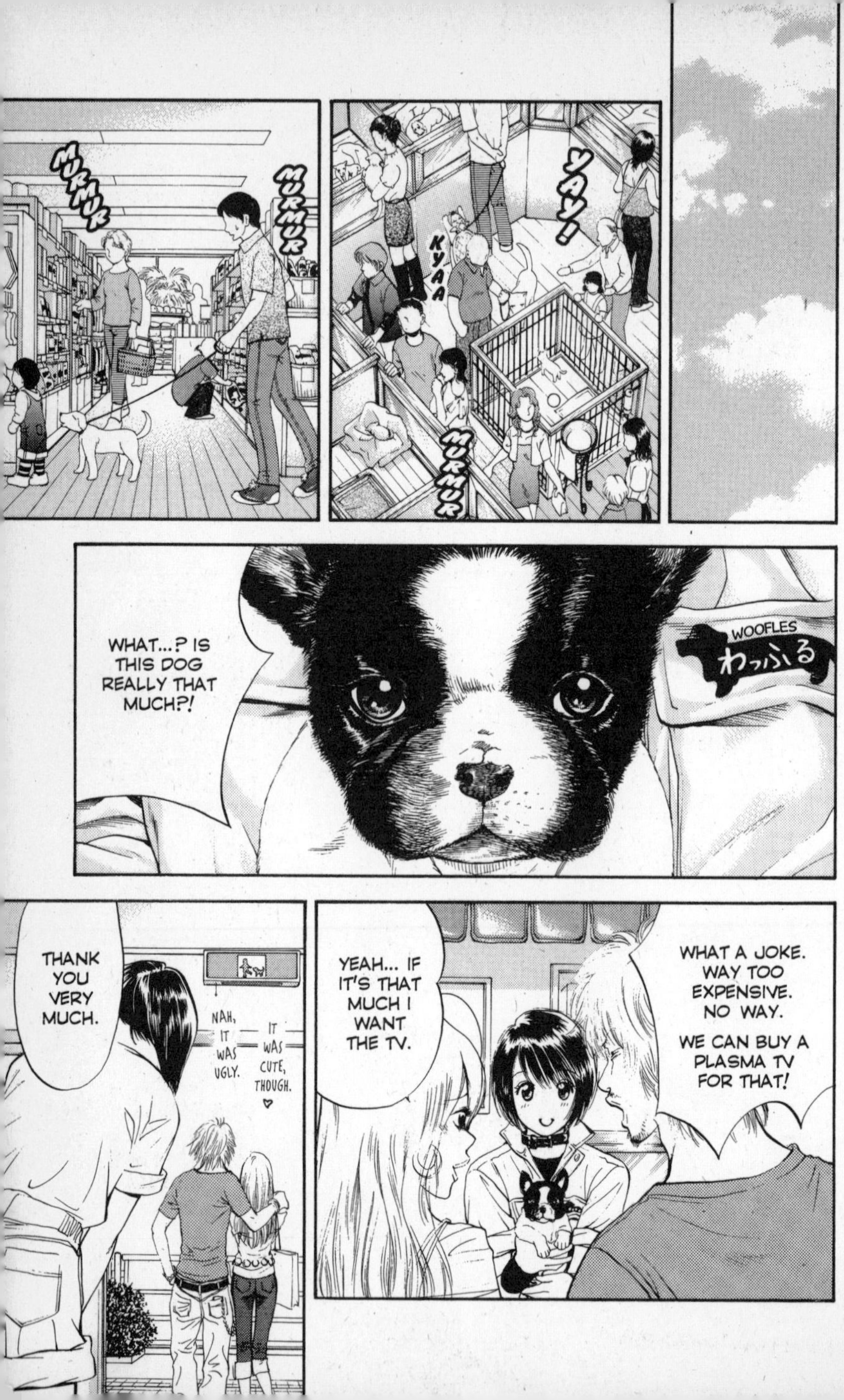
YAY!
KYAA
MURMUR
MURMUR
MURMUR
WHAT...? IS THIS DOG REALLY THAT MUCH?!
WOOFLES
わっふる
WHAT A JOKE. WAY TOO EXPENSIVE. NO WAY.
WE CAN BUY A PLASMA TV FOR THAT!
YEAH... IF IT'S THAT MUCH I WANT THE TV.
THANK YOU VERY MUCH.
IT WAS CUTE, THOUGH. ♥
NAH, IT WAS UGLY.

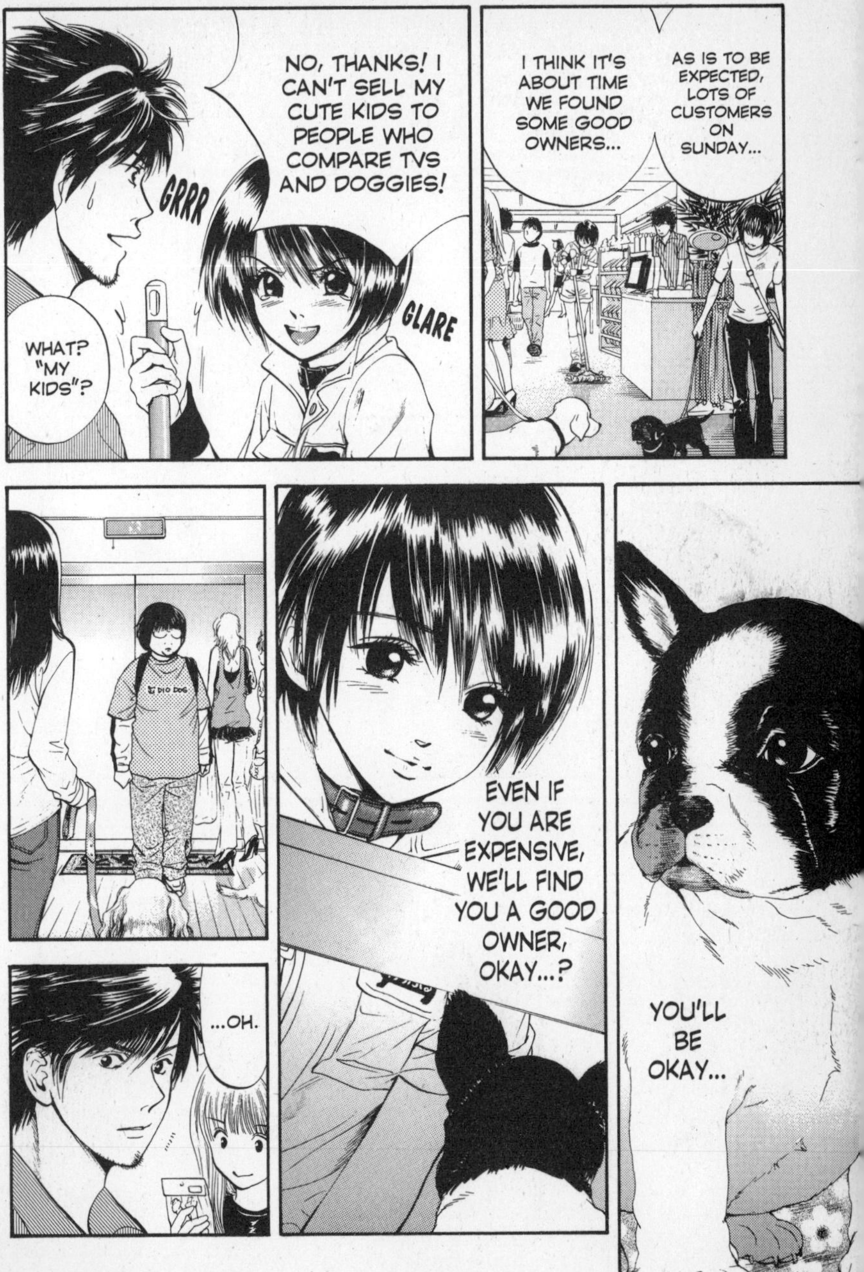
AS IS TO BE EXPECTED, LOTS OF CUSTOMERS ON SUNDAY...
I THINK IT'S ABOUT TIME WE FOUND SOME GOOD OWNERS...
NO, THANKS! I CAN'T SELL MY CUTE KIDS TO PEOPLE WHO COMPARE TVS AND DOGGIES!
GRRR
GLARE
WHAT? "MY KIDS"?
YOU'LL BE OKAY...
EVEN IF YOU ARE EXPENSIVE, WE'LL FIND YOU A GOOD OWNER, OKAY...?
DIO DOG
...OH.

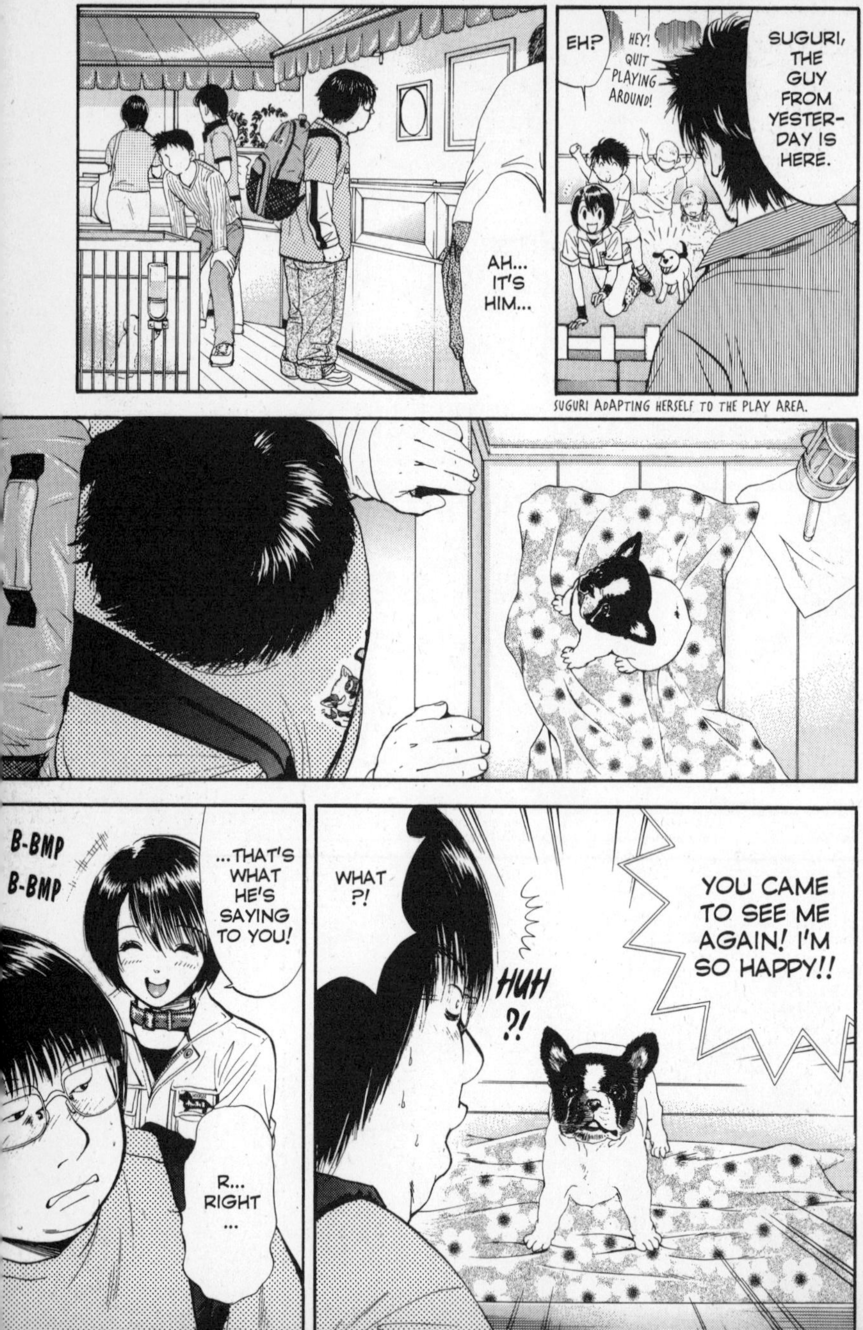
SUGURI, THE GUY FROM YESTERDAY IS HERE.
HEY! QUIT PLAYING AROUND!
EH?
SUGURI ADAPTING HERSELF TO THE PLAY AREA.
AH... IT'S HIM...
YOU CAME TO SEE ME AGAIN! I'M SO HAPPY!!
HUH ?!
WHAT ?!
...THAT'S WHAT HE'S SAYING TO YOU!
B-BMP B-BMP
R... RIGHT ...

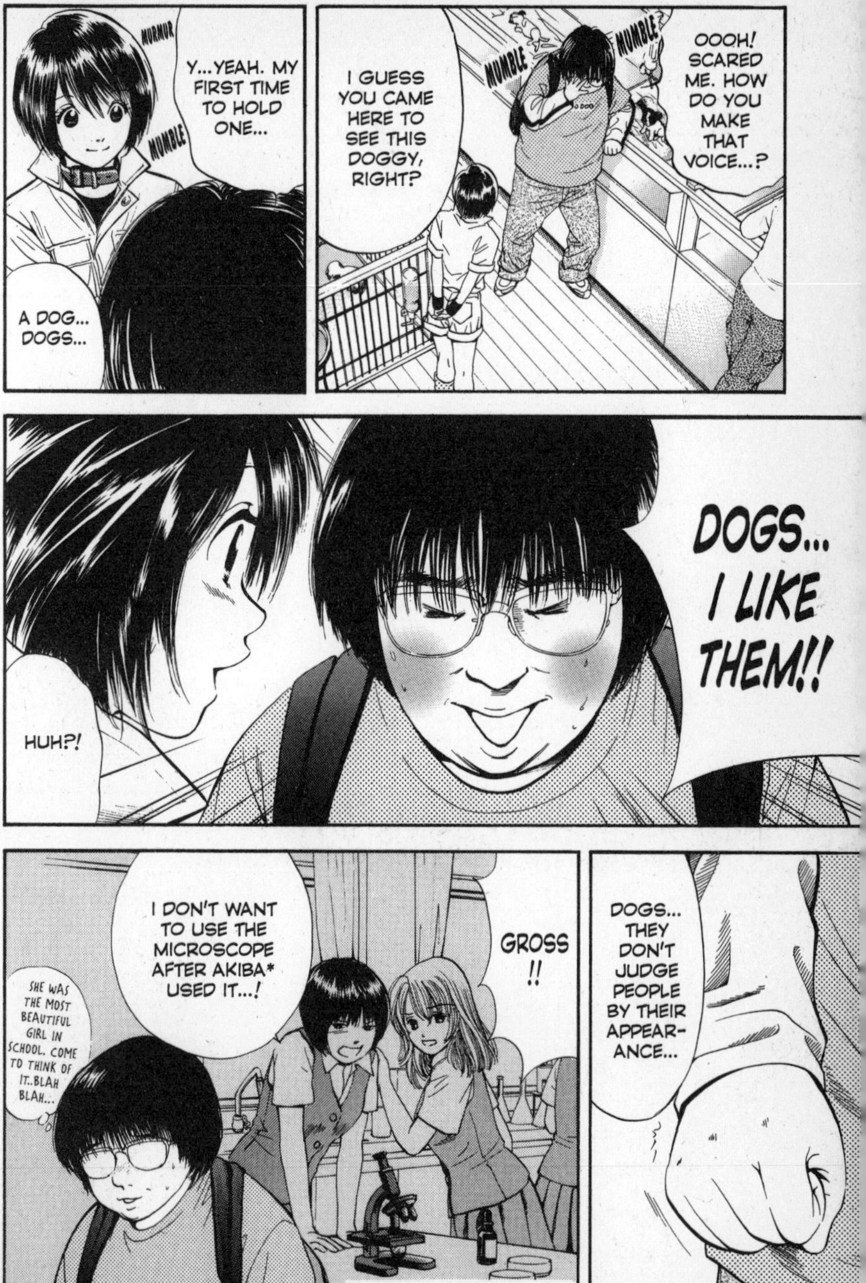
OOOH! SCARED ME. HOW DO YOU MAKE THAT VOICE...?
MUMBLE
MUMBLE
I GUESS YOU CAME HERE TO SEE THIS DOGGY, RIGHT?
MURMUR
Y...YEAH. MY FIRST TIME TO HOLD ONE...
MUMBLE
A DOG... DOGS...
DOGS... I LIKE THEM!!
HUH?!
DOGS... THEY DON'T JUDGE PEOPLE BY THEIR APPEARANCE...
GROSS !!
I DON'T WANT TO USE THE MICROSCOPE AFTER AKIBA* USED IT...!
SHE WAS THE MOST BEAUTIFUL GIRL IN SCHOOL. COME TO THINK OF IT..BLAH BLAH...

*"Akiba" is short for "Akihabara" in Tokyo where "otaku" or geeks congregate. Akiba may be substituted for "Nerd" or "Geek".

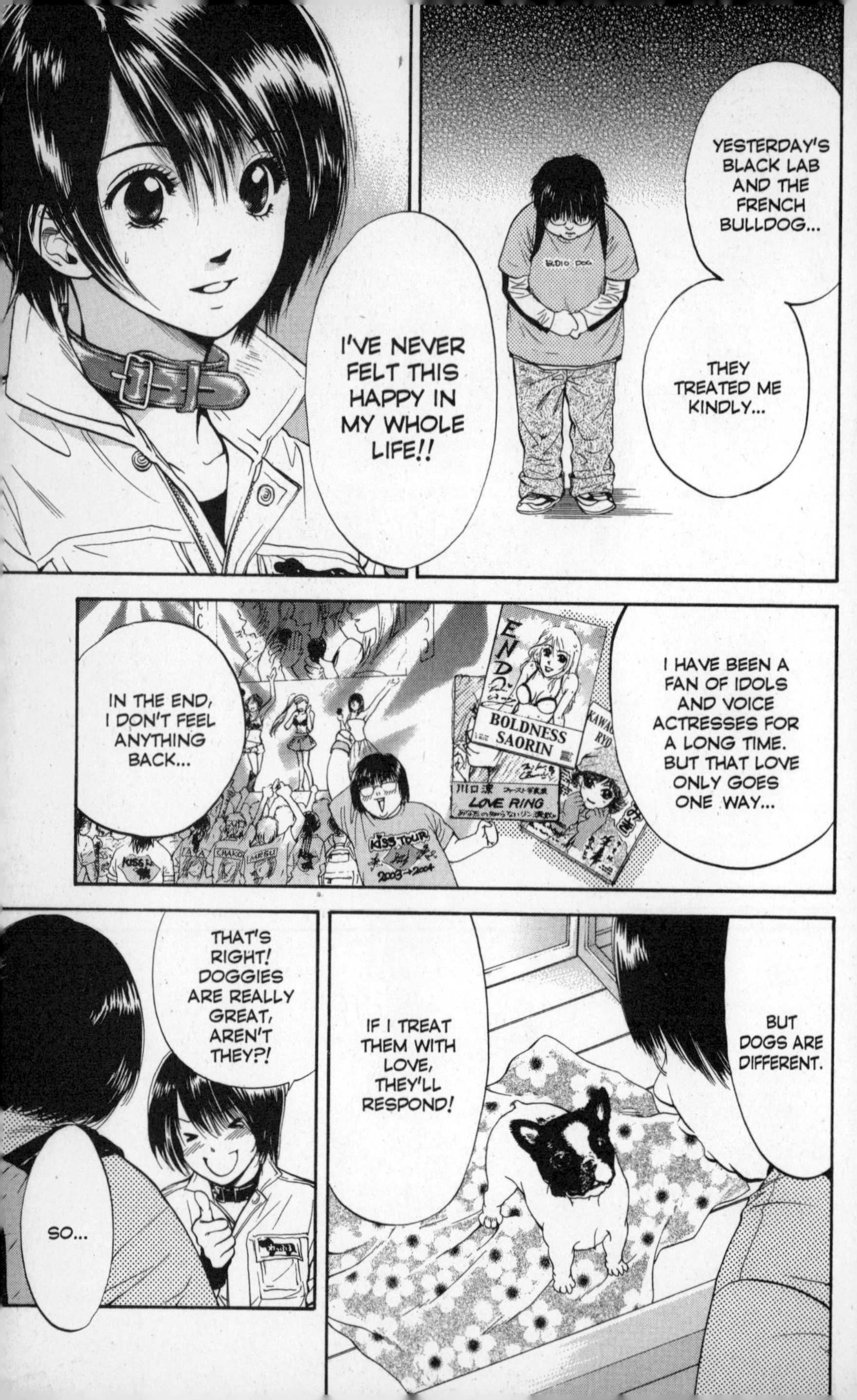
YESTERDAY'S BLACK LAB AND THE FRENCH BULLDOG...
THEY TREATED ME KINDLY...
I'VE NEVER FELT THIS HAPPY IN MY WHOLE LIFE!!
I HAVE BEEN A FAN OF IDOLS AND VOICE ACTRESSES FOR A LONG TIME. BUT THAT LOVE ONLY GOES ONE WAY...
BOLDNESS SAORIN
LOVE RING
IN THE END, I DON'T FEEL ANYTHING BACK...
BUT DOGS ARE DIFFERENT.
IF I TREAT THEM WITH LOVE, THEY'LL RESPOND!
THAT'S RIGHT! DOGGIES ARE REALLY GREAT, AREN'T THEY?!
SO...

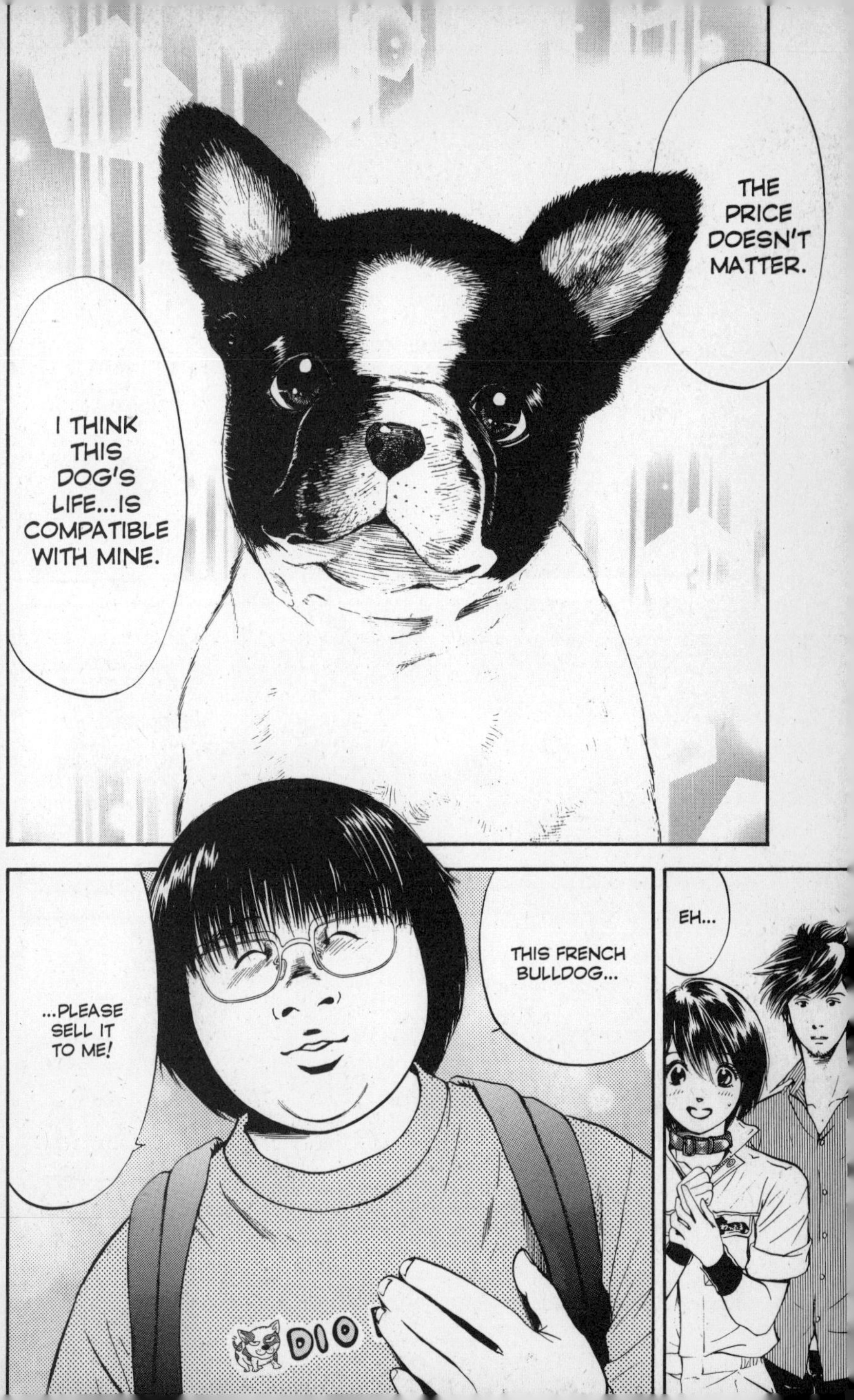
THE PRICE DOESN'T MATTER.
I THINK THIS DOG'S LIFE...IS COMPATIBLE WITH MINE.
EH...
THIS FRENCH BULLDOG...
...PLEASE SELL IT TO ME!
DIO

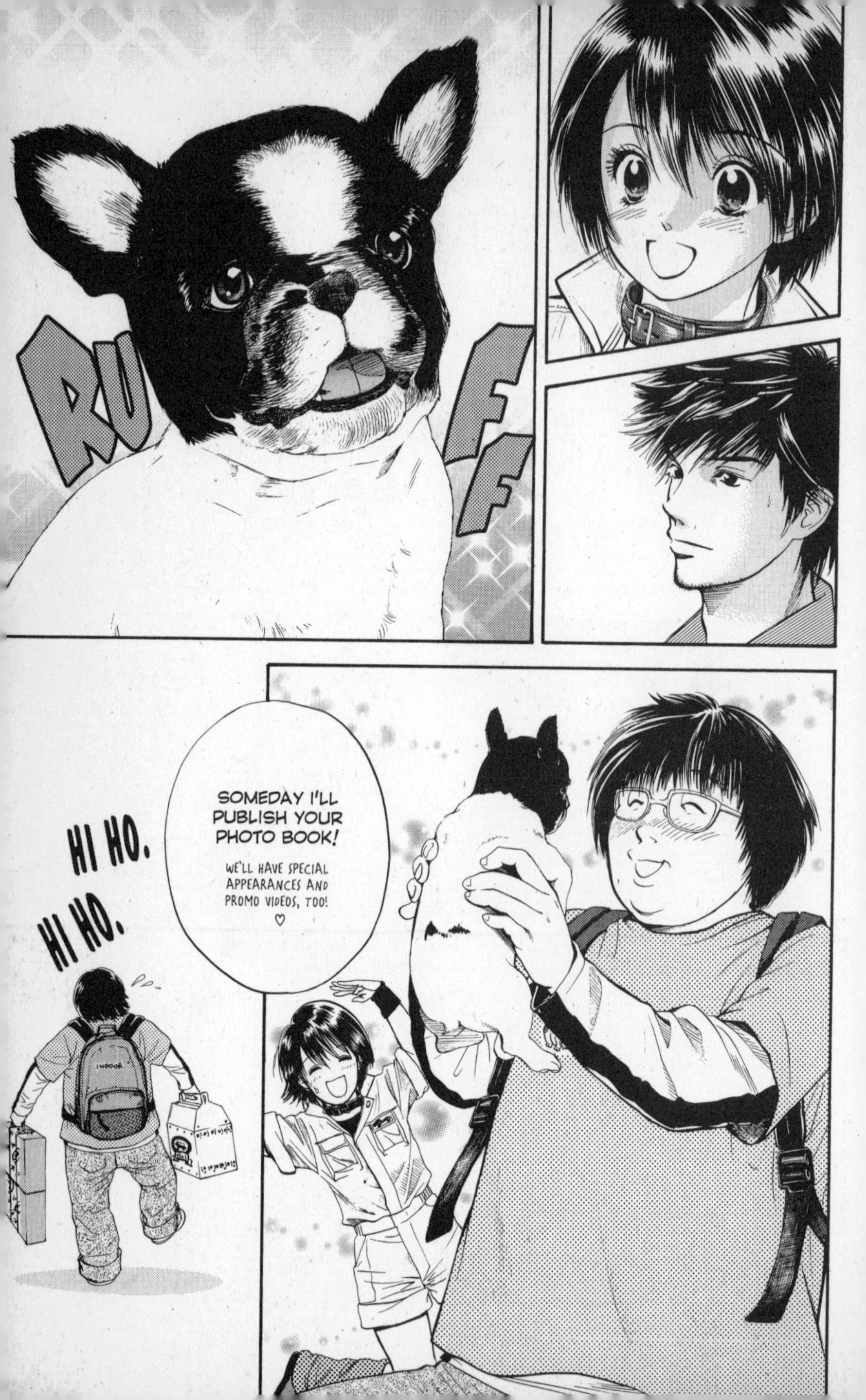
RUFFF
SOMEDAY I'LL PUBLISH YOUR PHOTO BOOK!
WE'LL HAVE SPECIAL APPEARANCES AND PROMO VIDEOS, TOO! ♡
HI HO.
HI HO.

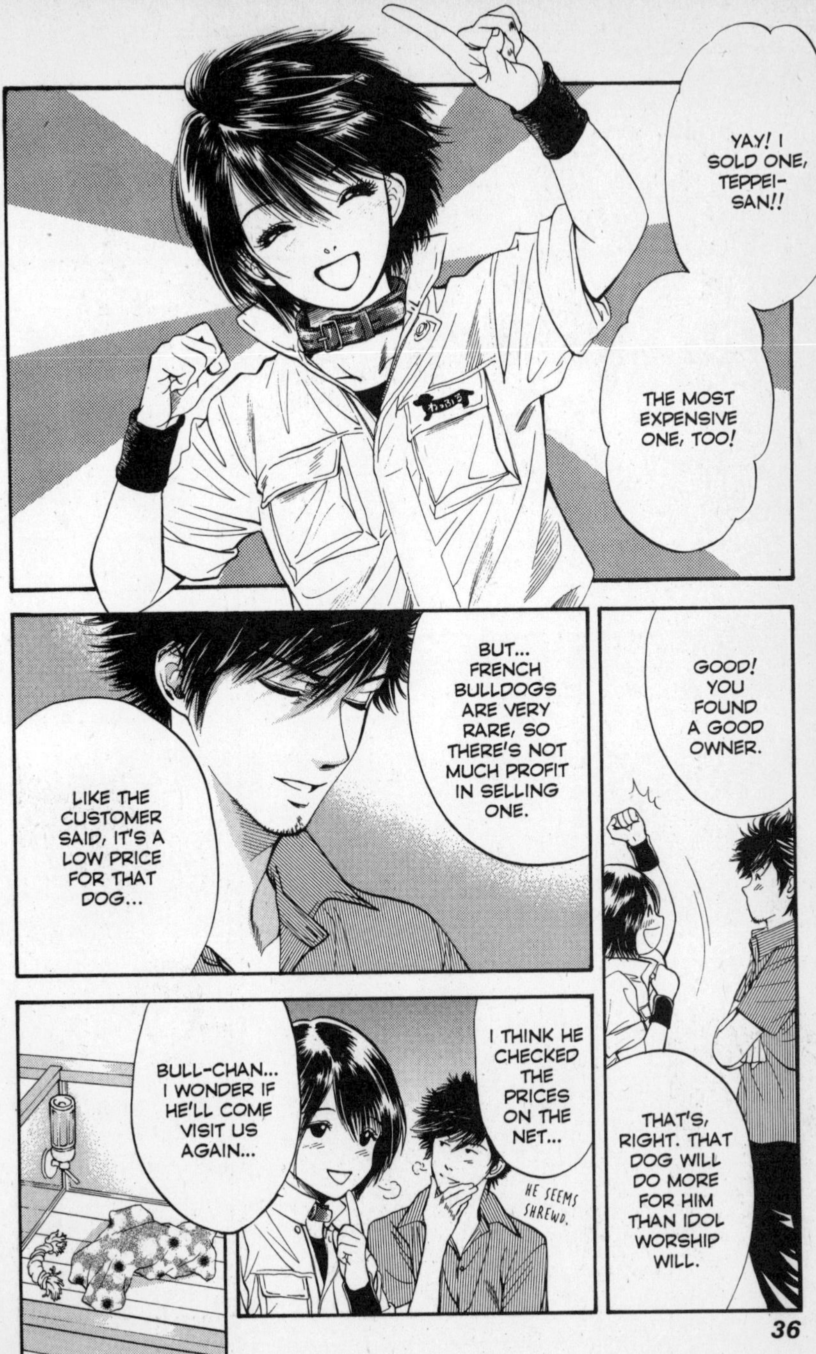

YAY! I SOLD ONE, TEPPEI-SAN!!
THE MOST EXPENSIVE ONE, TOO!
GOOD! YOU FOUND A GOOD OWNER.
THAT'S, RIGHT. THAT DOG WILL DO MORE FOR HIM THAN IDOL WORSHIP WILL.
BUT... FRENCH BULLDOGS ARE VERY RARE, SO THERE'S NOT MUCH PROFIT IN SELLING ONE.
LIKE THE CUSTOMER SAID, IT'S A LOW PRICE FOR THAT DOG...
I THINK HE CHECKED THE PRICES ON THE NET...
HE SEEMS SHREWD.
BULL-CHAN... I WONDER IF HE'LL COME VISIT US AGAIN...

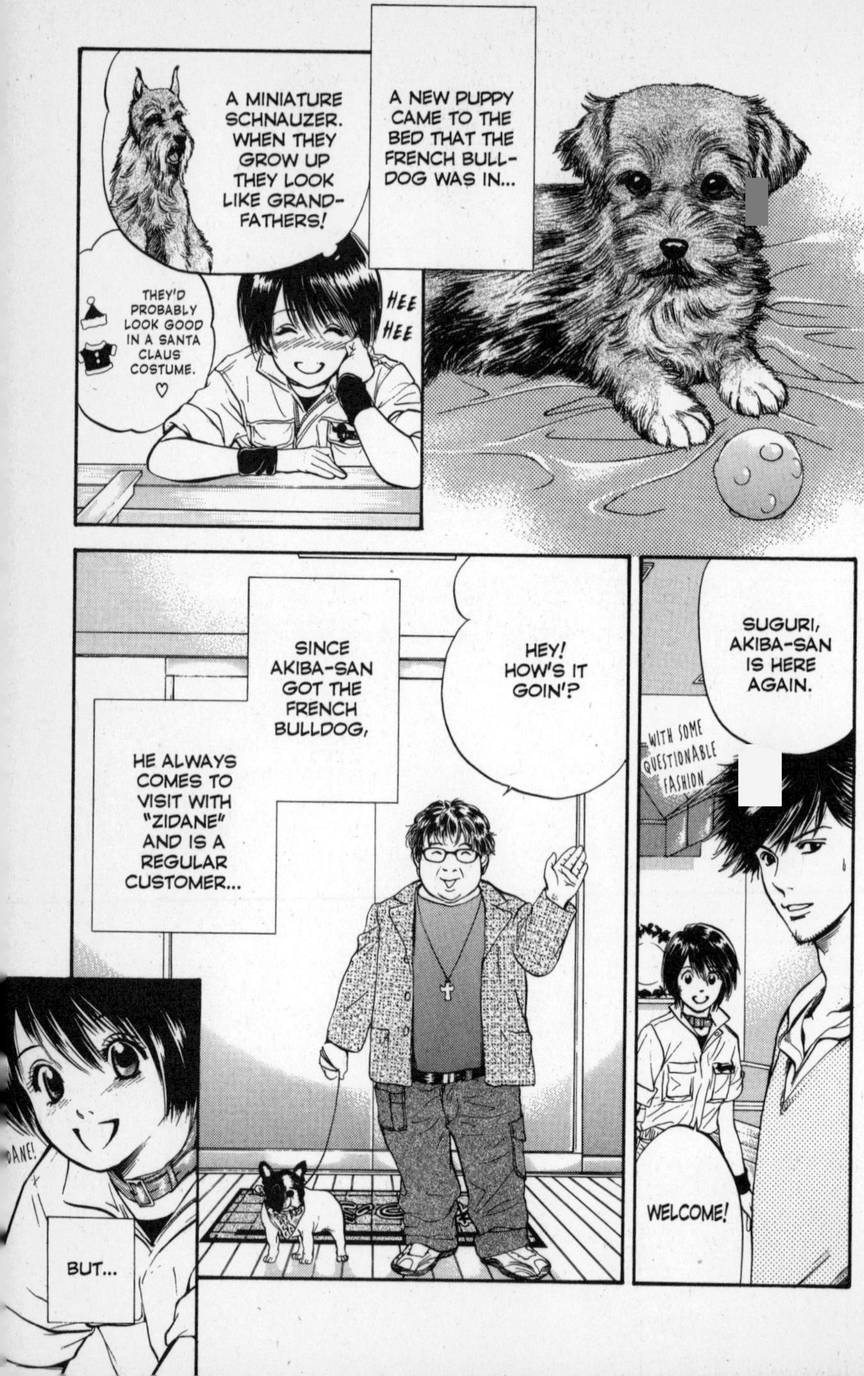
A NEW PUPPY CAME TO THE BED THAT THE FRENCH BULL-DOG WAS IN...
A MINIATURE SCHNAUZER. WHEN THEY GROW UP THEY LOOK LIKE GRAND-FATHERS!
HEE HEE
THEY'D PROBABLY LOOK GOOD IN A SANTA CLAUS COSTUME. ♡
SUGURI, AKIBA-SAN IS HERE AGAIN.
WITH SOME QUESTIONABLE FASHION
WELCOME!
HEY! HOW'S IT GOIN'?
SINCE AKIBA-SAN GOT THE FRENCH BULLDOG,
HE ALWAYS COMES TO VISIT WITH "ZIDANE" AND IS A REGULAR CUSTOMER...
BUT...

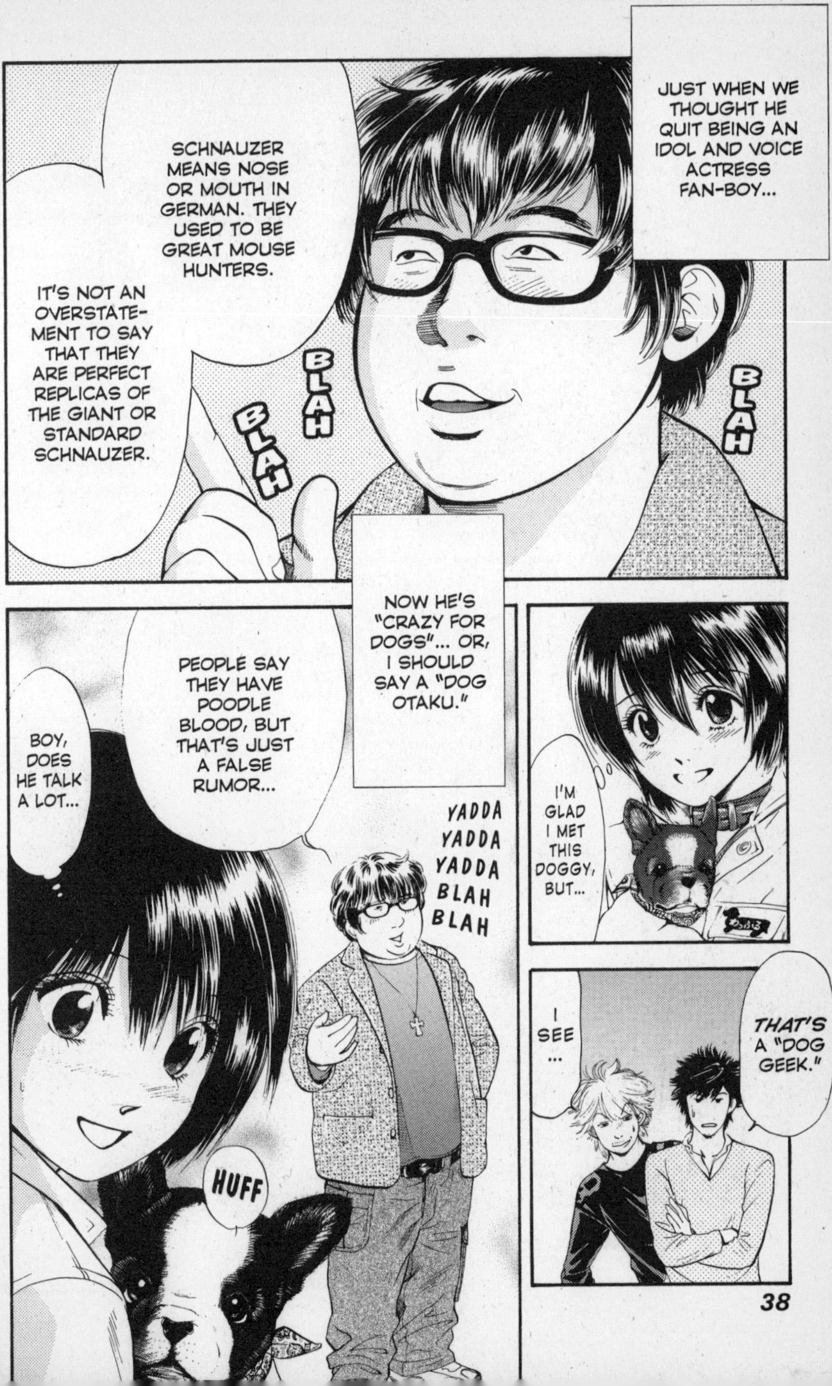
JUST WHEN WE THOUGHT HE QUIT BEING AN IDOL AND VOICE ACTRESS FAN-BOY...
BLAH
SCHNAUZER MEANS NOSE OR MOUTH IN GERMAN. THEY USED TO BE GREAT MOUSE HUNTERS.
BLAH BLAH
IT'S NOT AN OVERSTATE-MENT TO SAY THAT THEY ARE PERFECT REPLICAS OF THE GIANT OR STANDARD SCHNAUZER.
NOW HE'S "CRAZY FOR DOGS"... OR, I SHOULD SAY A "DOG OTAKU."
I'M GLAD I MET THIS DOGGY, BUT...
THAT'S A "DOG GEEK."
I SEE ...
YADDA YADDA YADDA BLAH BLAH
PEOPLE SAY THEY HAVE POODLE BLOOD, BUT THAT'S JUST A FALSE RUMOR...
BOY, DOES HE TALK A LOT...
HUFF

CHAPTER 11
MAKIN' MONEY?!

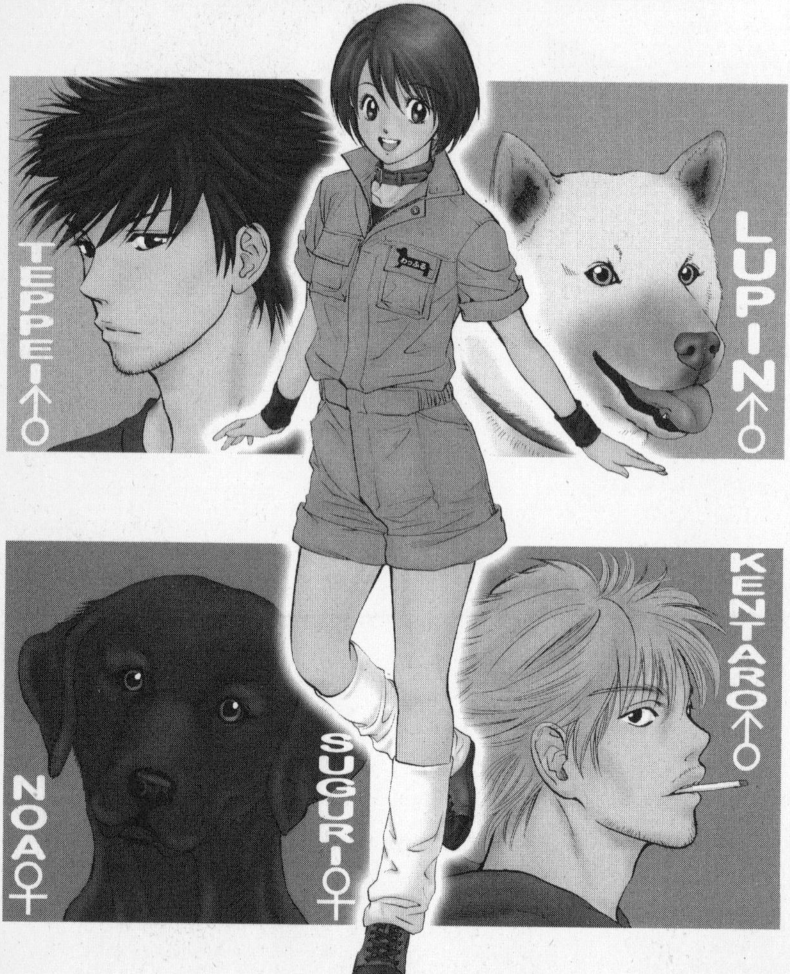
LUPIN ♂
TEPPEI ♂
KENTARO ♂
SUGURI ♀
NOA ♀

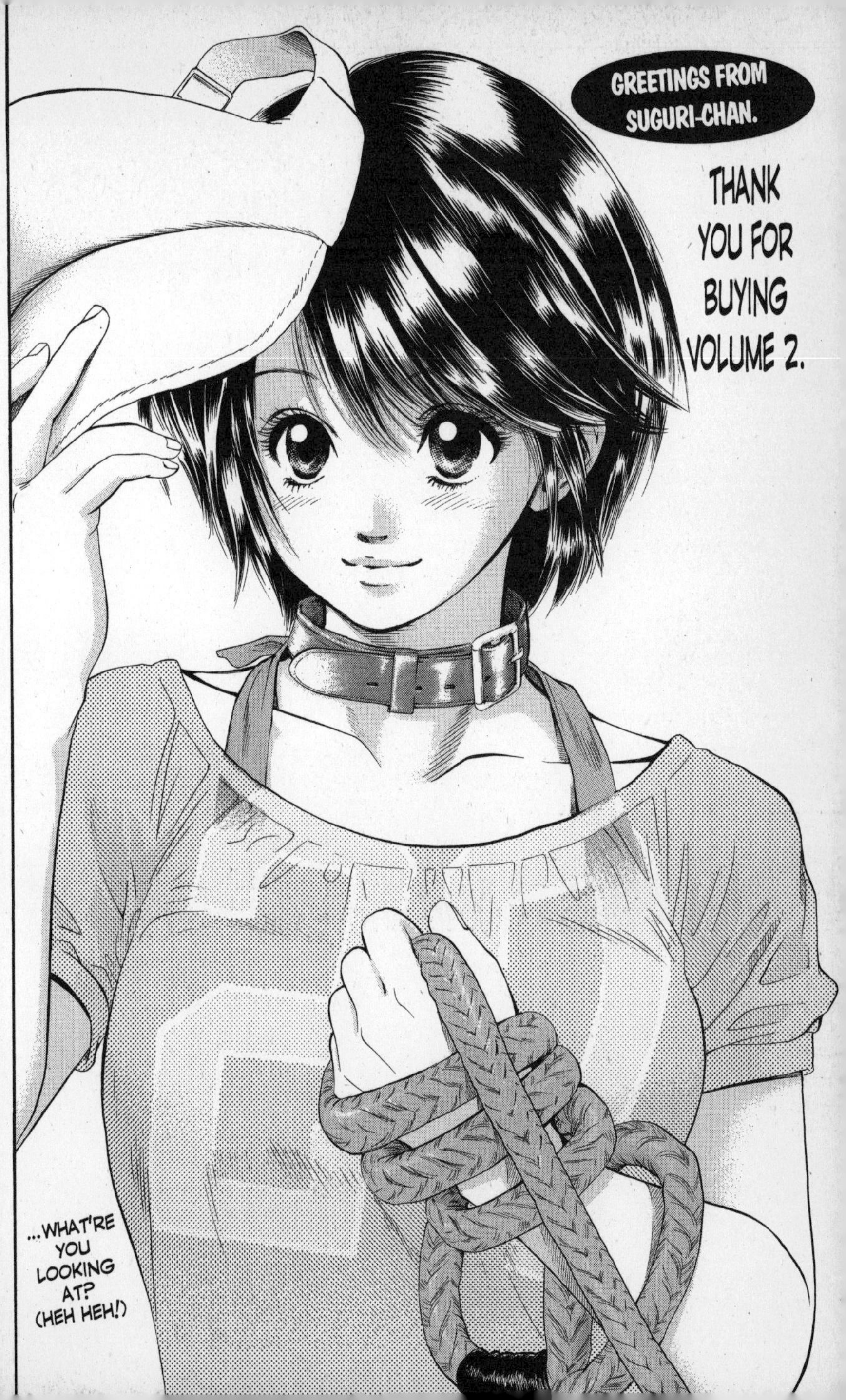
GREETINGS FROM SUGURI-CHAN.
THANK YOU FOR BUYING VOLUME 2.
...WHAT'RE YOU LOOKING AT? (HEH HEH!)

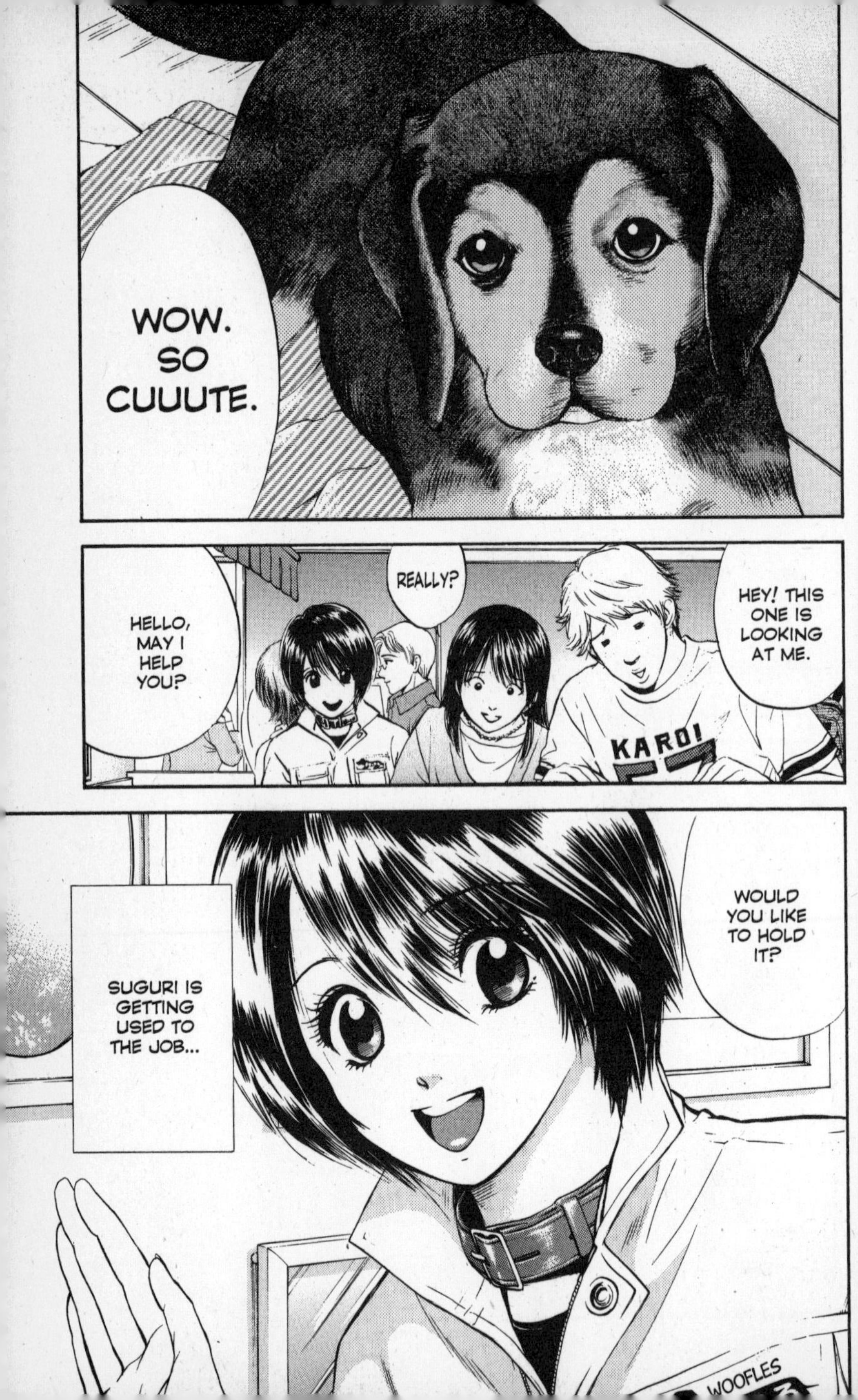
WOW. SO CUUUTE.
HEY! THIS ONE IS LOOKING AT ME.
KAROI
REALLY?
HELLO, MAY I HELP YOU?
WOULD YOU LIKE TO HOLD IT?
SUGURI IS GETTING USED TO THE JOB...
WOOFLES

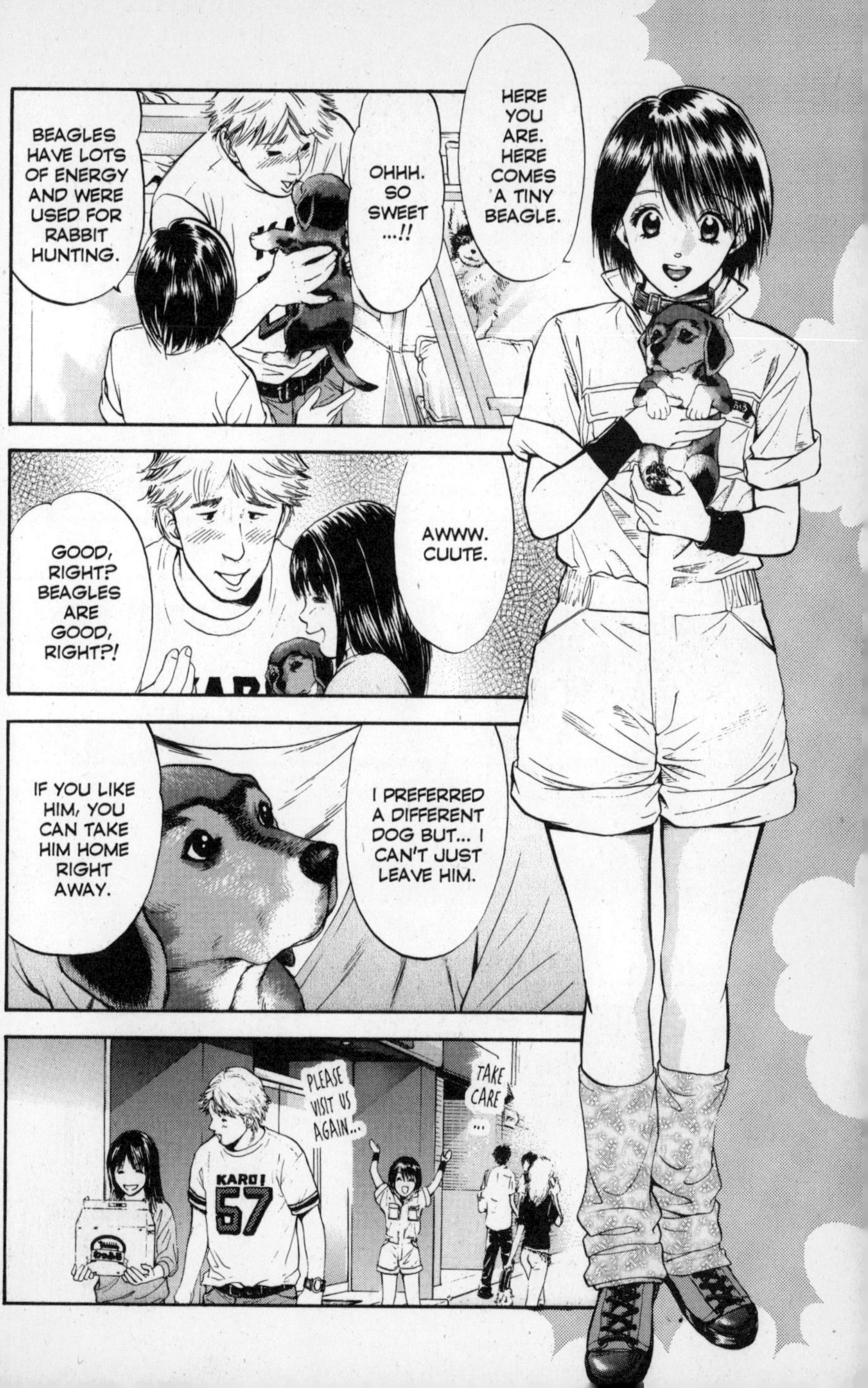
HERE YOU ARE. HERE COMES A TINY BEAGLE.
OHHH. SO SWEET ...!!
BEAGLES HAVE LOTS OF ENERGY AND WERE USED FOR RABBIT HUNTING.
AWWW. CUUTE.
GOOD, RIGHT? BEAGLES ARE GOOD, RIGHT?!
I PREFERRED A DIFFERENT DOG BUT... I CAN'T JUST LEAVE HIM.
IF YOU LIKE HIM, YOU CAN TAKE HIM HOME RIGHT AWAY.
TAKE CARE ...
PLEASE VISIT US AGAIN...
KARO! 67

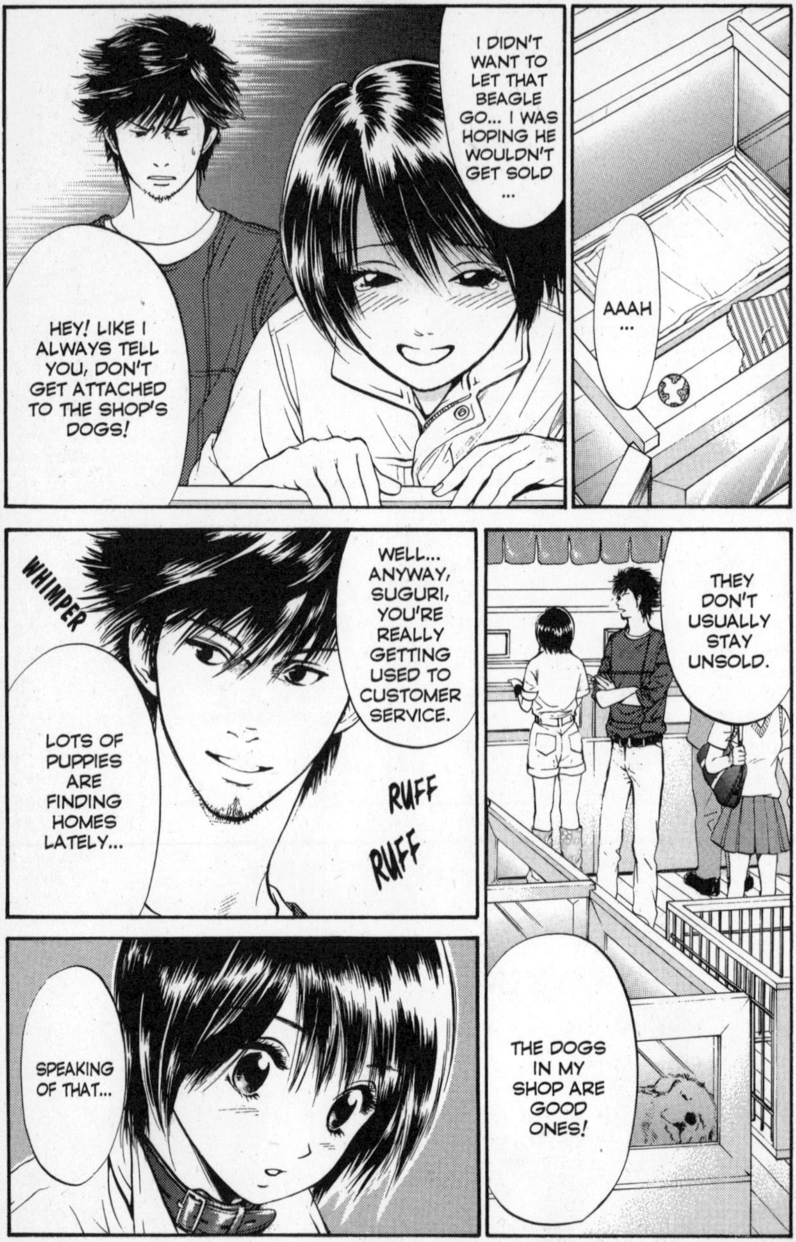
AAAH ...
I DIDN'T WANT TO LET THAT BEAGLE GO... I WAS HOPING HE WOULDN'T GET SOLD ...
HEY! LIKE I ALWAYS TELL YOU, DON'T GET ATTACHED TO THE SHOP'S DOGS!
THEY DON'T USUALLY STAY UNSOLD.
THE DOGS IN MY SHOP ARE GOOD ONES!
WELL... ANYWAY, SUGURI, YOU'RE REALLY GETTING USED TO CUSTOMER SERVICE.
WHIMPER
LOTS OF PUPPIES ARE FINDING HOMES LATELY...
RUFF
RUFF
SPEAKING OF THAT...

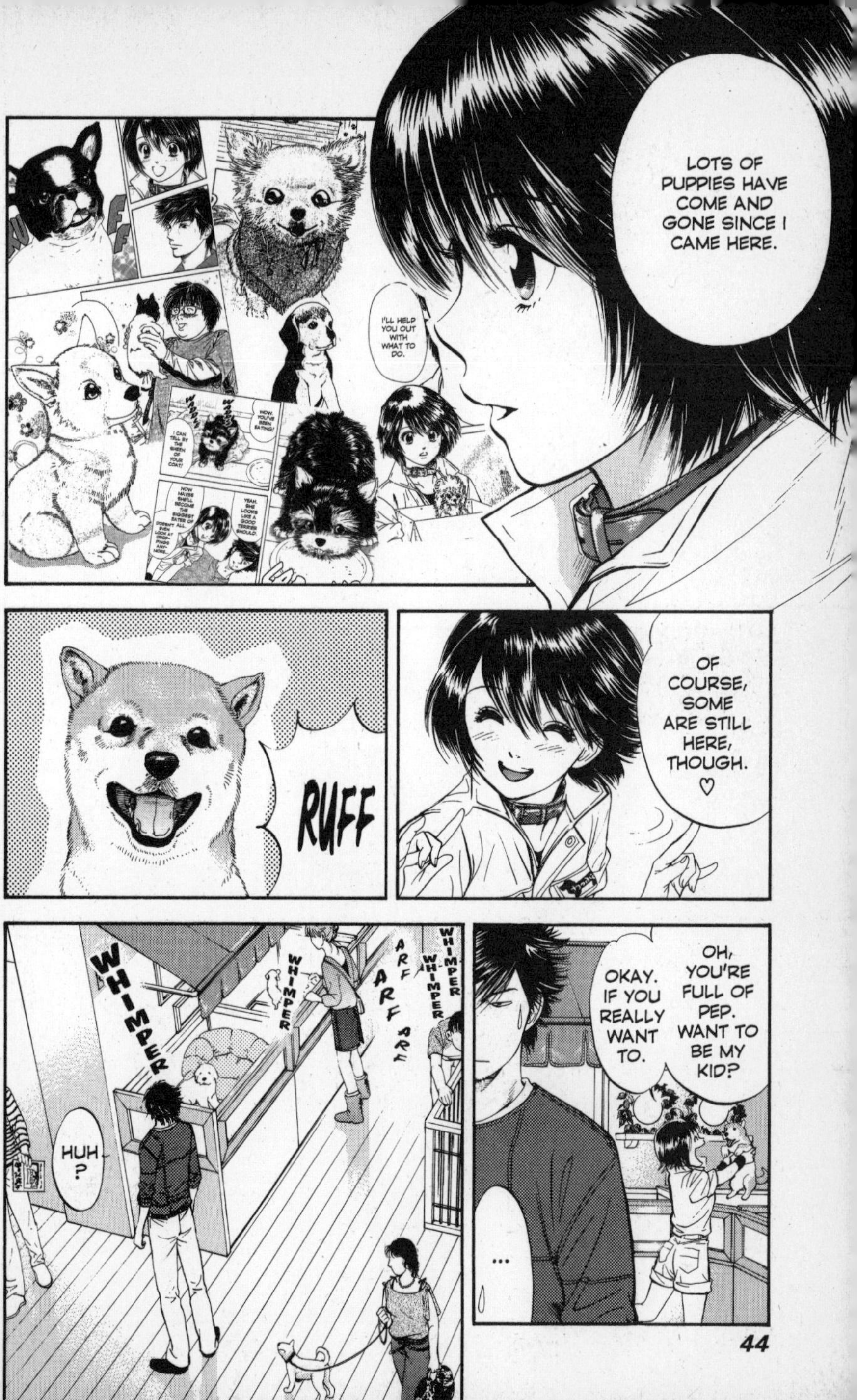
LOTS OF PUPPIES HAVE COME AND GONE SINCE I CAME HERE.
I'LL HELP YOU OUT WITH WHAT TO DO.
WOW, YOU'VE BEEN EATING!
I CAN TELL BY THE SHEEN OF YOUR COAT!
YEAH, SHE LOOKS LIKE A GOOD TERRIER SHOULD.
NOW MAYBE SHE'LL BECOME THE BIGGEST EATER OF ALL.
DOESN'T EVEN LOOK AT DROPPINGS ANYMORE...
OF COURSE, SOME ARE STILL HERE, THOUGH. ♡
RUFF
OH, YOU'RE FULL OF PEP. WANT TO BE MY KID?
OKAY. IF YOU REALLY WANT TO.
...
WHIMPER
ARF ARF ARF
WHIMPER
WHIMPER
WHIMPER
HUH?

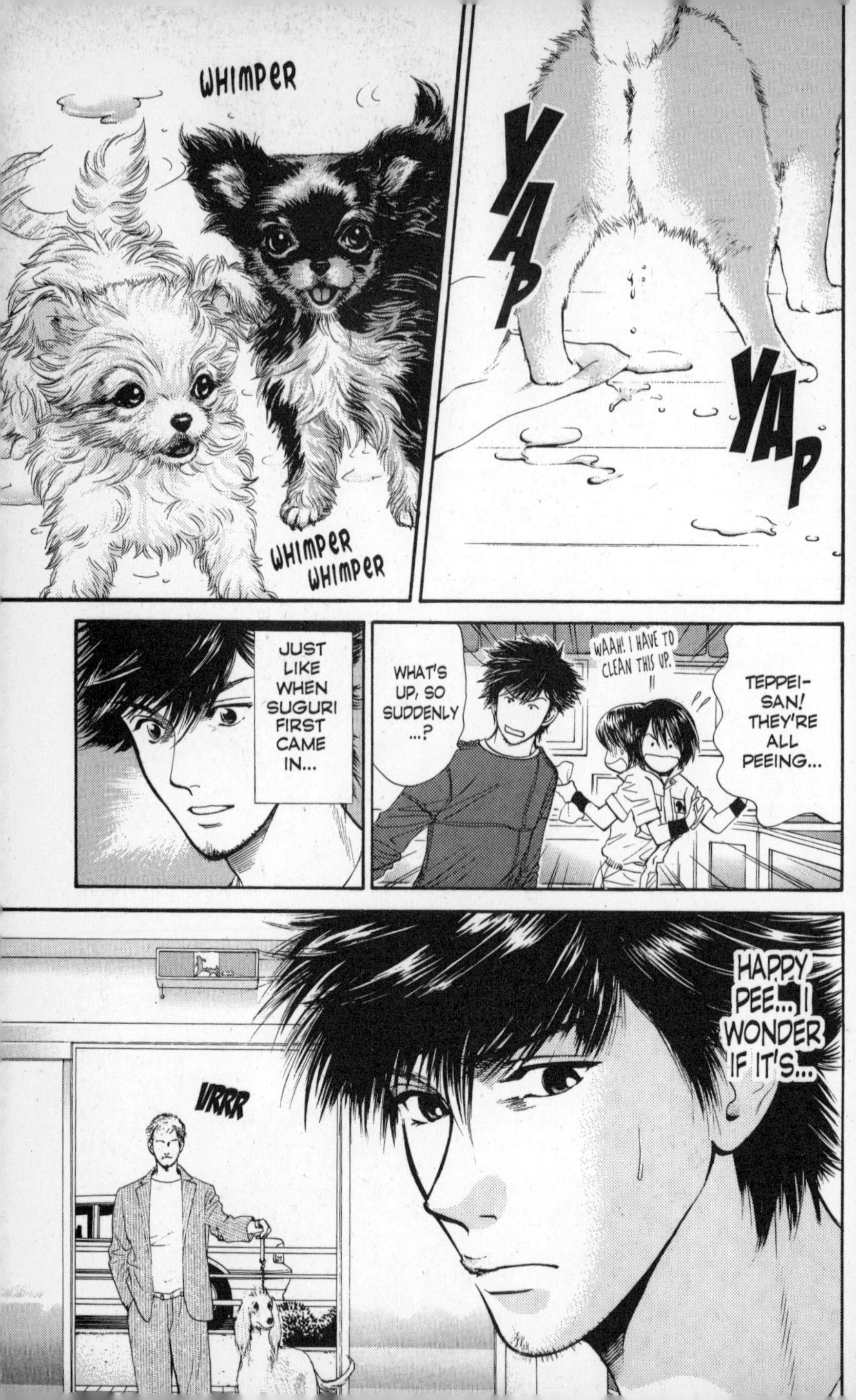
YAP
YAP
WHIMPER
WHIMPER
WHIMPER
TEPPEI-SAN! THEY'RE ALL PEEING...
WAAH! I HAVE TO CLEAN THIS UP.
WHAT'S UP, SO SUDDENLY...?
JUST LIKE WHEN SUGURI FIRST CAME IN...
HAPPY PEE... I WONDER IF IT'S...
VRRR

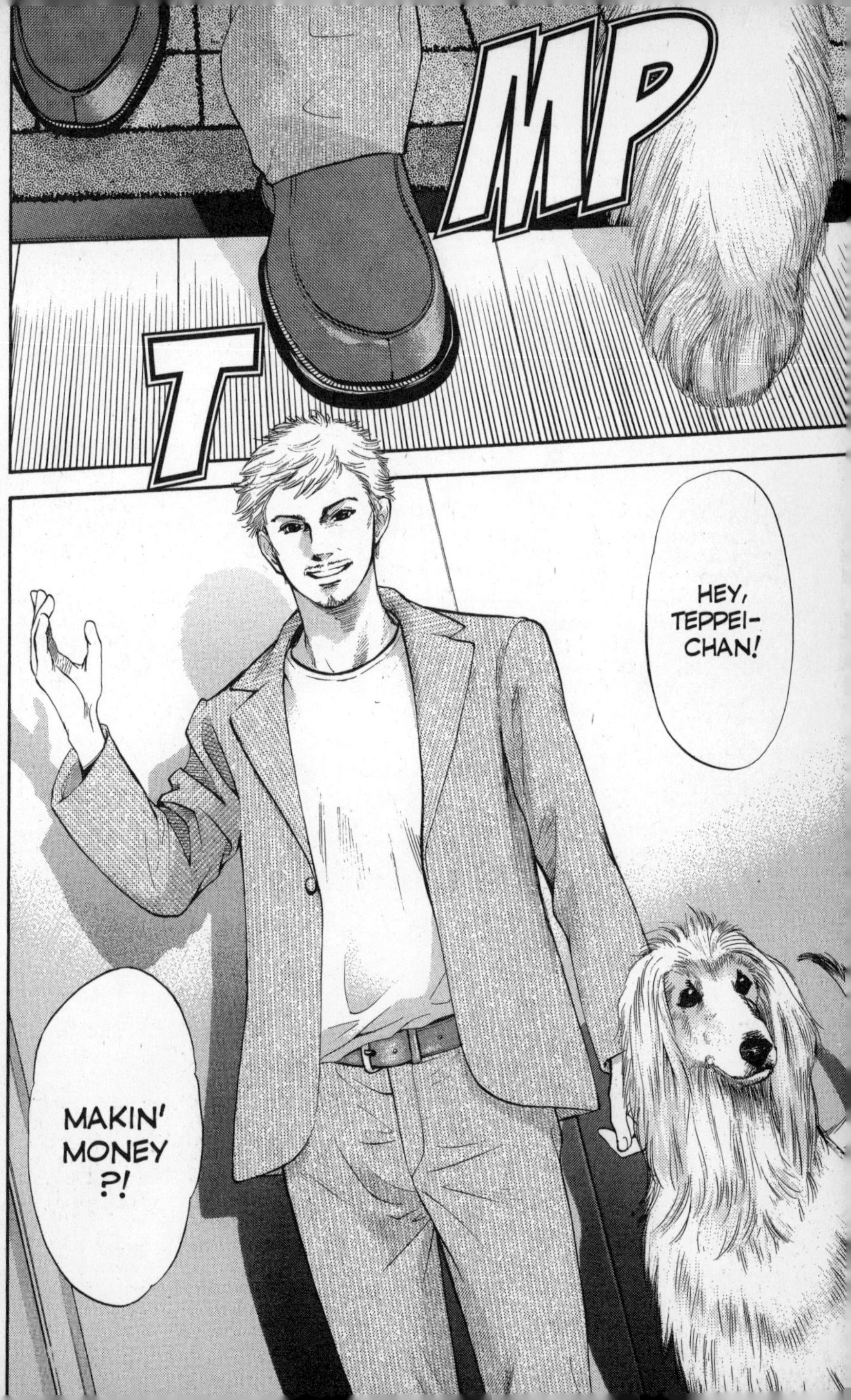
T MP
HEY, TEPPEI-CHAN!
MAKIN' MONEY ?!

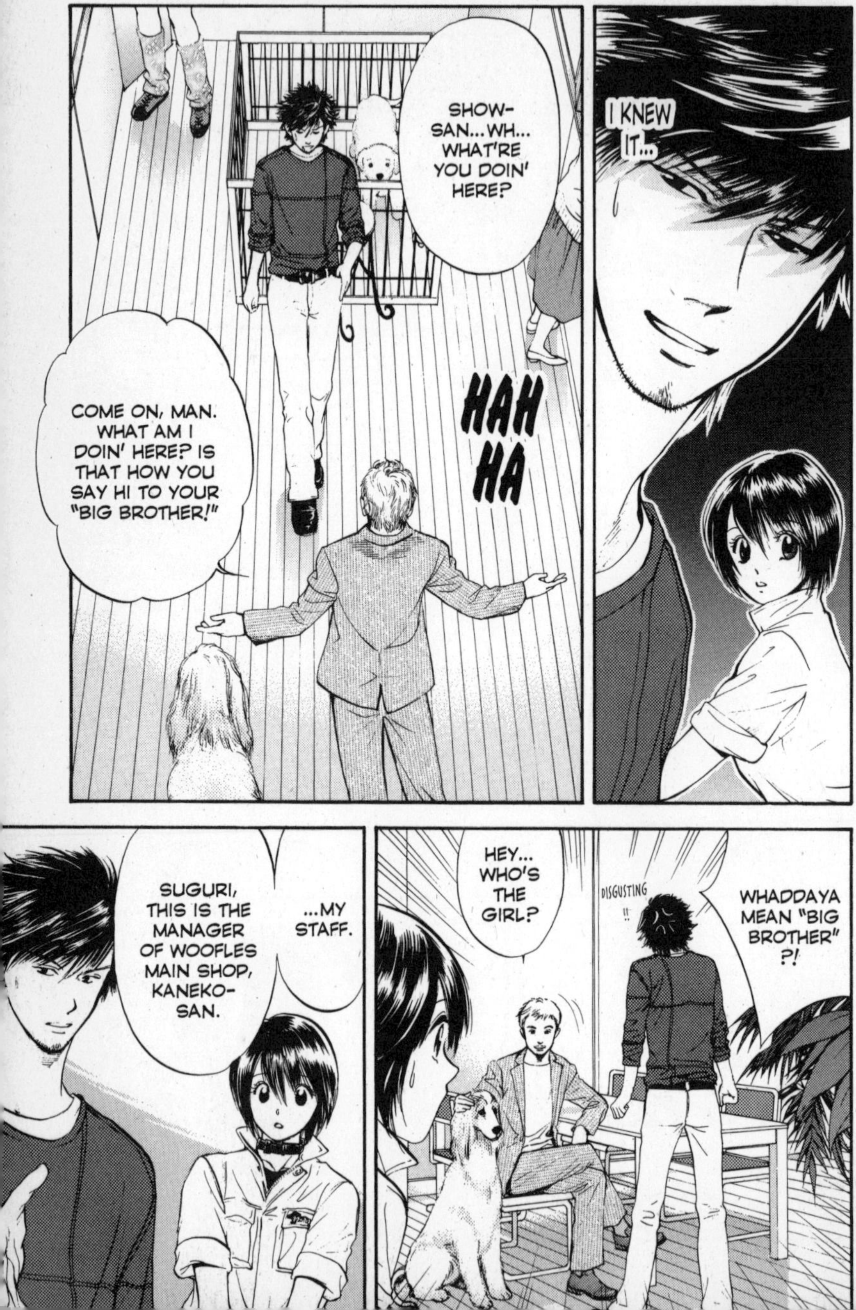
I KNEW IT...
SHOW-SAN...WH... WHAT'RE YOU DOIN' HERE?
HAH HA
COME ON, MAN. WHAT AM I DOIN' HERE? IS THAT HOW YOU SAY HI TO YOUR "BIG BROTHER!"
WHADDAYA MEAN "BIG BROTHER" ?!
DISGUSTING !!
HEY... WHO'S THE GIRL?
...MY STAFF.
SUGURI, THIS IS THE MANAGER OF WOOFLES MAIN SHOP, KANEKO-SAN.

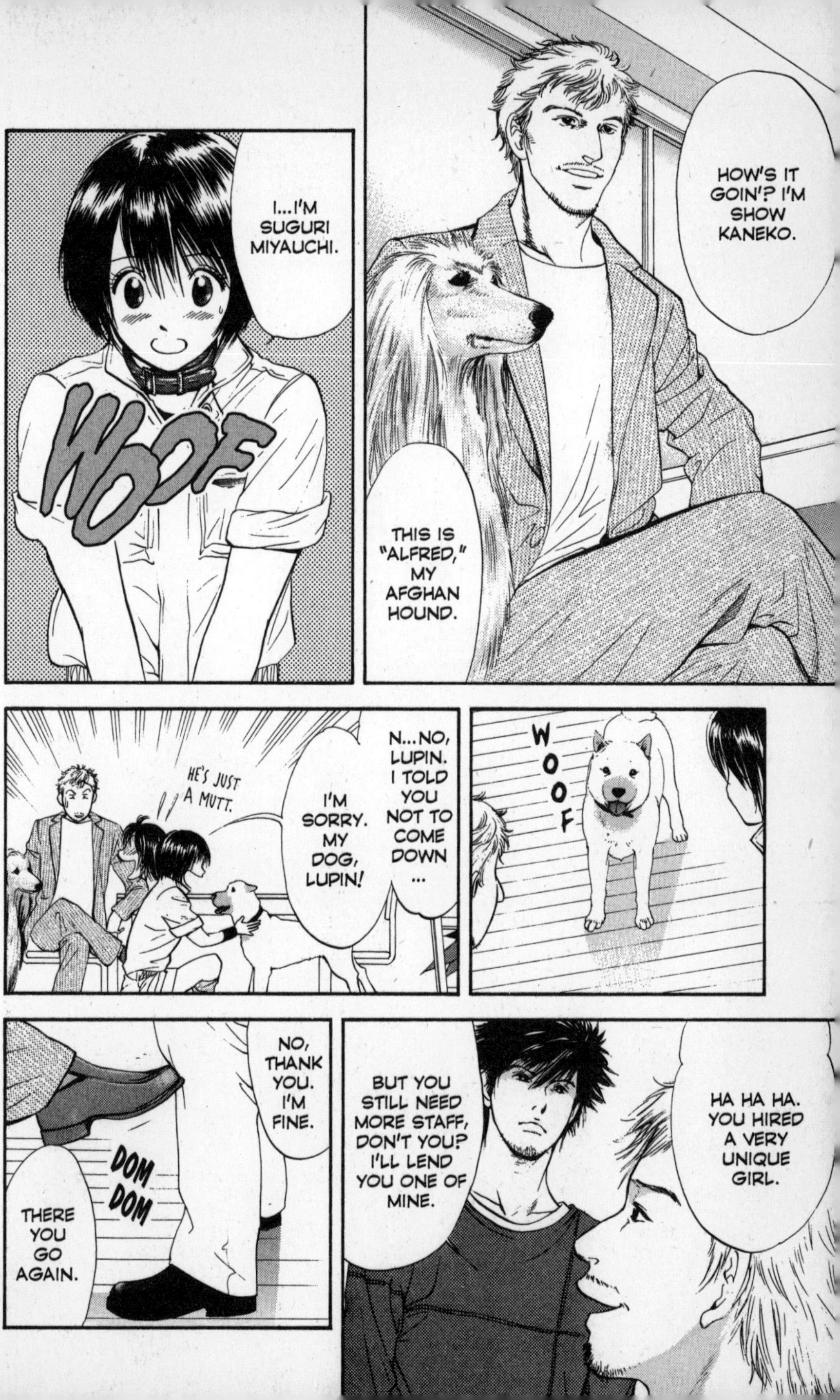
HOW'S IT GOIN'? I'M SHOW KANEKO.
THIS IS "ALFRED," MY AFGHAN HOUND.
I...I'M SUGURI MIYAUCHI.
WOOF
WOOF
N...NO, LUPIN. I TOLD YOU NOT TO COME DOWN ...
I'M SORRY. MY DOG, LUPIN!
HE'S JUST A MUTT.
HA HA HA. YOU HIRED A VERY UNIQUE GIRL.
BUT YOU STILL NEED MORE STAFF, DON'T YOU? I'LL LEND YOU ONE OF MINE.
NO, THANK YOU. I'M FINE.
DOM DOM
THERE YOU GO AGAIN.

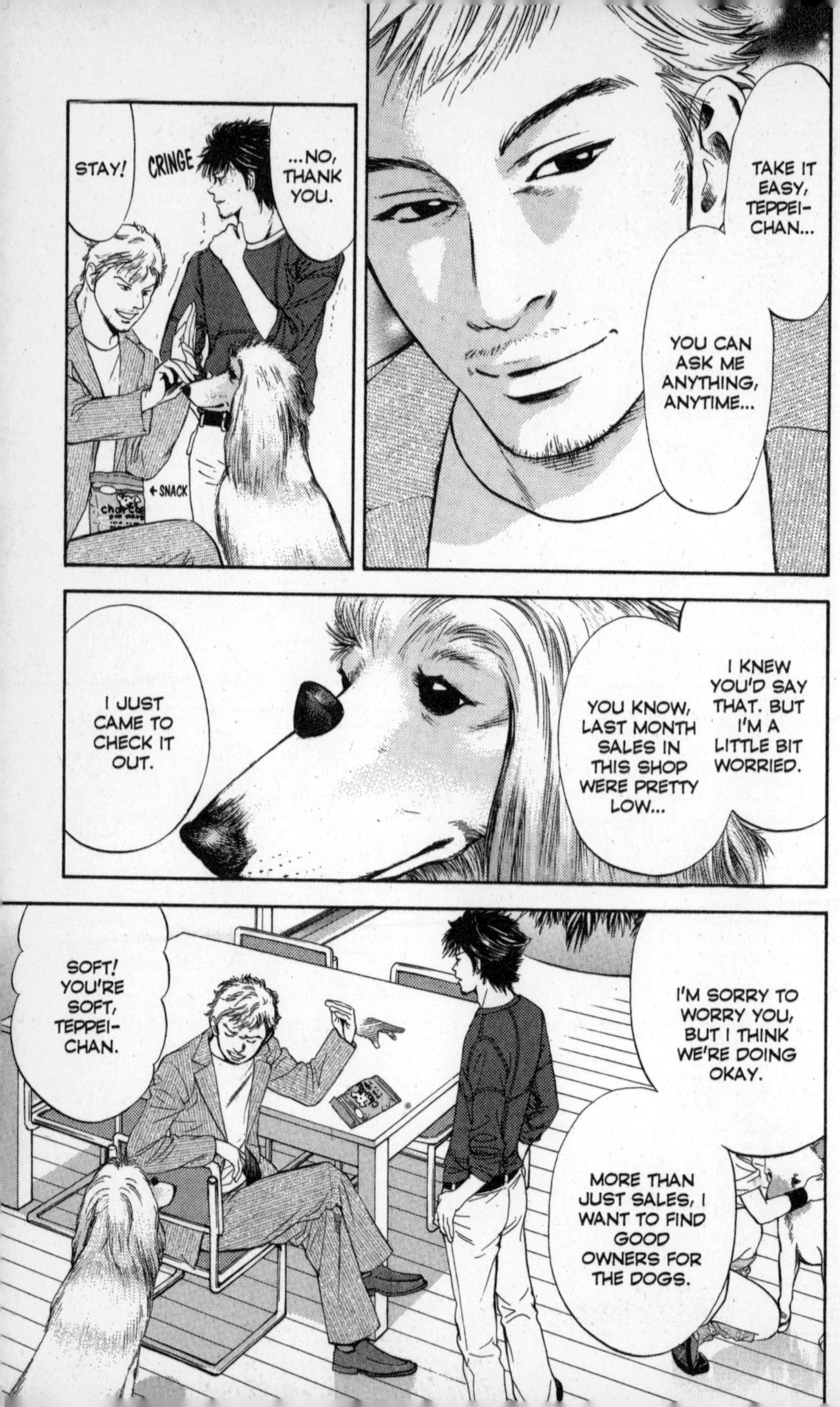
TAKE IT EASY, TEPPEI-CHAN...
YOU CAN ASK ME ANYTHING, ANYTIME...
...NO, THANK YOU.
CRINGE
STAY!
← SNACK
I KNEW YOU'D SAY THAT. BUT I'M A LITTLE BIT WORRIED.
YOU KNOW, LAST MONTH SALES IN THIS SHOP WERE PRETTY LOW...
I JUST CAME TO CHECK IT OUT.
I'M SORRY TO WORRY YOU, BUT I THINK WE'RE DOING OKAY.
MORE THAN JUST SALES, I WANT TO FIND GOOD OWNERS FOR THE DOGS.
SOFT! YOU'RE SOFT, TEPPEI-CHAN.

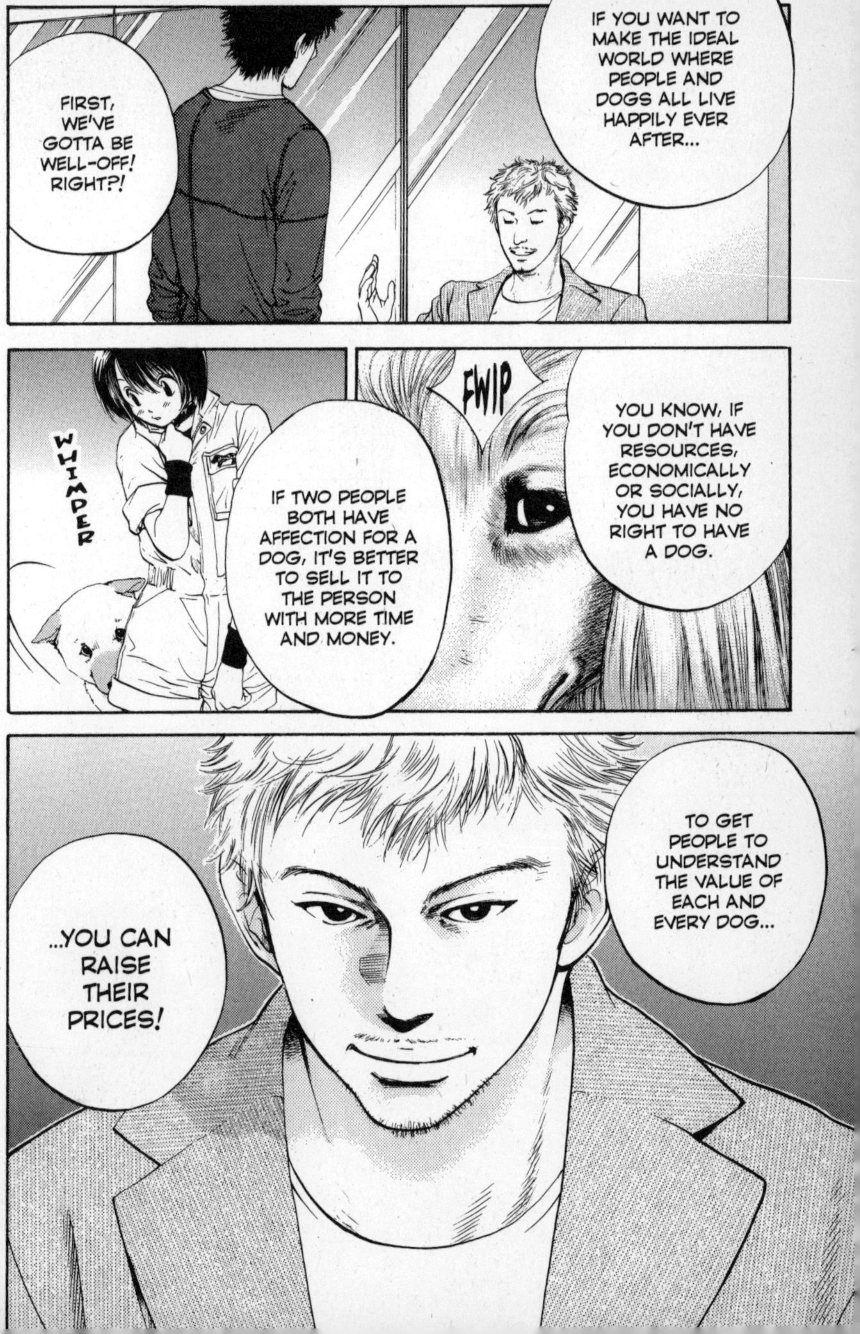
IF YOU WANT TO MAKE THE IDEAL WORLD WHERE PEOPLE AND DOGS ALL LIVE HAPPILY EVER AFTER...
FIRST, WE'VE GOTTA BE WELL-OFF! RIGHT?!
FWIP
YOU KNOW, IF YOU DON'T HAVE RESOURCES, ECONOMICALLY OR SOCIALLY, YOU HAVE NO RIGHT TO HAVE A DOG.
IF TWO PEOPLE BOTH HAVE AFFECTION FOR A DOG, IT'S BETTER TO SELL IT TO THE PERSON WITH MORE TIME AND MONEY.
WHIMPER
TO GET PEOPLE TO UNDERSTAND THE VALUE OF EACH AND EVERY DOG...
...YOU CAN RAISE THEIR PRICES!

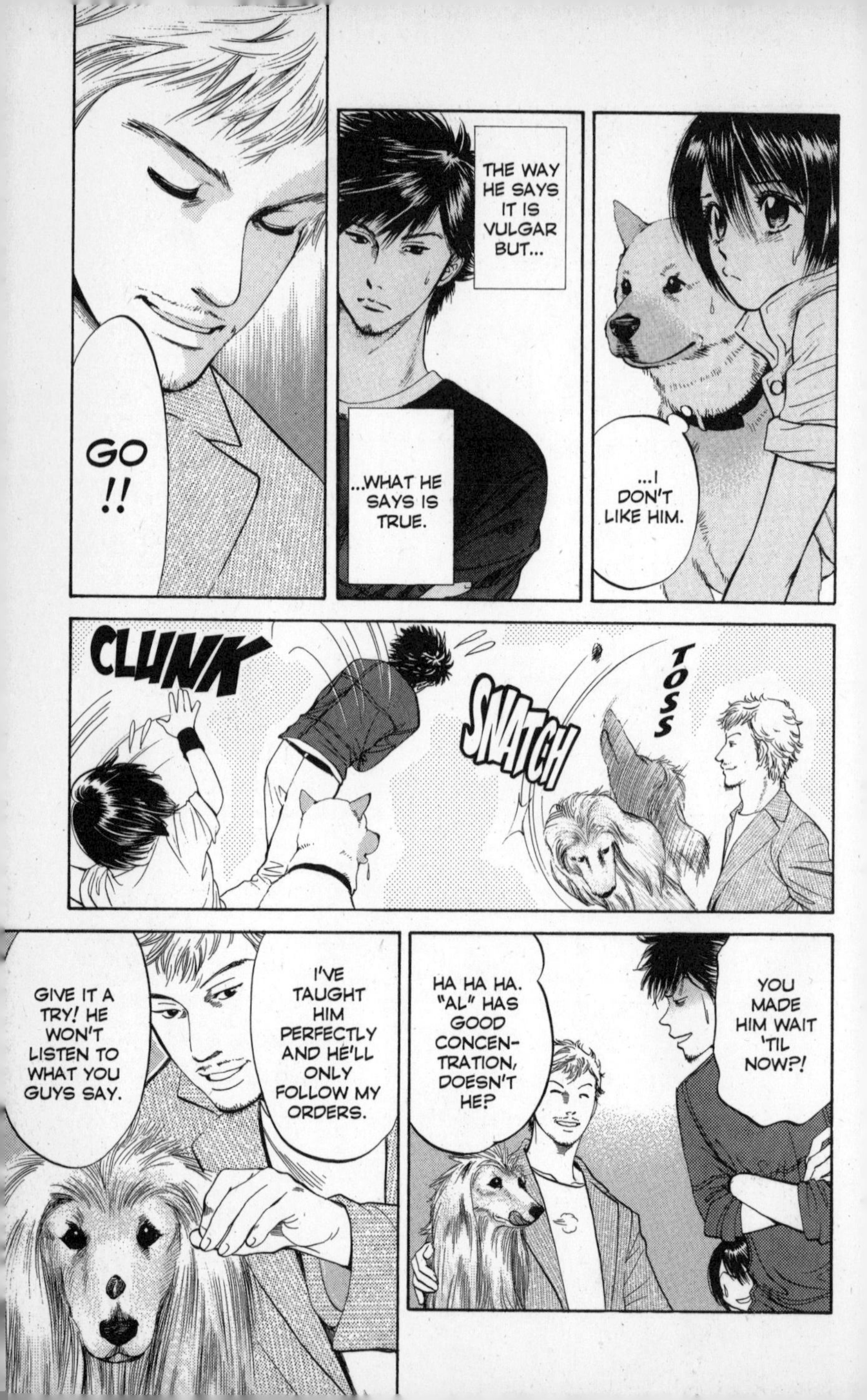
...I DON'T LIKE HIM.
THE WAY HE SAYS IT IS VULGAR BUT...
...WHAT HE SAYS IS TRUE.
GO!!
TOSS
SNATCH
CLUNK
YOU MADE HIM WAIT 'TIL NOW?!
HA HA HA. "AL" HAS GOOD CONCEN-TRATION, DOESN'T HE?
I'VE TAUGHT HIM PERFECTLY AND HE'LL ONLY FOLLOW MY ORDERS.
GIVE IT A TRY! HE WON'T LISTEN TO WHAT YOU GUYS SAY.

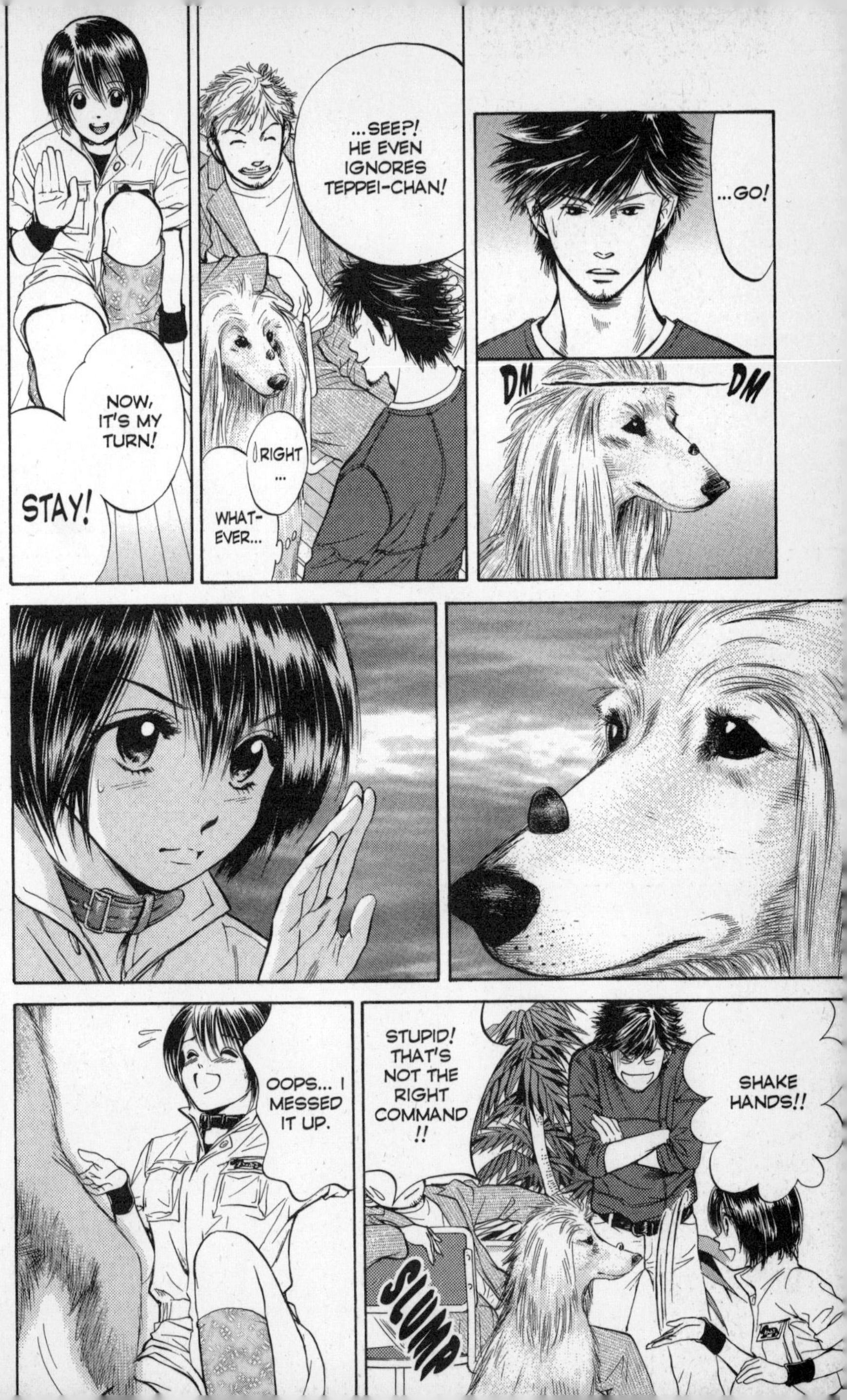
...GO!
DM DM
...SEE?! HE EVEN IGNORES TEPPEI-CHAN!
RIGHT ...
WHATEVER...
NOW, IT'S MY TURN!
STAY!
SHAKE HANDS!!
STUPID! THAT'S NOT THE RIGHT COMMAND !!
SLUMP
OOPS... I MESSED IT UP.

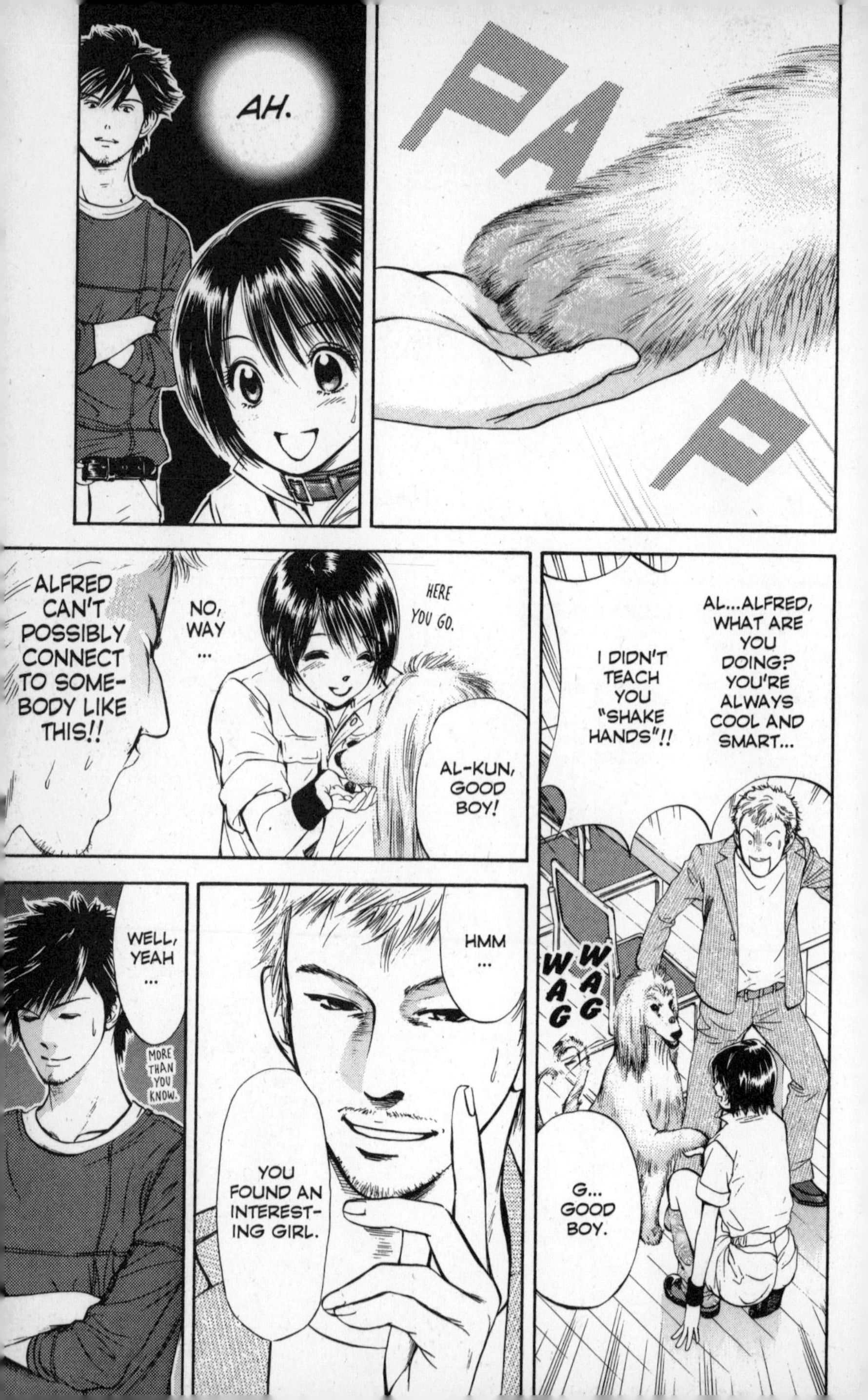
PAP
AH.
AL...ALFRED, WHAT ARE YOU DOING? YOU'RE ALWAYS COOL AND SMART...
I DIDN'T TEACH YOU "SHAKE HANDS"!!
WAG WAG
G... GOOD BOY.
HERE YOU GO.
AL-KUN, GOOD BOY!
NO, WAY ...
ALFRED CAN'T POSSIBLY CONNECT TO SOME-BODY LIKE THIS!!
HMM ...
YOU FOUND AN INTEREST-ING GIRL.
WELL, YEAH ...
MORE THAN YOU KNOW.

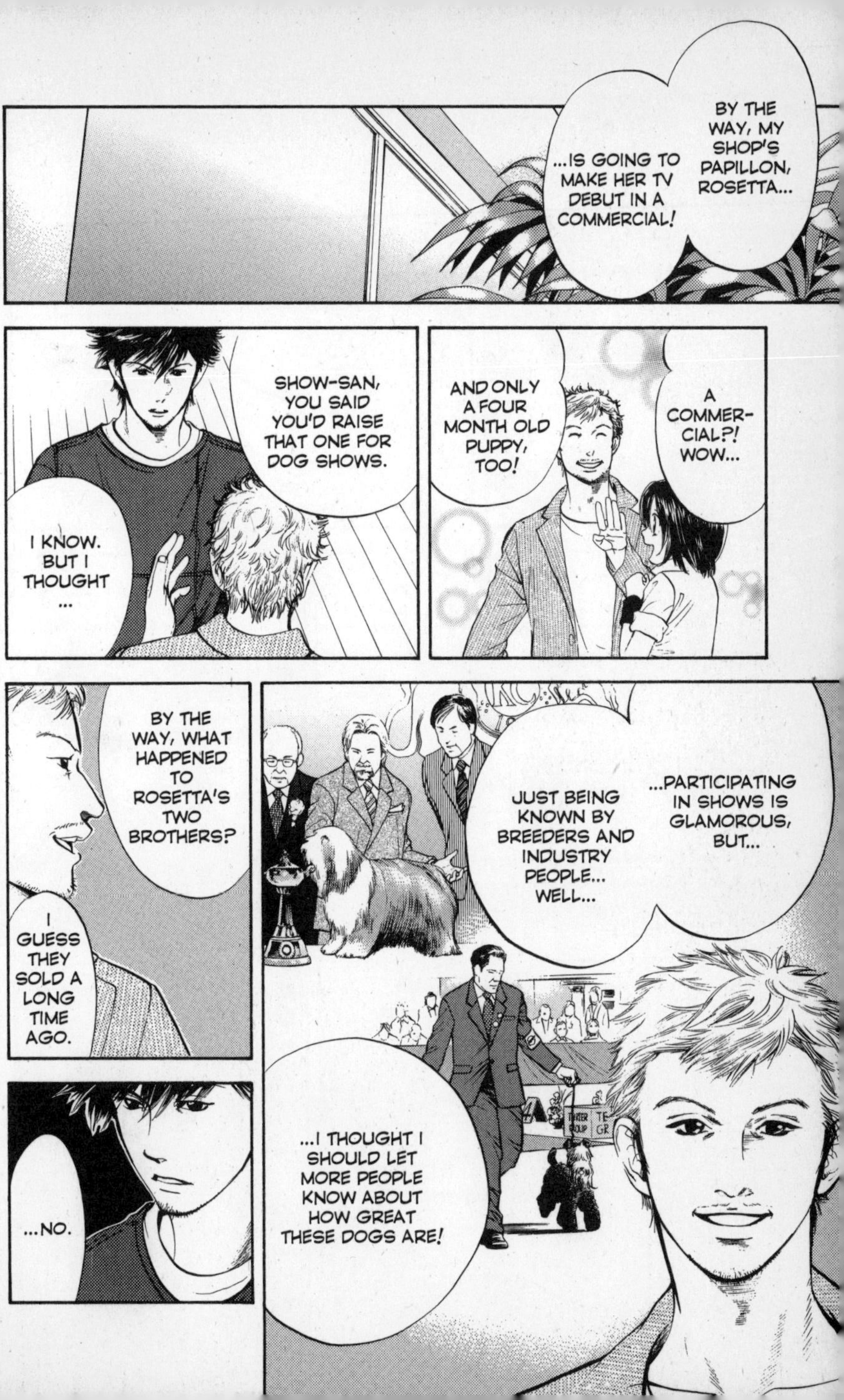
BY THE WAY, MY SHOP'S PAPILLON, ROSETTA...
...IS GOING TO MAKE HER TV DEBUT IN A COMMERCIAL!
A COMMERCIAL?! WOW...
AND ONLY A FOUR MONTH OLD PUPPY, TOO!
SHOW-SAN, YOU SAID YOU'D RAISE THAT ONE FOR DOG SHOWS.
I KNOW. BUT I THOUGHT ...
...PARTICIPATING IN SHOWS IS GLAMOROUS, BUT...
JUST BEING KNOWN BY BREEDERS AND INDUSTRY PEOPLE... WELL...
...I THOUGHT I SHOULD LET MORE PEOPLE KNOW ABOUT HOW GREAT THESE DOGS ARE!
BY THE WAY, WHAT HAPPENED TO ROSETTA'S TWO BROTHERS?
I GUESS THEY SOLD A LONG TIME AGO.
...NO.

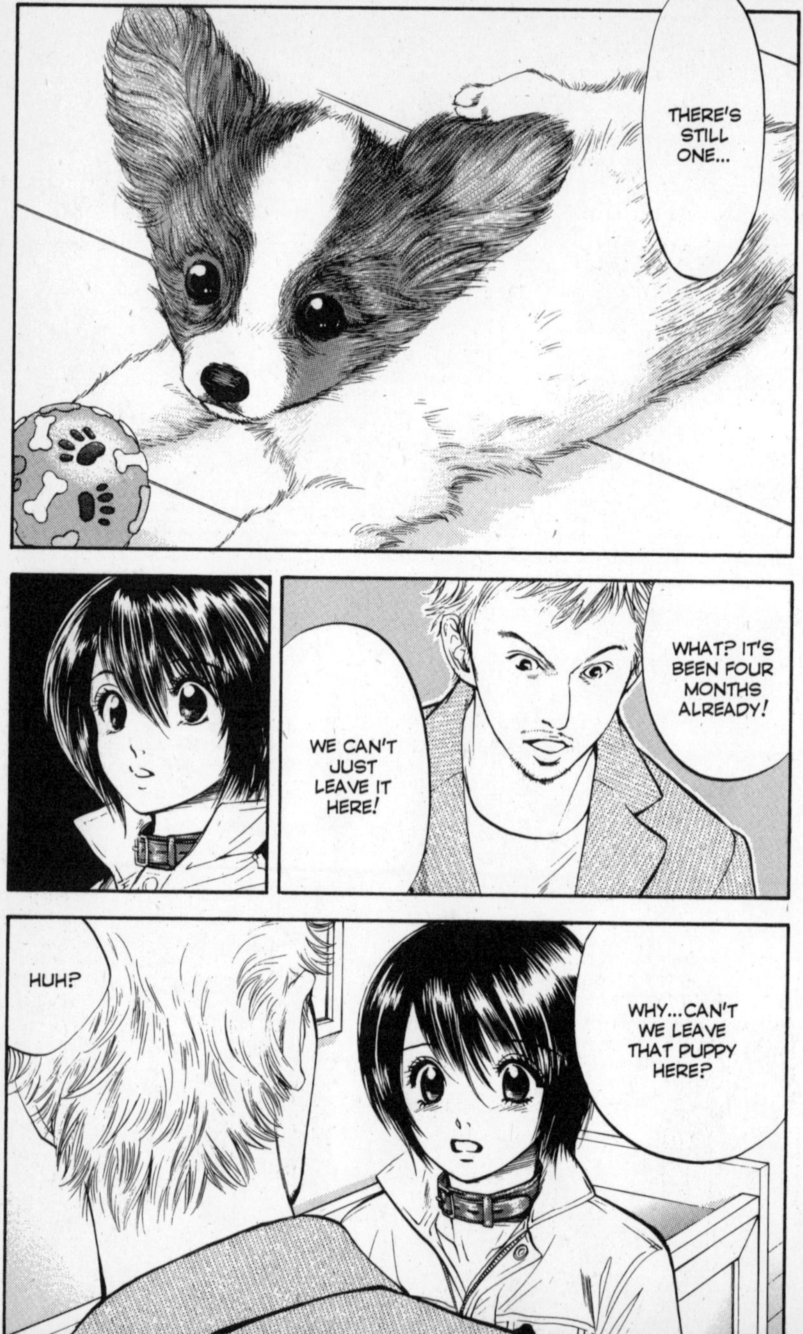
THERE'S STILL ONE...
WHAT? IT'S BEEN FOUR MONTHS ALREADY!
WE CAN'T JUST LEAVE IT HERE!
WHY...CAN'T WE LEAVE THAT PUPPY HERE?
HUH?

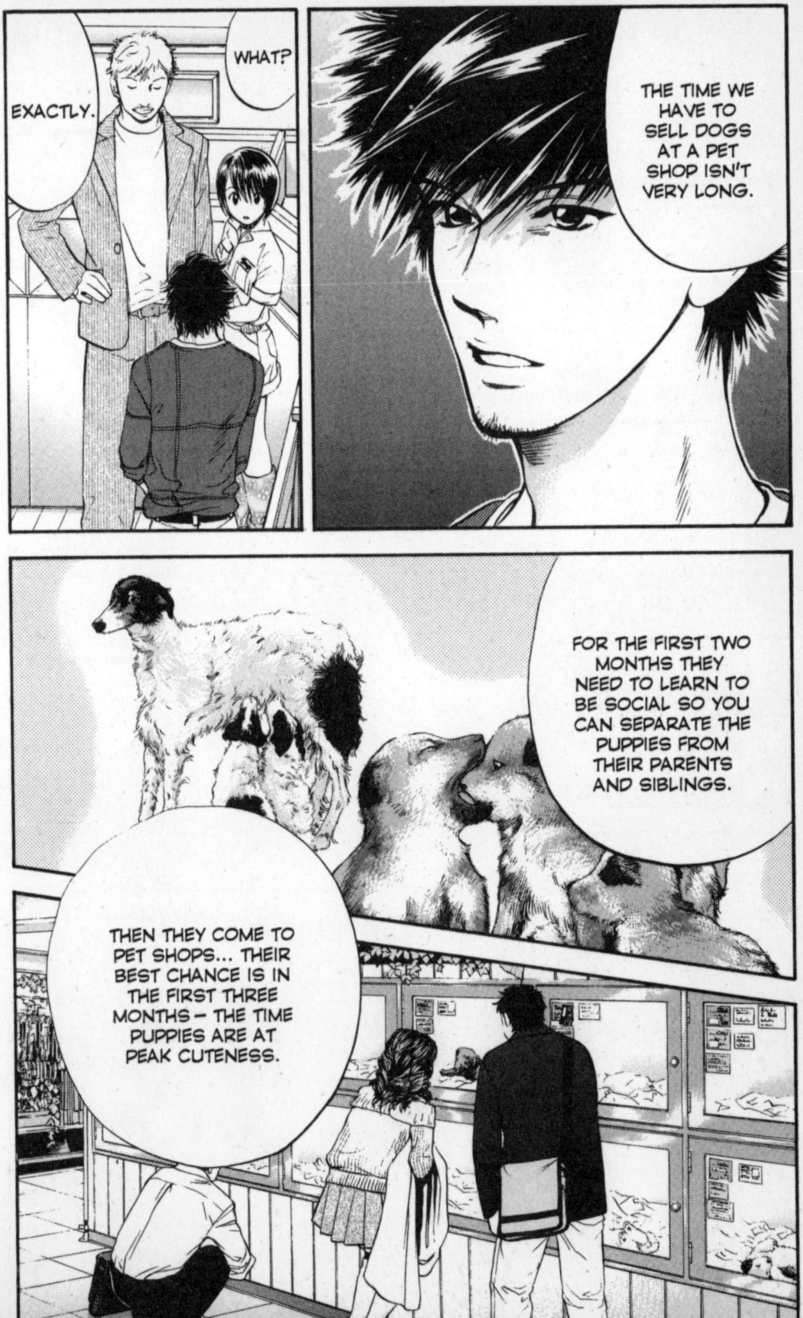
THE TIME WE HAVE TO SELL DOGS AT A PET SHOP ISN'T VERY LONG.
WHAT?
EXACTLY.
FOR THE FIRST TWO MONTHS THEY NEED TO LEARN TO BE SOCIAL SO YOU CAN SEPARATE THE PUPPIES FROM THEIR PARENTS AND SIBLINGS.
THEN THEY COME TO PET SHOPS... THEIR BEST CHANCE IS IN THE FIRST THREE MONTHS — THE TIME PUPPIES ARE AT PEAK CUTENESS.

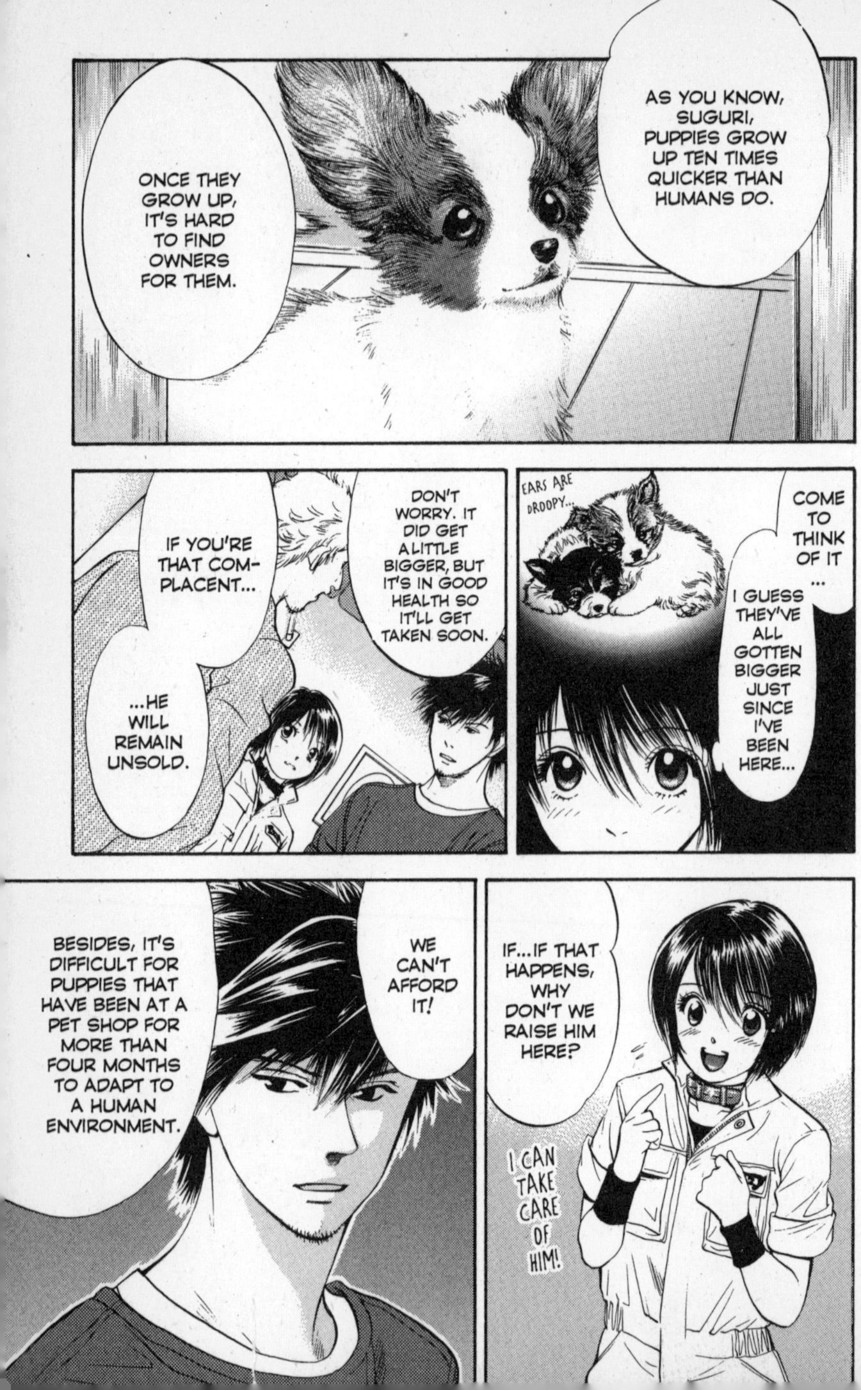
AS YOU KNOW, SUGURI, PUPPIES GROW UP TEN TIMES QUICKER THAN HUMANS DO.
ONCE THEY GROW UP, IT'S HARD TO FIND OWNERS FOR THEM.
COME TO THINK OF IT ...
I GUESS THEY'VE ALL GOTTEN BIGGER JUST SINCE I'VE BEEN HERE...
EARS ARE DROOPY...
DON'T WORRY. IT DID GET A LITTLE BIGGER, BUT IT'S IN GOOD HEALTH SO IT'LL GET TAKEN SOON.
IF YOU'RE THAT COM-PLACENT...
...HE WILL REMAIN UNSOLD.
IF...IF THAT HAPPENS, WHY DON'T WE RAISE HIM HERE?
I CAN TAKE CARE OF HIM!
WE CAN'T AFFORD IT!
BESIDES, IT'S DIFFICULT FOR PUPPIES THAT HAVE BEEN AT A PET SHOP FOR MORE THAN FOUR MONTHS TO ADAPT TO A HUMAN ENVIRONMENT.

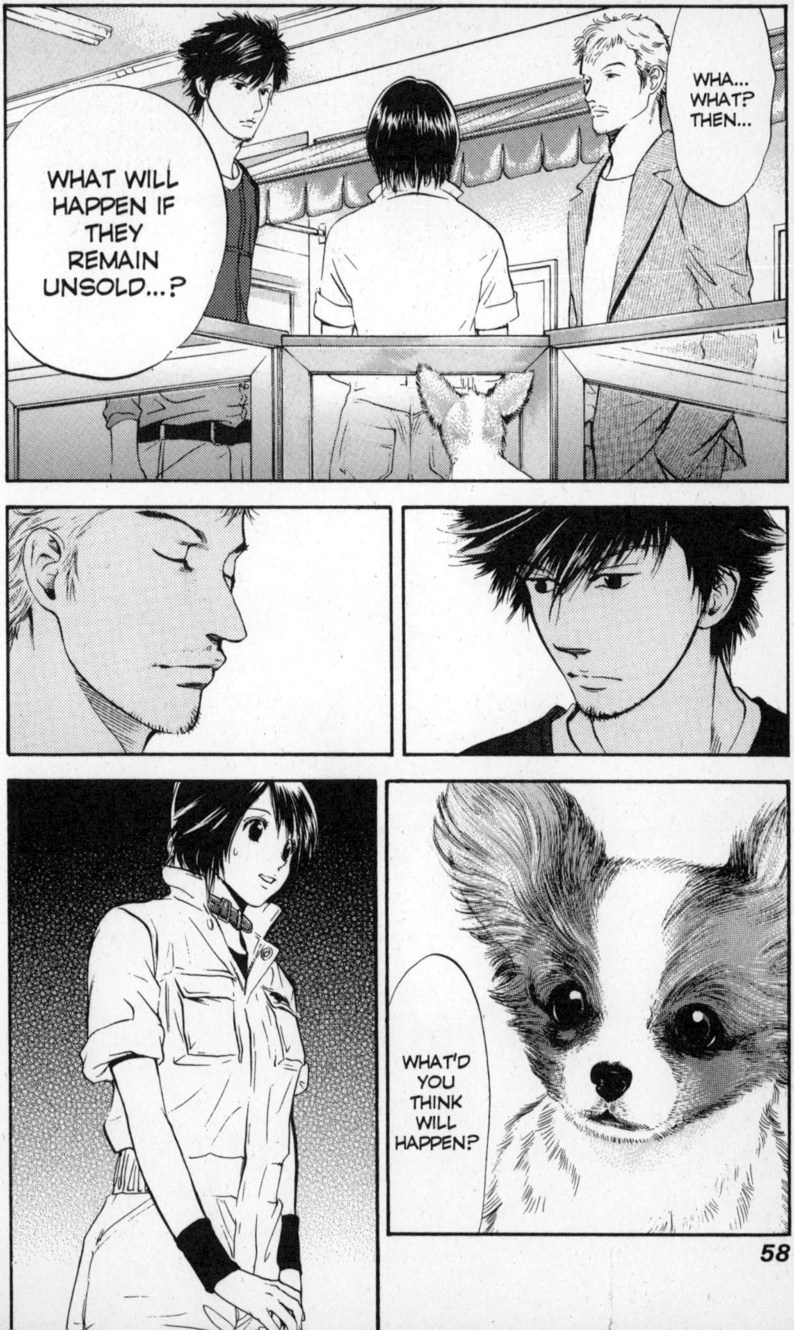
WHA... WHAT? THEN...
WHAT WILL HAPPEN IF THEY REMAIN UNSOLD...?
WHAT'D YOU THINK WILL HAPPEN?

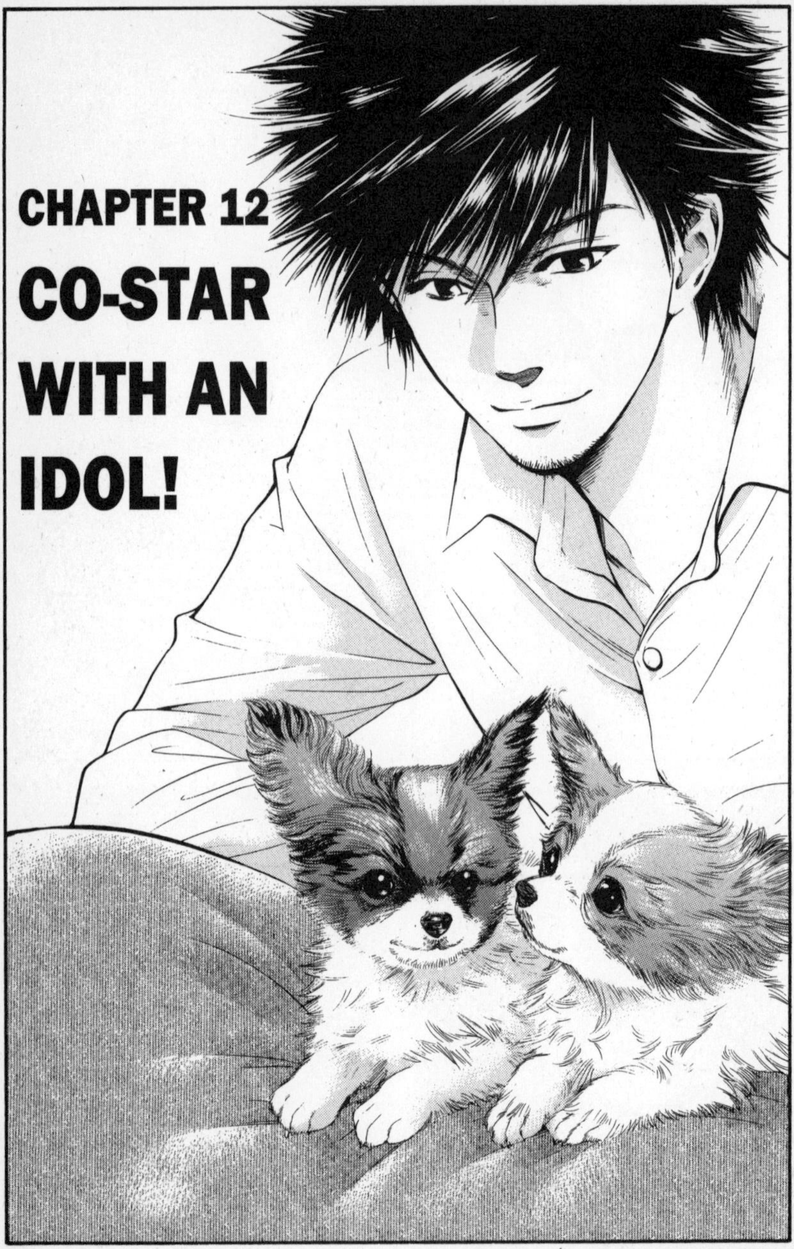
CHAPTER 12
CO-STAR WITH AN IDOL!

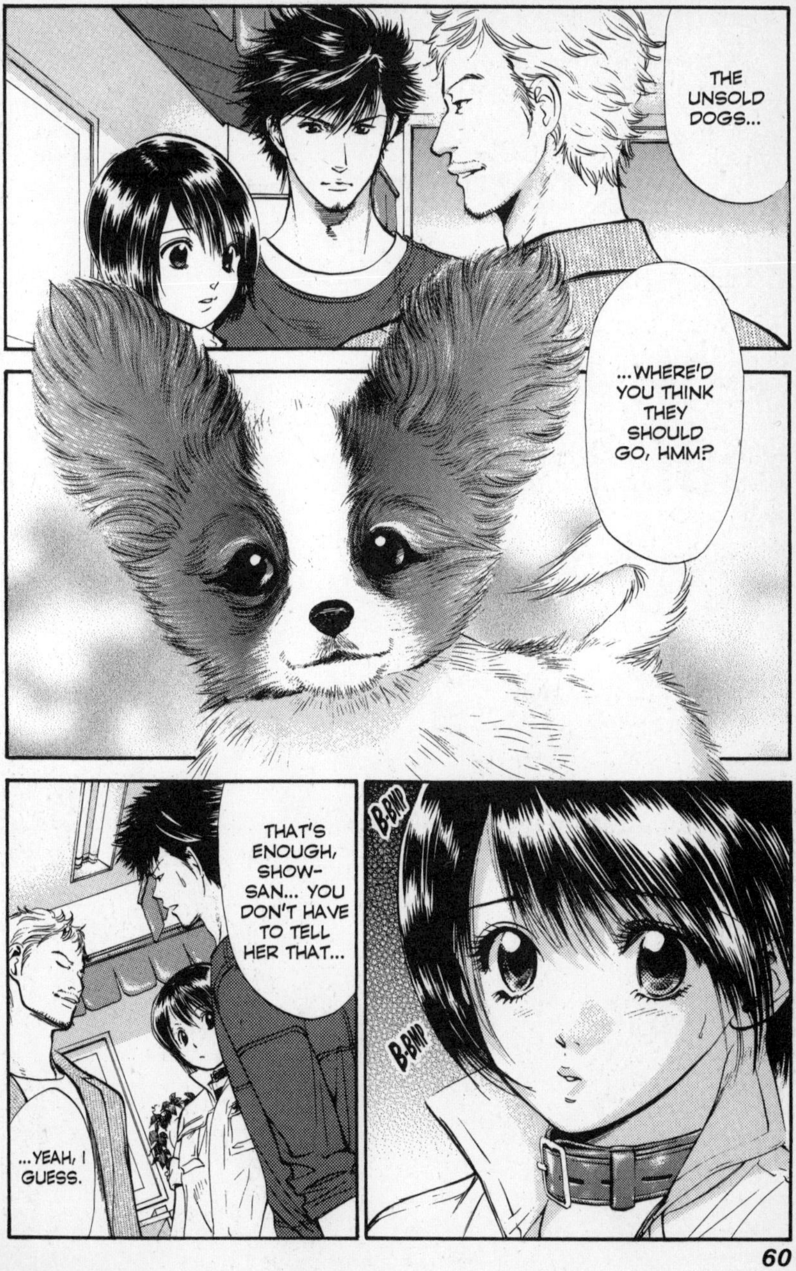
THE UNSOLD DOGS...
...WHERE'D YOU THINK THEY SHOULD GO, HMM?
B-BMP
B-BMP
THAT'S ENOUGH, SHOW-SAN... YOU DON'T HAVE TO TELL HER THAT...
...YEAH, I GUESS.

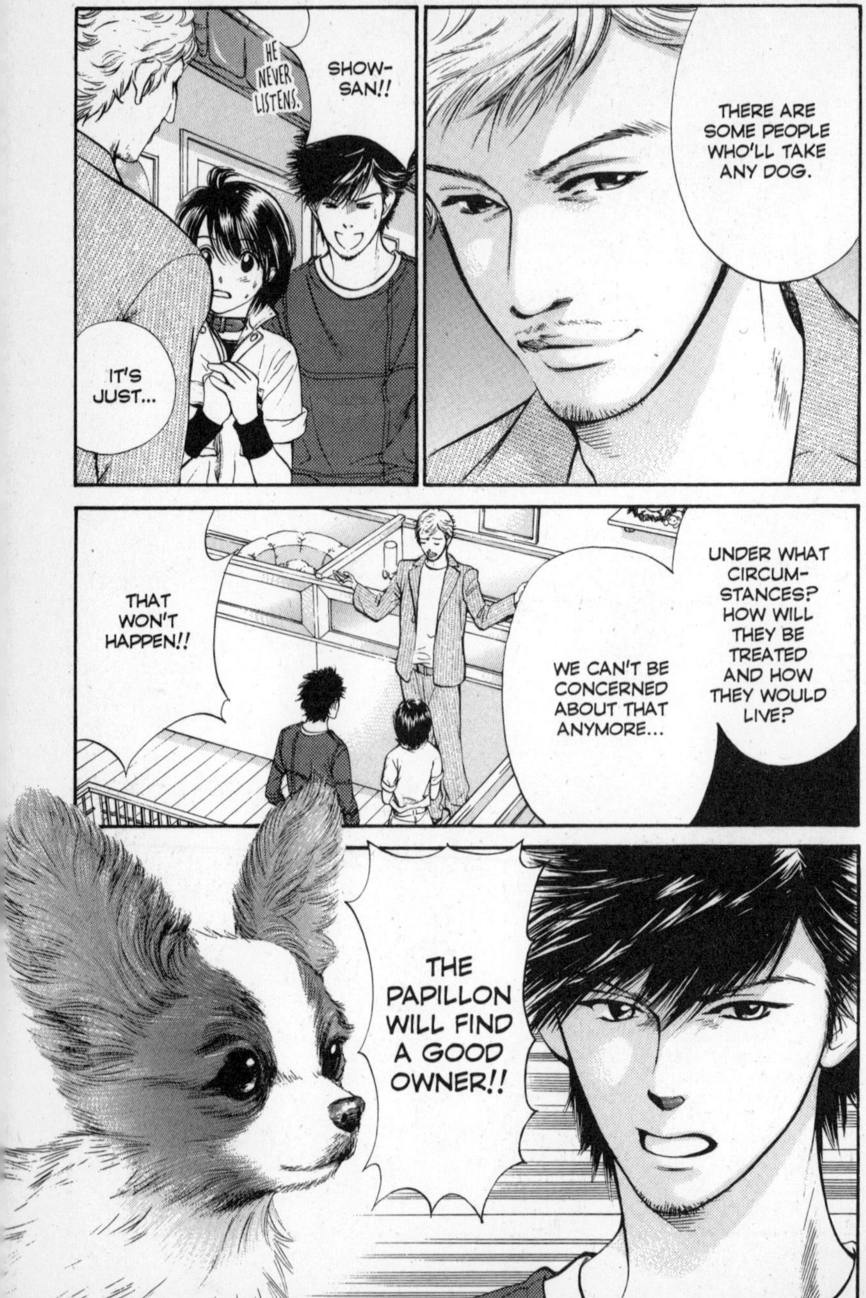
THERE ARE SOME PEOPLE WHO'LL TAKE ANY DOG.
SHOW-SAN!!
HE NEVER LISTENS.
IT'S JUST...
UNDER WHAT CIRCUM-STANCES? HOW WILL THEY BE TREATED AND HOW THEY WOULD LIVE?
WE CAN'T BE CONCERNED ABOUT THAT ANYMORE...
THAT WON'T HAPPEN!!
THE PAPILLON WILL FIND A GOOD OWNER!!

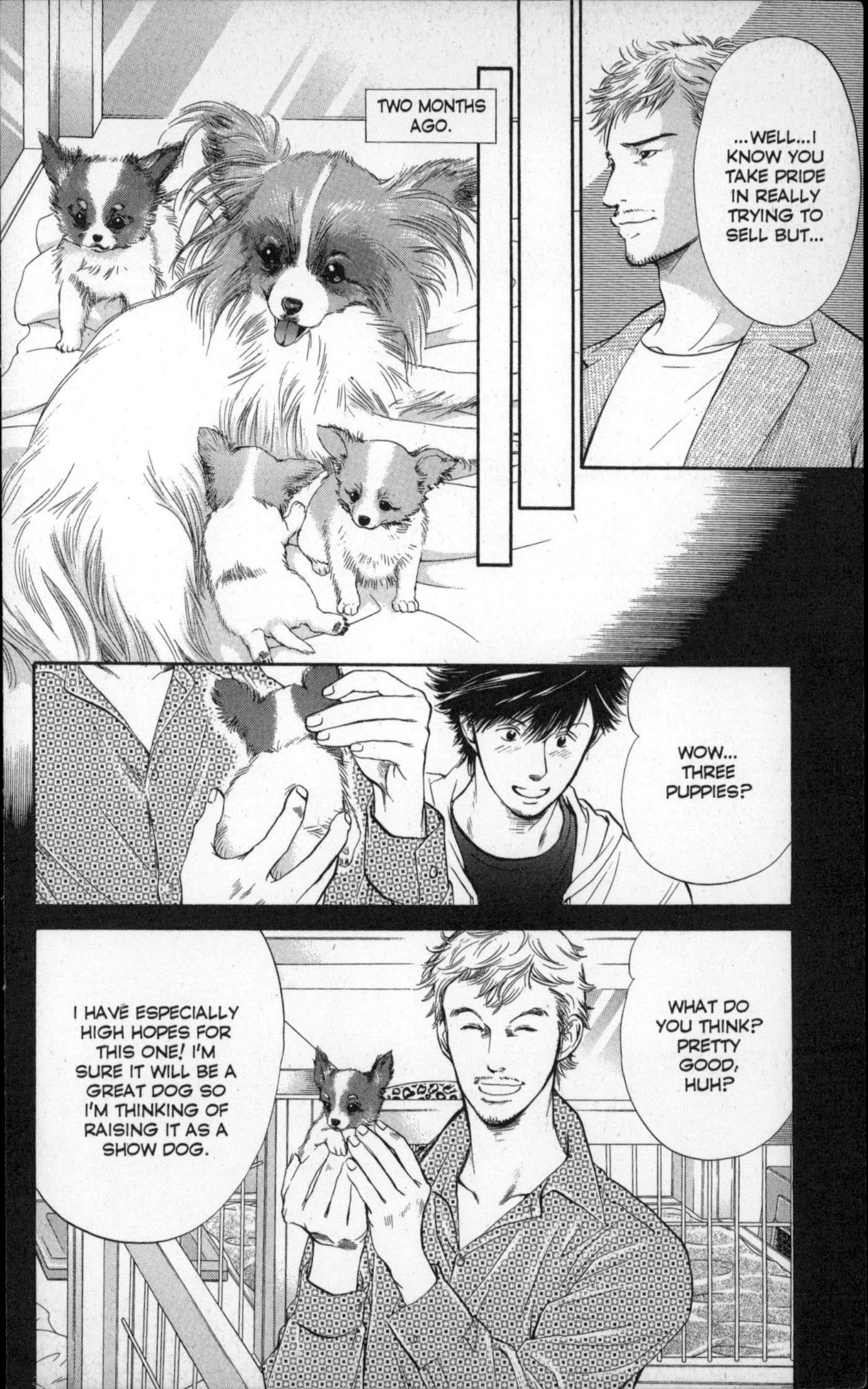
...WELL...I KNOW YOU TAKE PRIDE IN REALLY TRYING TO SELL BUT...
TWO MONTHS AGO.
WOW... THREE PUPPIES?
WHAT DO YOU THINK? PRETTY GOOD, HUH?
I HAVE ESPECIALLY HIGH HOPES FOR THIS ONE! I'M SURE IT WILL BE A GREAT DOG SO I'M THINKING OF RAISING IT AS A SHOW DOG.

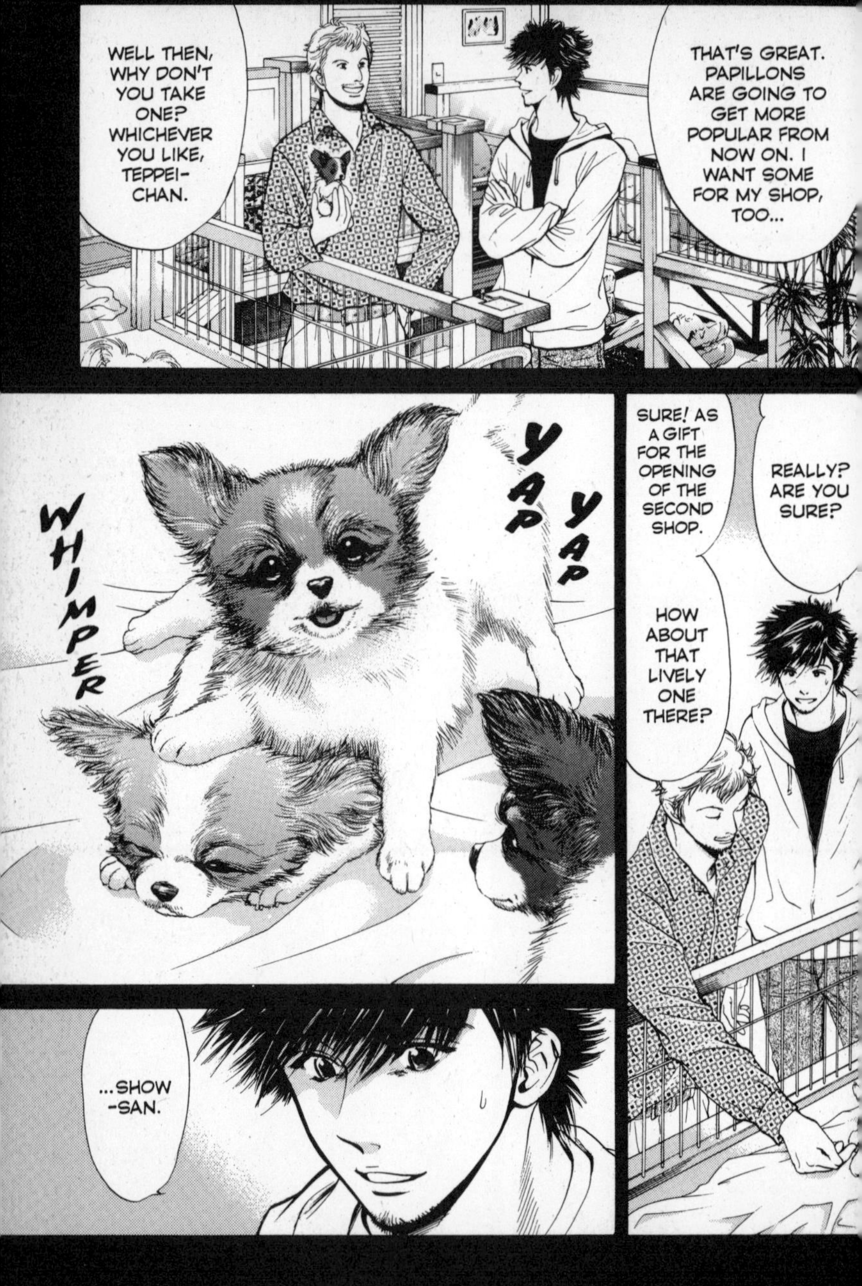
THAT'S GREAT. PAPILLONS ARE GOING TO GET MORE POPULAR FROM NOW ON. I WANT SOME FOR MY SHOP, TOO...
WELL THEN, WHY DON'T YOU TAKE ONE? WHICHEVER YOU LIKE, TEPPEI-CHAN.
REALLY? ARE YOU SURE?
SURE! AS A GIFT FOR THE OPENING OF THE SECOND SHOP.
HOW ABOUT THAT LIVELY ONE THERE?
YAP YAP
WHIMPER
...SHOW-SAN.

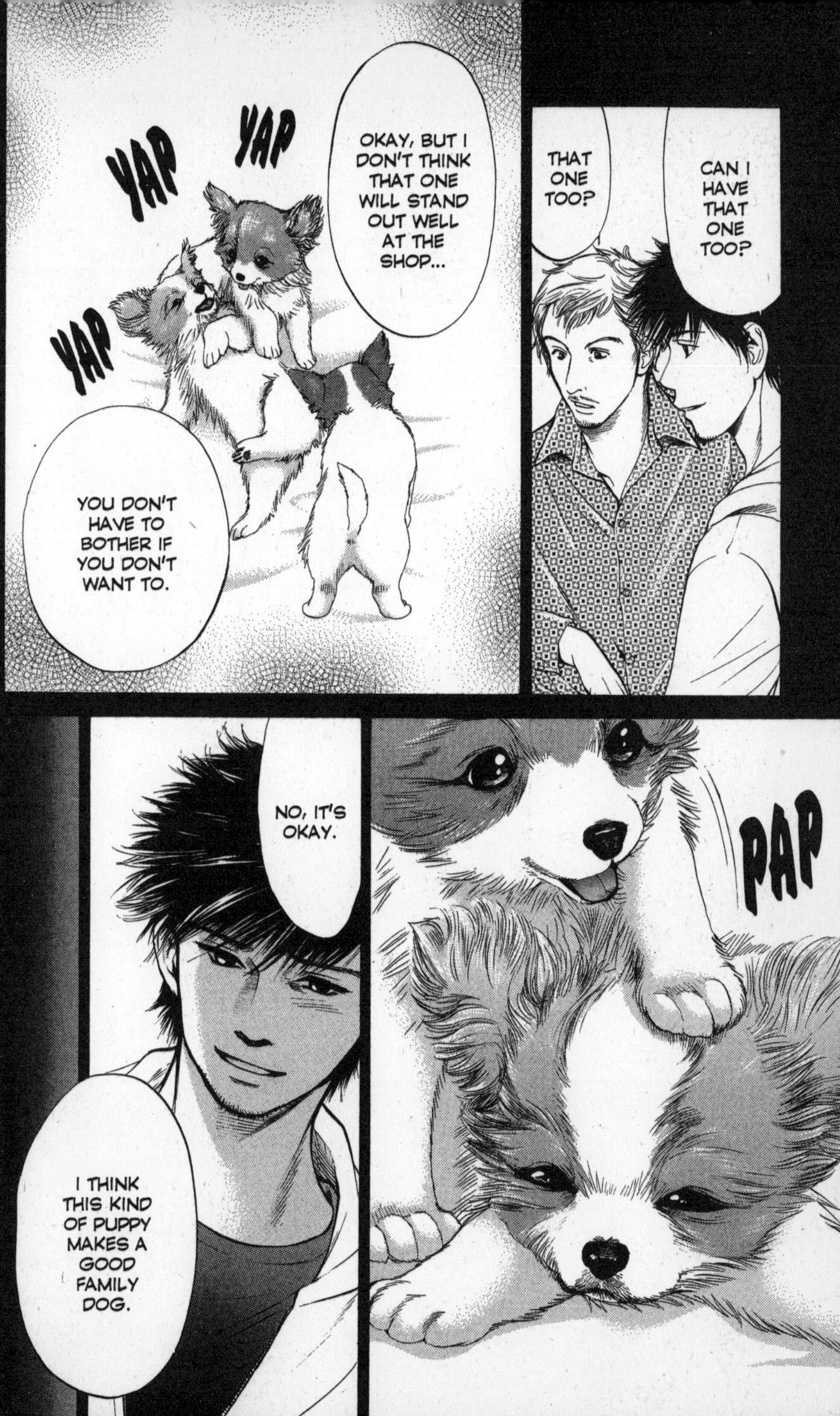
CAN I HAVE THAT ONE TOO?
THAT ONE TOO?
OKAY, BUT I DON'T THINK THAT ONE WILL STAND OUT WELL AT THE SHOP...
YAP YAP
YAP
YOU DON'T HAVE TO BOTHER IF YOU DON'T WANT TO.
PAP
NO, IT'S OKAY.
I THINK THIS KIND OF PUPPY MAKES A GOOD FAMILY DOG.

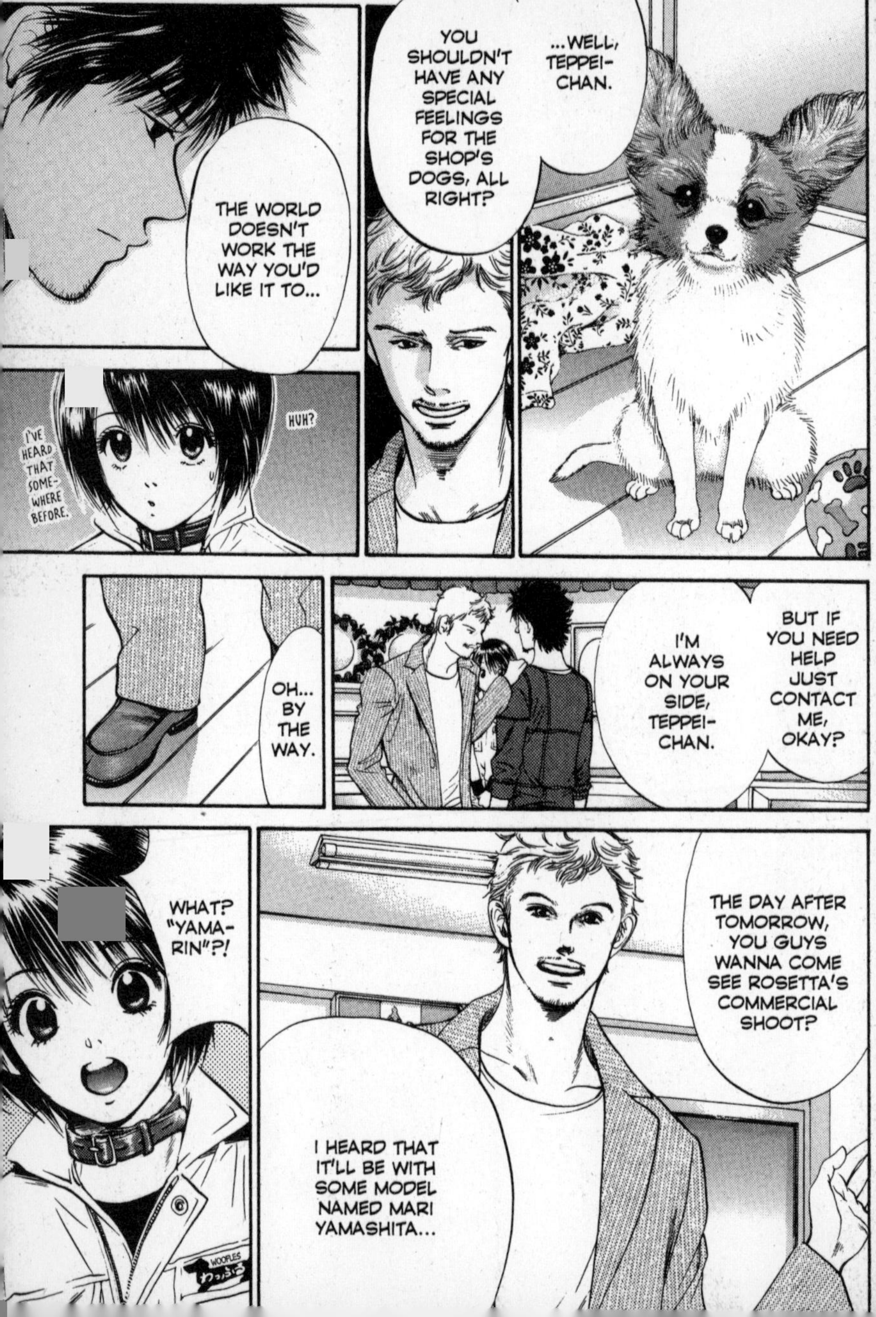
...WELL, TEPPEI-CHAN.
YOU SHOULDN'T HAVE ANY SPECIAL FEELINGS FOR THE SHOP'S DOGS, ALL RIGHT?
THE WORLD DOESN'T WORK THE WAY YOU'D LIKE IT TO...
HUH?
I'VE HEARD THAT SOME-WHERE BEFORE.
BUT IF YOU NEED HELP JUST CONTACT ME, OKAY?
I'M ALWAYS ON YOUR SIDE, TEPPEI-CHAN.
OH... BY THE WAY.
THE DAY AFTER TOMORROW, YOU GUYS WANNA COME SEE ROSETTA'S COMMERCIAL SHOOT?
I HEARD THAT IT'LL BE WITH SOME MODEL NAMED MARI YAMASHITA...
WHAT? "YAMA-RIN"?!
WOOFLES

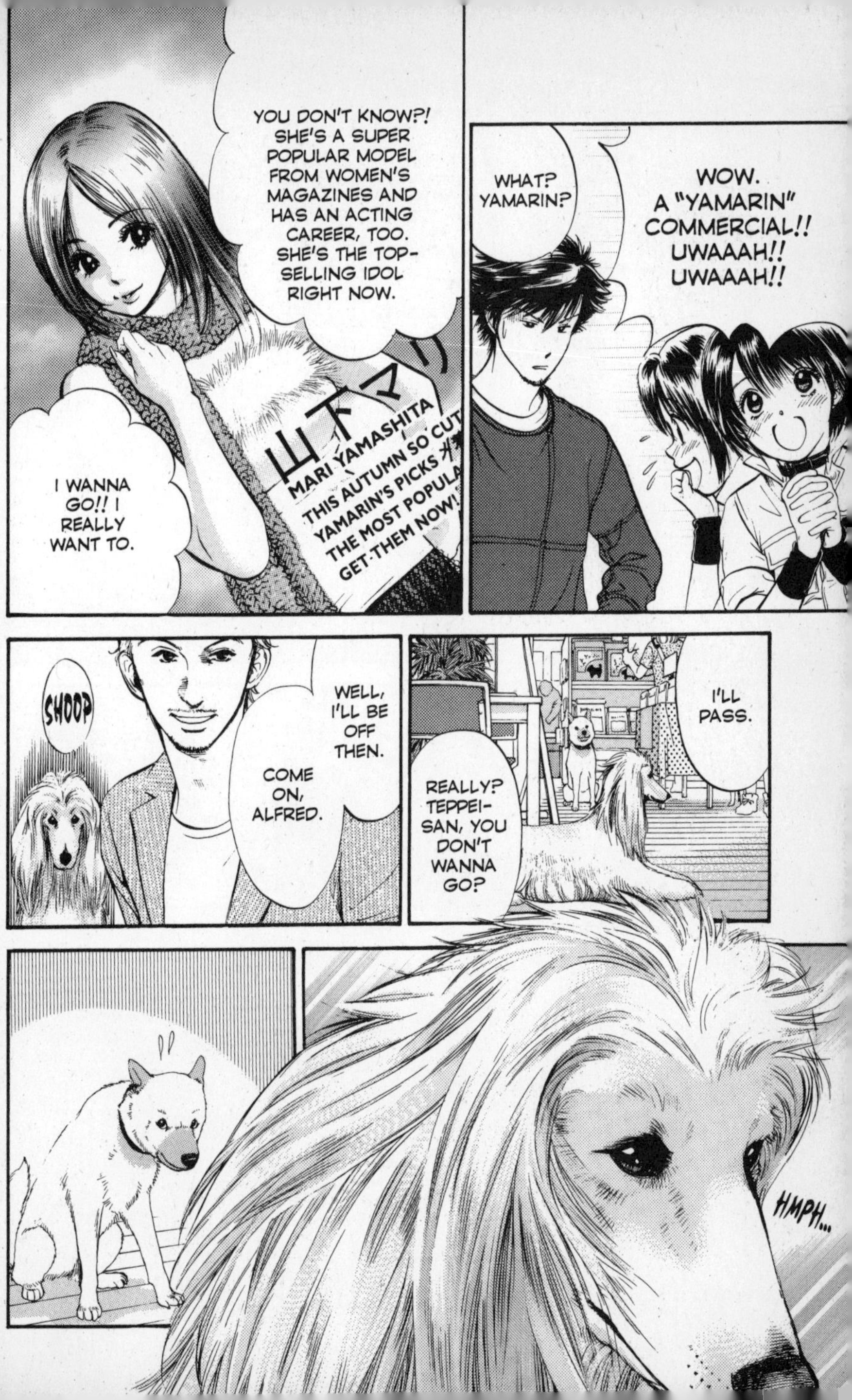
WOW. A "YAMARIN" COMMERCIAL!! UWAAAH!! UWAAAH!!
WHAT? YAMARIN?
YOU DON'T KNOW?! SHE'S A SUPER POPULAR MODEL FROM WOMEN'S MAGAZINES AND HAS AN ACTING CAREER, TOO. SHE'S THE TOP-SELLING IDOL RIGHT NOW.
山下マ
MARI YAMASHITA
THIS AUTUMN SO CUT
YAMARIN'S PICKS
THE MOST POPULA
GET THEM NOW!
I WANNA GO!! I REALLY WANT TO.
I'LL PASS.
REALLY? TEPPEI-SAN, YOU DON'T WANNA GO?
WELL, I'LL BE OFF THEN.
COME ON, ALFRED.
SHOOP
HMPH...

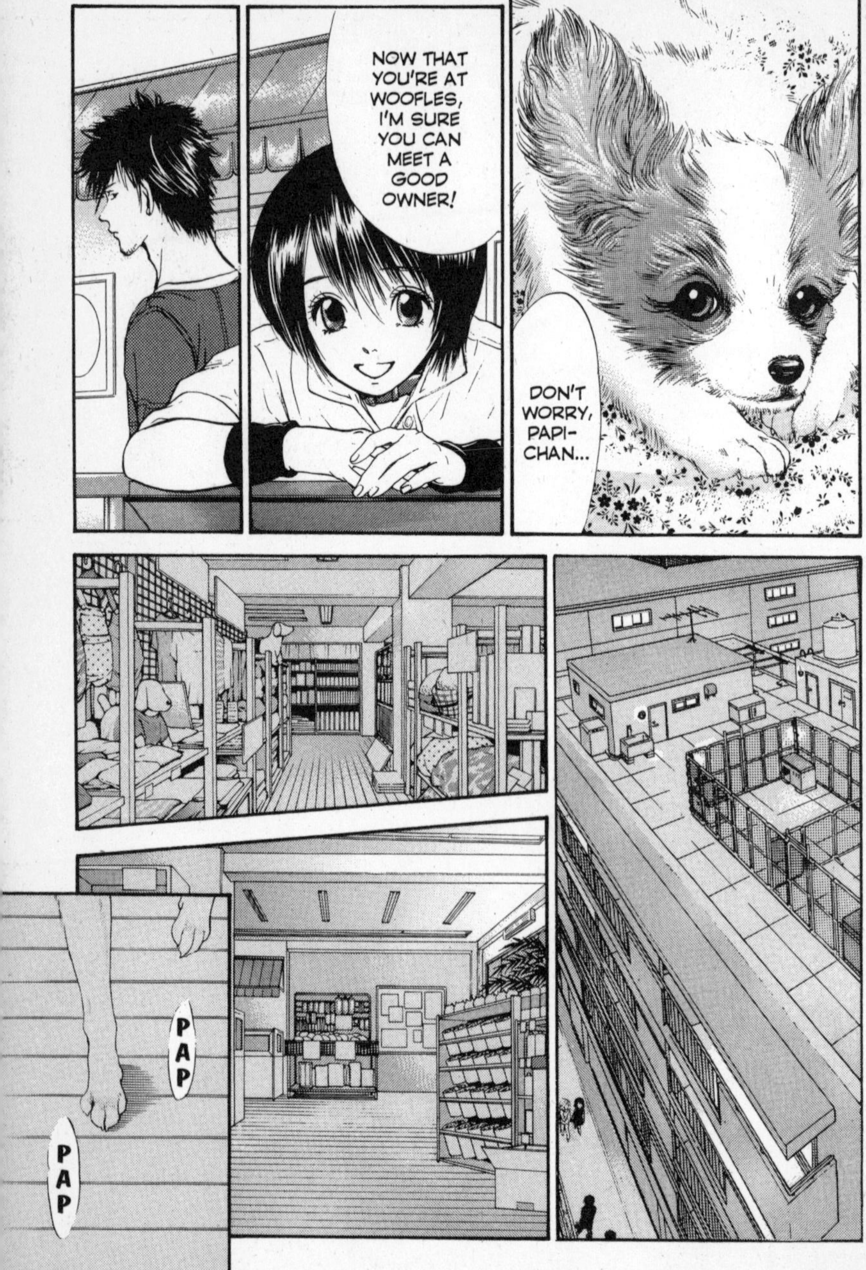
DON'T WORRY, PAPI-CHAN...
NOW THAT YOU'RE AT WOOFLES, I'M SURE YOU CAN MEET A GOOD OWNER!
PAP
PAP

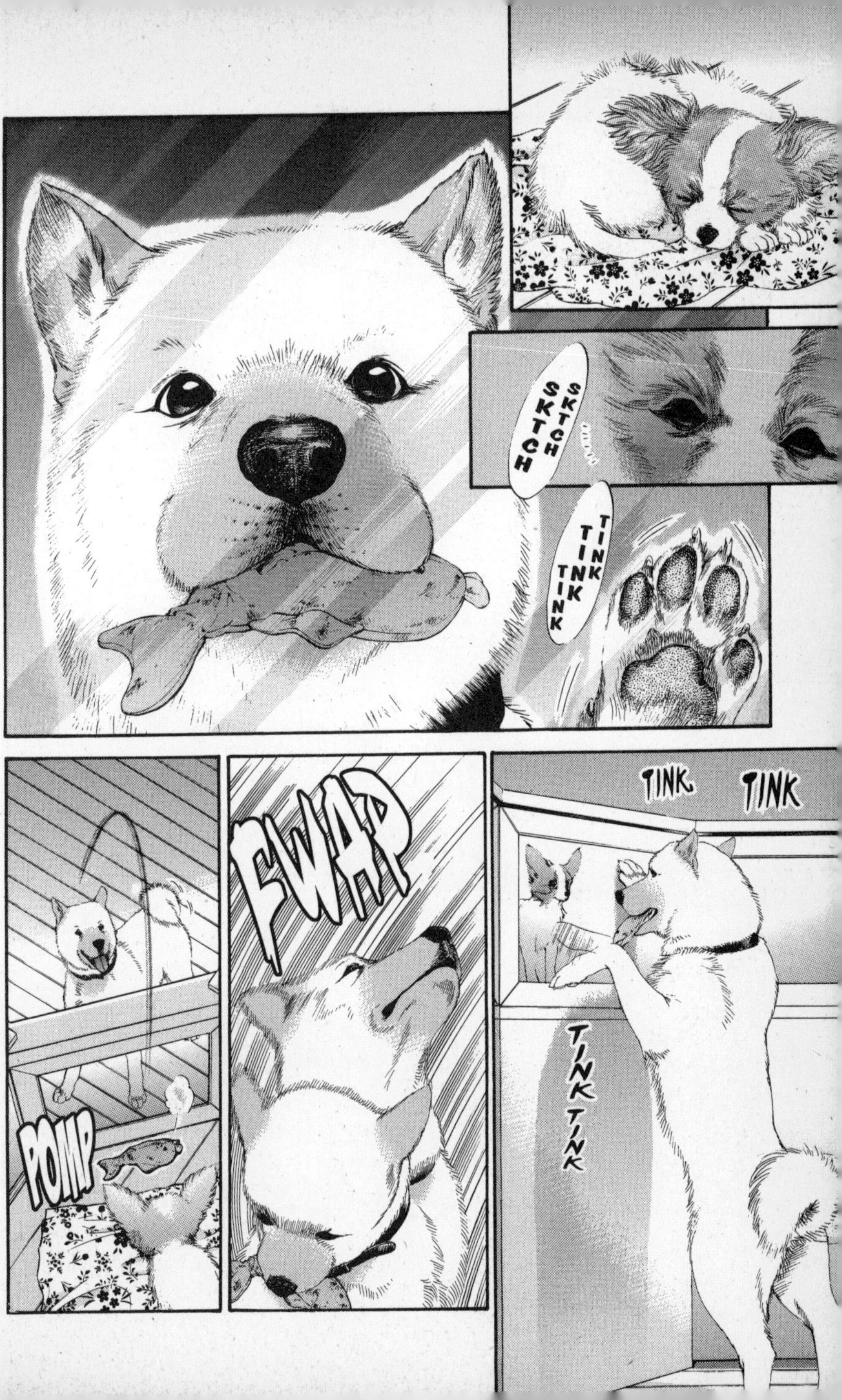
SKTCH SKTCH
TINK TINK TINK TINK
TINK TINK
TINK TINK
FWAP
POMP

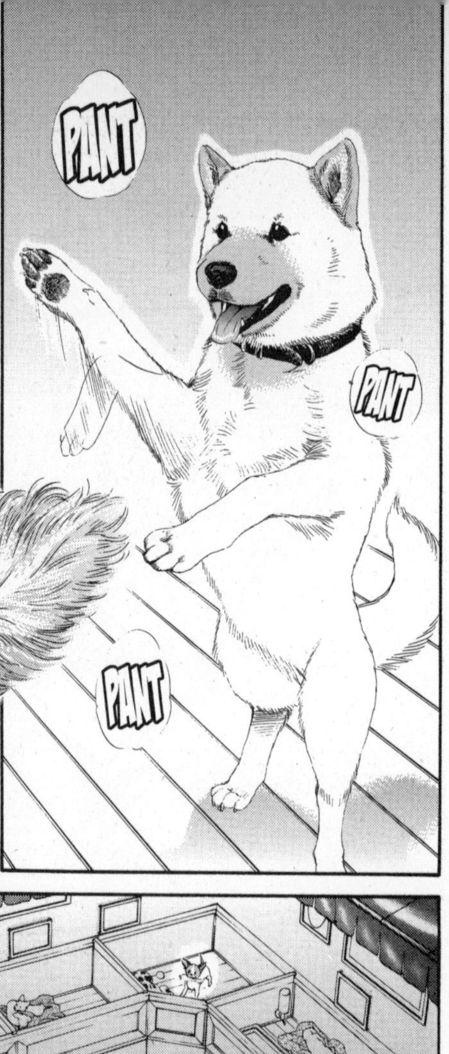
PANT
PANT
PANT
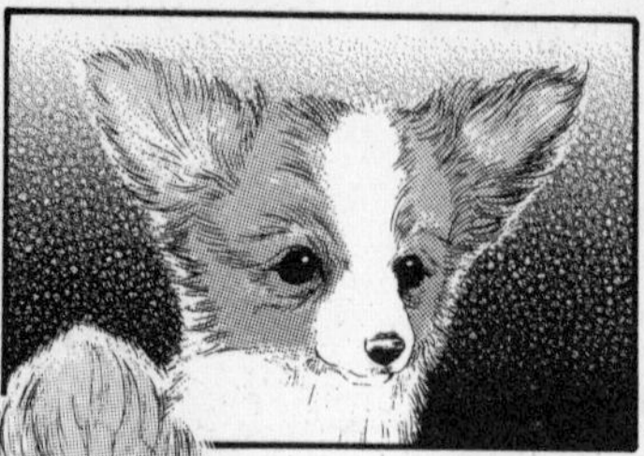
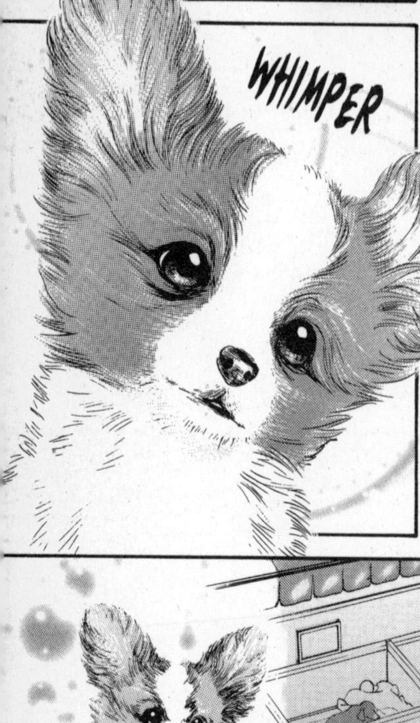
WHIMPER
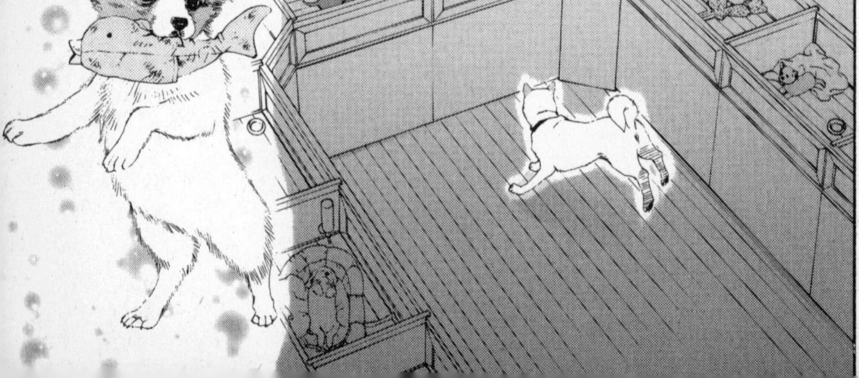

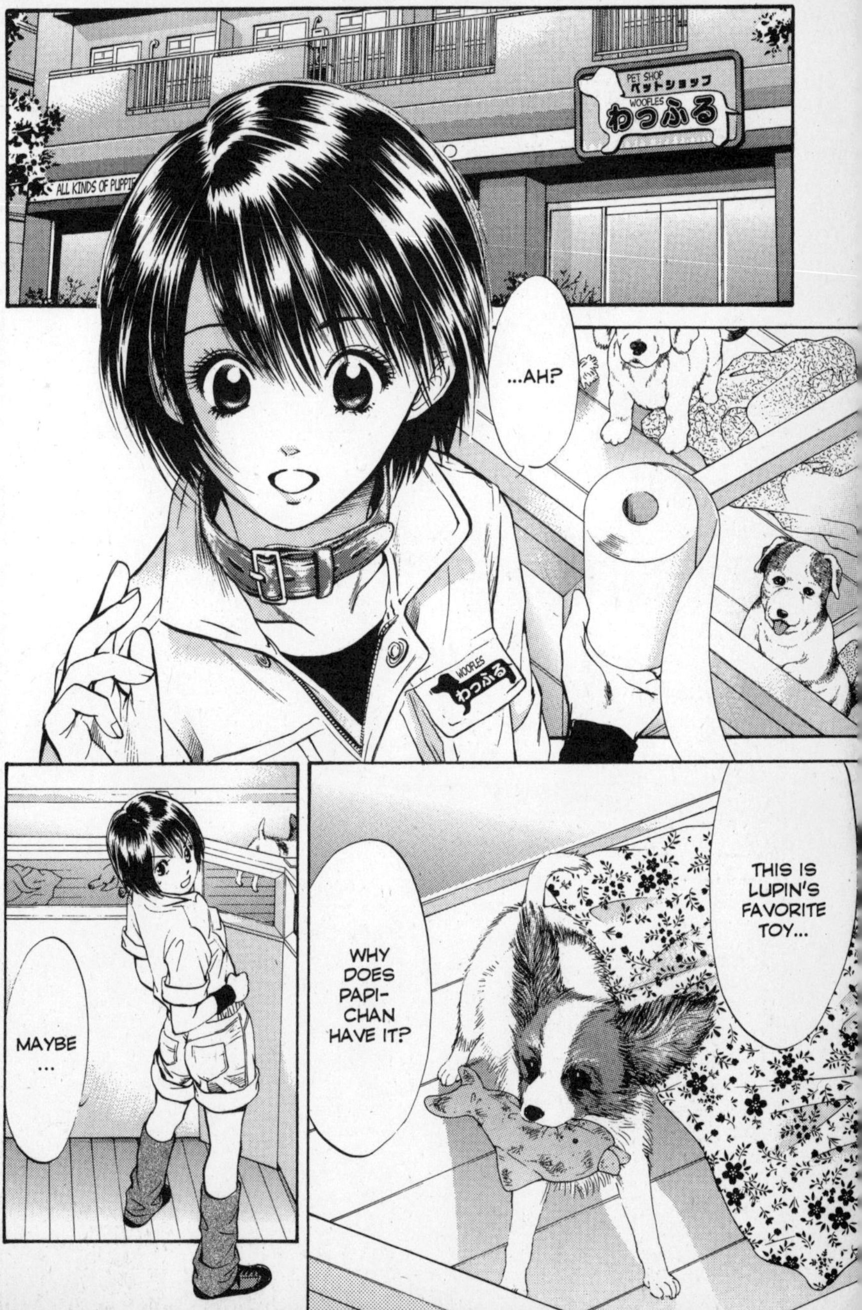
PET SHOP
ペットショップ
WOOFLES
わっふる
ALL KINDS OF PUPPIE
...AH?
WOOFLES
わっふる
THIS IS LUPIN'S FAVORITE TOY...
WHY DOES PAPI-CHAN HAVE IT?
MAYBE ...

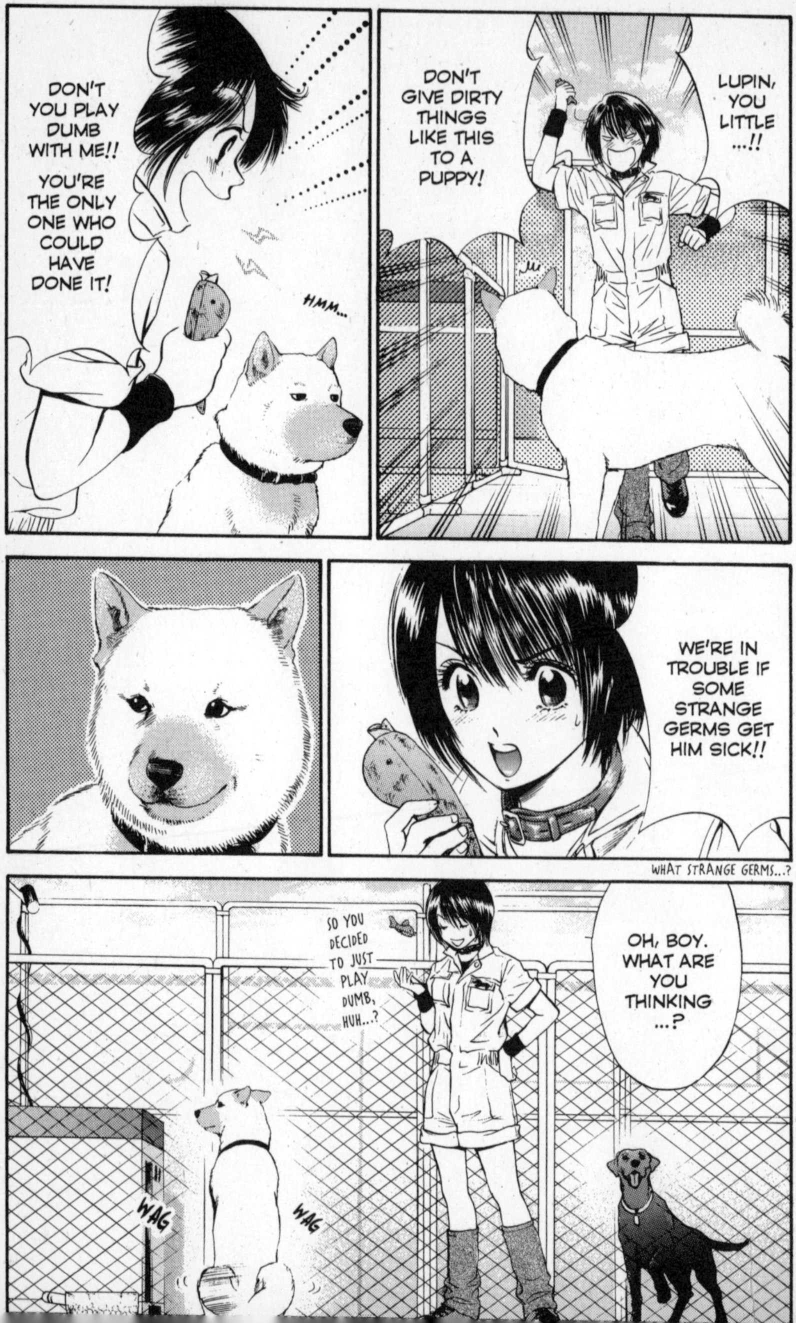
LUPIN, YOU LITTLE ...!!
DON'T GIVE DIRTY THINGS LIKE THIS TO A PUPPY!
HMM...
DON'T YOU PLAY DUMB WITH ME!!
YOU'RE THE ONLY ONE WHO COULD HAVE DONE IT!
WE'RE IN TROUBLE IF SOME STRANGE GERMS GET HIM SICK!!
WHAT STRANGE GERMS...?
OH, BOY. WHAT ARE YOU THINKING ...?
SO YOU DECIDED TO JUST PLAY DUMB, HUH...?
WAG
WAG

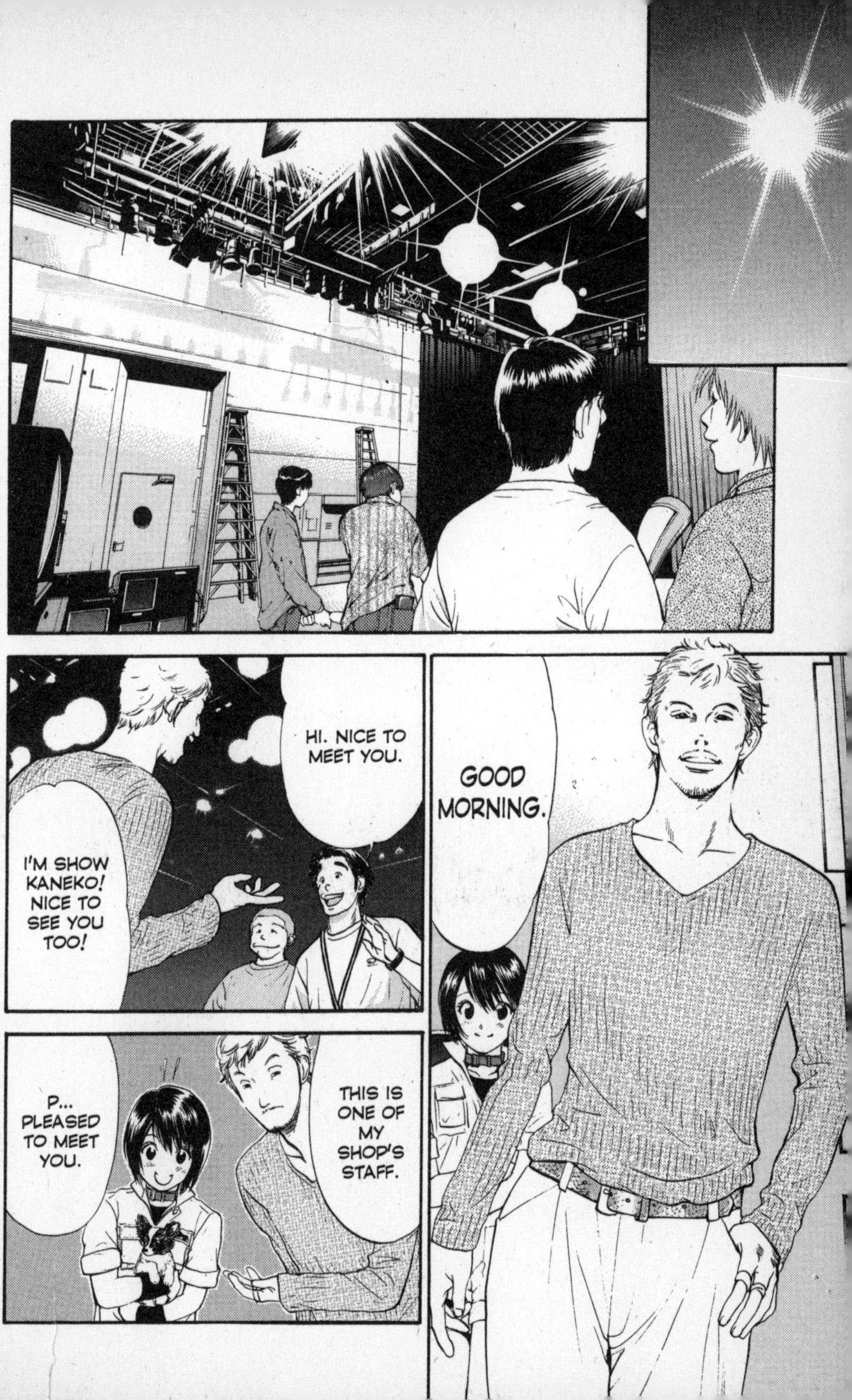
GOOD MORNING.
HI. NICE TO MEET YOU.
I'M SHOW KANEKO! NICE TO SEE YOU TOO!
THIS IS ONE OF MY SHOP'S STAFF.
P... PLEASED TO MEET YOU.

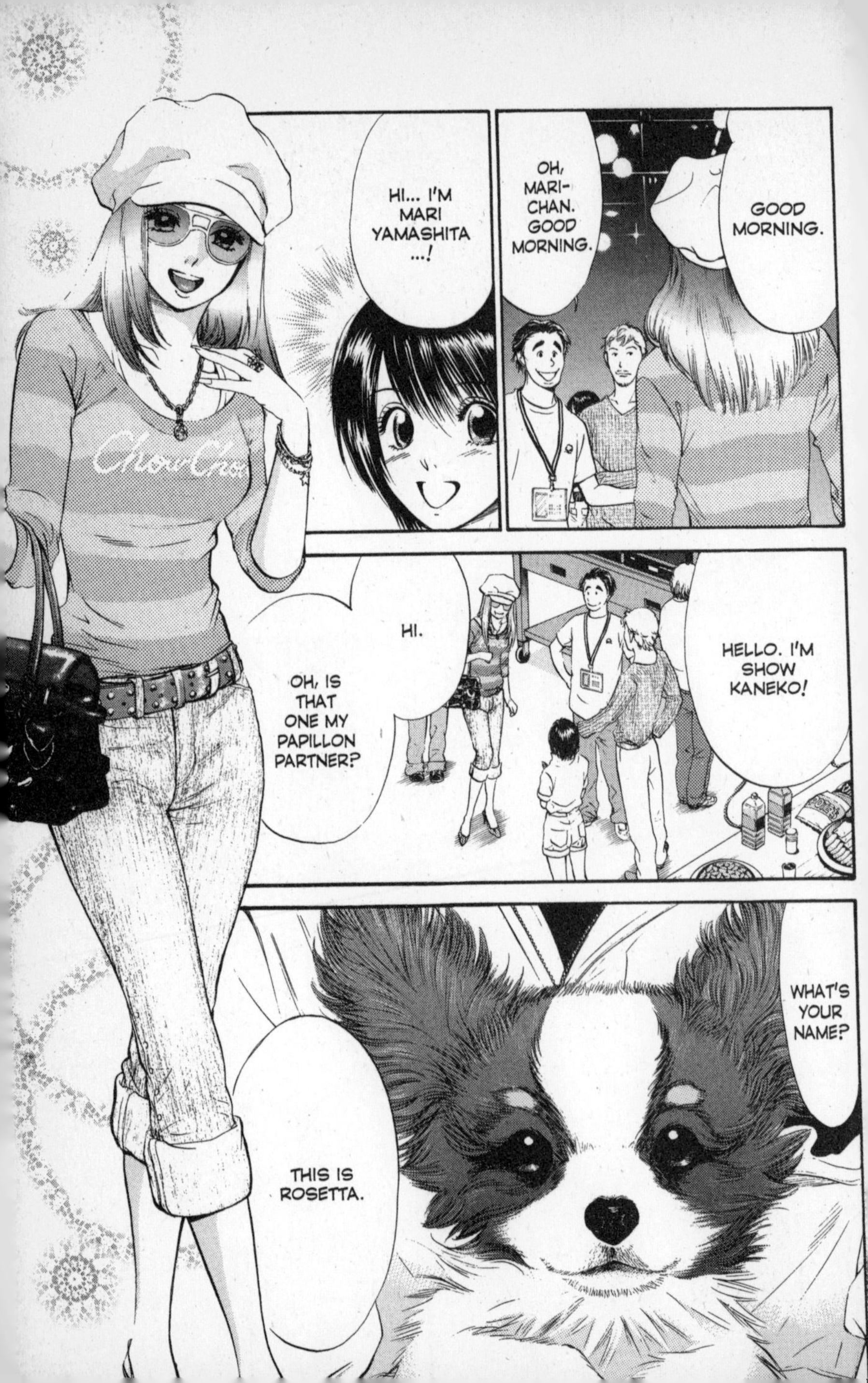
GOOD MORNING.
OH, MARI-CHAN. GOOD MORNING.
HI... I'M MARI YAMASHITA ...!
HELLO. I'M SHOW KANEKO!
HI.
OH, IS THAT ONE MY PAPILLON PARTNER?
WHAT'S YOUR NAME?
THIS IS ROSETTA.

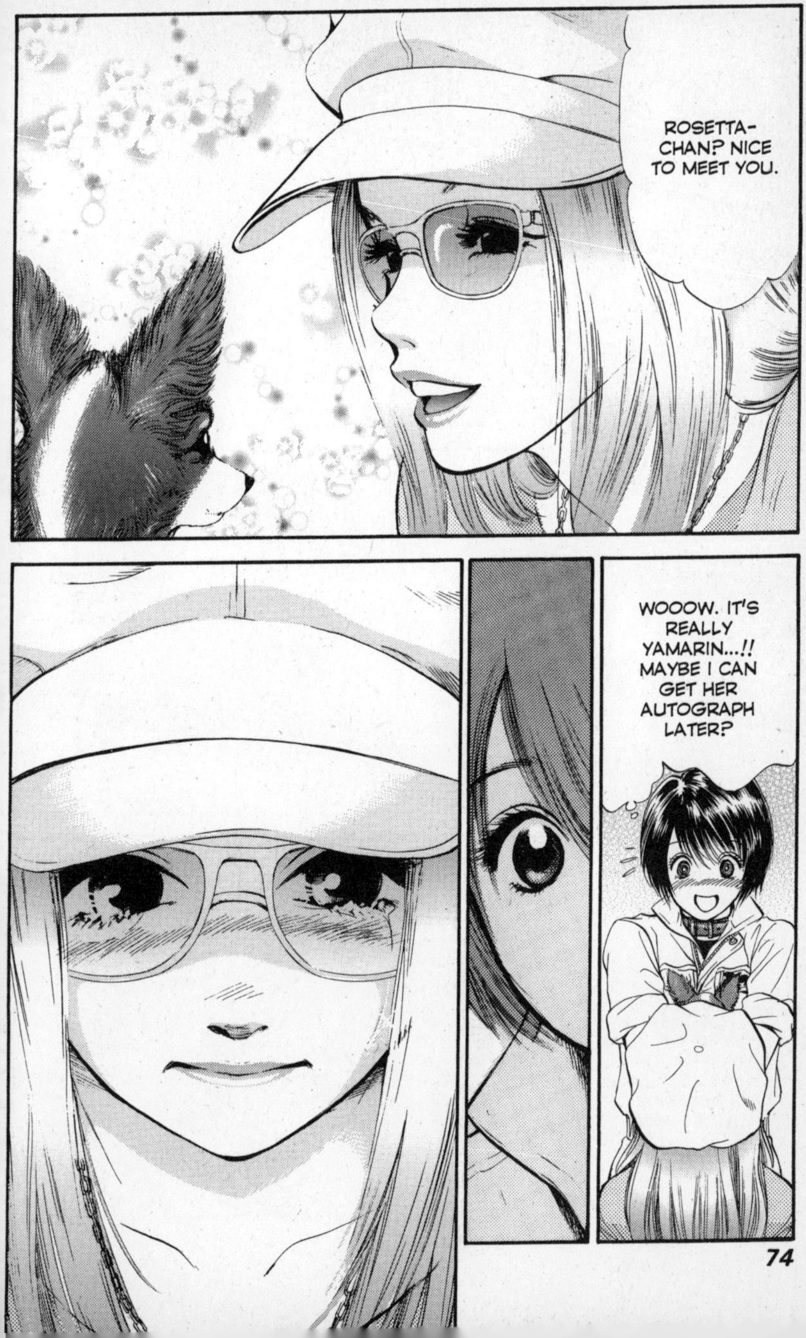
ROSETTA-CHAN? NICE TO MEET YOU.
WOOOW. IT'S REALLY YAMARIN...!! MAYBE I CAN GET HER AUTOGRAPH LATER?

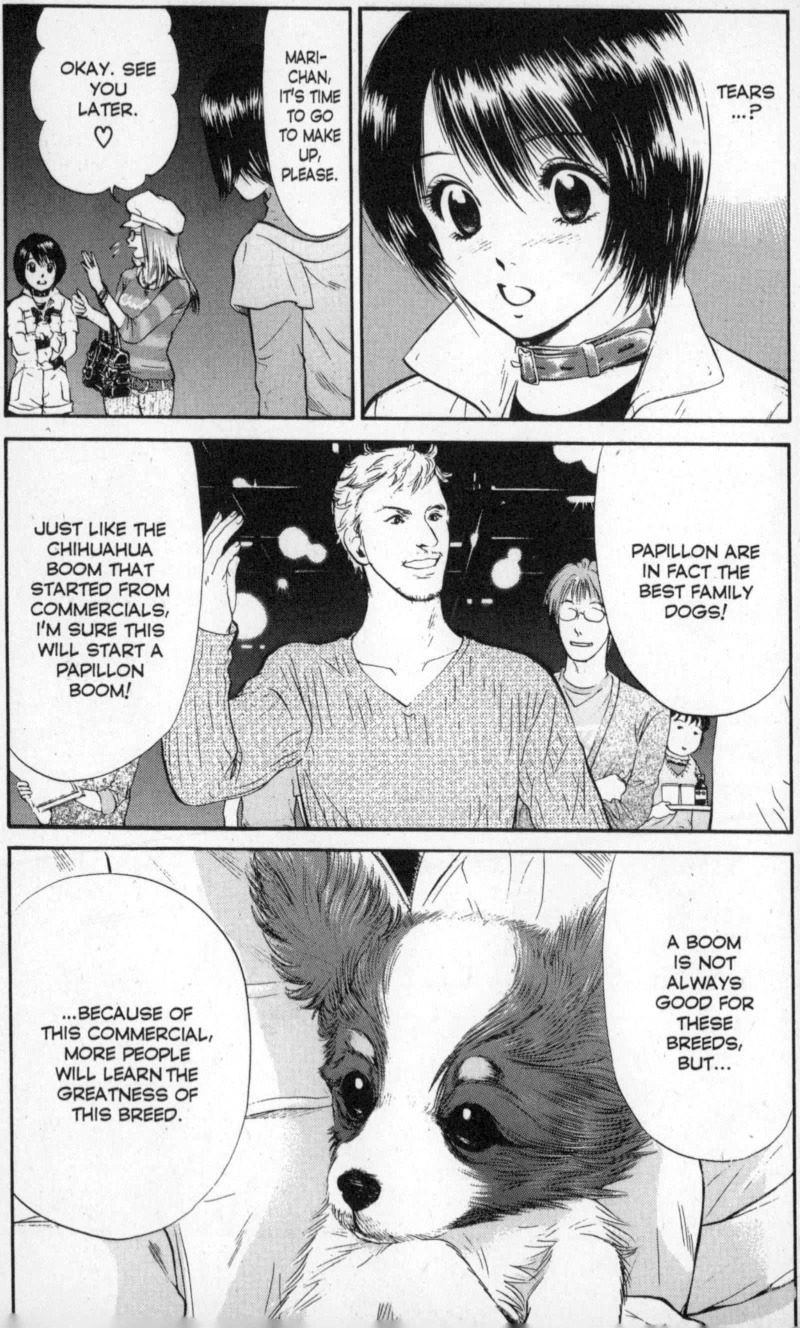
TEARS ...?
MARI-CHAN, IT'S TIME TO GO TO MAKE UP, PLEASE.
OKAY. SEE YOU LATER. ♡
PAPILLON ARE IN FACT THE BEST FAMILY DOGS!
JUST LIKE THE CHIHUAHUA BOOM THAT STARTED FROM COMMERCIALS, I'M SURE THIS WILL START A PAPILLON BOOM!
A BOOM IS NOT ALWAYS GOOD FOR THESE BREEDS, BUT...
...BECAUSE OF THIS COMMERCIAL, MORE PEOPLE WILL LEARN THE GREATNESS OF THIS BREED.

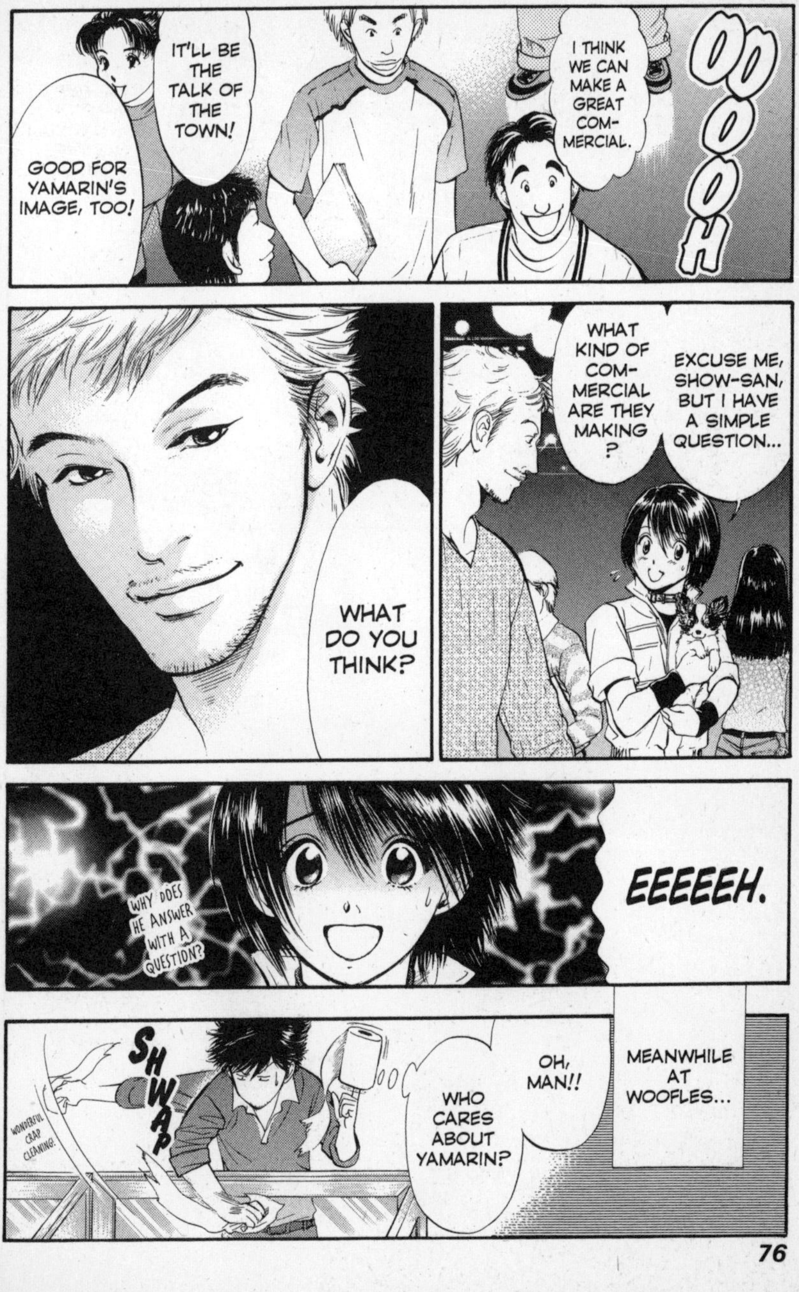
OOOOOH
I THINK WE CAN MAKE A GREAT COM-MERCIAL.
IT'LL BE THE TALK OF THE TOWN!
GOOD FOR YAMARIN'S IMAGE, TOO!
EXCUSE ME, SHOW-SAN, BUT I HAVE A SIMPLE QUESTION...
WHAT KIND OF COM-MERCIAL ARE THEY MAKING?
WHAT DO YOU THINK?
EEEEEH.
WHY DOES HE ANSWER WITH A QUESTION?
MEANWHILE AT WOOFLES...
OH, MAN!!
WHO CARES ABOUT YAMARIN?
SHWAP
WONDERFUL CRAP CLEANING.

CHAPTER 13 EVEN THE CRUSTS ARE FLUFFY

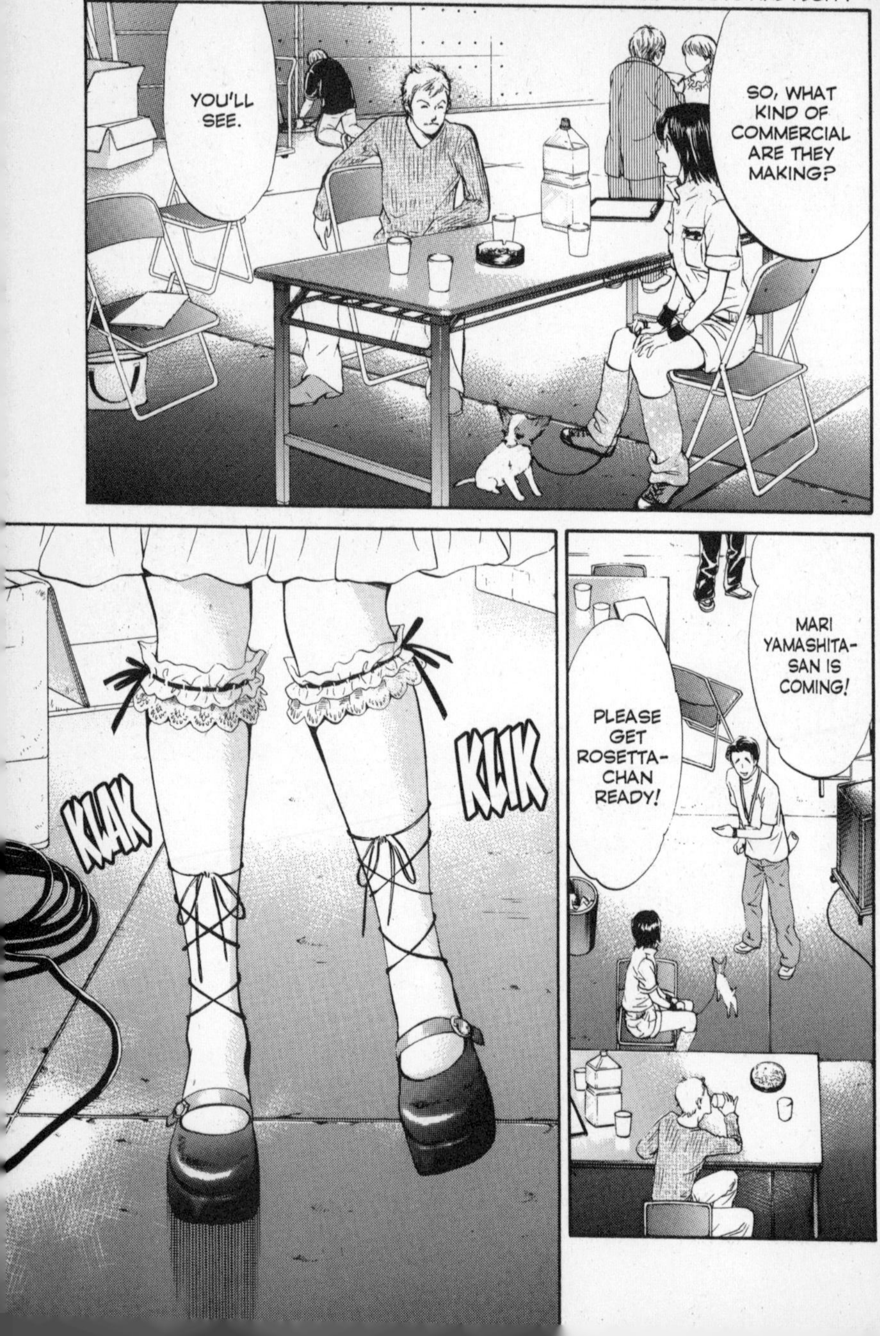
SO, WHAT KIND OF COMMERCIAL ARE THEY MAKING?
YOU'LL SEE.
MARI YAMASHITA-SAN IS COMING!
PLEASE GET ROSETTA-CHAN READY!
KLIK
KLAK

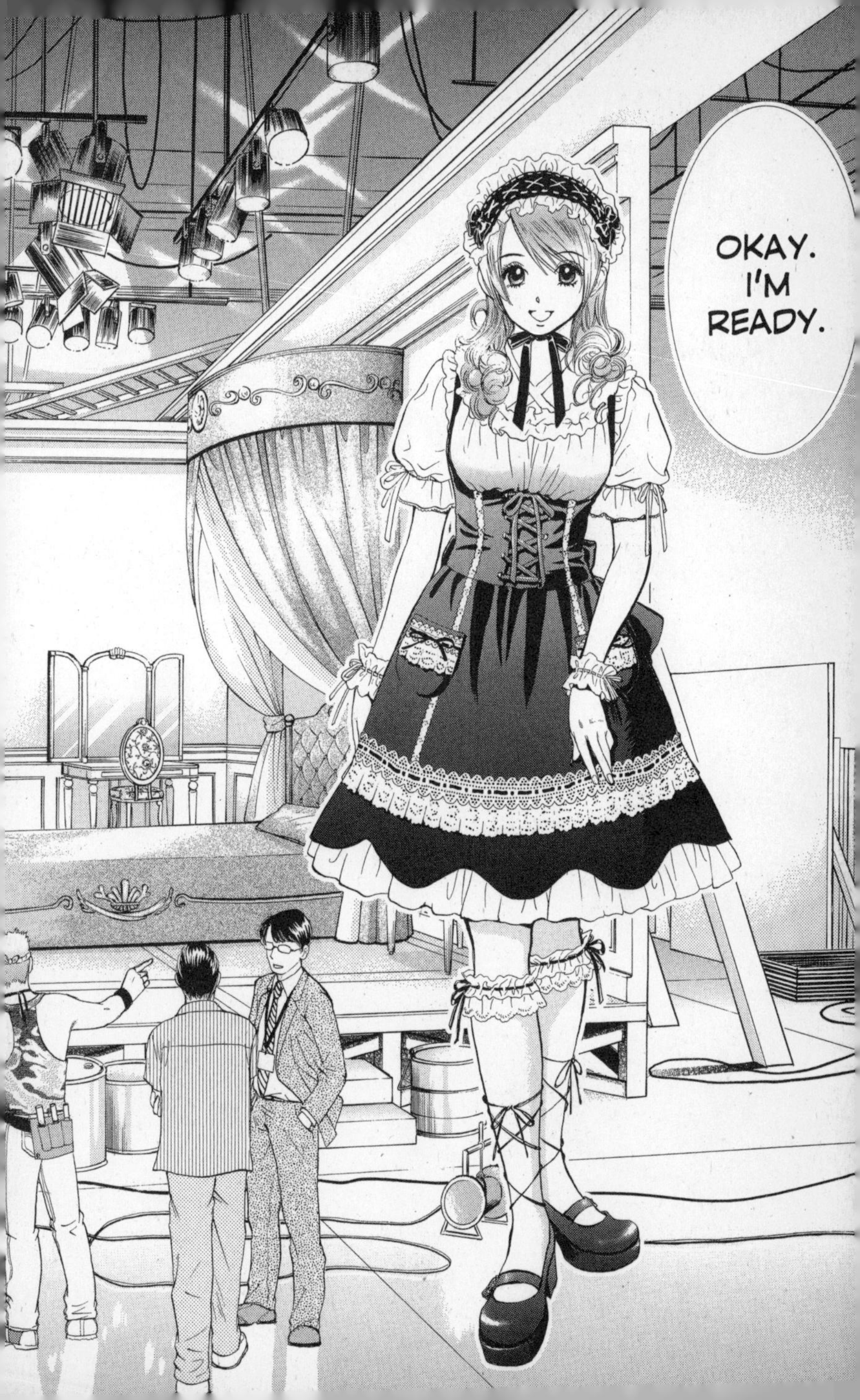
OKAY. I'M READY.

CHAPTER 13
EVEN THE CRUSTS ARE FLUFFY ♡

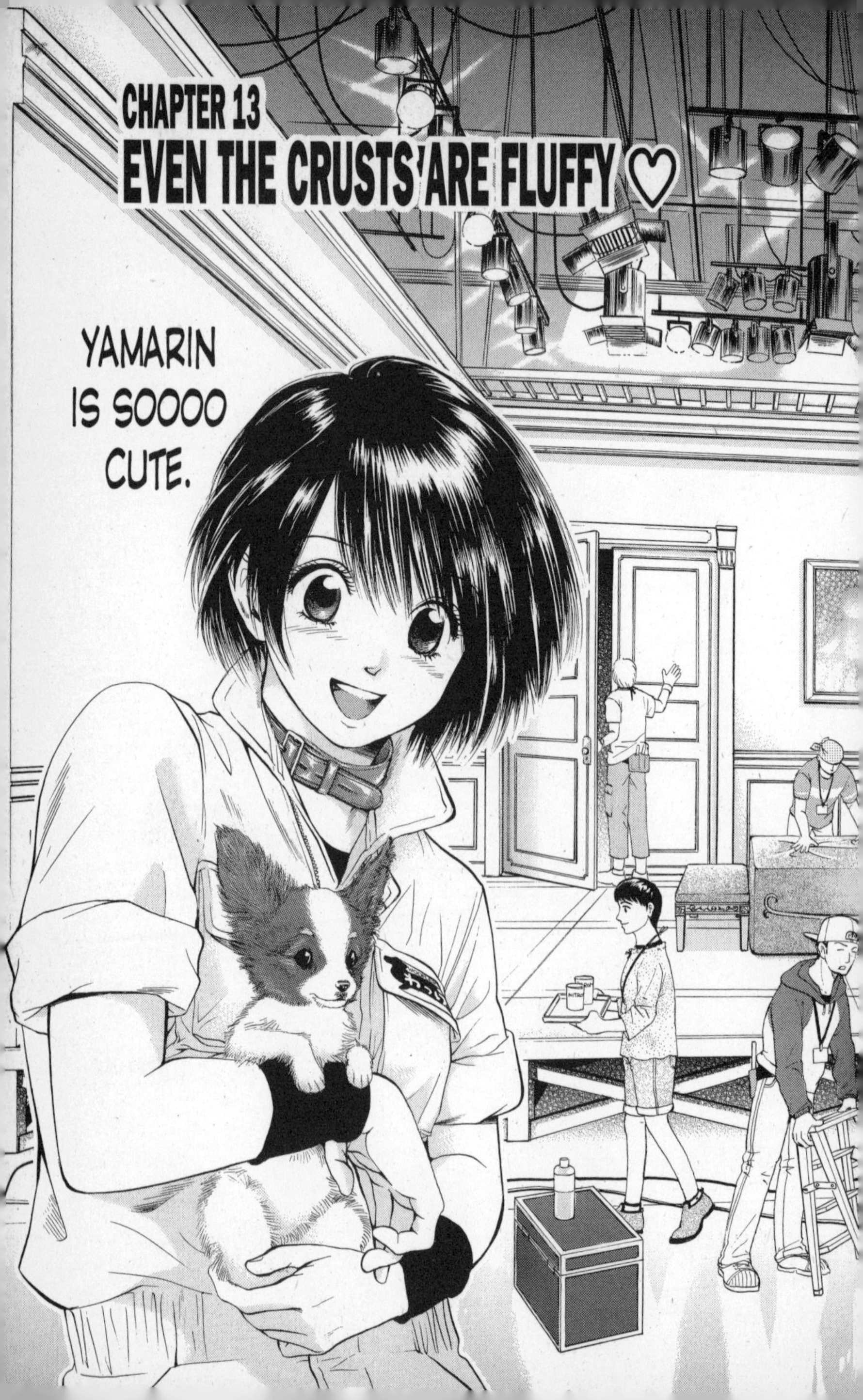
YAMARIN IS SOOOO CUTE.

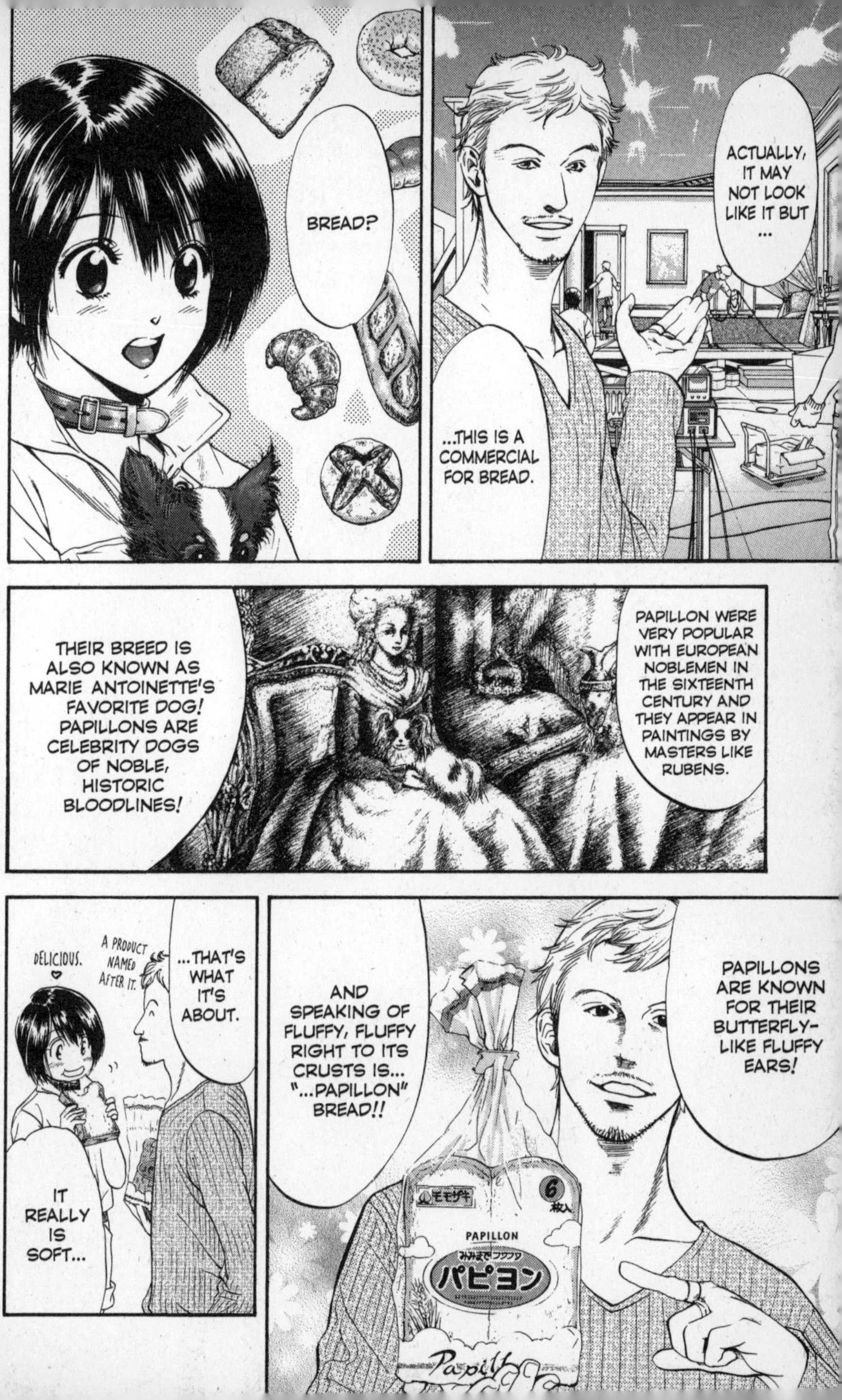
ACTUALLY, IT MAY NOT LOOK LIKE IT BUT ...
...THIS IS A COMMERCIAL FOR BREAD.
BREAD?
PAPILLON WERE VERY POPULAR WITH EUROPEAN NOBLEMEN IN THE SIXTEENTH CENTURY AND THEY APPEAR IN PAINTINGS BY MASTERS LIKE RUBENS.
THEIR BREED IS ALSO KNOWN AS MARIE ANTOINETTE'S FAVORITE DOG! PAPILLONS ARE CELEBRITY DOGS OF NOBLE, HISTORIC BLOODLINES!
PAPILLONS ARE KNOWN FOR THEIR BUTTERFLY-LIKE FLUFFY EARS!
AND SPEAKING OF FLUFFY, FLUFFY RIGHT TO ITS CRUSTS IS... "...PAPILLON" BREAD!!
モモザキ
6 枚入
PAPILLON
みみまでフワフワ
パピヨン
...THAT'S WHAT IT'S ABOUT.
A PRODUCT NAMED AFTER IT.
DELICIOUS.
IT REALLY IS SOFT...

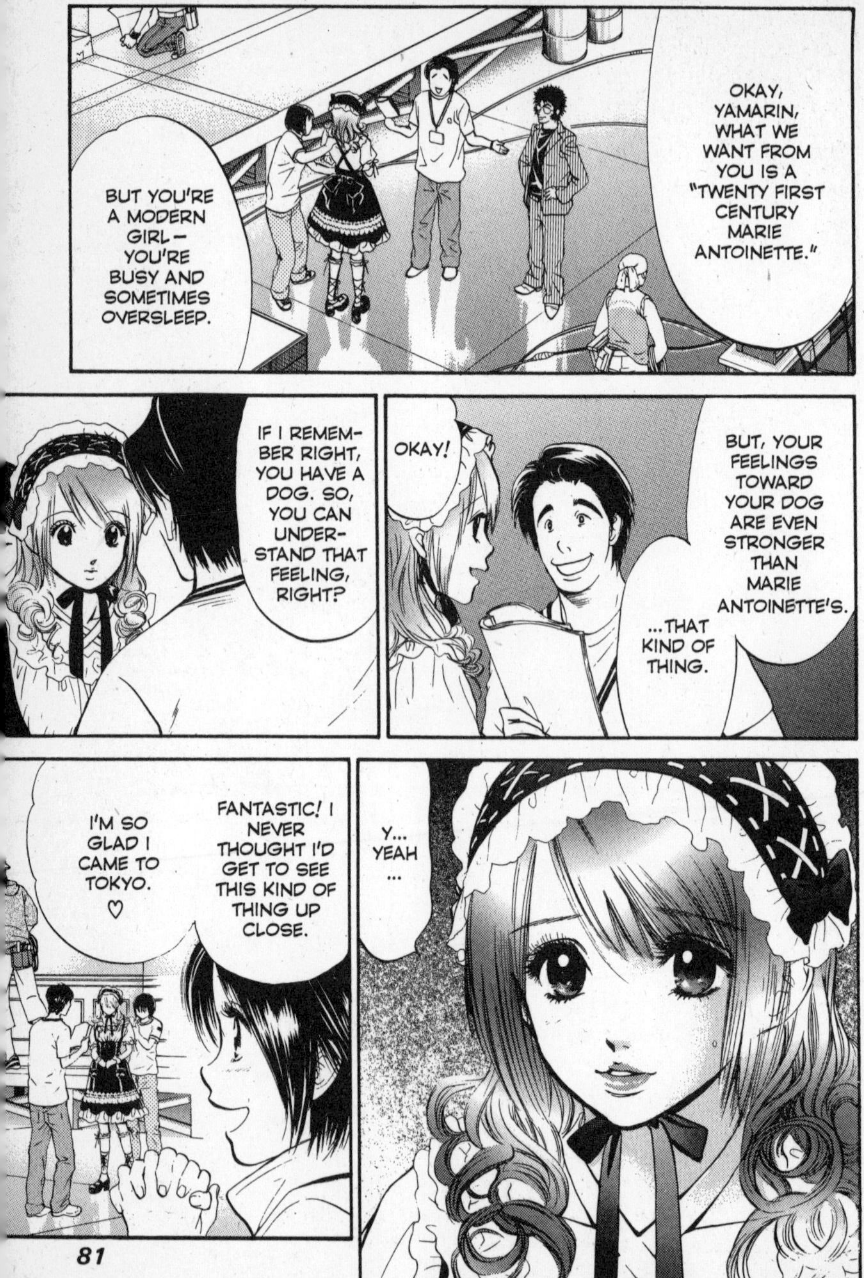
OKAY, YAMARIN, WHAT WE WANT FROM YOU IS A "TWENTY FIRST CENTURY MARIE ANTOINETTE."
BUT YOU'RE A MODERN GIRL— YOU'RE BUSY AND SOMETIMES OVERSLEEP.
BUT, YOUR FEELINGS TOWARD YOUR DOG ARE EVEN STRONGER THAN MARIE ANTOINETTE'S.
...THAT KIND OF THING.
OKAY!
IF I REMEMBER RIGHT, YOU HAVE A DOG. SO, YOU CAN UNDERSTAND THAT FEELING, RIGHT?
Y... YEAH ...
FANTASTIC! I NEVER THOUGHT I'D GET TO SEE THIS KIND OF THING UP CLOSE.
I'M SO GLAD I CAME TO TOKYO. ♡

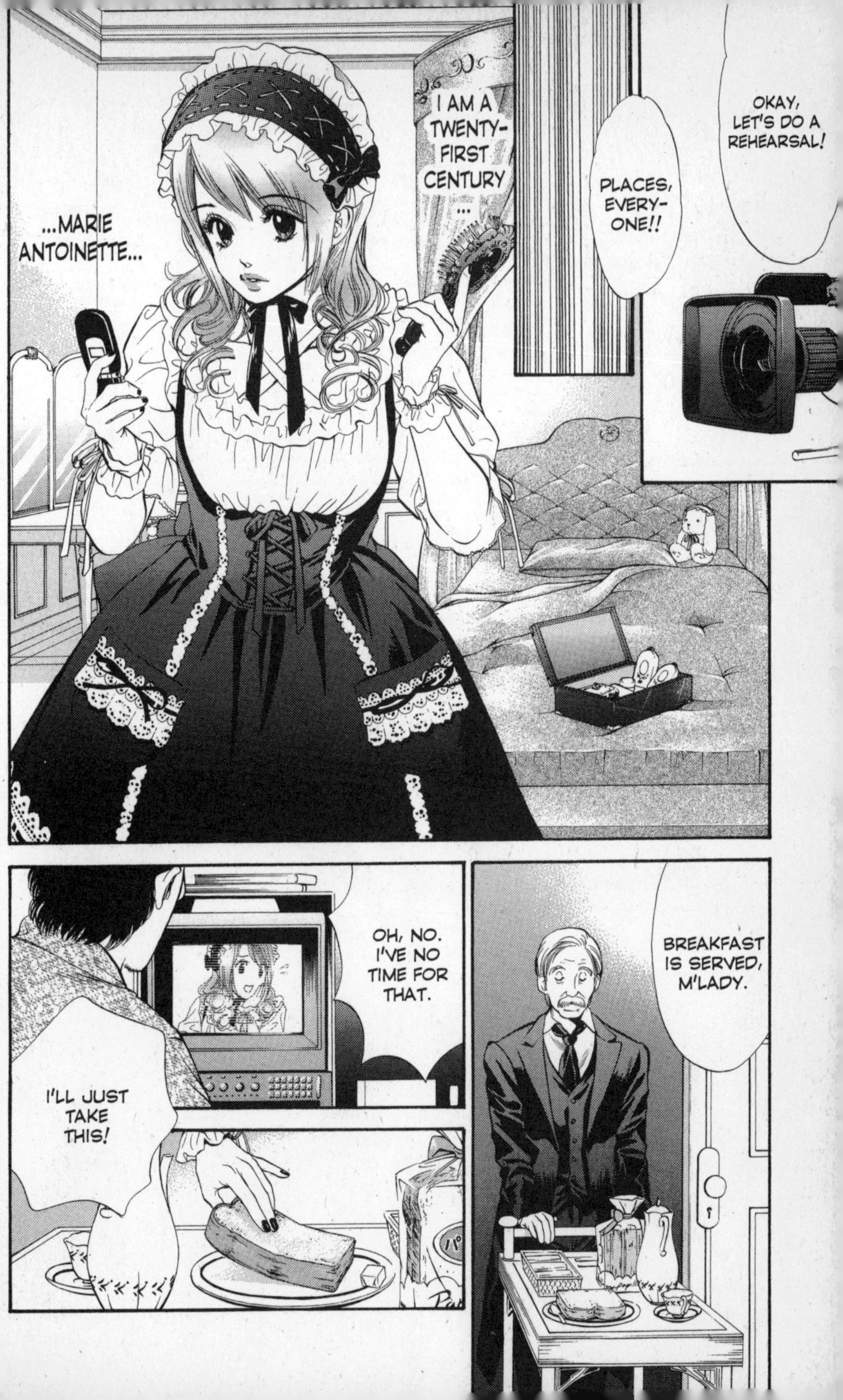
OKAY, LET'S DO A REHEARSAL!
PLACES, EVERYONE!!
I AM A TWENTY-FIRST CENTURY ...
...MARIE ANTOINETTE...
BREAKFAST IS SERVED, M'LADY.
OH, NO. I'VE NO TIME FOR THAT.
I'LL JUST TAKE THIS!

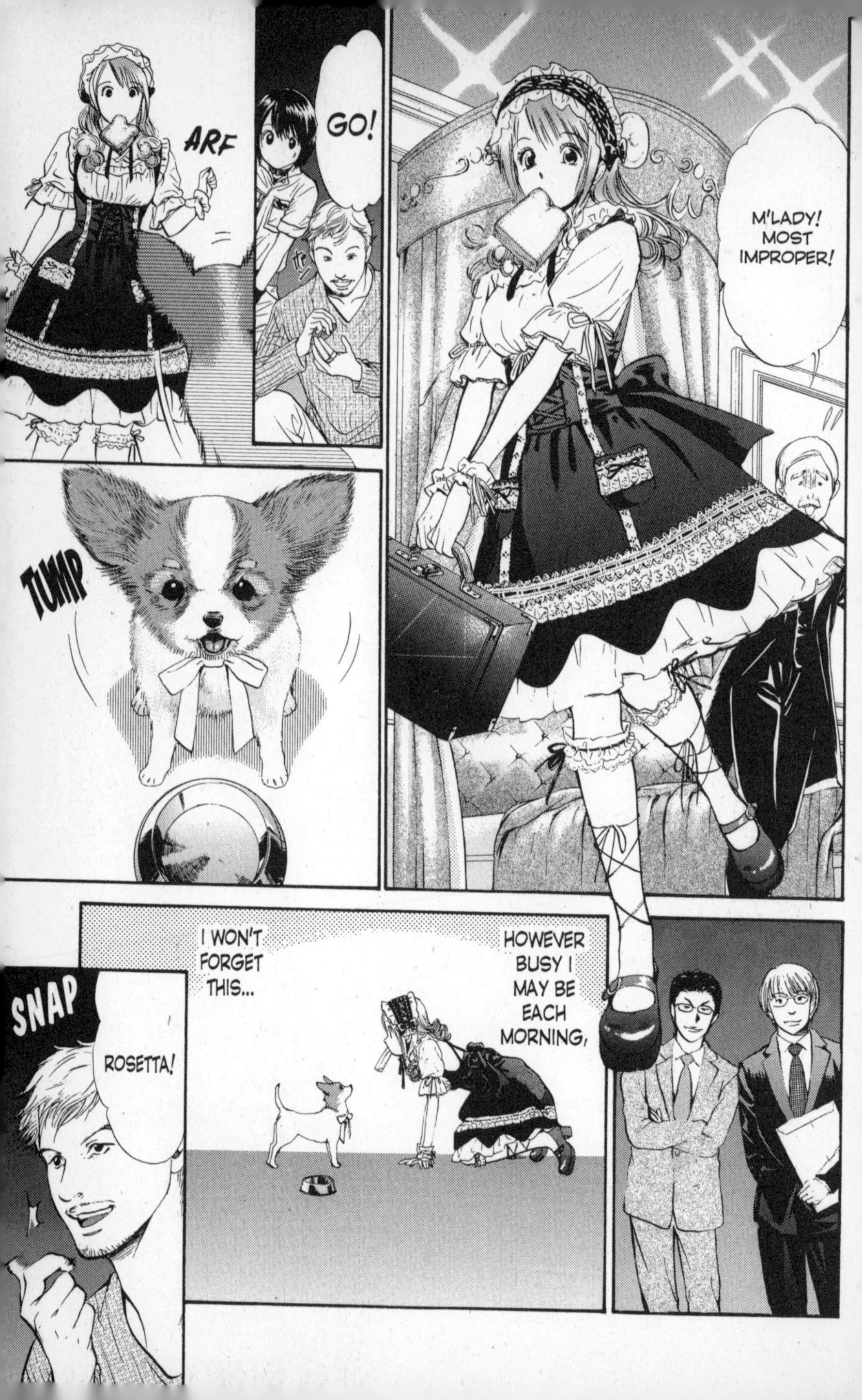
M'LADY! MOST IMPROPER!
GO!
ARF
TUMP
HOWEVER BUSY I MAY BE EACH MORNING,
I WON'T FORGET THIS...
SNAP
ROSETTA!

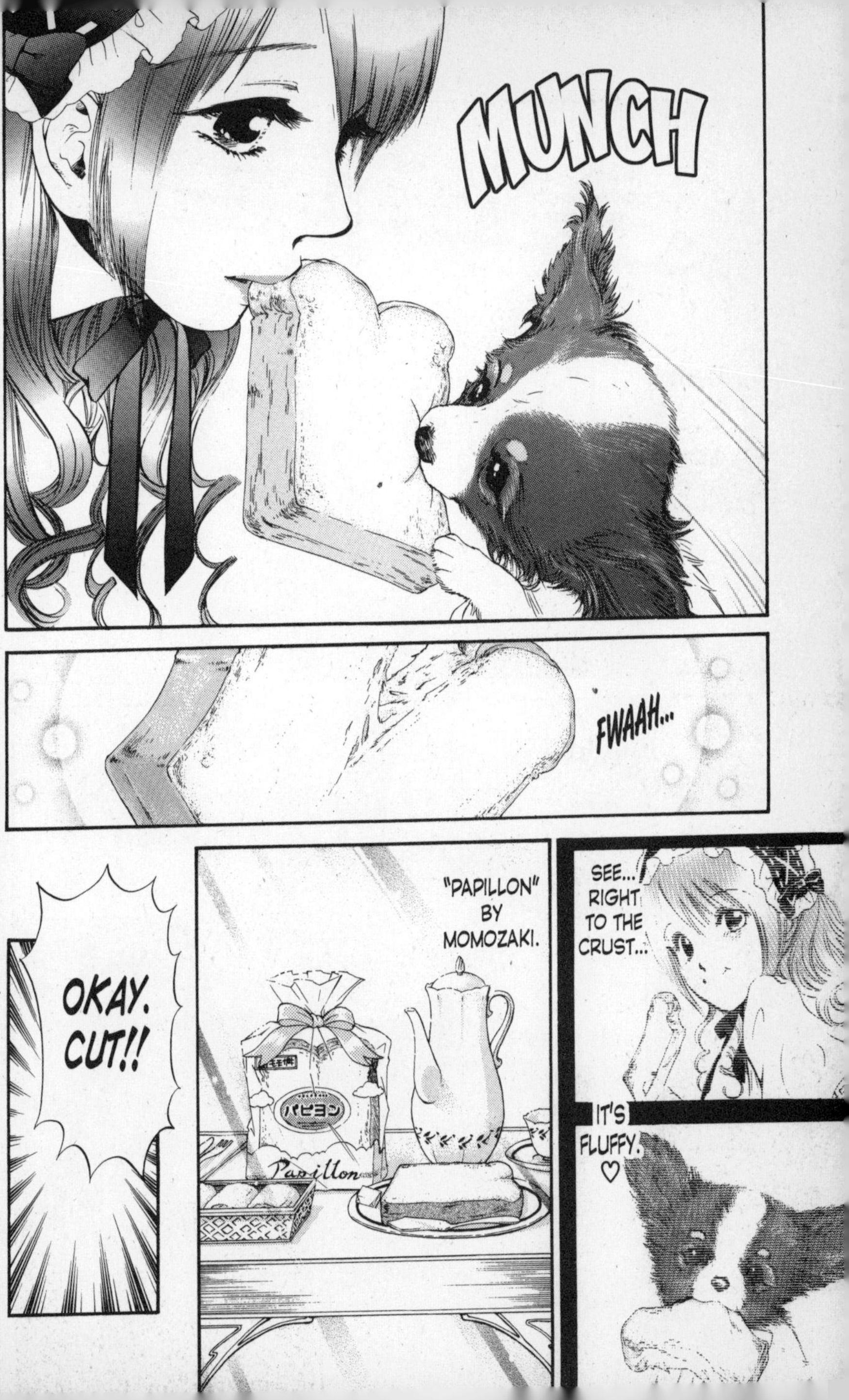
MUNCH
FWAAH...
SEE... RIGHT TO THE CRUST...
IT'S FLUFFY. ♡
"PAPILLON" BY MOMOZAKI.
パピヨン
Papillon
OKAY. CUT!!

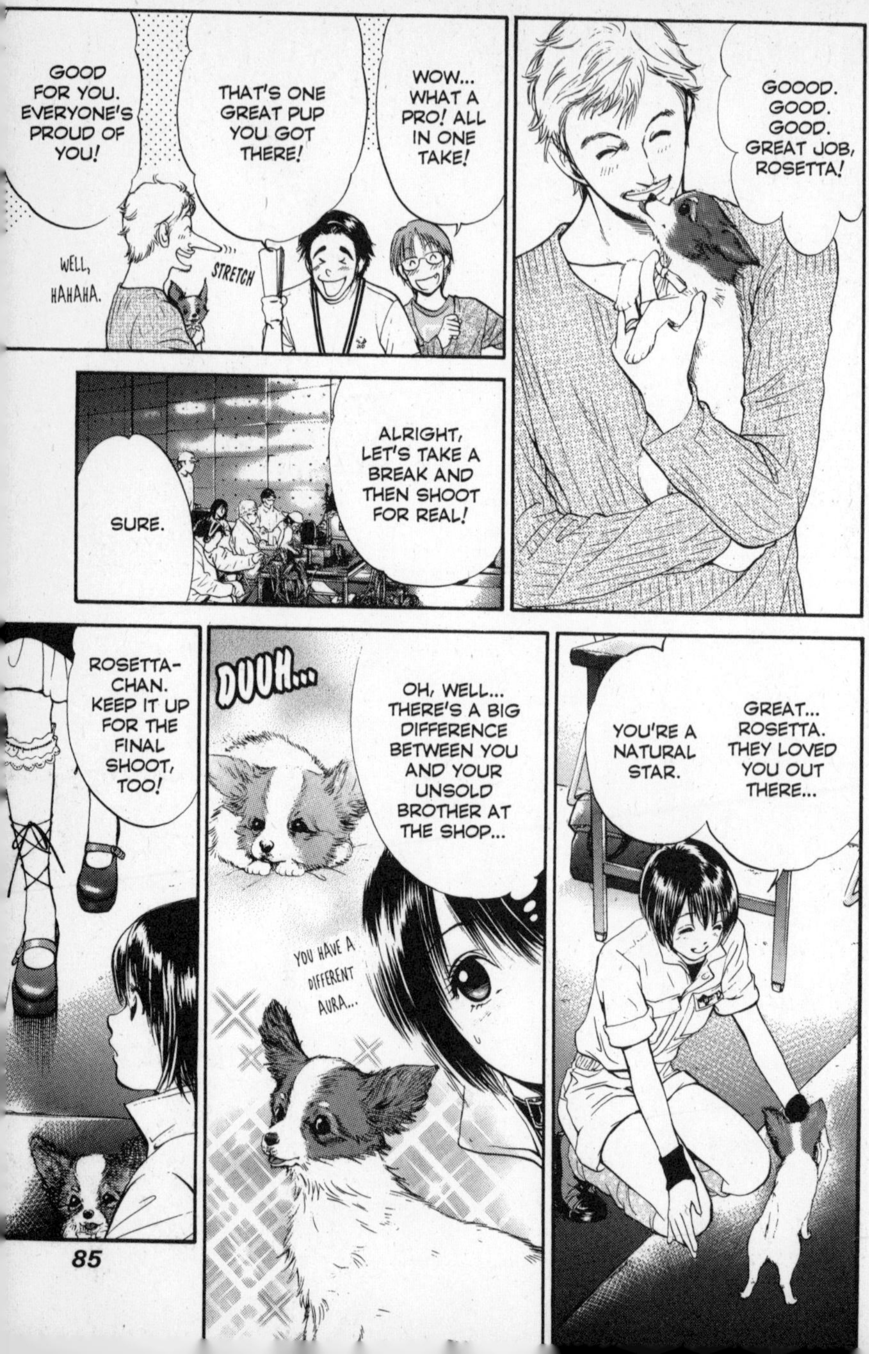
GOOOD. GOOD. GOOD. GREAT JOB, ROSETTA!
WOW... WHAT A PRO! ALL IN ONE TAKE!
THAT'S ONE GREAT PUP YOU GOT THERE!
GOOD FOR YOU. EVERYONE'S PROUD OF YOU!
STRETCH
WELL, HAHAHA.
ALRIGHT, LET'S TAKE A BREAK AND THEN SHOOT FOR REAL!
SURE.
GREAT... ROSETTA. THEY LOVED YOU OUT THERE...
YOU'RE A NATURAL STAR.
DUUH...
OH, WELL... THERE'S A BIG DIFFERENCE BETWEEN YOU AND YOUR UNSOLD BROTHER AT THE SHOP...
YOU HAVE A DIFFERENT AURA...
ROSETTA-CHAN. KEEP IT UP FOR THE FINAL SHOOT, TOO!

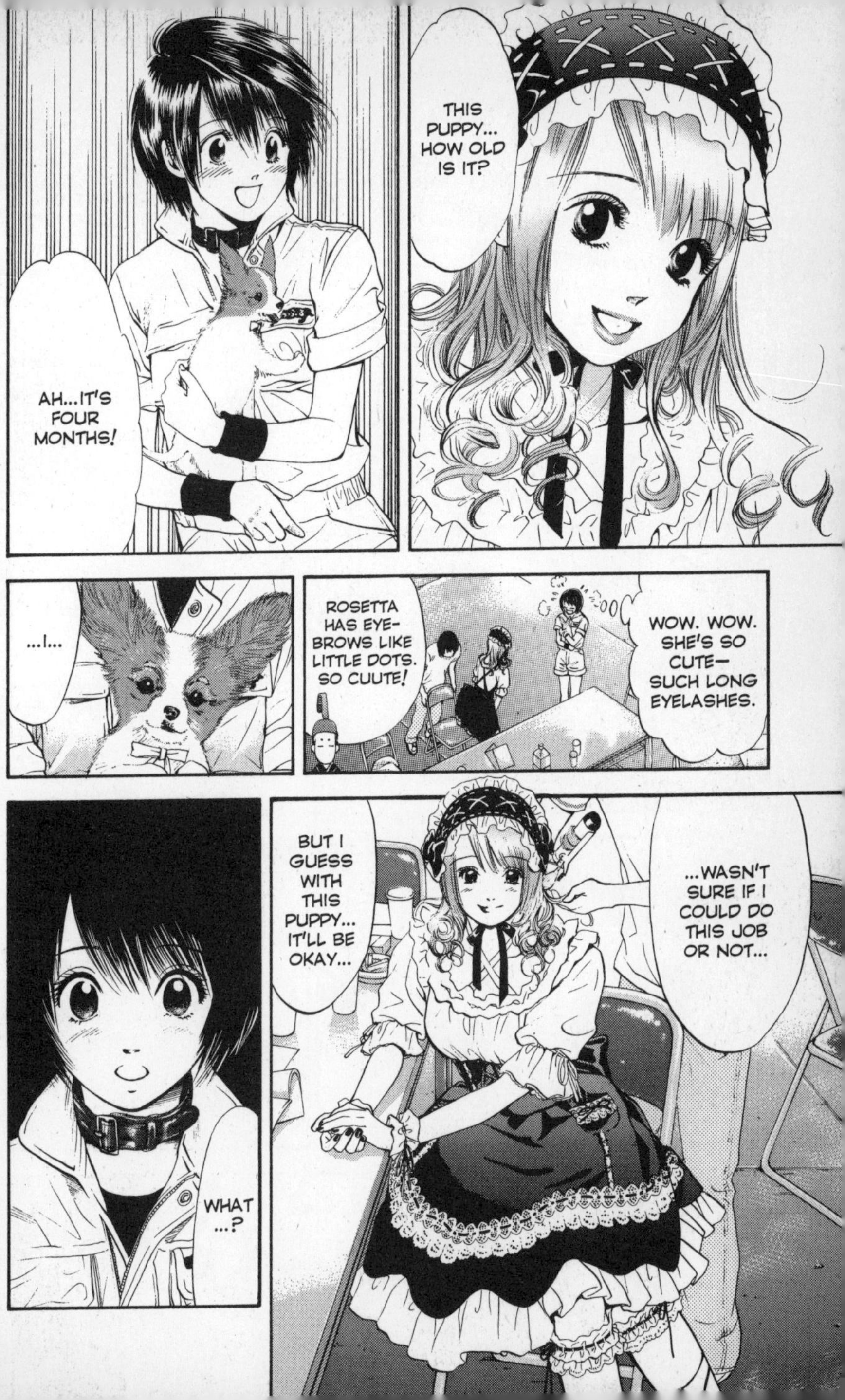
THIS PUPPY... HOW OLD IS IT?
AH...IT'S FOUR MONTHS!
WOW. WOW. SHE'S SO CUTE— SUCH LONG EYELASHES.
ROSETTA HAS EYE-BROWS LIKE LITTLE DOTS. SO CUUTE!
...I...
...WASN'T SURE IF I COULD DO THIS JOB OR NOT...
BUT I GUESS WITH THIS PUPPY... IT'LL BE OKAY...
WHAT ...?

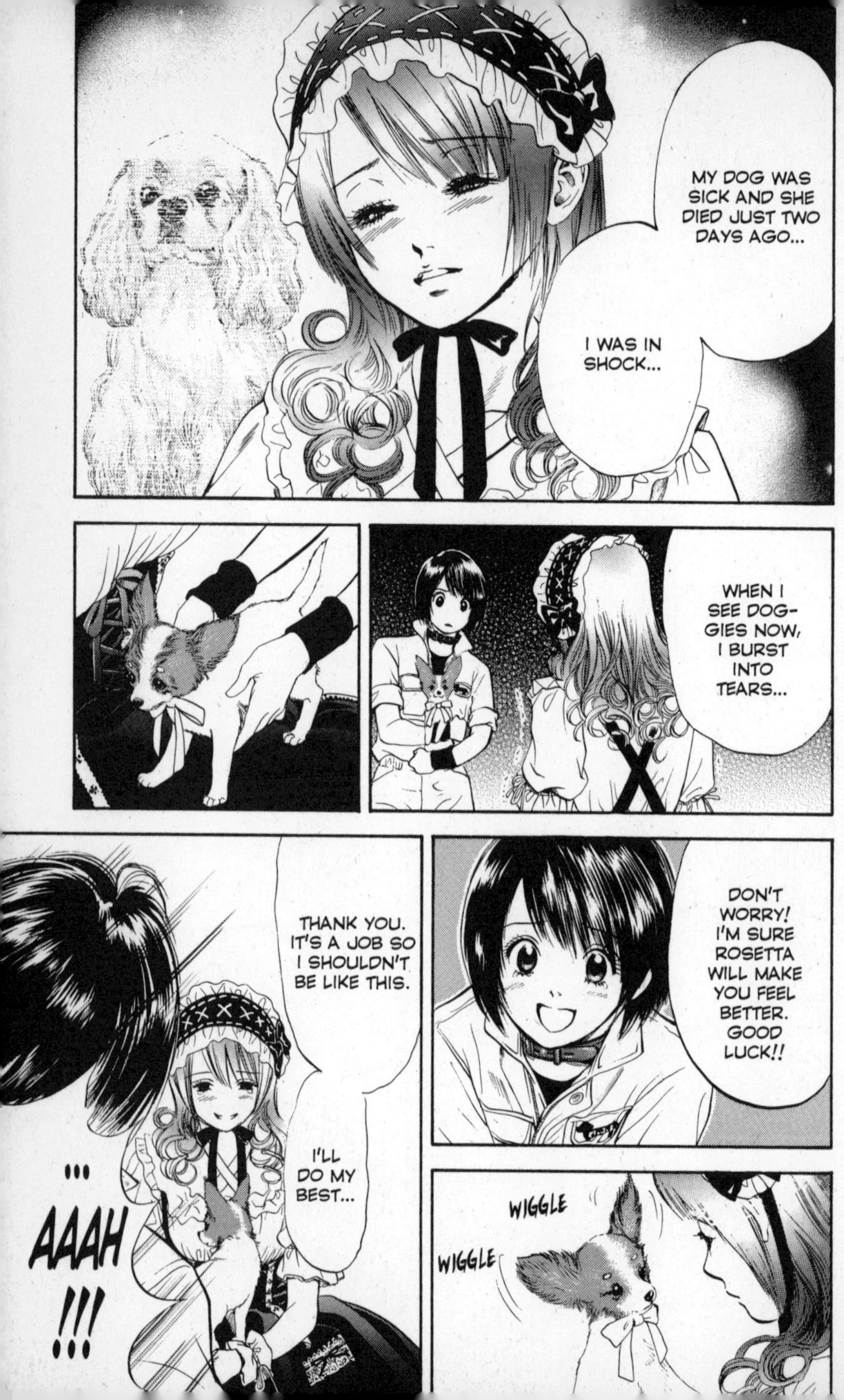
MY DOG WAS SICK AND SHE DIED JUST TWO DAYS AGO...
I WAS IN SHOCK...
WHEN I SEE DOG-GIES NOW, I BURST INTO TEARS...
DON'T WORRY! I'M SURE ROSETTA WILL MAKE YOU FEEL BETTER. GOOD LUCK!!
WIGGLE
WIGGLE
THANK YOU. IT'S A JOB SO I SHOULDN'T BE LIKE THIS.
I'LL DO MY BEST...
... AAAH !!!

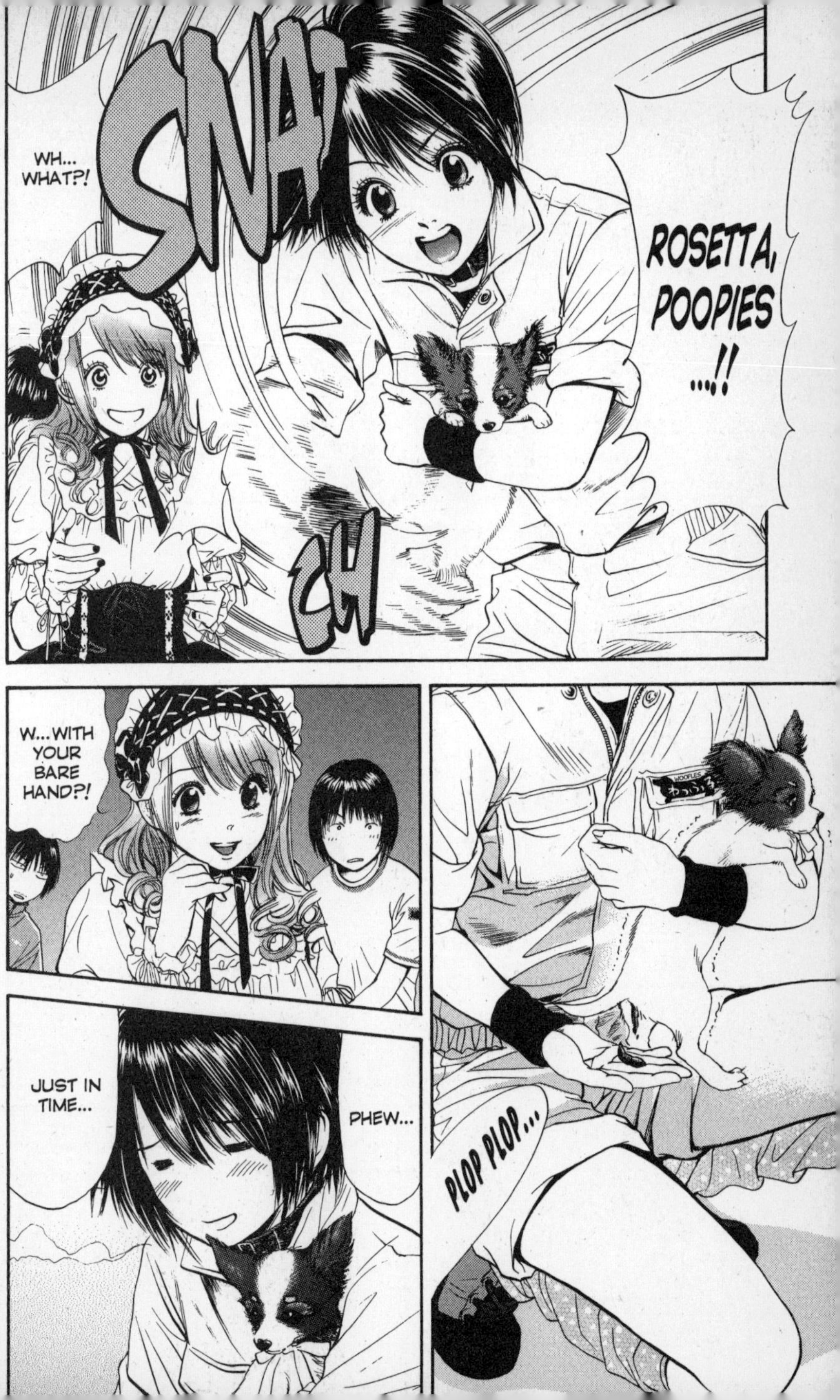
ROSETTA, POOPIES ...!!
SNATCH
WH... WHAT?!
PLOP PLOP...
W...WITH YOUR BARE HAND?!
PHEW...
JUST IN TIME...

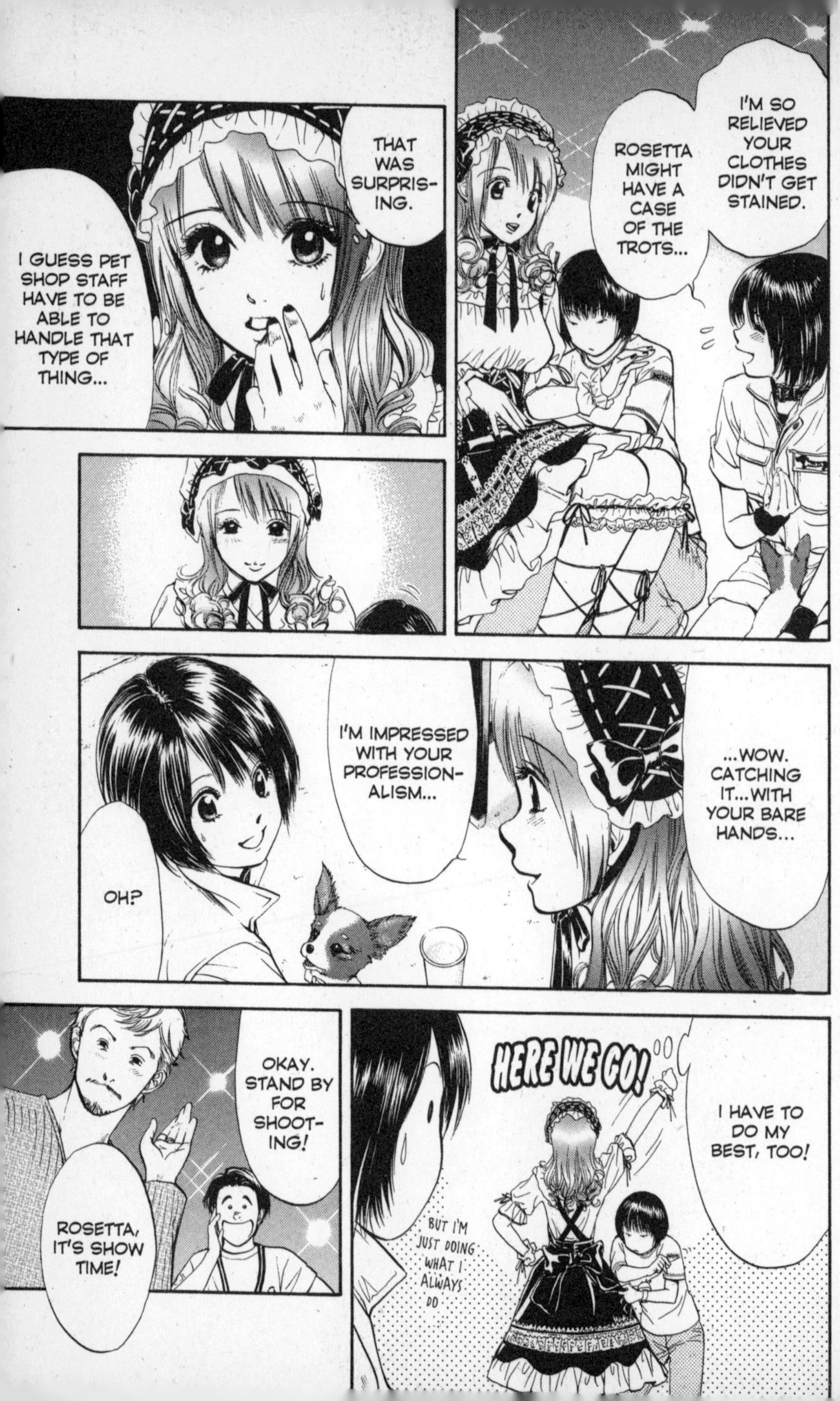
I'M SO RELIEVED YOUR CLOTHES DIDN'T GET STAINED.
ROSETTA MIGHT HAVE A CASE OF THE TROTS...
THAT WAS SURPRIS-ING.
I GUESS PET SHOP STAFF HAVE TO BE ABLE TO HANDLE THAT TYPE OF THING...
...WOW. CATCHING IT...WITH YOUR BARE HANDS...
I'M IMPRESSED WITH YOUR PROFESSION-ALISM...
OH?
HERE WE GO!
I HAVE TO DO MY BEST, TOO!
BUT I'M JUST DOING WHAT I ALWAYS DO
OKAY. STAND BY FOR SHOOT-ING!
ROSETTA, IT'S SHOW TIME!

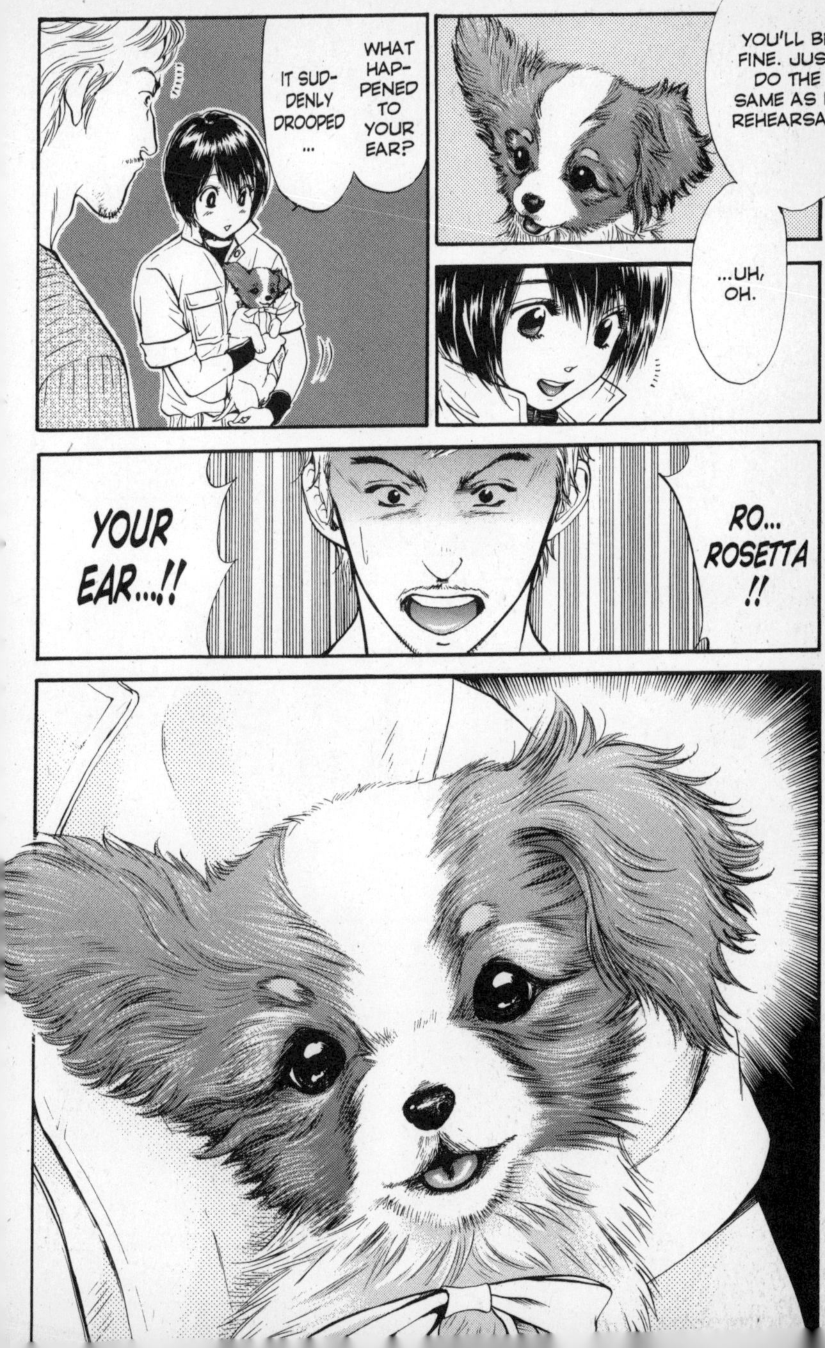
YOU'LL BE FINE. JUST DO THE SAME AS IN REHEARSAL.
...UH, OH.
WHAT HAP-PENED TO YOUR EAR?
IT SUD-DENLY DROOPED ...
RO... ROSETTA !!
YOUR EAR...!!

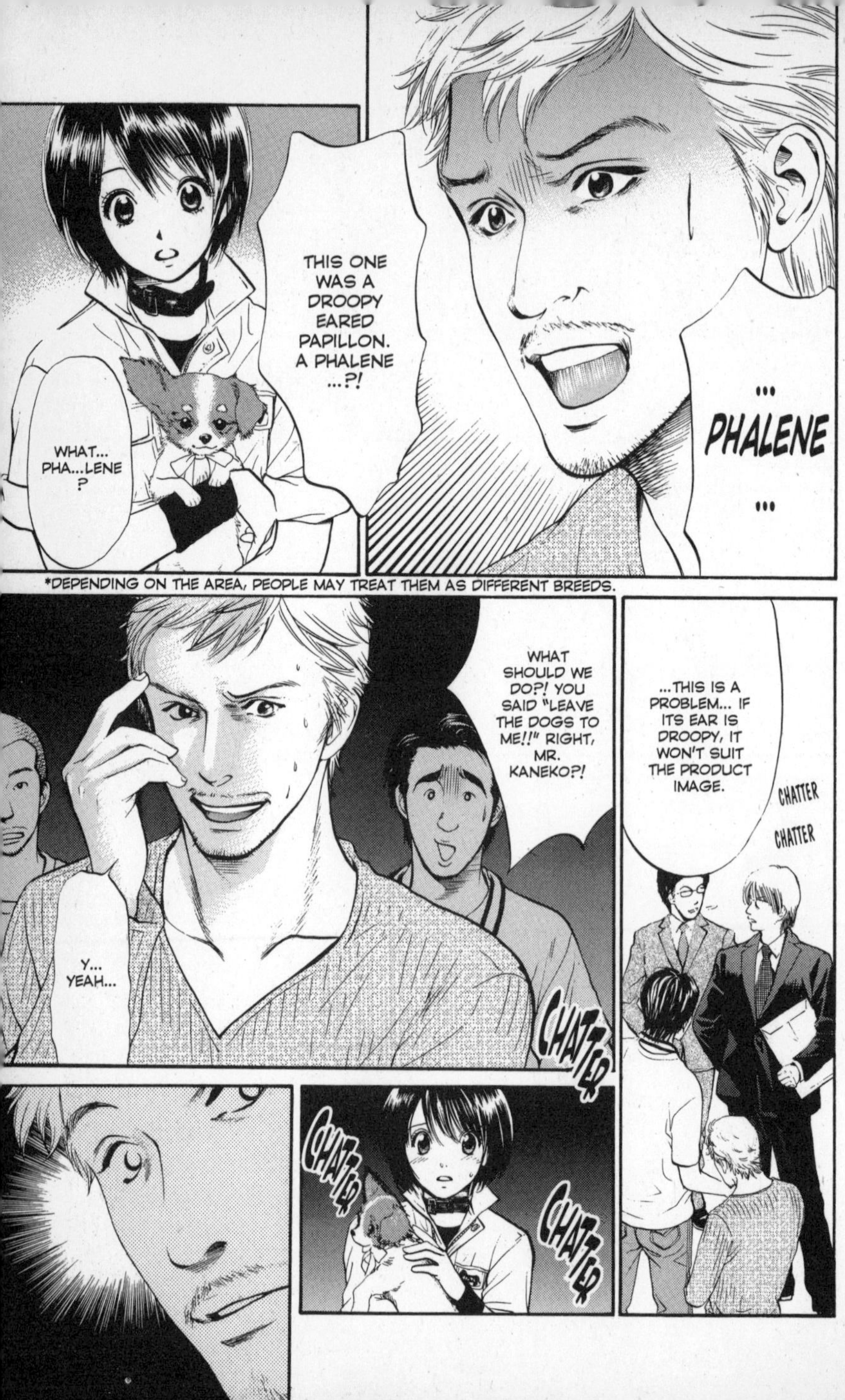
...PHALENE...
THIS ONE WAS A DROOPY EARED PAPILLON. A PHALENE ...?!
WHAT... PHA...LENE?
...THIS IS A PROBLEM... IF ITS EAR IS DROOPY, IT WON'T SUIT THE PRODUCT IMAGE.
CHATTER
CHATTER
WHAT SHOULD WE DO?! YOU SAID "LEAVE THE DOGS TO ME!!" RIGHT, MR. KANEKO?!
Y... YEAH...
CHATTER
CHATTER
CHATTER

*DEPENDING ON THE AREA, PEOPLE MAY TREAT THEM AS DIFFERENT BREEDS.

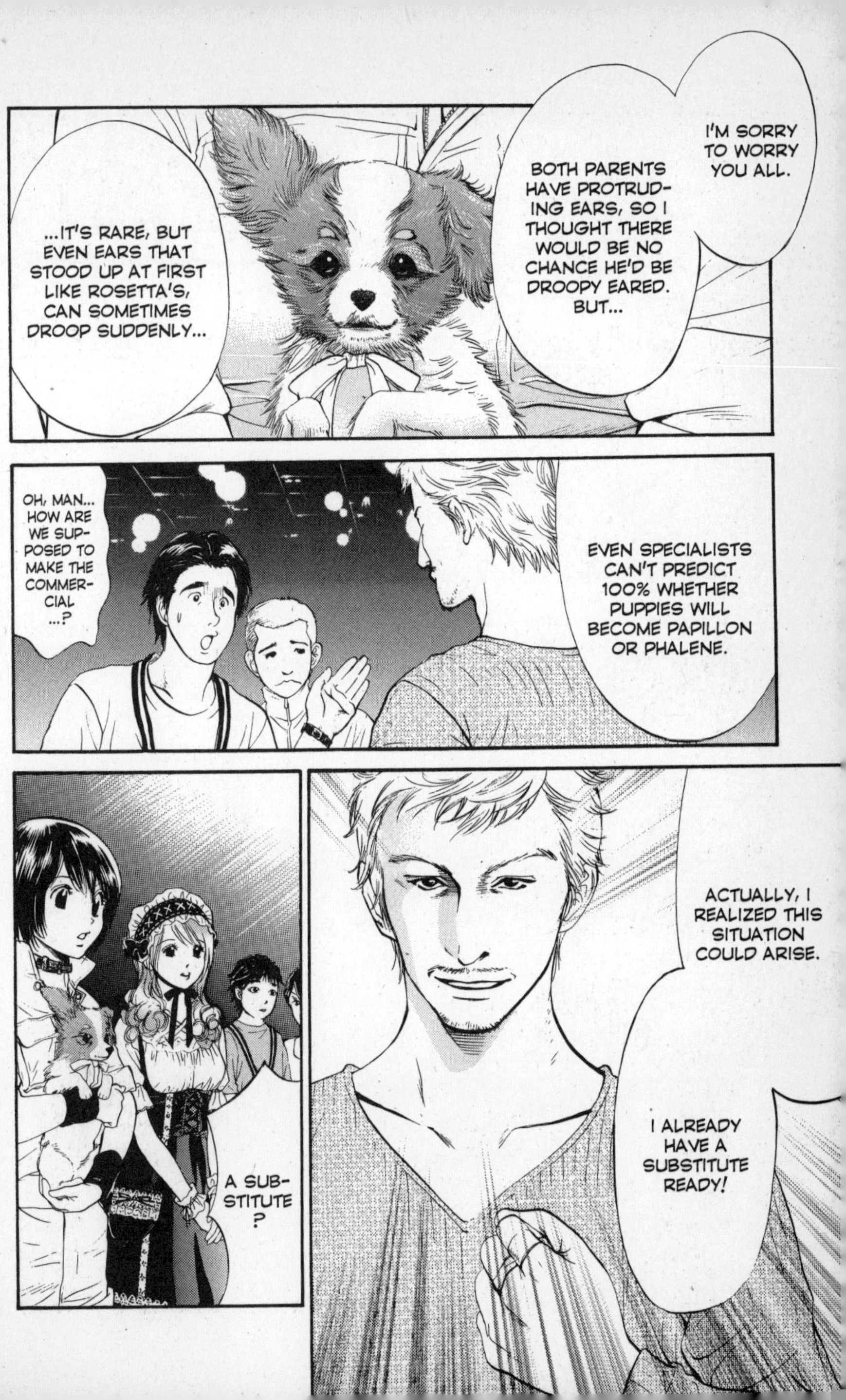
I'M SORRY TO WORRY YOU ALL.
BOTH PARENTS HAVE PROTRUDING EARS, SO I THOUGHT THERE WOULD BE NO CHANCE HE'D BE DROOPY EARED. BUT...
...IT'S RARE, BUT EVEN EARS THAT STOOD UP AT FIRST LIKE ROSETTA'S, CAN SOMETIMES DROOP SUDDENLY...
EVEN SPECIALISTS CAN'T PREDICT 100% WHETHER PUPPIES WILL BECOME PAPILLON OR PHALENE.
OH, MAN... HOW ARE WE SUPPOSED TO MAKE THE COMMERCIAL ...?
ACTUALLY, I REALIZED THIS SITUATION COULD ARISE.
I ALREADY HAVE A SUBSTITUTE READY!
A SUBSTITUTE ?

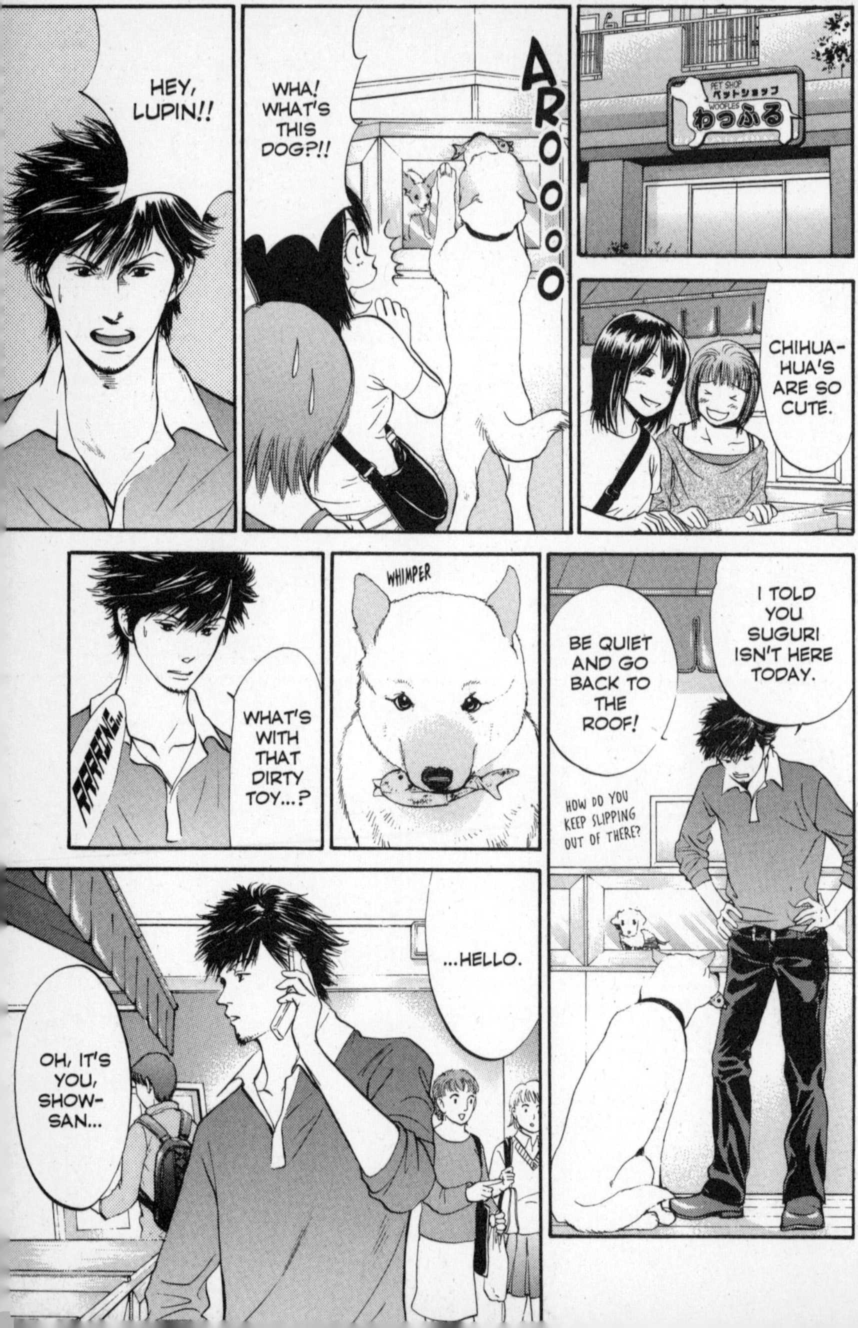
PET SHOP
ペットショップ
WOOFLES
わっふる
CHIHUA-HUA'S ARE SO CUTE.
AROOOOO
WHA! WHAT'S THIS DOG?!!
HEY, LUPIN!!
I TOLD YOU SUGURI ISN'T HERE TODAY.
BE QUIET AND GO BACK TO THE ROOF!
HOW DO YOU KEEP SLIPPING OUT OF THERE?
WHIMPER
WHAT'S WITH THAT DIRTY TOY...?
RRRRING...
...HELLO.
OH, IT'S YOU, SHOW-SAN...

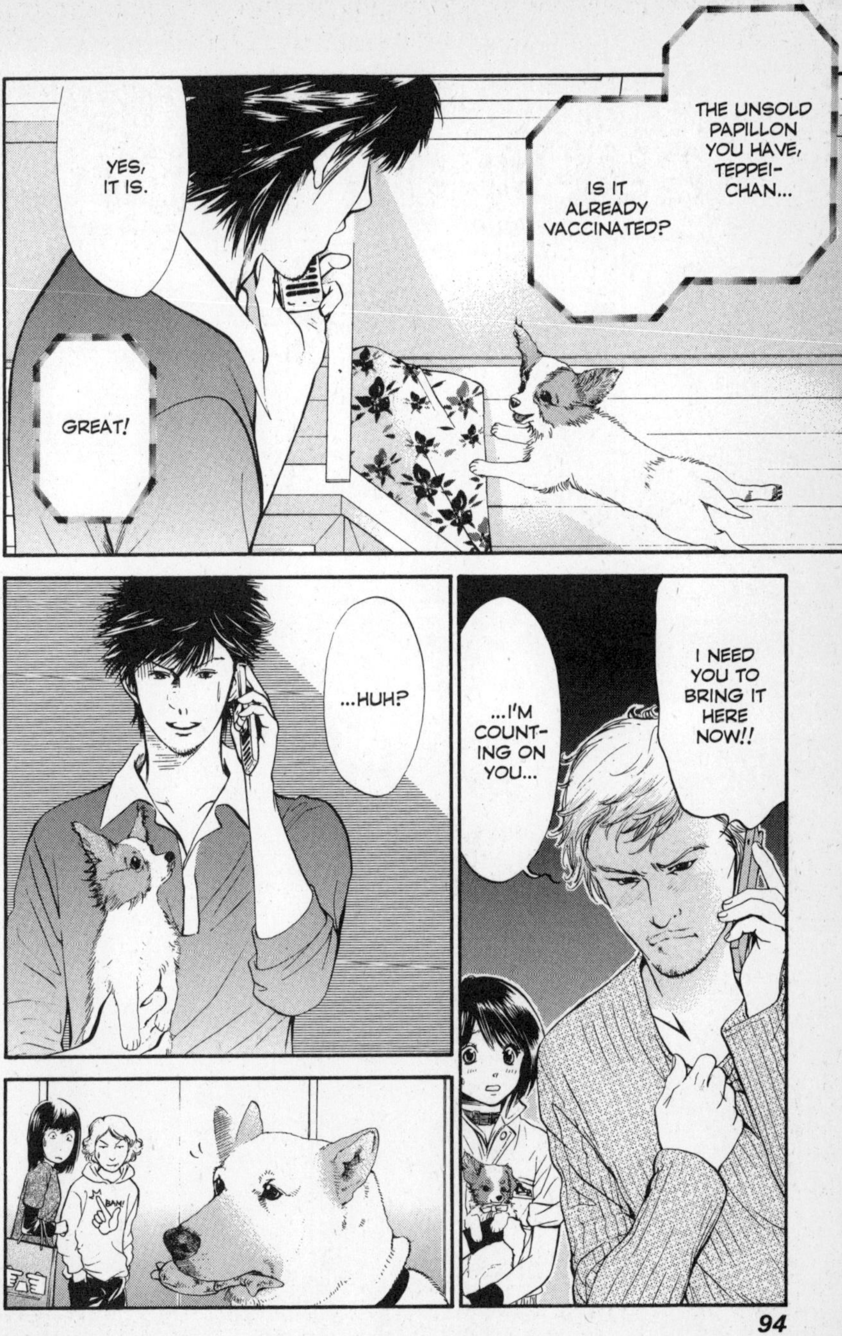
THE UNSOLD PAPILLON YOU HAVE, TEPPEI-CHAN...
IS IT ALREADY VACCINATED?
YES, IT IS.
GREAT!
I NEED YOU TO BRING IT HERE NOW!!
...I'M COUNTING ON YOU...
...HUH?

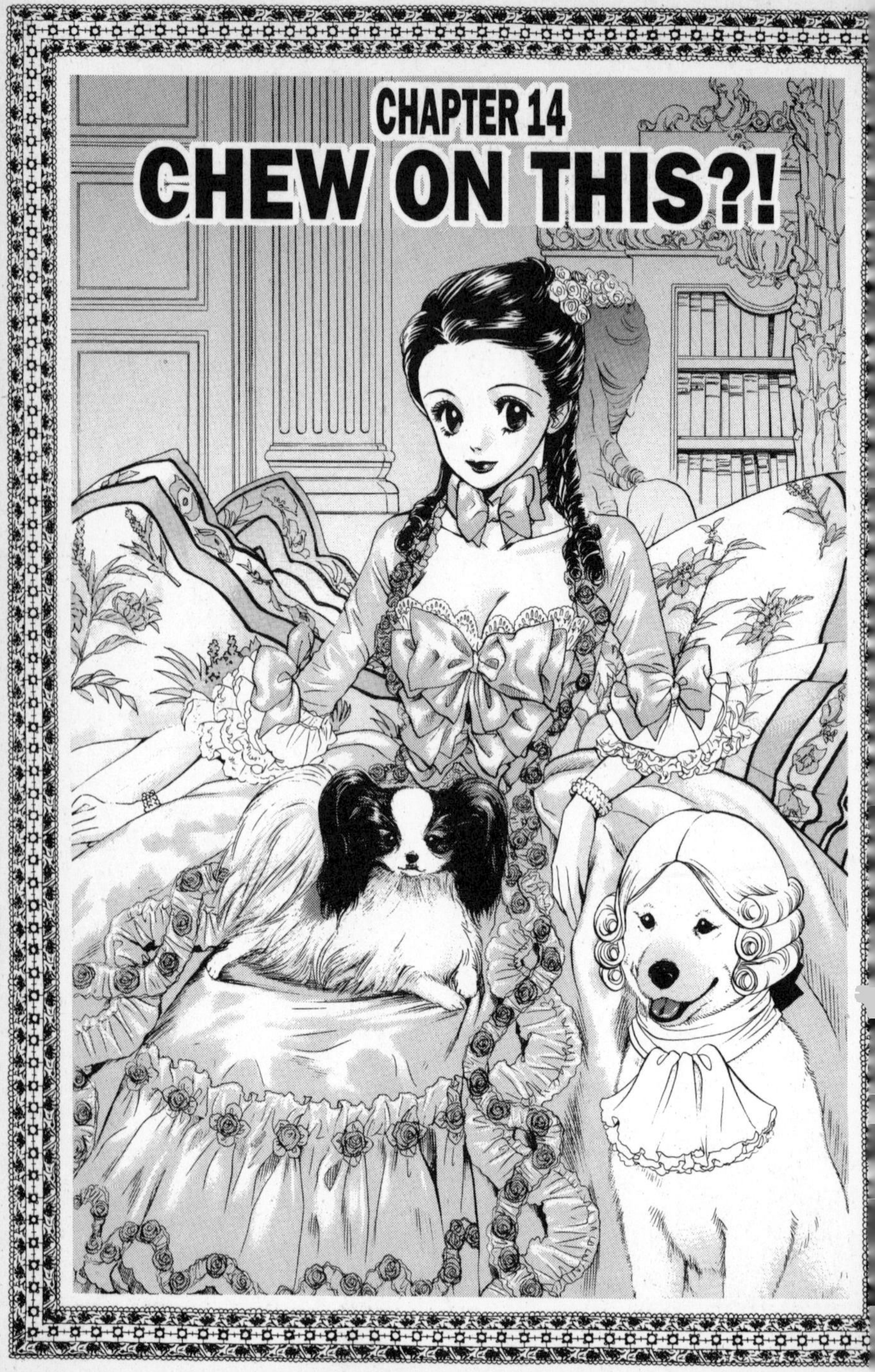
CHAPTER 14
CHEW ON THIS?!

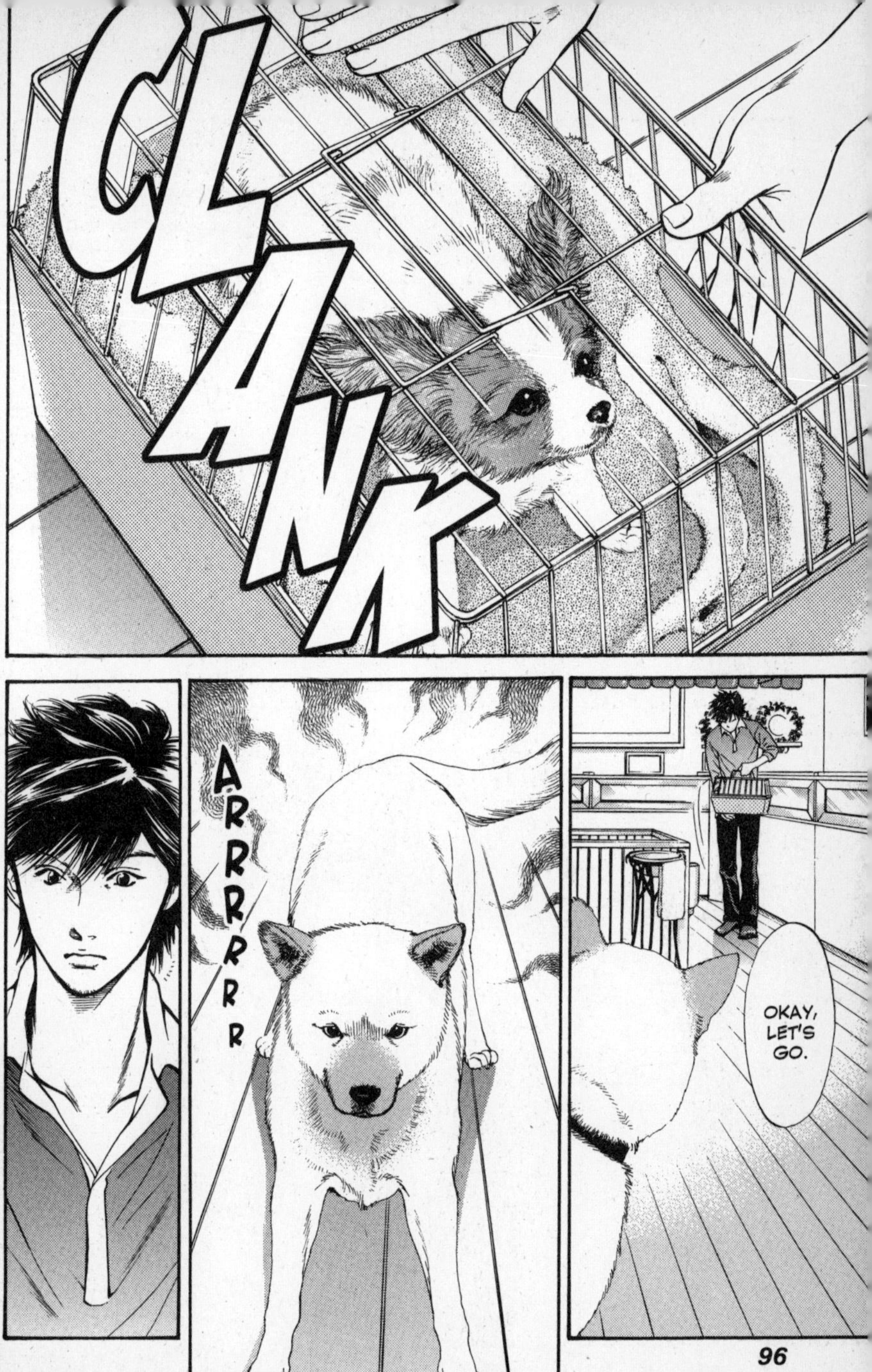
CLANK
OKAY, LET'S GO.
ARRRRRRR

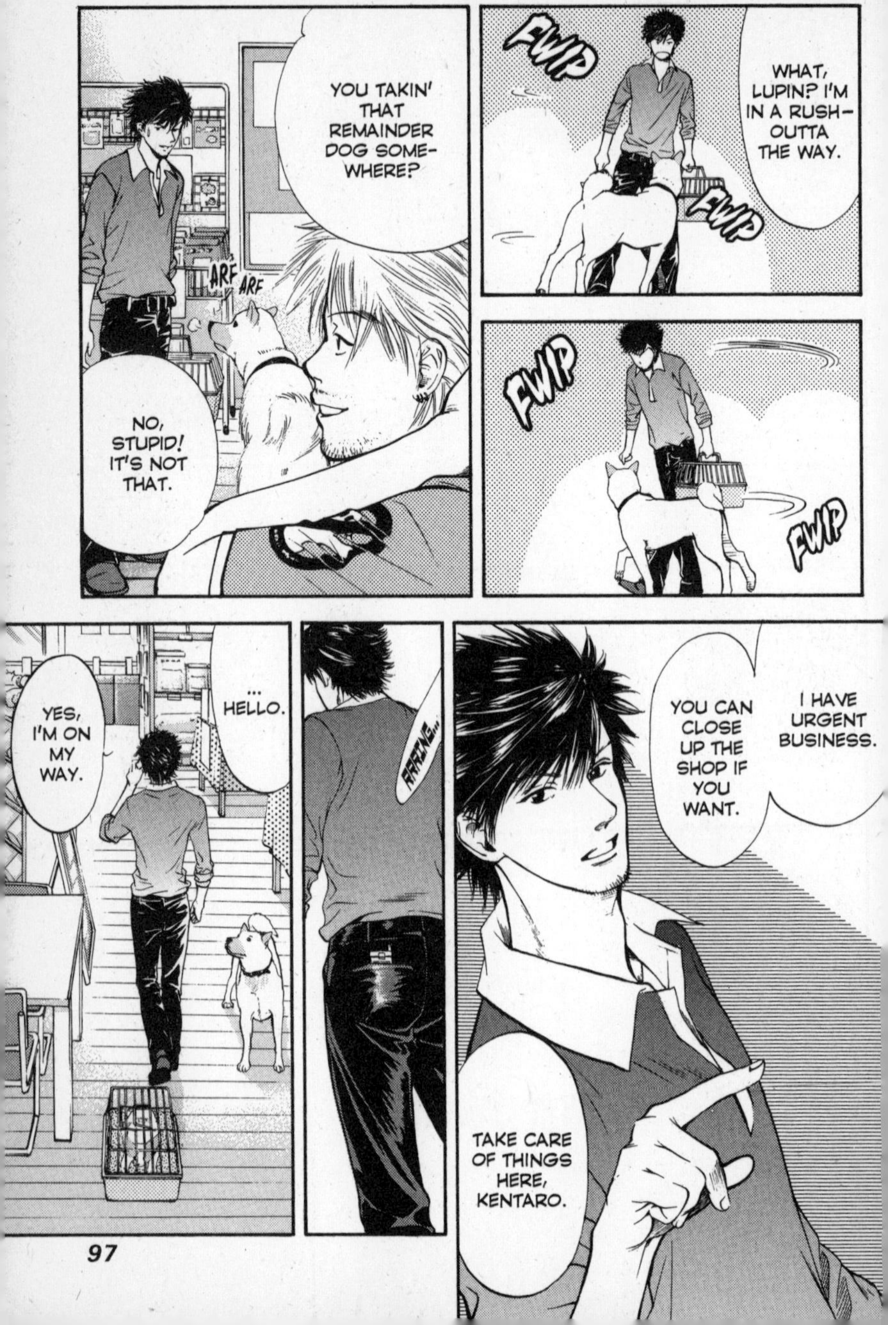
FWIP
WHAT, LUPIN? I'M IN A RUSH— OUTTA THE WAY.
FWIP
FWIP
FWIP
YOU TAKIN' THAT REMAINDER DOG SOME-WHERE?
ARF ARF
NO, STUPID! IT'S NOT THAT.
I HAVE URGENT BUSINESS.
YOU CAN CLOSE UP THE SHOP IF YOU WANT.
TAKE CARE OF THINGS HERE, KENTARO.
FRRRING...
... HELLO.
YES, I'M ON MY WAY.

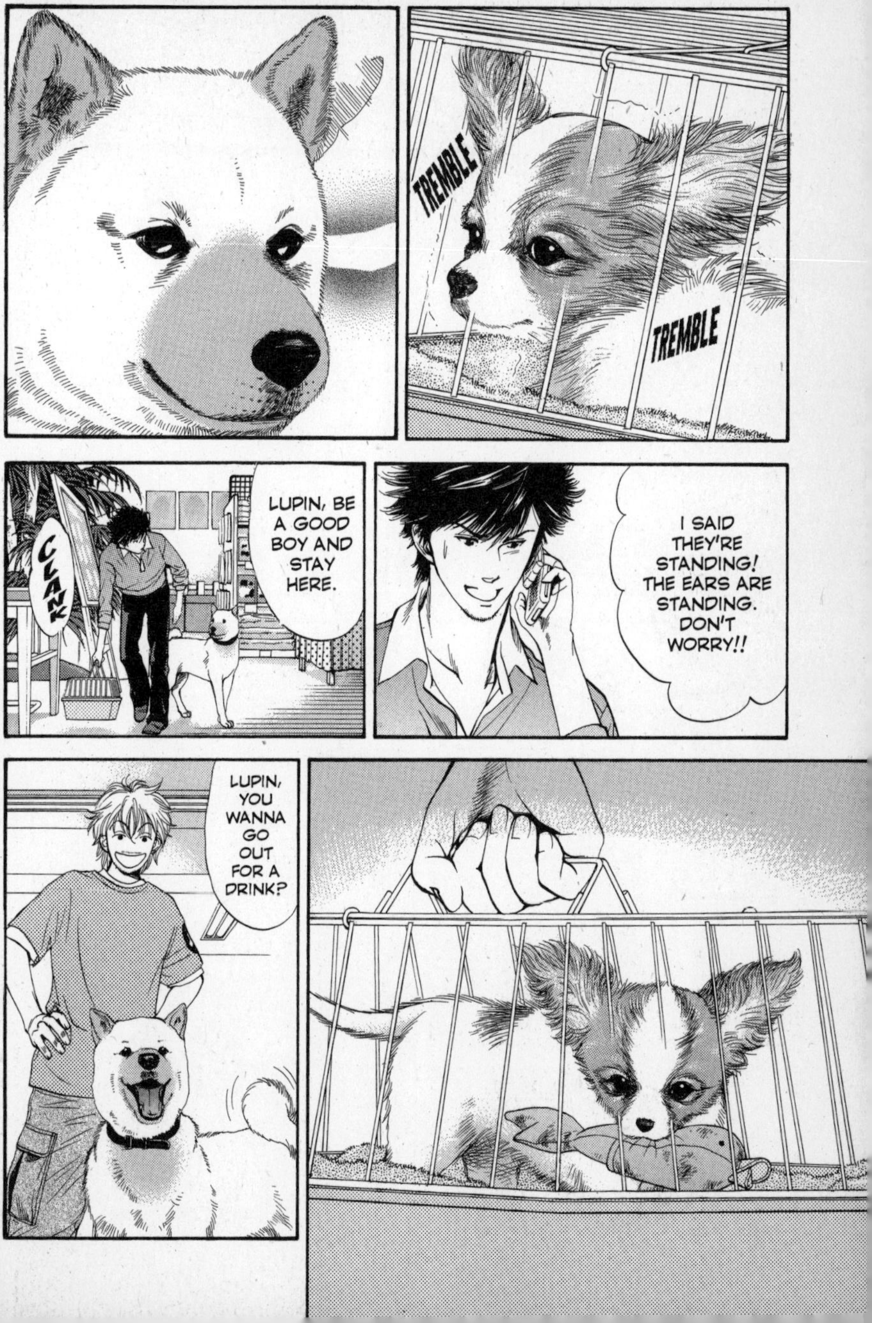
TREMBLE
TREMBLE
I SAID THEY'RE STANDING! THE EARS ARE STANDING. DON'T WORRY!!
LUPIN, BE A GOOD BOY AND STAY HERE.
CLANK
LUPIN, YOU WANNA GO OUT FOR A DRINK?

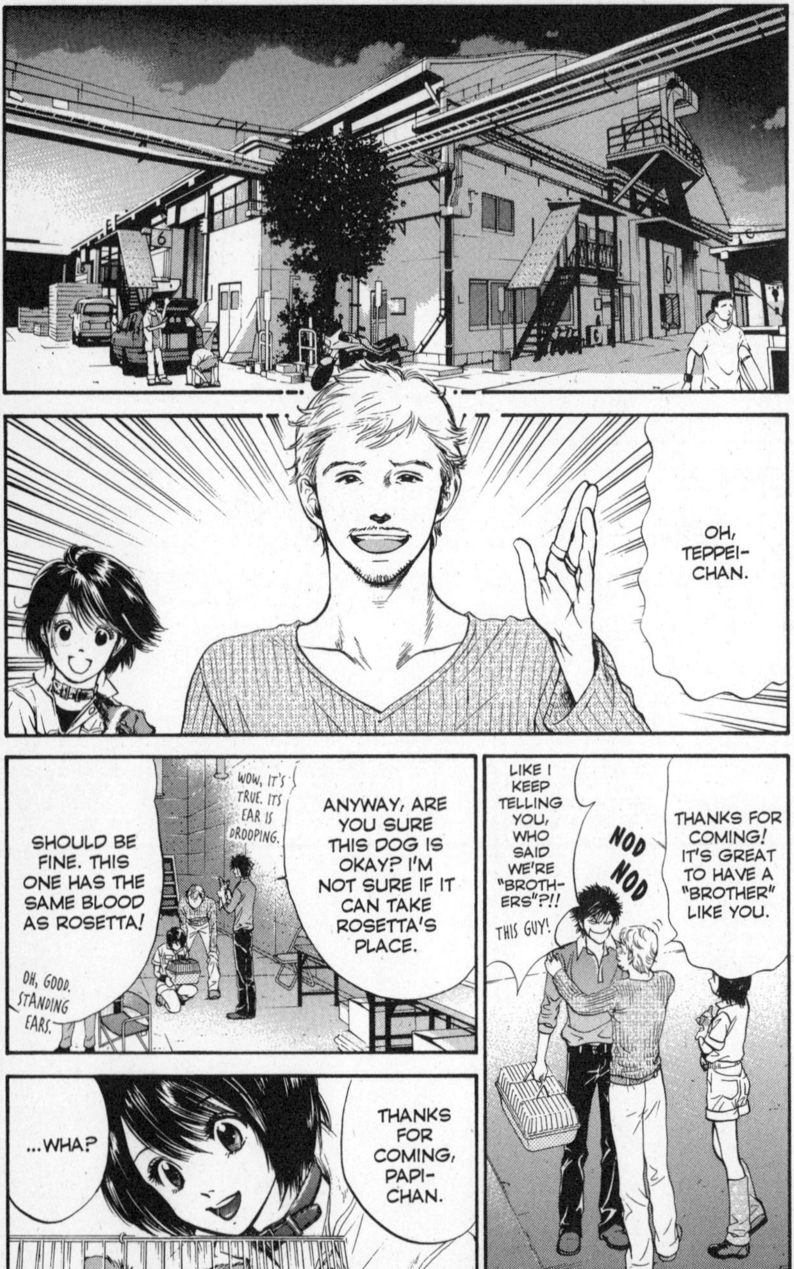
OH, TEPPEI-CHAN.
THANKS FOR COMING! IT'S GREAT TO HAVE A "BROTHER" LIKE YOU.
NOD NOD
LIKE I KEEP TELLING YOU, WHO SAID WE'RE "BROTHERS"?!!
THIS GUY!
ANYWAY, ARE YOU SURE THIS DOG IS OKAY? I'M NOT SURE IF IT CAN TAKE ROSETTA'S PLACE.
WOW, IT'S TRUE. ITS EAR IS DROOPING.
SHOULD BE FINE. THIS ONE HAS THE SAME BLOOD AS ROSETTA!
OH, GOOD. STANDING EARS.
THANKS FOR COMING, PAPI-CHAN.
...WHA?

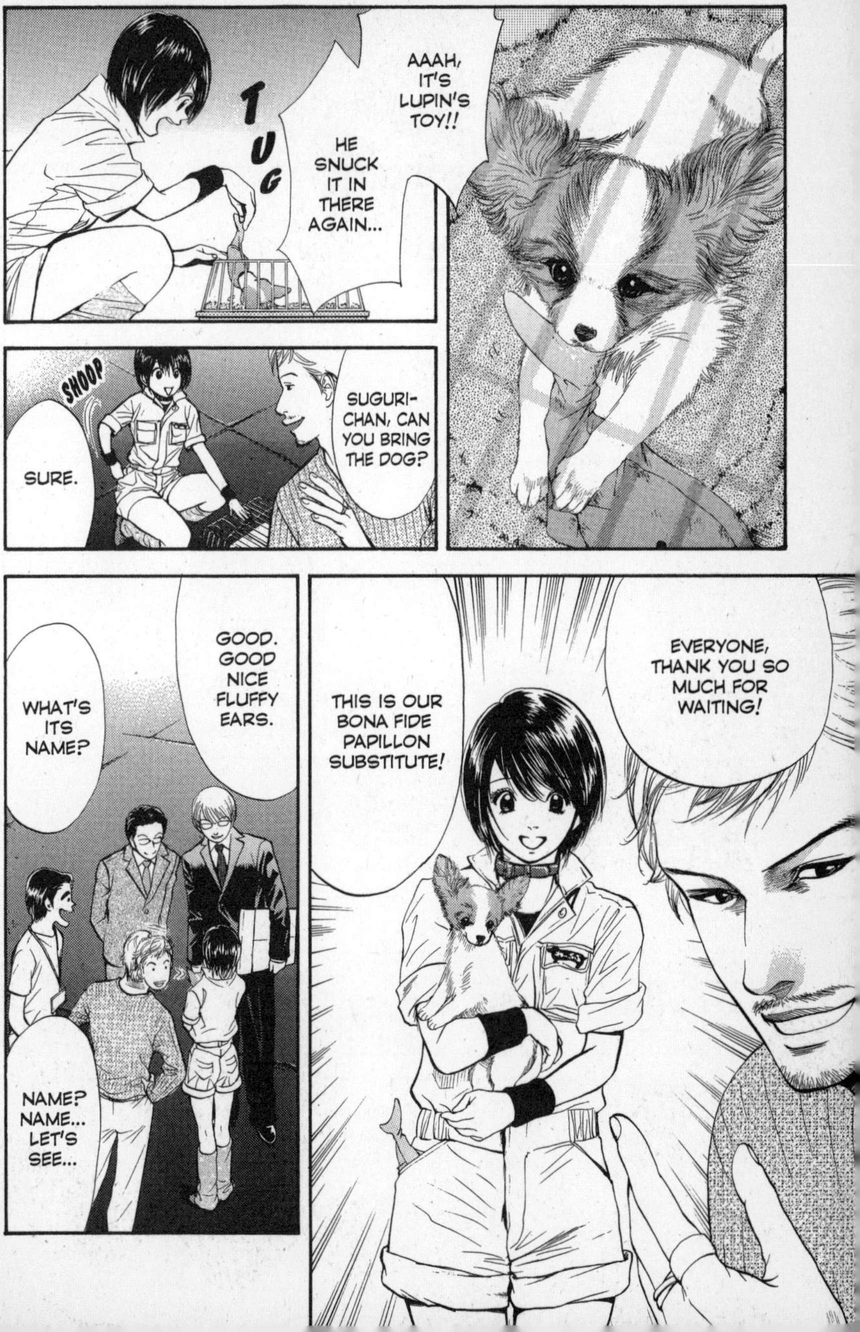
AAAH, IT'S LUPIN'S TOY!!
HE SNUCK IT IN THERE AGAIN...
TUG
SUGURI-CHAN, CAN YOU BRING THE DOG?
SHOOP
SURE.
EVERYONE, THANK YOU SO MUCH FOR WAITING!
THIS IS OUR BONA FIDE PAPILLON SUBSTITUTE!
GOOD. GOOD NICE FLUFFY EARS.
WHAT'S ITS NAME?
NAME? NAME... LET'S SEE...

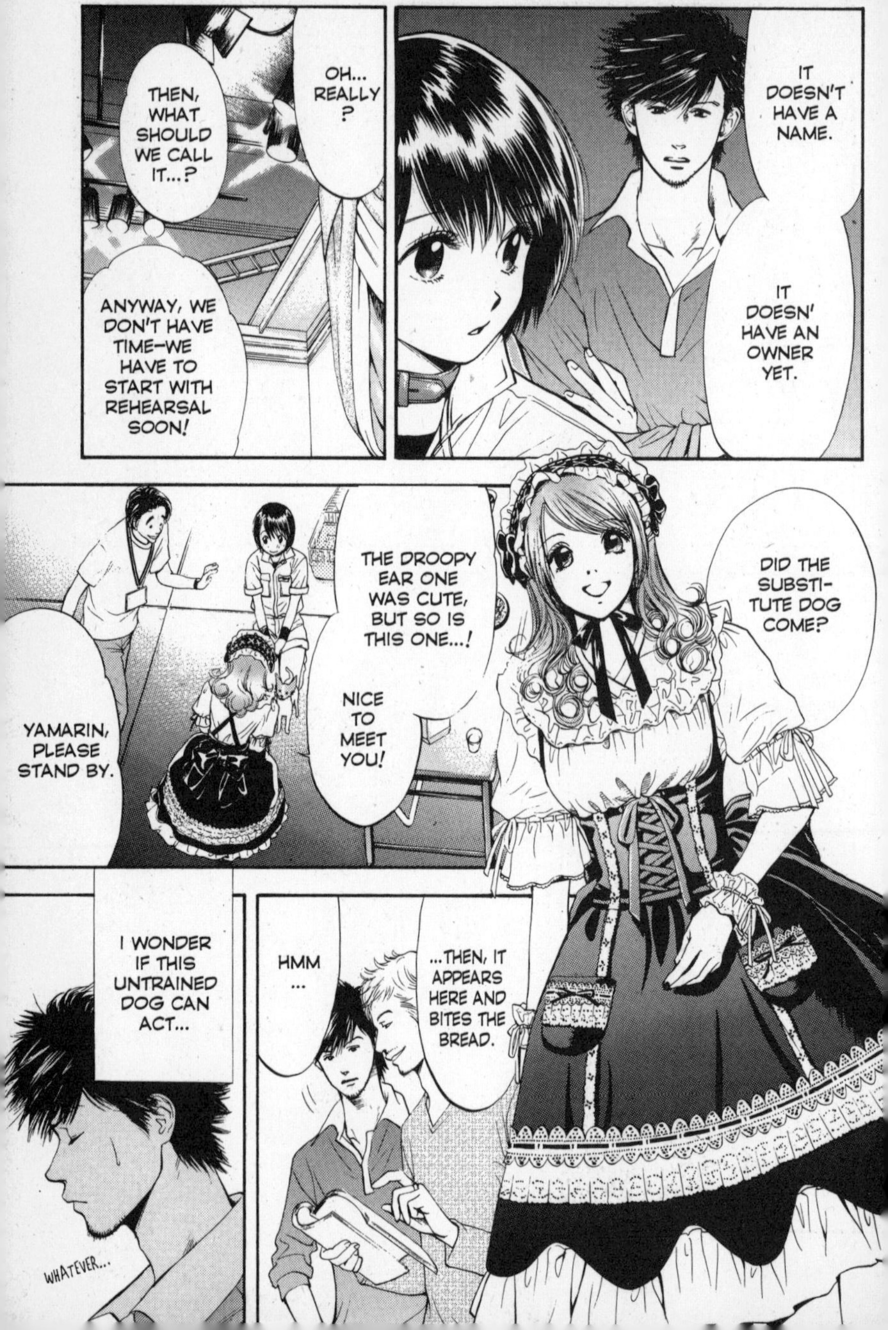
IT DOESN'T HAVE A NAME.
IT DOESN' HAVE AN OWNER YET.
OH... REALLY?
THEN, WHAT SHOULD WE CALL IT...?
ANYWAY, WE DON'T HAVE TIME—WE HAVE TO START WITH REHEARSAL SOON!
DID THE SUBSTI-TUTE DOG COME?
THE DROOPY EAR ONE WAS CUTE, BUT SO IS THIS ONE...!
NICE TO MEET YOU!
YAMARIN, PLEASE STAND BY.
...THEN, IT APPEARS HERE AND BITES THE BREAD.
HMM ...
I WONDER IF THIS UNTRAINED DOG CAN ACT...
WHATEVER...

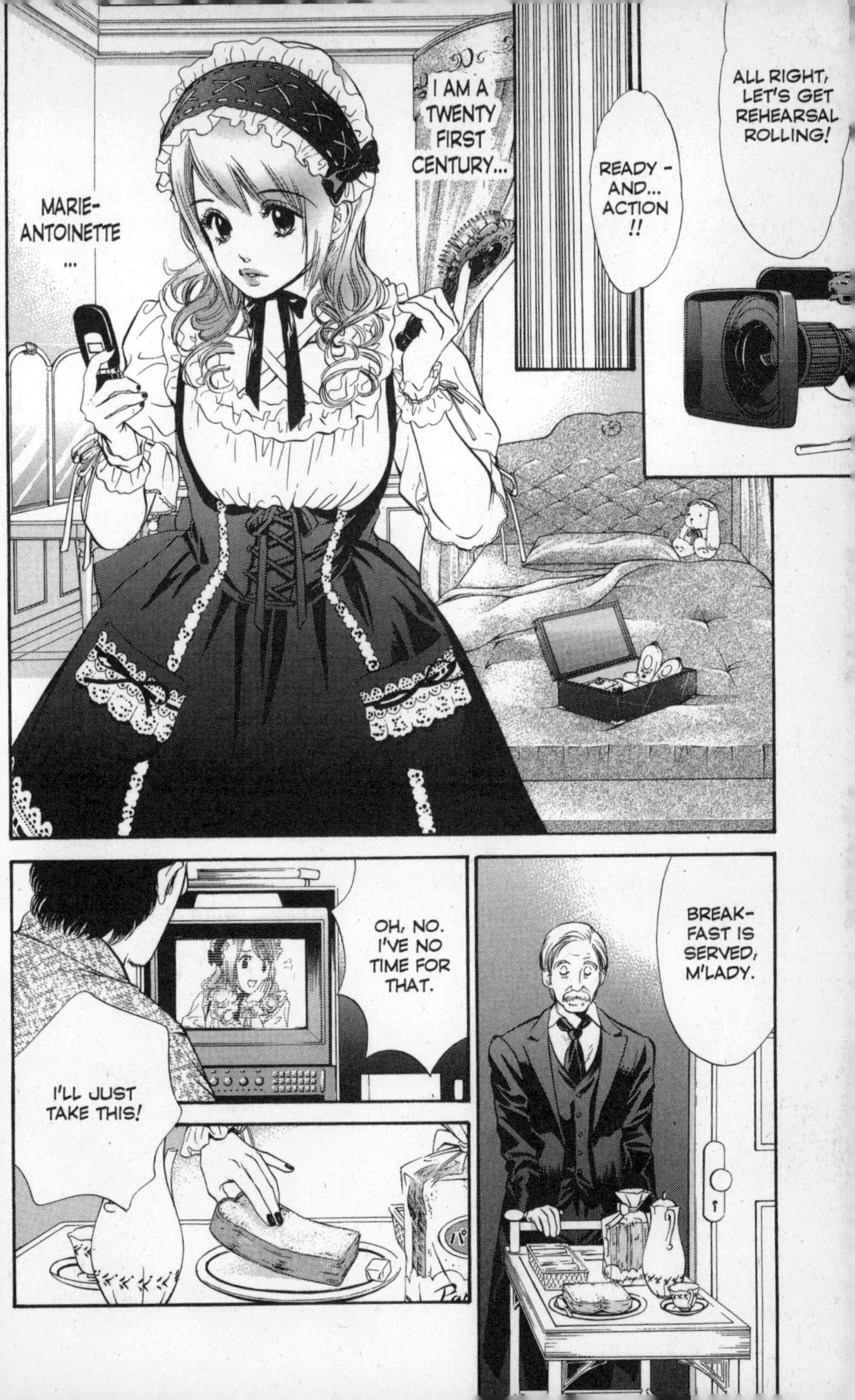
ALL RIGHT, LET'S GET REHEARSAL ROLLING!
READY - AND... ACTION !!
I AM A TWENTY FIRST CENTURY...
MARIE-ANTOINETTE ...
BREAK-FAST IS SERVED, M'LADY.
OH, NO. I'VE NO TIME FOR THAT.
I'LL JUST TAKE THIS!

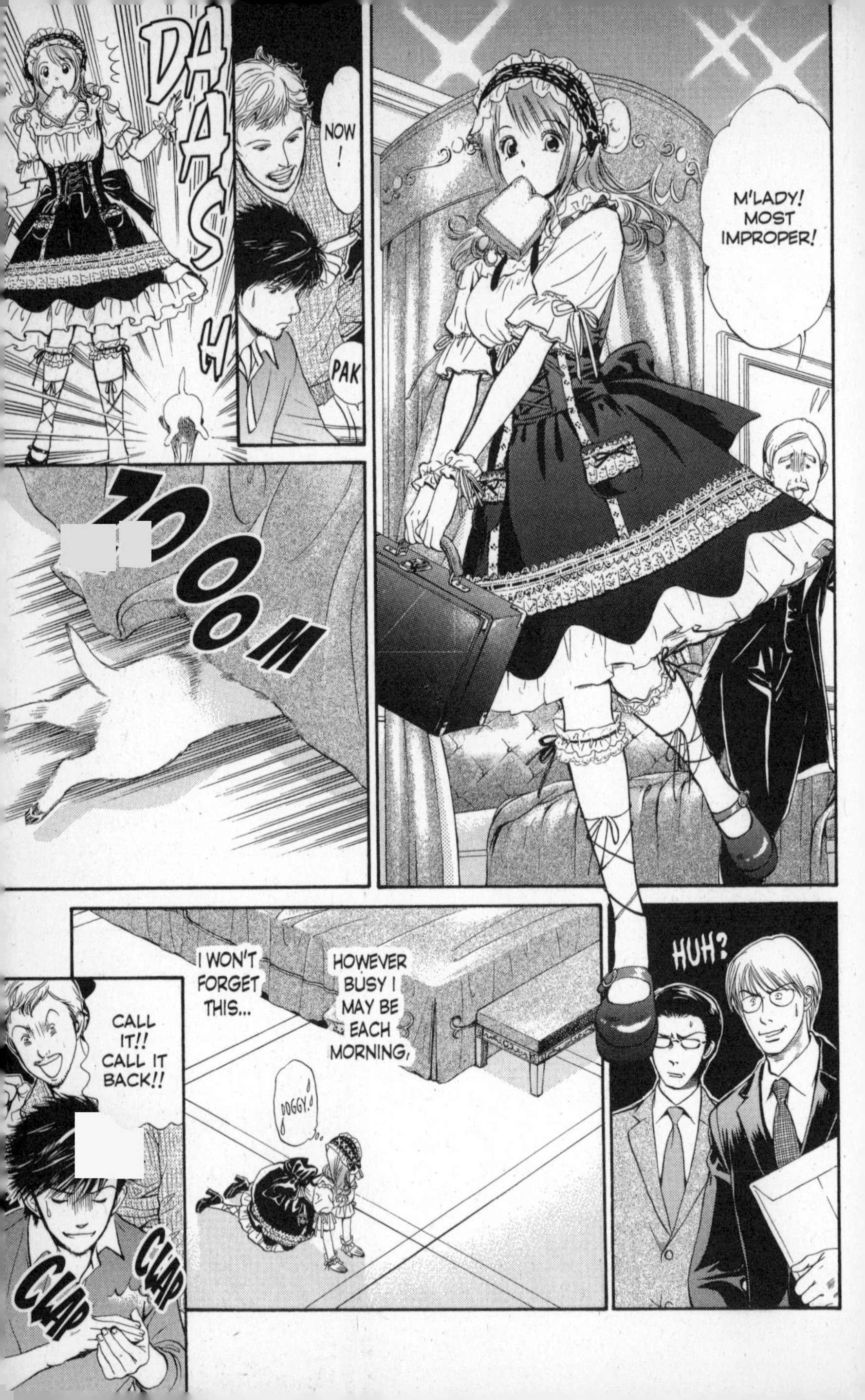
M'LADY! MOST IMPROPER!
NOW!
PAK
DAASH
ZOOOM
HUH?
HOWEVER BUSY I MAY BE EACH MORNING,
I WON'T FORGET THIS...
DOGGY.
CALL IT!! CALL IT BACK!!
CLAP
CLAP

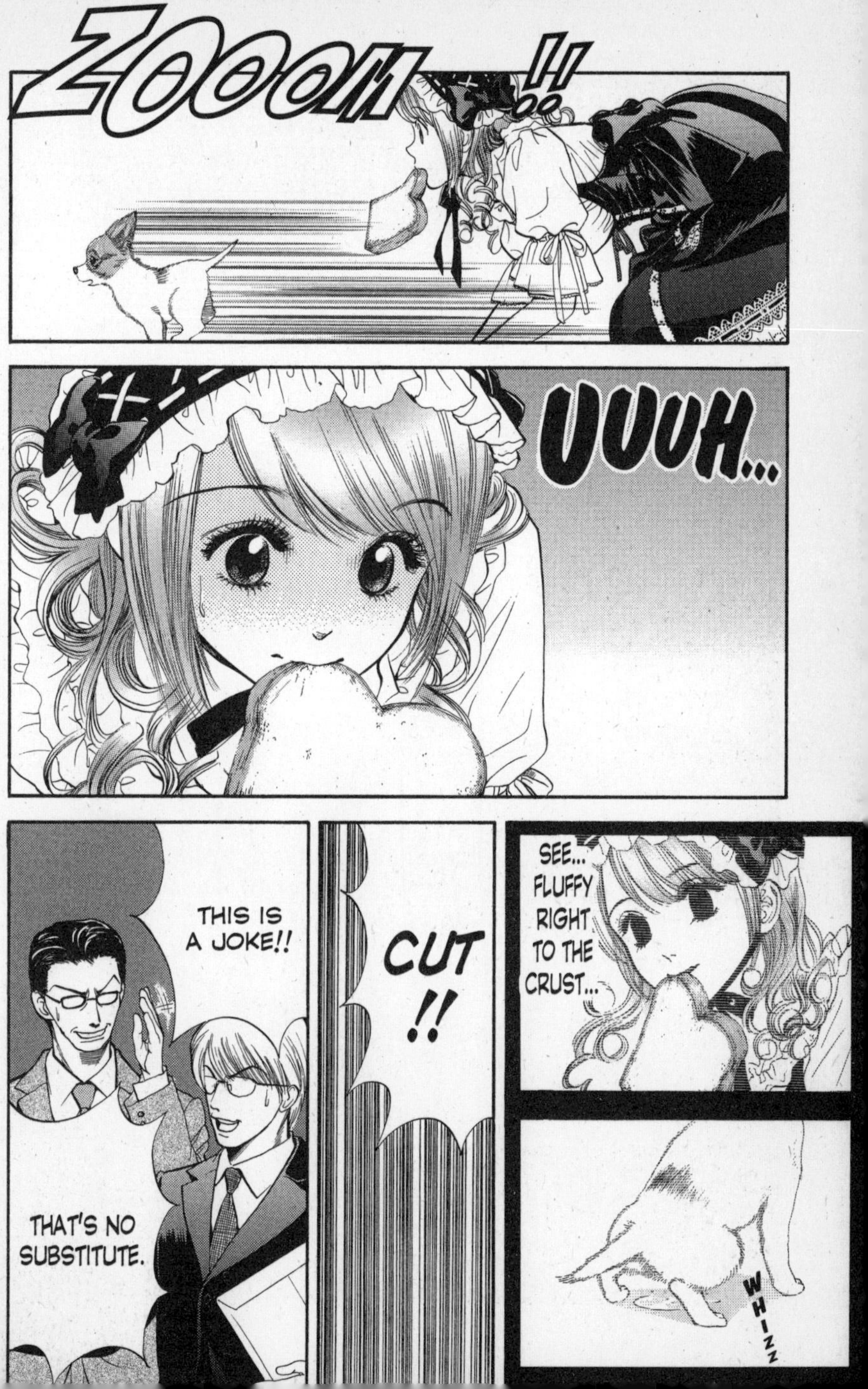
ZOOOM!!
UUUH...
SEE... FLUFFY RIGHT TO THE CRUST...
WHIZZ
CUT!!
THIS IS A JOKE!!
THAT'S NO SUBSTITUTE.

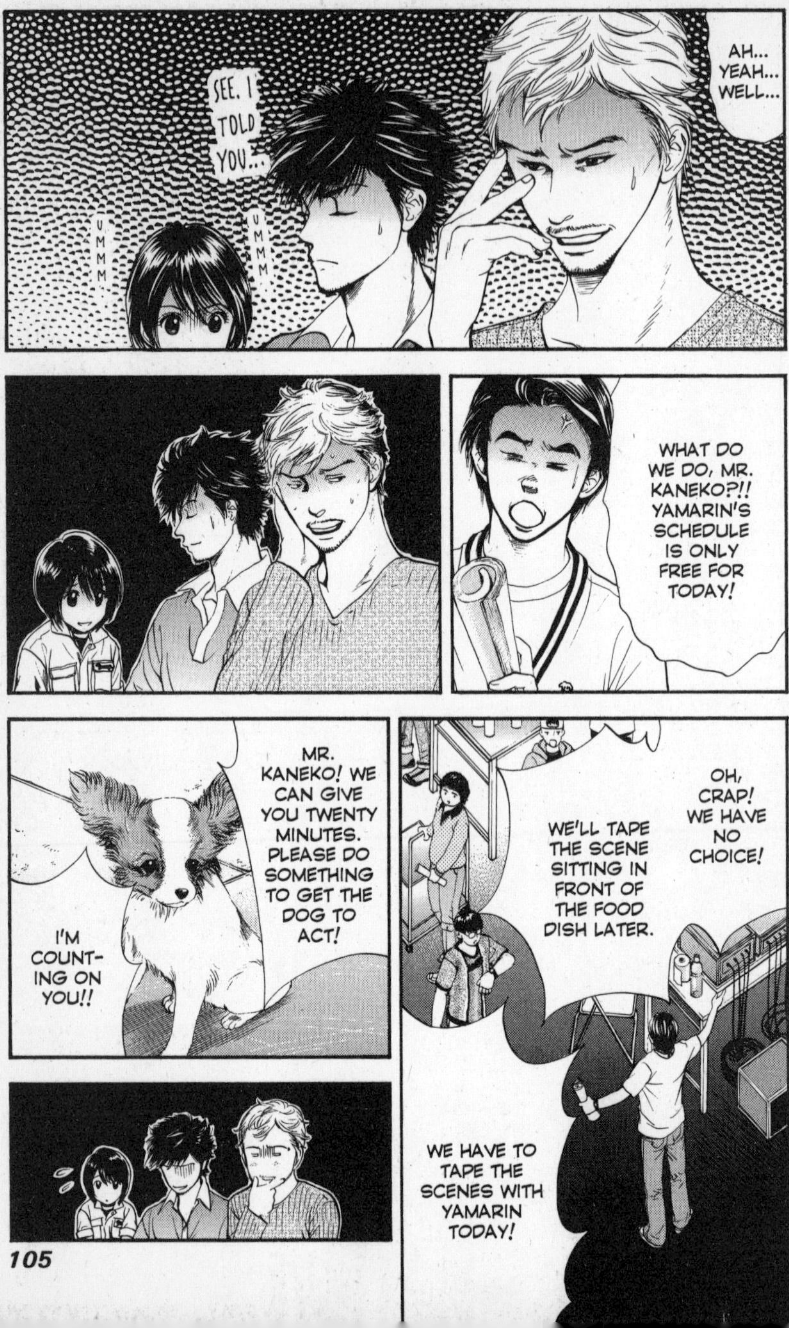
AH... YEAH... WELL...
SEE. I TOLD YOU...
UMMM
UMMM
WHAT DO WE DO, MR. KANEKO?!! YAMARIN'S SCHEDULE IS ONLY FREE FOR TODAY!
OH, CRAP! WE HAVE NO CHOICE!
WE'LL TAPE THE SCENE SITTING IN FRONT OF THE FOOD DISH LATER.
WE HAVE TO TAPE THE SCENES WITH YAMARIN TODAY!
MR. KANEKO! WE CAN GIVE YOU TWENTY MINUTES. PLEASE DO SOMETHING TO GET THE DOG TO ACT!
I'M COUNTING ON YOU!!

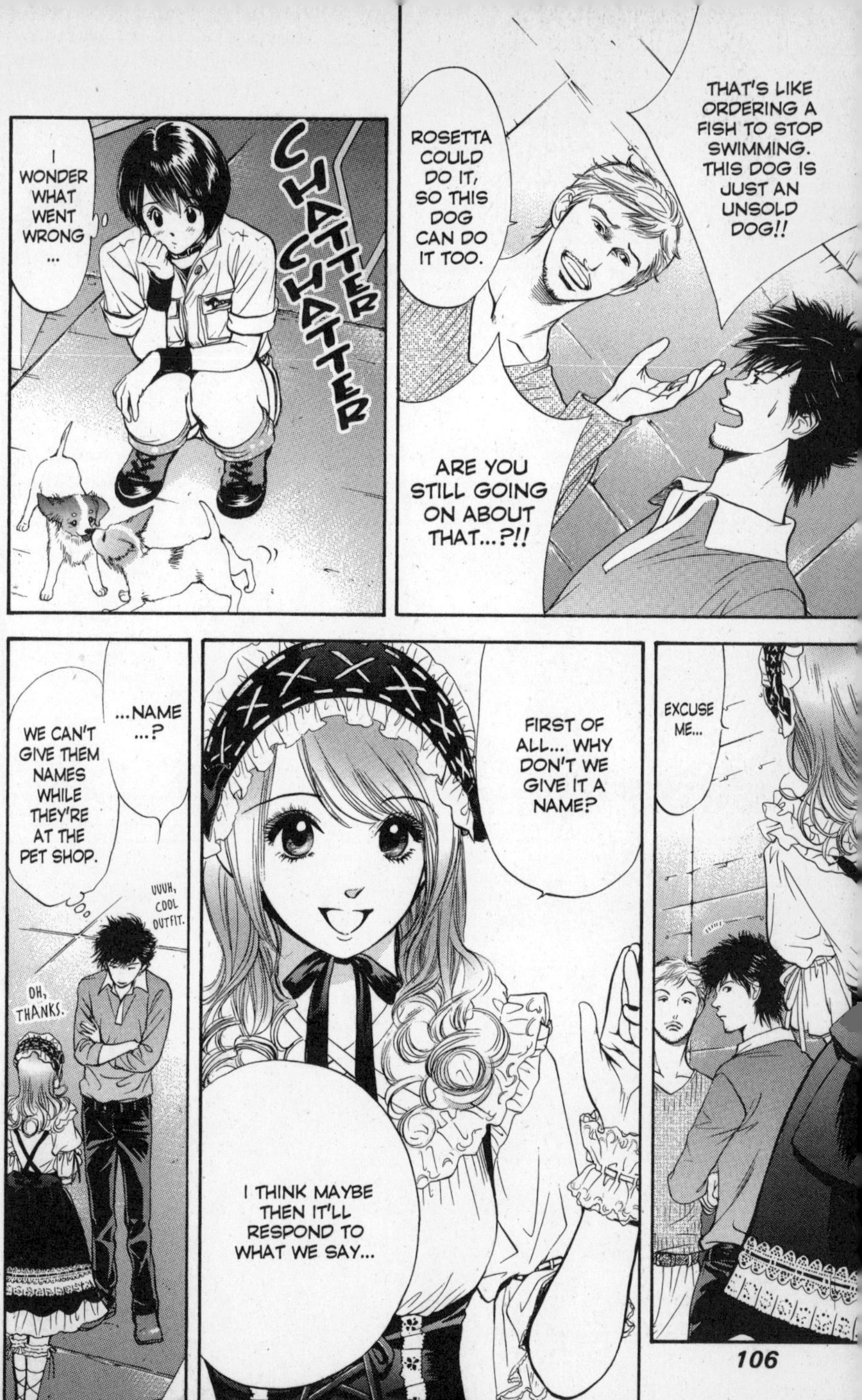

THAT'S LIKE ORDERING A FISH TO STOP SWIMMING. THIS DOG IS JUST AN UNSOLD DOG!!
ROSETTA COULD DO IT, SO THIS DOG CAN DO IT TOO.
ARE YOU STILL GOING ON ABOUT THAT...?!!
CHATTER CHATTER
I WONDER WHAT WENT WRONG ...
EXCUSE ME...
FIRST OF ALL... WHY DON'T WE GIVE IT A NAME?
I THINK MAYBE THEN IT'LL RESPOND TO WHAT WE SAY...
...NAME ...?
WE CAN'T GIVE THEM NAMES WHILE THEY'RE AT THE PET SHOP.
UUUH, COOL OUTFIT.
OH, THANKS.

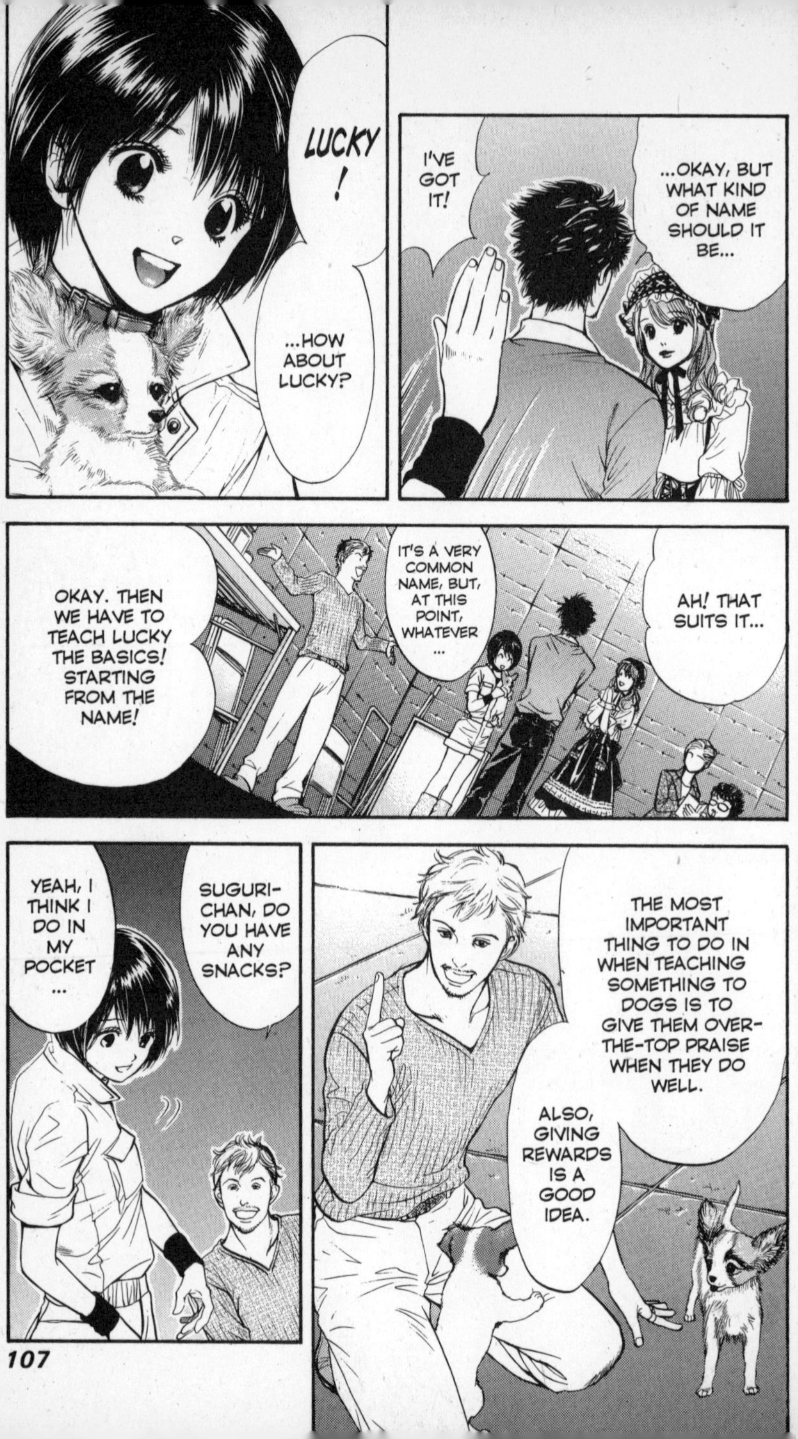
...OKAY, BUT WHAT KIND OF NAME SHOULD IT BE...
I'VE GOT IT!
LUCKY!
...HOW ABOUT LUCKY?
AH! THAT SUITS IT...
IT'S A VERY COMMON NAME, BUT, AT THIS POINT, WHATEVER...
OKAY. THEN WE HAVE TO TEACH LUCKY THE BASICS! STARTING FROM THE NAME!
THE MOST IMPORTANT THING TO DO IN WHEN TEACHING SOMETHING TO DOGS IS TO GIVE THEM OVER-THE-TOP PRAISE WHEN THEY DO WELL.
ALSO, GIVING REWARDS IS A GOOD IDEA.
SUGURI-CHAN, DO YOU HAVE ANY SNACKS?
YEAH, I THINK I DO IN MY POCKET...

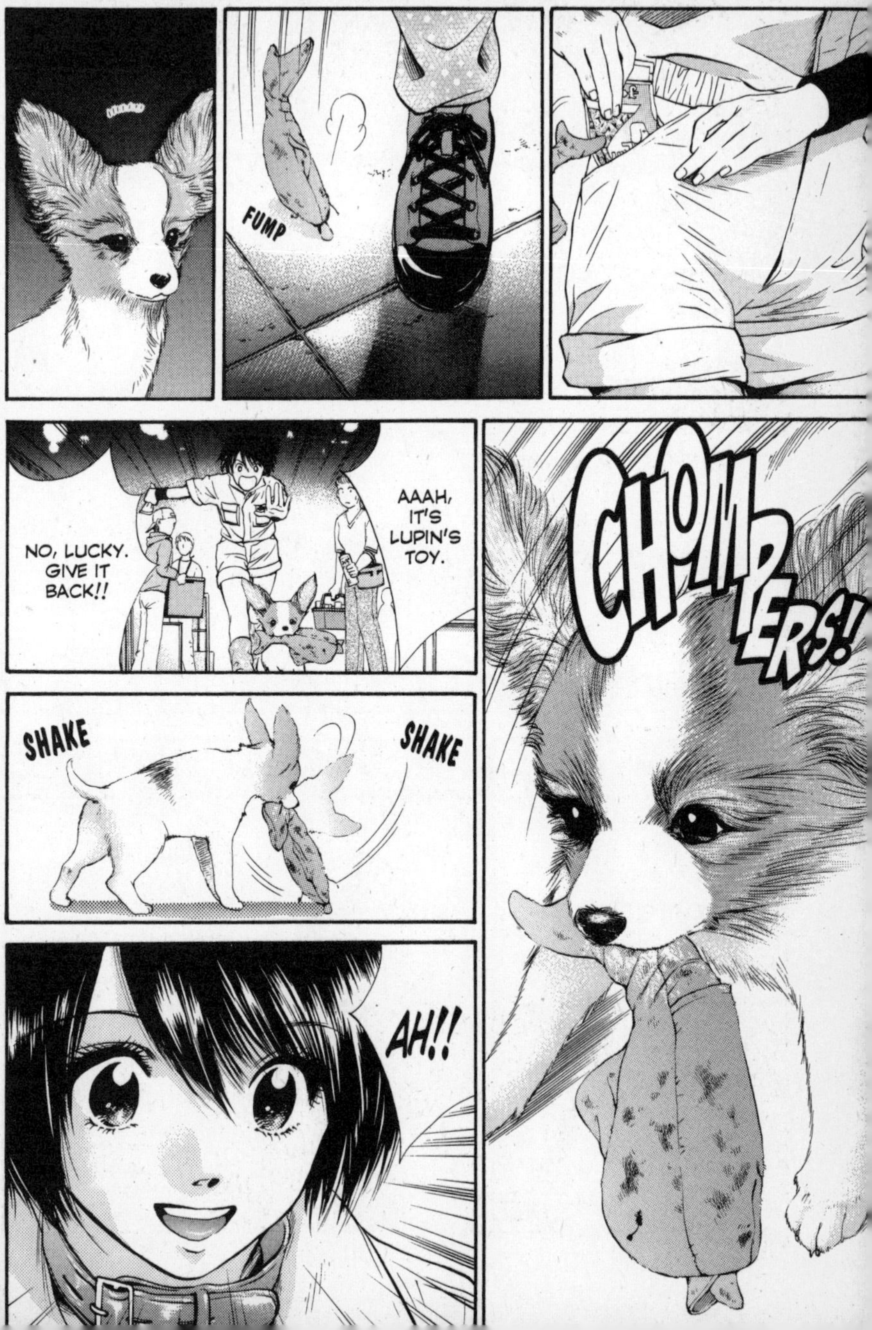
FUMP
CHOMPERS!
AAAH, IT'S LUPIN'S TOY.
NO, LUCKY. GIVE IT BACK!!
SHAKE
SHAKE
AH!!

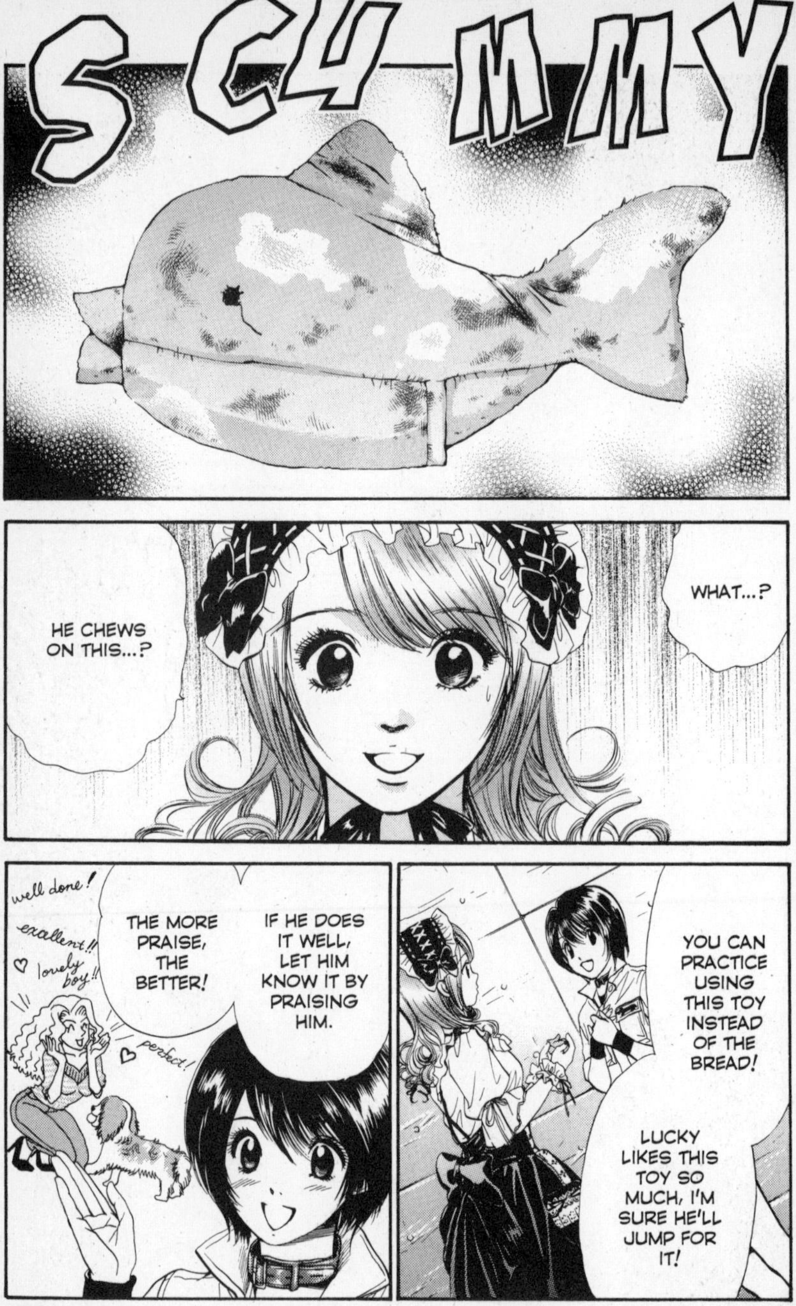
SCUMMY
WHAT...?
HE CHEWS ON THIS...?
YOU CAN PRACTICE USING THIS TOY INSTEAD OF THE BREAD!
LUCKY LIKES THIS TOY SO MUCH, I'M SURE HE'LL JUMP FOR IT!
IF HE DOES IT WELL, LET HIM KNOW IT BY PRAISING HIM.
THE MORE PRAISE, THE BETTER!
well done!
exallent!!
lovely boy!!
perfect!

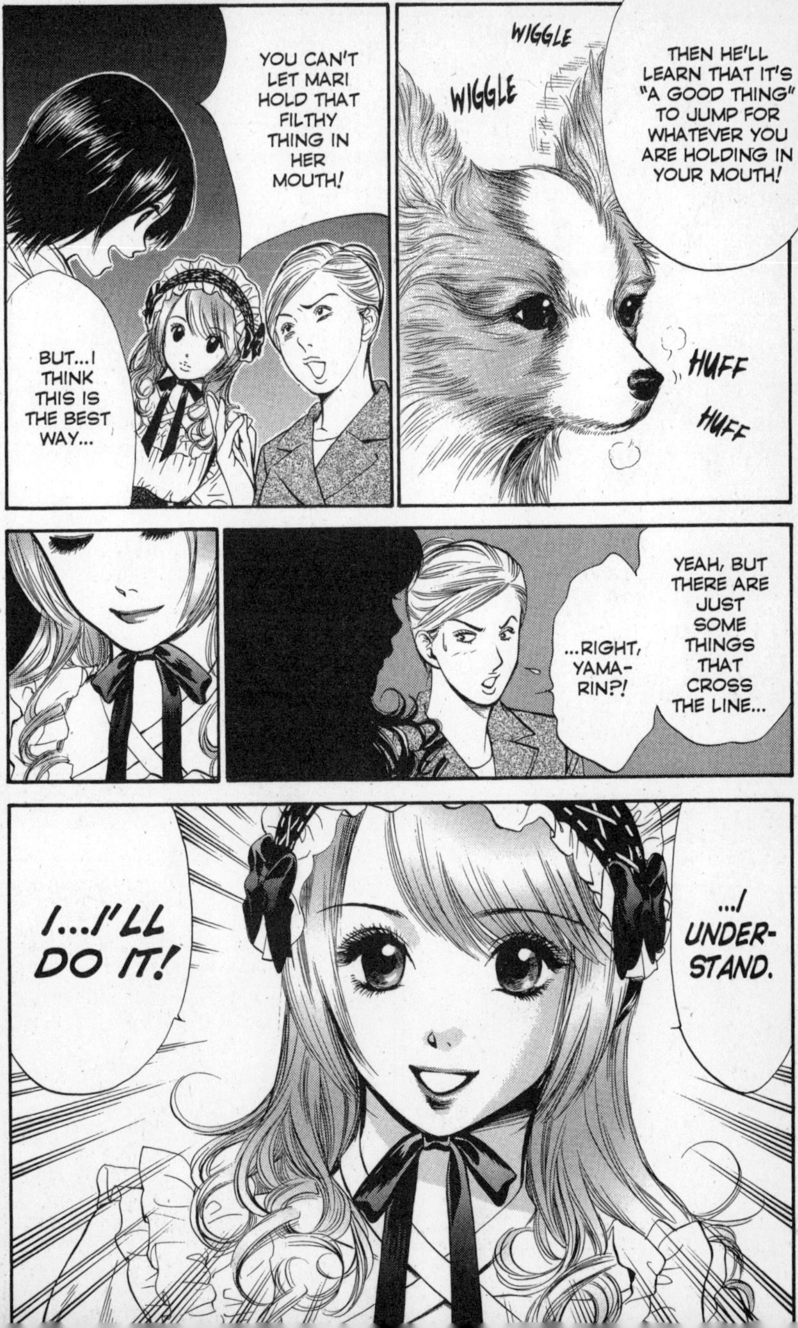
THEN HE'LL LEARN THAT IT'S "A GOOD THING" TO JUMP FOR WHATEVER YOU ARE HOLDING IN YOUR MOUTH!
WIGGLE
WIGGLE
HUFF
HUFF
YOU CAN'T LET MARI HOLD THAT FILTHY THING IN HER MOUTH!
BUT...I THINK THIS IS THE BEST WAY...
YEAH, BUT THERE ARE JUST SOME THINGS THAT CROSS THE LINE...
...RIGHT, YAMA-RIN?!
...I UNDER-STAND.
I...I'LL DO IT!

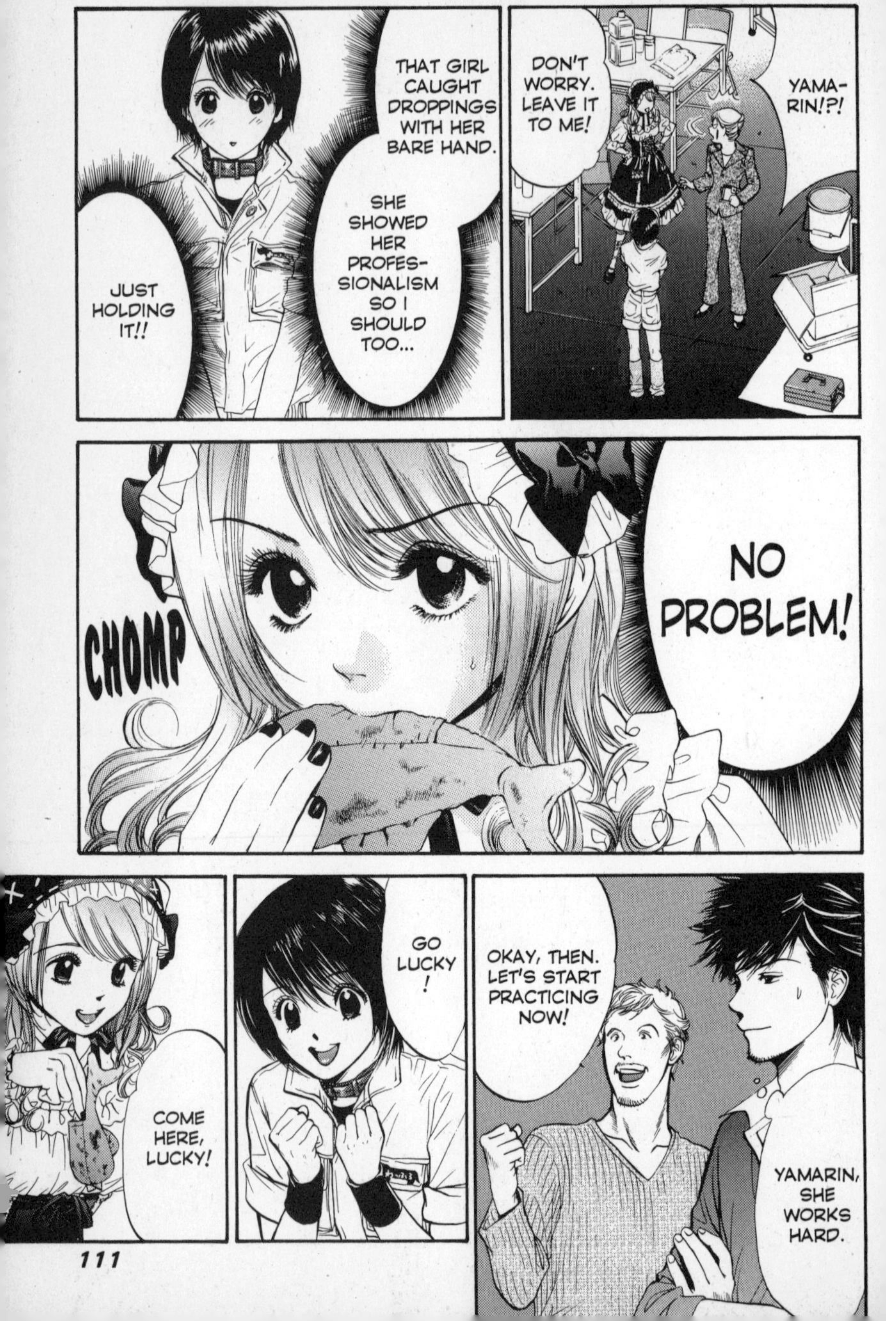
YAMA-RIN!?!
DON'T WORRY. LEAVE IT TO ME!
THAT GIRL CAUGHT DROPPINGS WITH HER BARE HAND.
SHE SHOWED HER PROFES-SIONALISM SO I SHOULD TOO...
JUST HOLDING IT!!
NO PROBLEM!
CHOMP
OKAY, THEN. LET'S START PRACTICING NOW!
YAMARIN, SHE WORKS HARD.
GO LUCKY!
COME HERE, LUCKY!

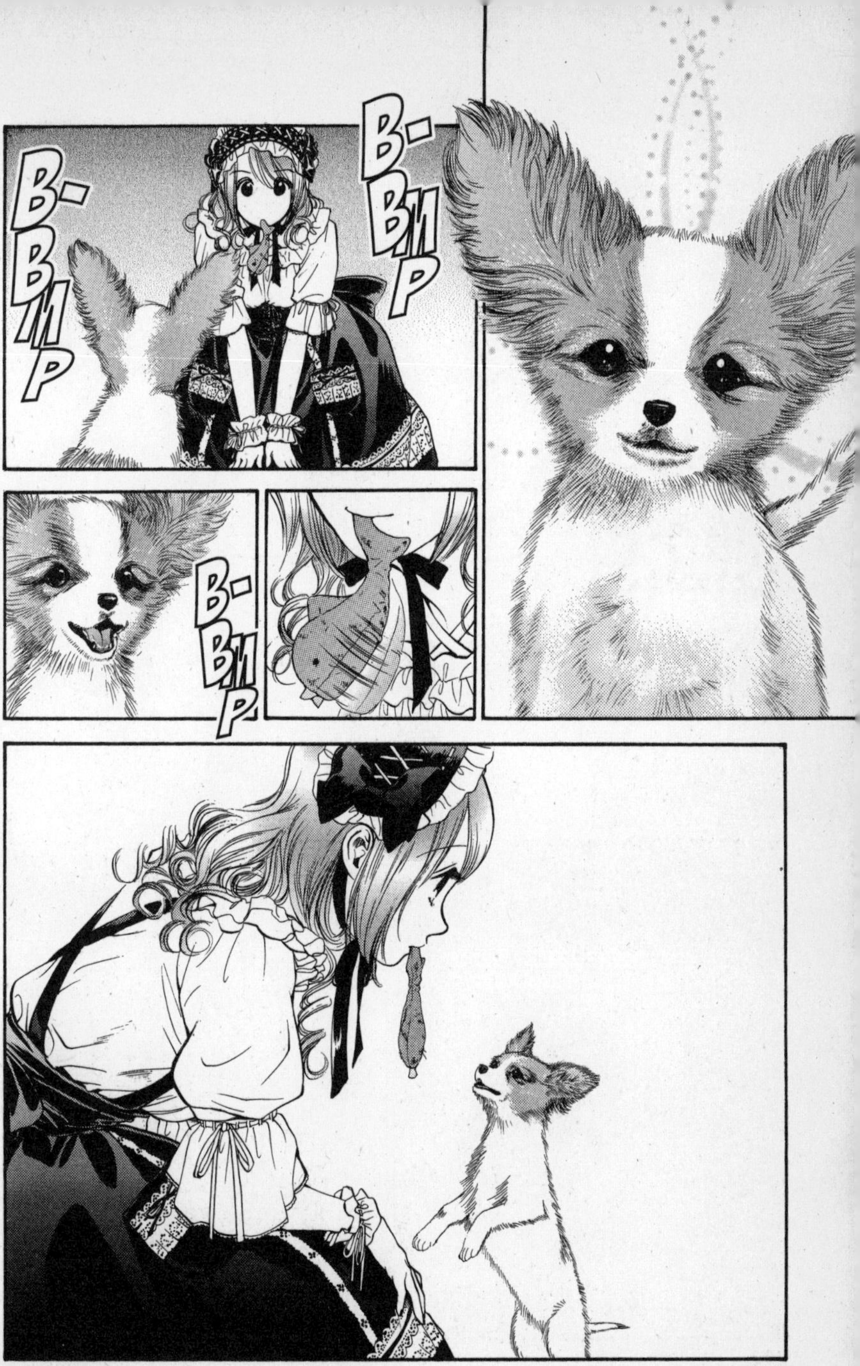
B-BMP
B-BMP
B-BMP

CHAPTER 15
THE 31ST MIRACLE!

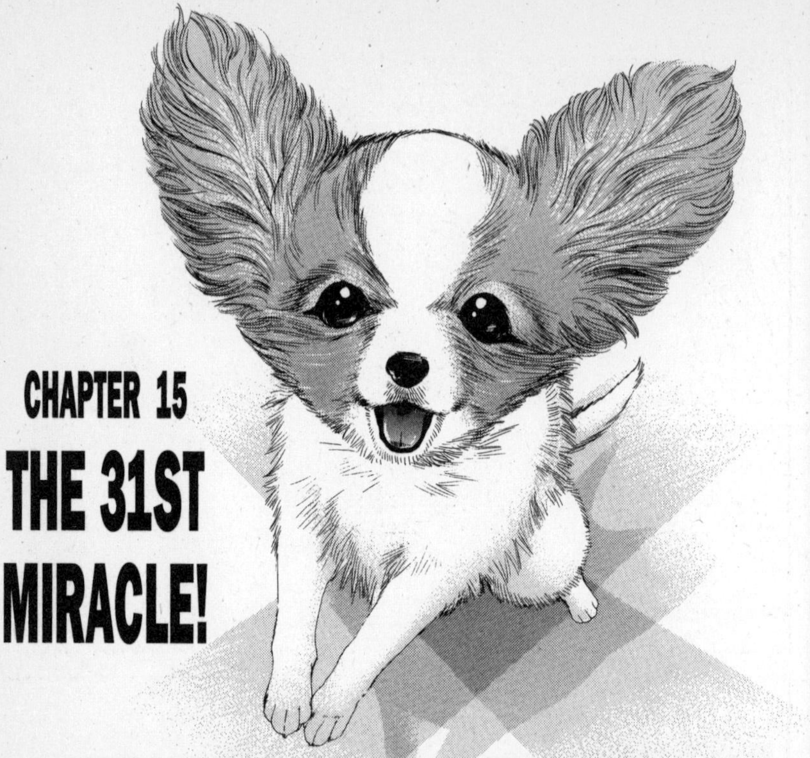

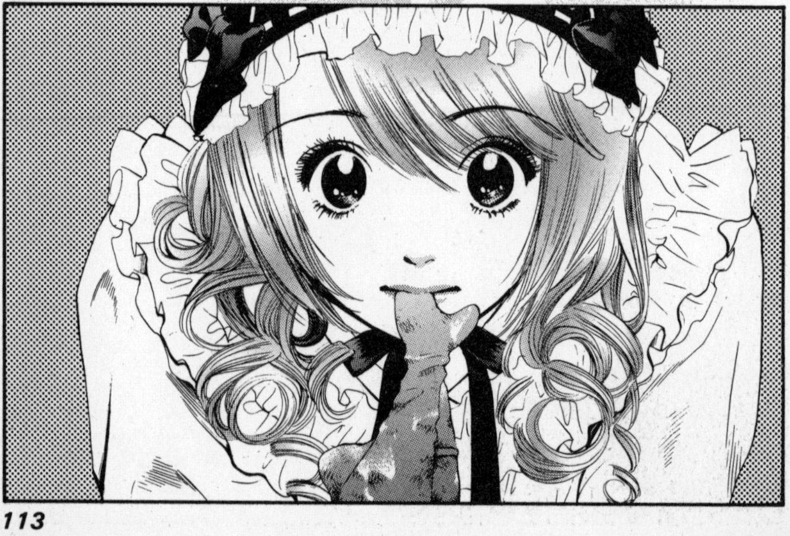

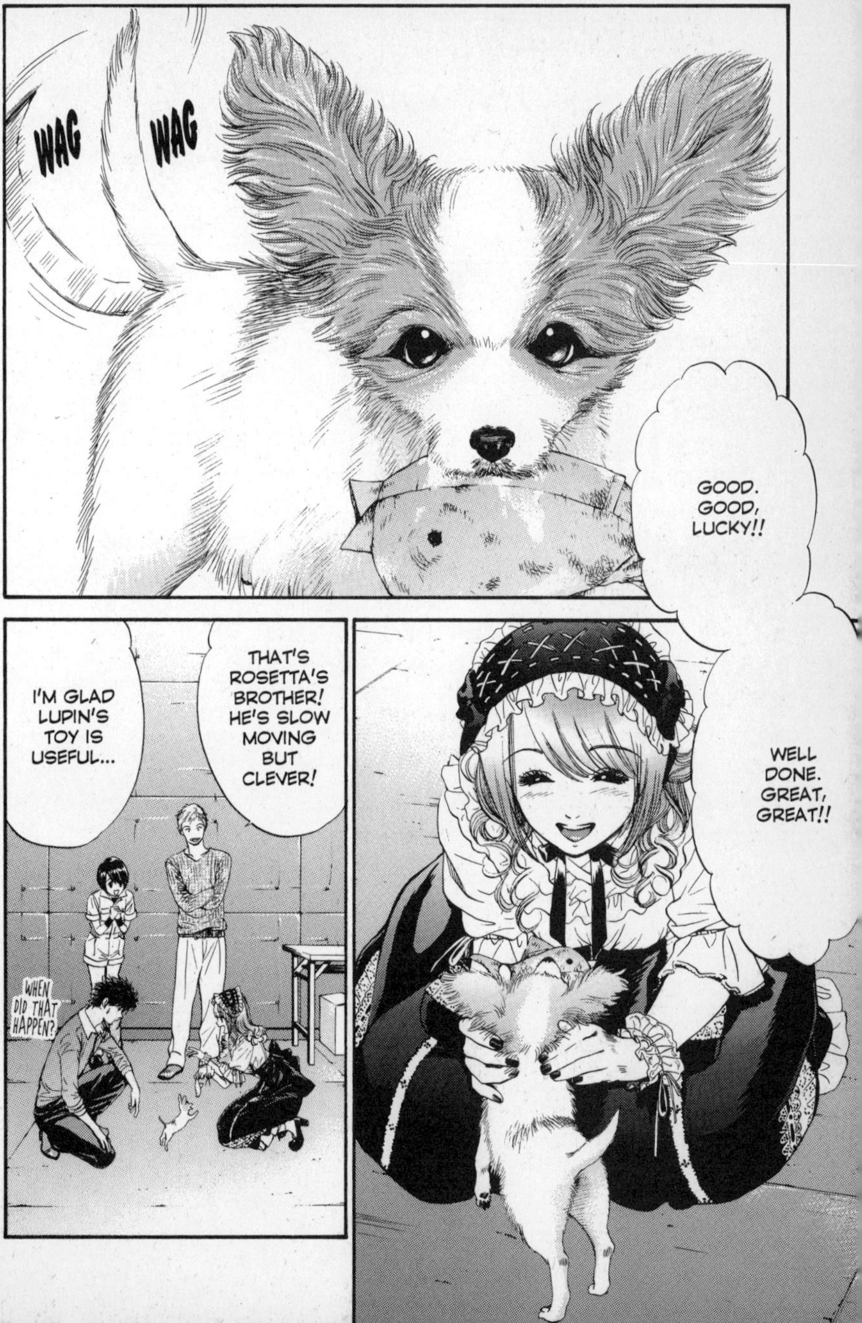
WAG
WAG
GOOD. GOOD, LUCKY!!
WELL DONE. GREAT, GREAT!!
THAT'S ROSETTA'S BROTHER! HE'S SLOW MOVING BUT CLEVER!
I'M GLAD LUPIN'S TOY IS USEFUL...
WHEN DID THAT HAPPEN?

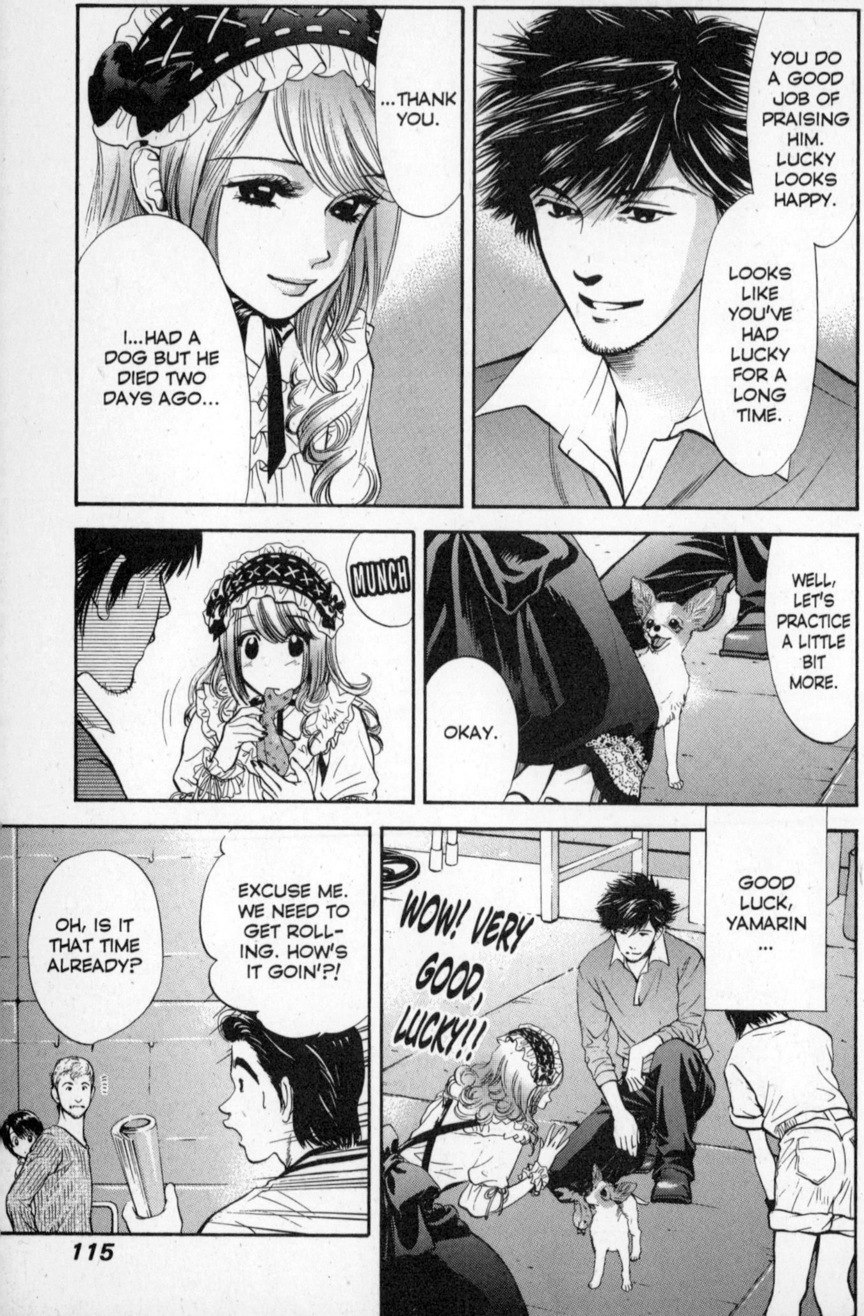
YOU DO A GOOD JOB OF PRAISING HIM. LUCKY LOOKS HAPPY.
LOOKS LIKE YOU'VE HAD LUCKY FOR A LONG TIME.
...THANK YOU.
I...HAD A DOG BUT HE DIED TWO DAYS AGO...
WELL, LET'S PRACTICE A LITTLE BIT MORE.
OKAY.
MUNCH
GOOD LUCK, YAMARIN ...
WOW! VERY GOOD, LUCKY!!
EXCUSE ME. WE NEED TO GET ROLL-ING. HOW'S IT GOIN'?!
OH, IS IT THAT TIME ALREADY?

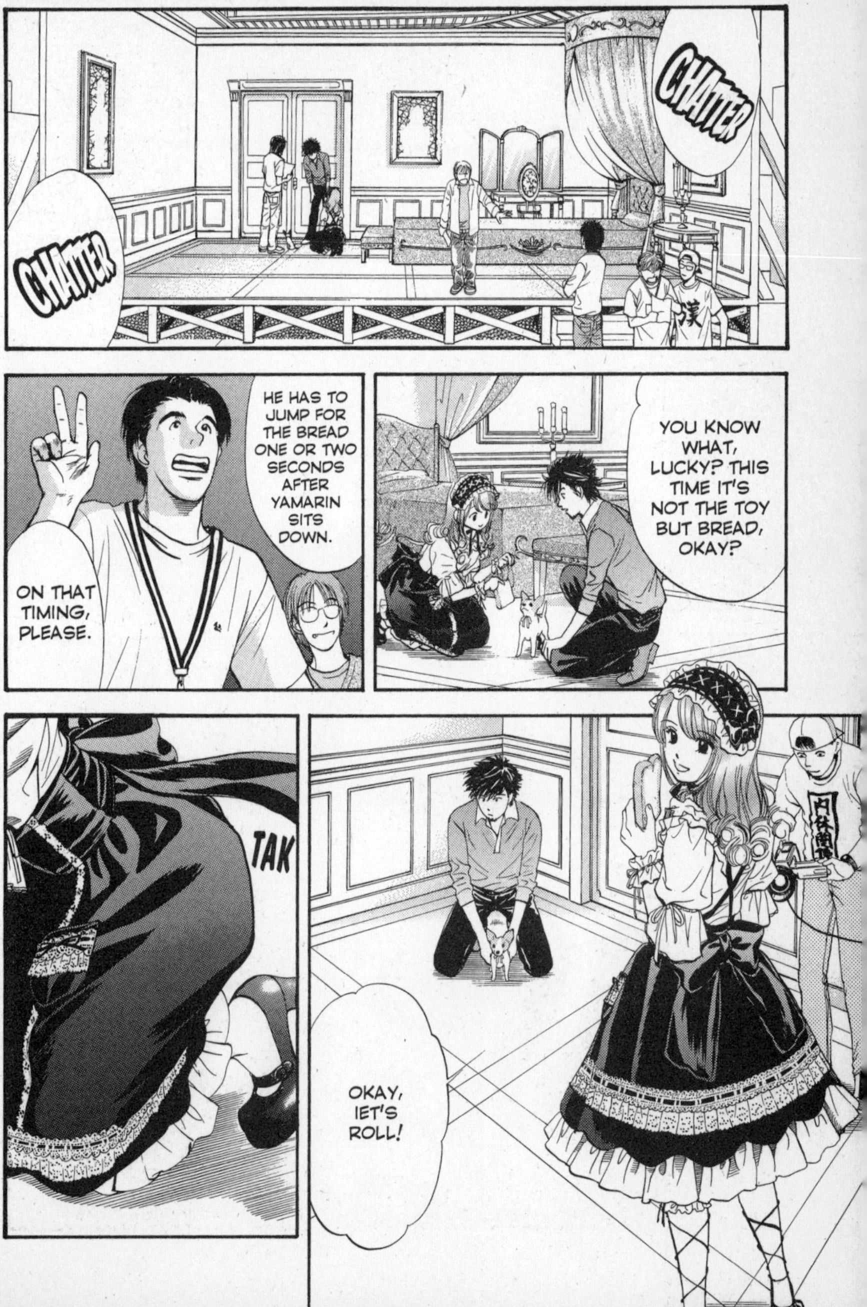
CHATTER
CHATTER
YOU KNOW WHAT, LUCKY? THIS TIME IT'S NOT THE TOY BUT BREAD, OKAY?
HE HAS TO JUMP FOR THE BREAD ONE OR TWO SECONDS AFTER YAMARIN SITS DOWN.
ON THAT TIMING, PLEASE.
OKAY, IET'S ROLL!
TAK

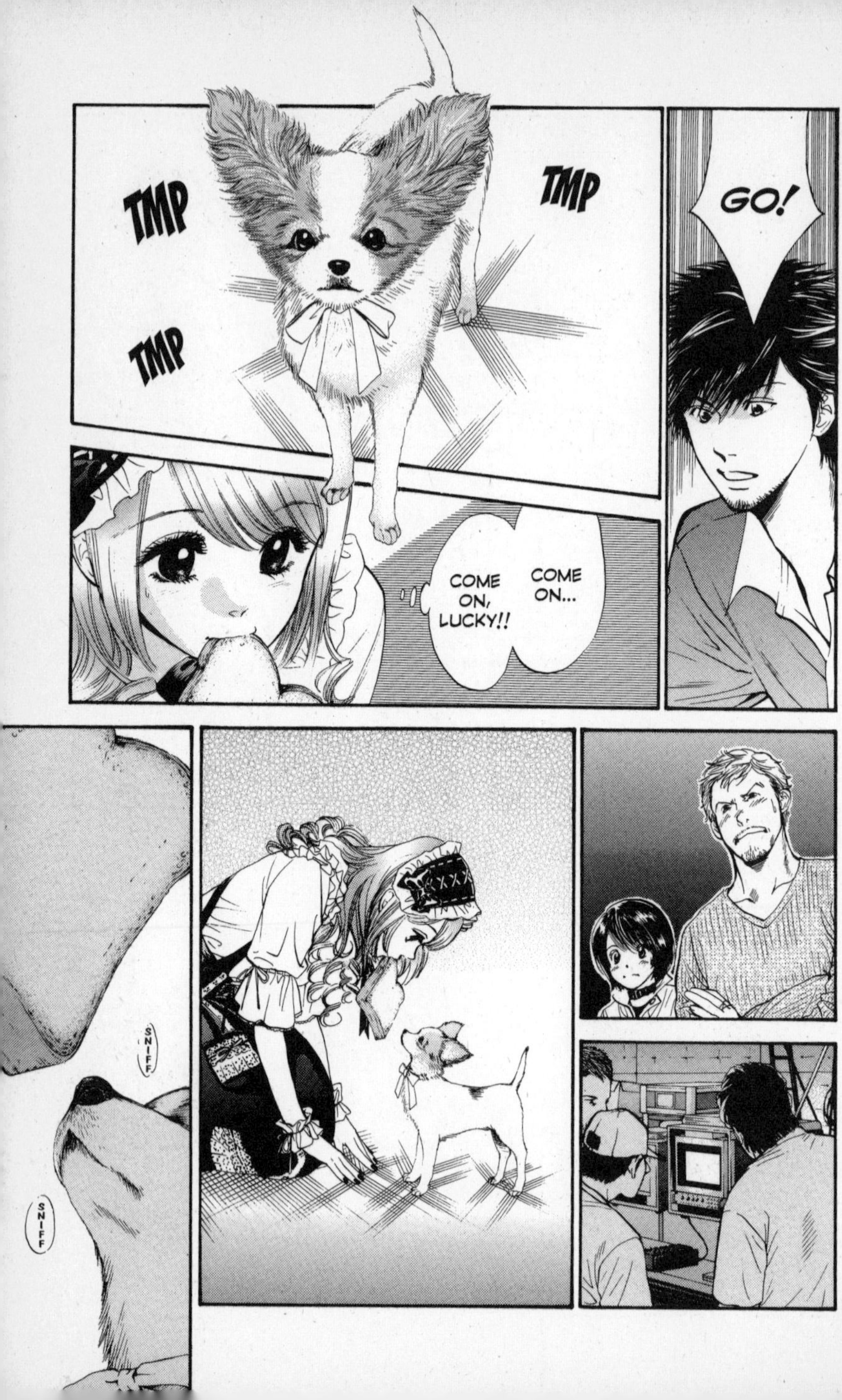
GO!
TMP
TMP
TMP
COME ON, LUCKY!! COME ON...
SNIFF
SNIFF

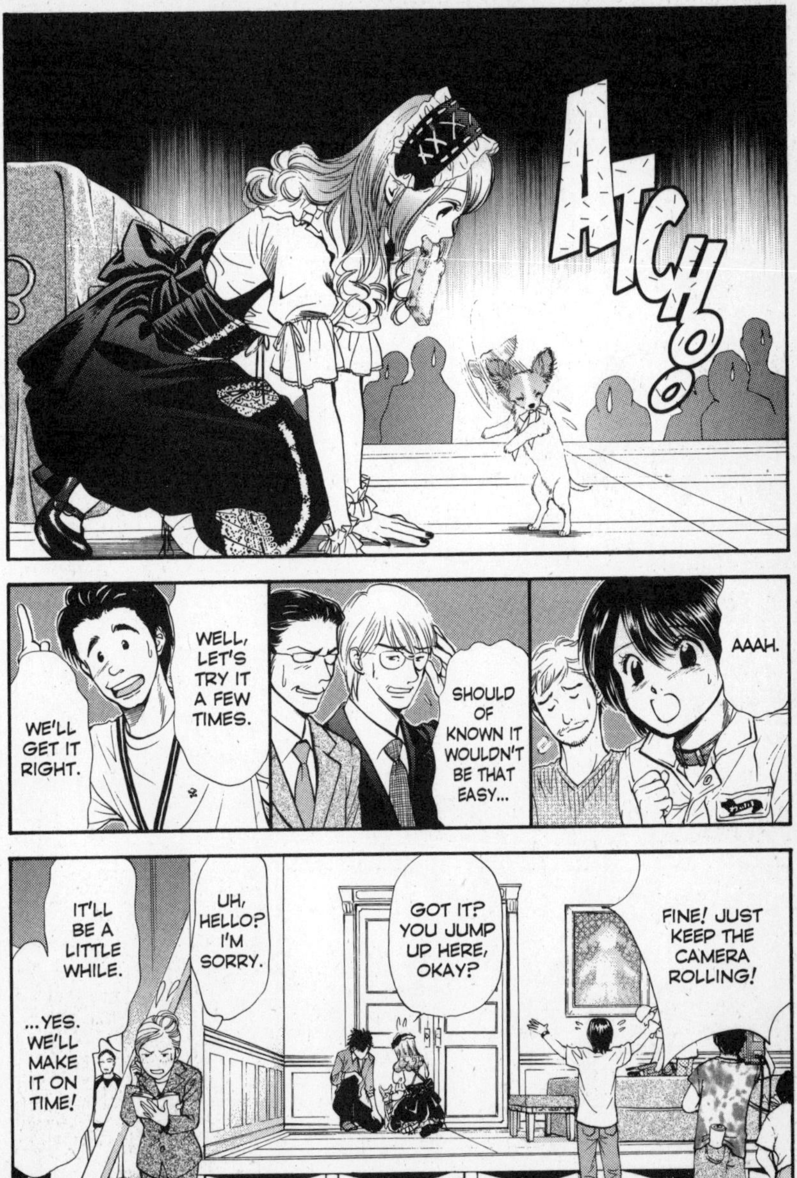
ATCHOO
AAAH.
SHOULD OF KNOWN IT WOULDN'T BE THAT EASY...
WELL, LET'S TRY IT A FEW TIMES.
WE'LL GET IT RIGHT.
FINE! JUST KEEP THE CAMERA ROLLING!
GOT IT? YOU JUMP UP HERE, OKAY?
UH, HELLO? I'M SORRY.
IT'LL BE A LITTLE WHILE.
...YES. WE'LL MAKE IT ON TIME!

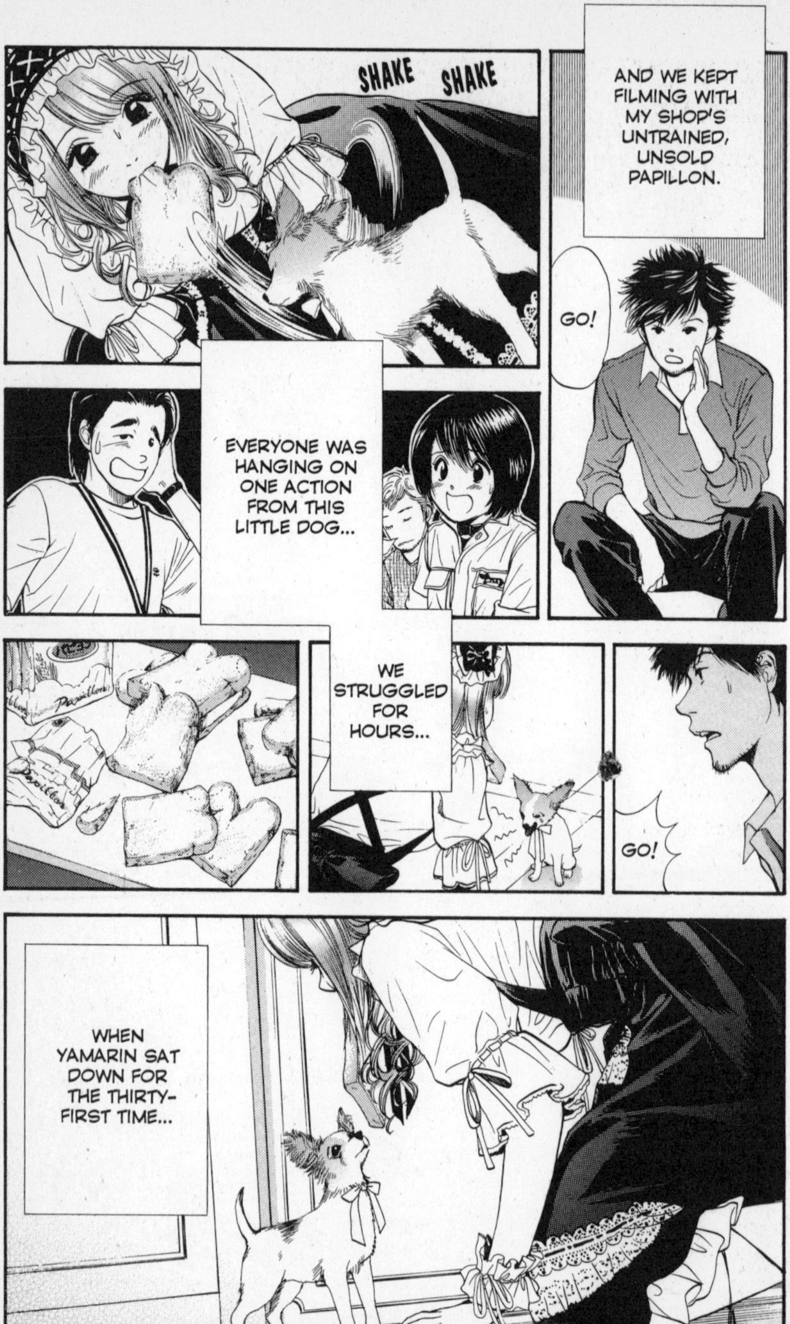
AND WE KEPT FILMING WITH MY SHOP'S UNTRAINED, UNSOLD PAPILLON.
GO!
SHAKE SHAKE
EVERYONE WAS HANGING ON ONE ACTION FROM THIS LITTLE DOG...
GO!
WE STRUGGLED FOR HOURS...
Papillon
Papillon
WHEN YAMARIN SAT DOWN FOR THE THIRTY-FIRST TIME...

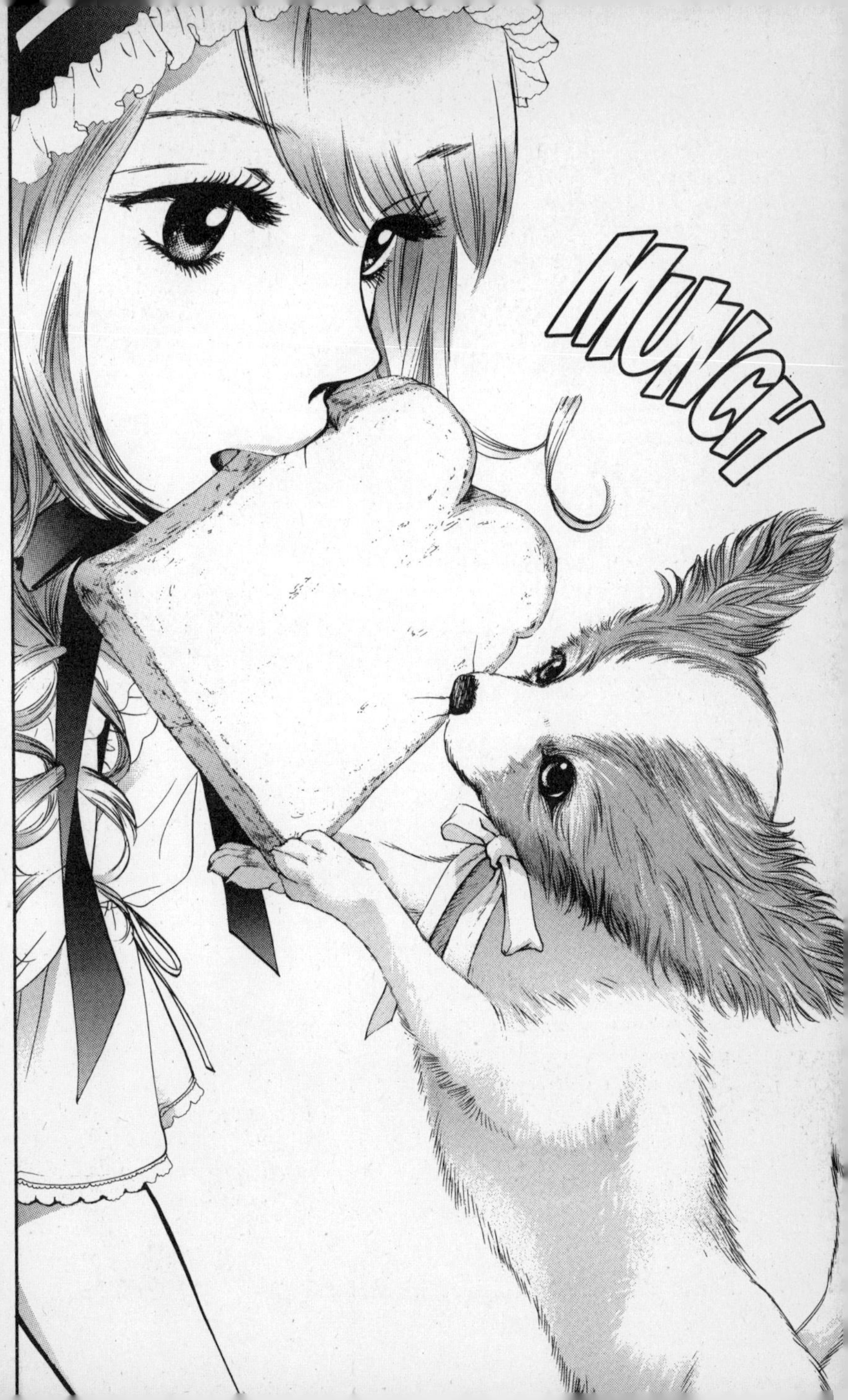
MUNCH

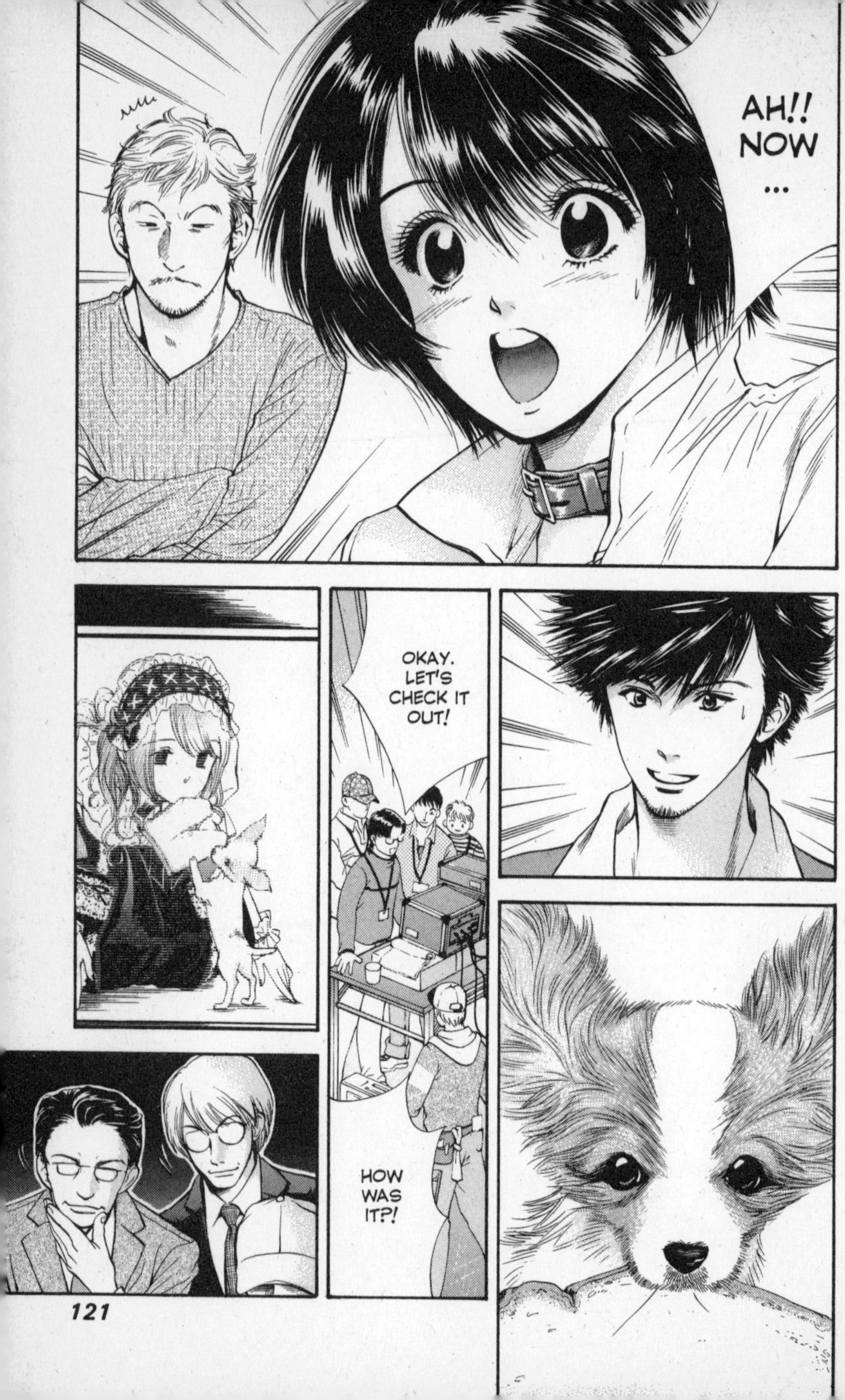
AH!! NOW ...
OKAY. LET'S CHECK IT OUT!
HOW WAS IT?!

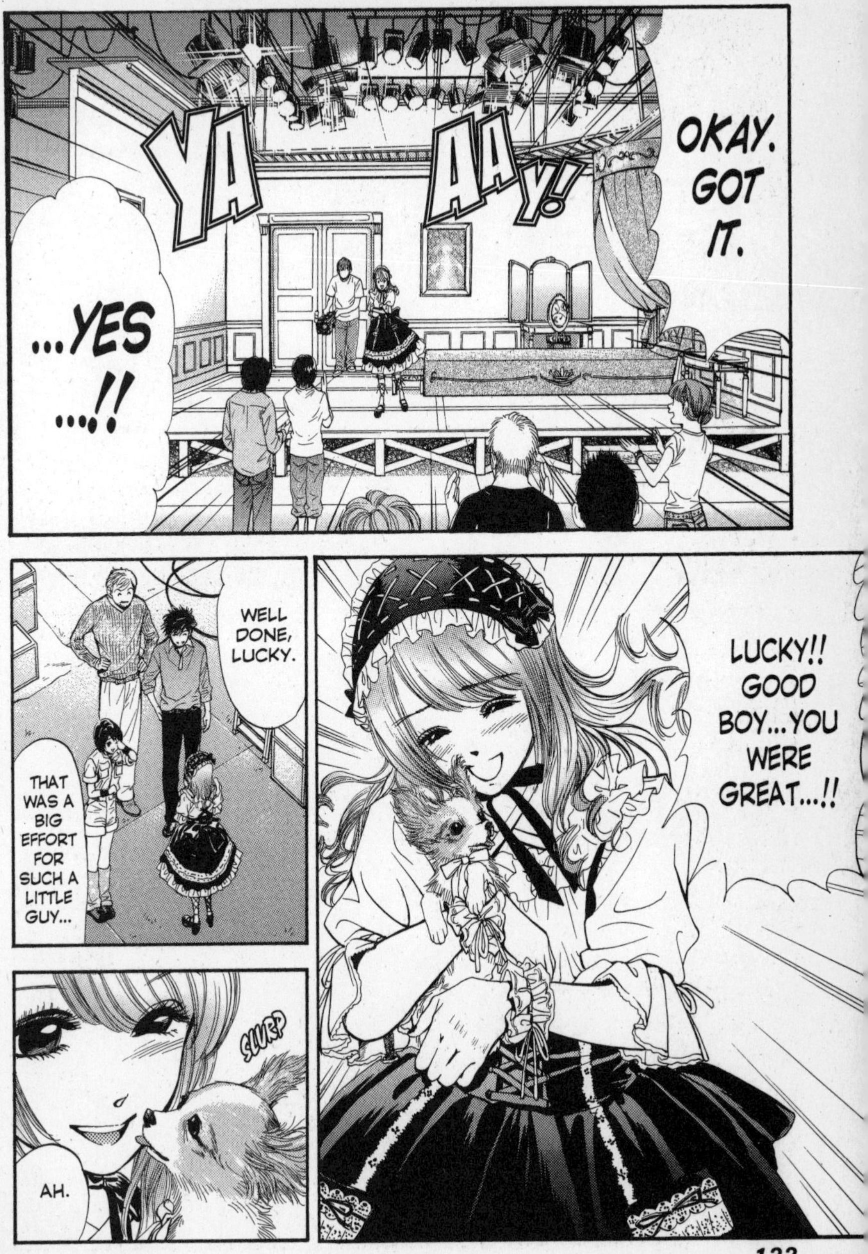
OKAY. GOT IT.
YA AAY!
...YES ...!!
LUCKY!! GOOD BOY...YOU WERE GREAT...!!
WELL DONE, LUCKY.
THAT WAS A BIG EFFORT FOR SUCH A LITTLE GUY...
SLURP
AH.

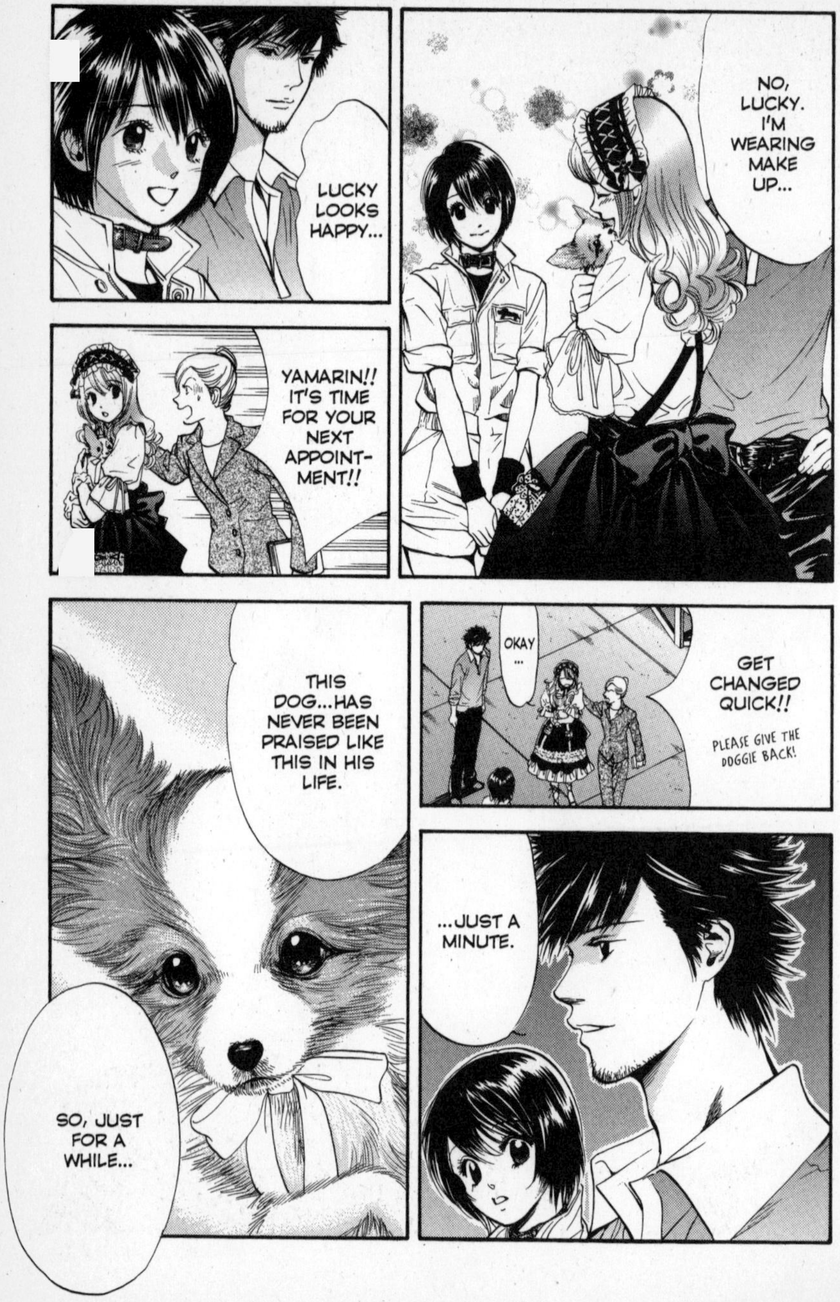
NO, LUCKY. I'M WEARING MAKE UP...
LUCKY LOOKS HAPPY...
YAMARIN!! IT'S TIME FOR YOUR NEXT APPOINT-MENT!!
GET CHANGED QUICK!!
PLEASE GIVE THE DOGGIE BACK!
OKAY ...
...JUST A MINUTE.
THIS DOG...HAS NEVER BEEN PRAISED LIKE THIS IN HIS LIFE.
SO, JUST FOR A WHILE...

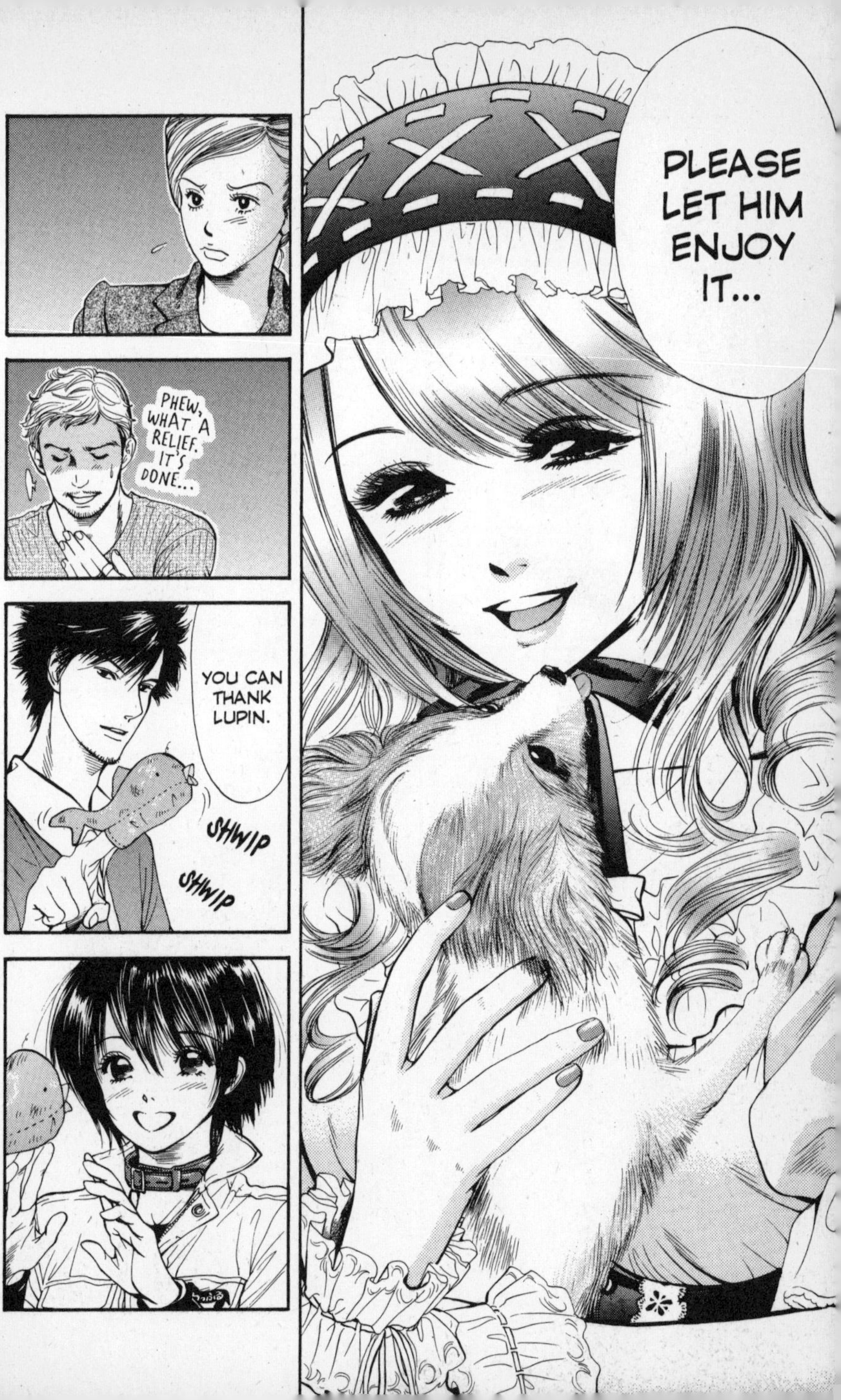
PLEASE LET HIM ENJOY IT...
PHEW, WHAT A RELIEF. IT'S DONE...
YOU CAN THANK LUPIN.
SHWIP
SHWIP

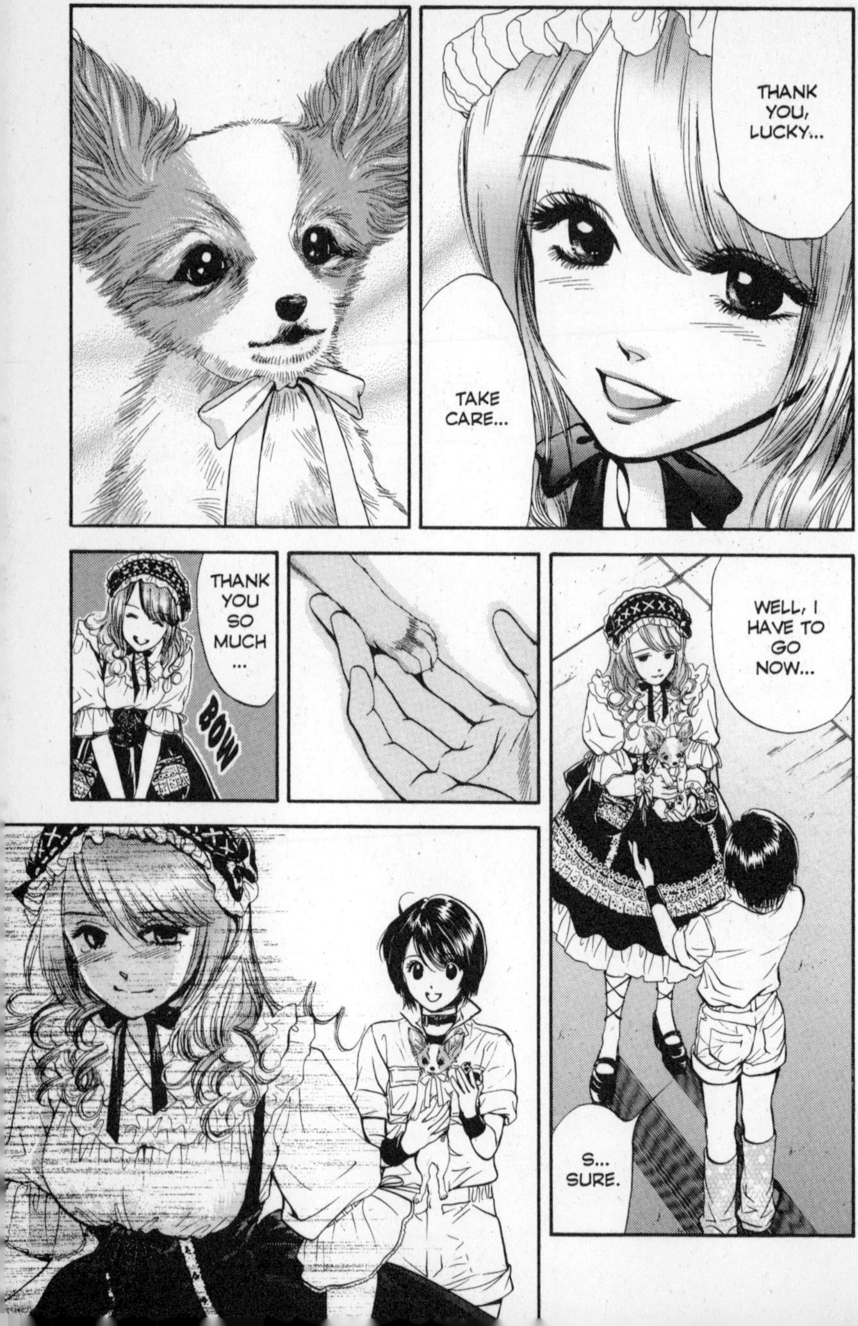
THANK YOU, LUCKY...
TAKE CARE...
WELL, I HAVE TO GO NOW...
S... SURE.
THANK YOU SO MUCH ...
BOW

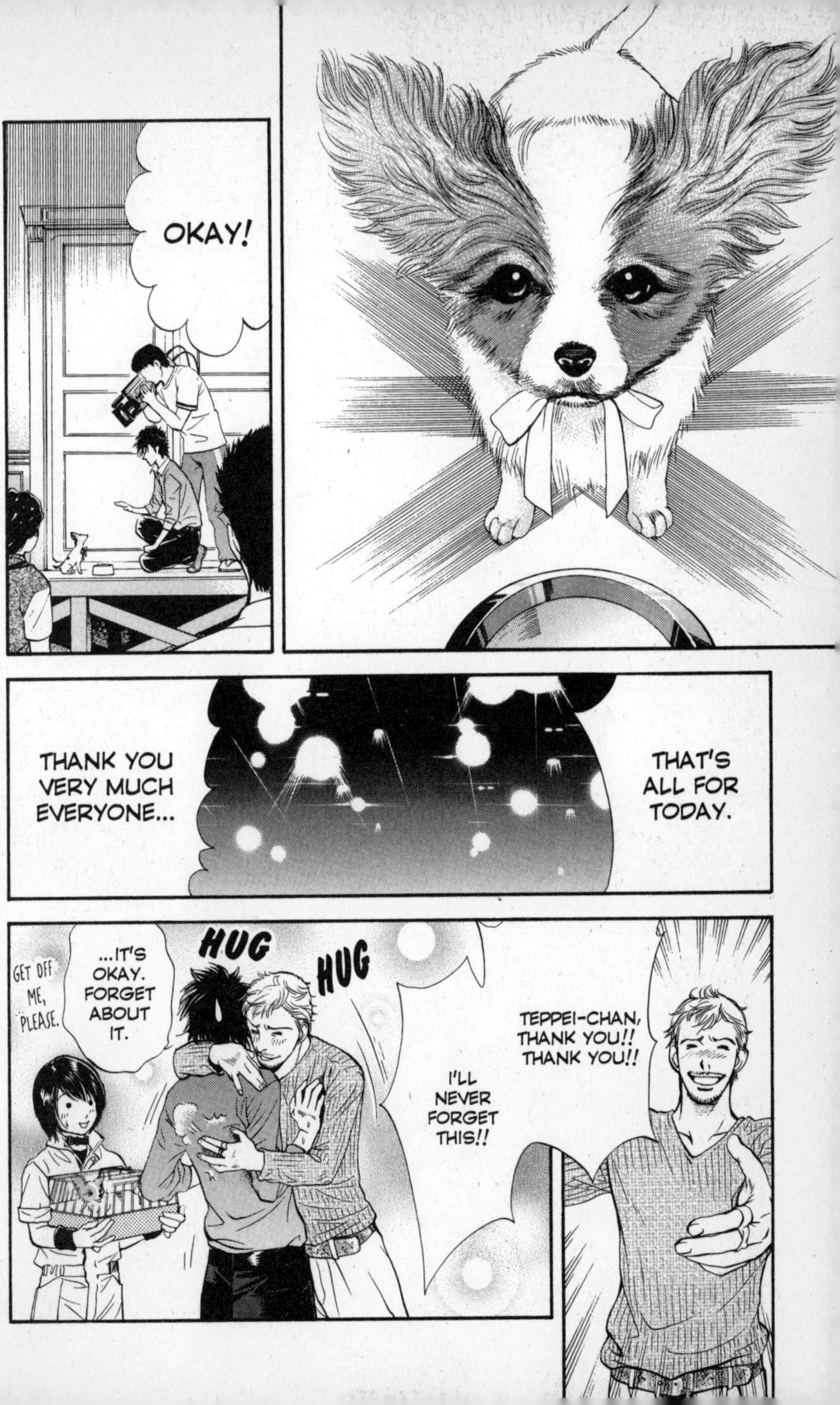
OKAY!
THAT'S ALL FOR TODAY.
THANK YOU VERY MUCH EVERYONE...
TEPPEI-CHAN, THANK YOU!! THANK YOU!!
I'LL NEVER FORGET THIS!!
HUG
HUG
...IT'S OKAY. FORGET ABOUT IT.
GET OFF ME, PLEASE.

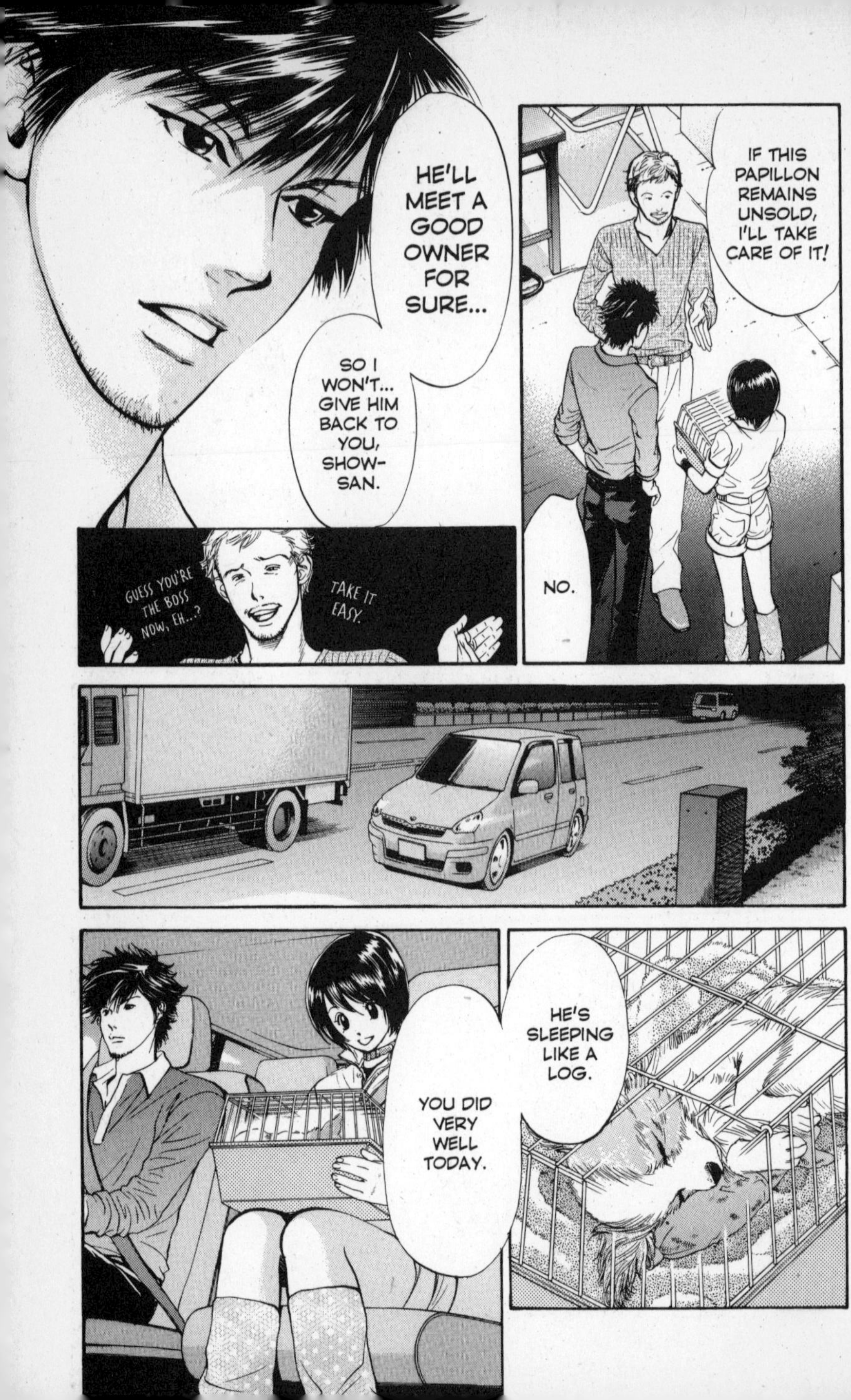
IF THIS PAPILLON REMAINS UNSOLD, I'LL TAKE CARE OF IT!
NO.
HE'LL MEET A GOOD OWNER FOR SURE...
SO I WON'T... GIVE HIM BACK TO YOU, SHOW-SAN.
TAKE IT EASY.
GUESS YOU'RE THE BOSS NOW, EH...?
HE'S SLEEPING LIKE A LOG.
YOU DID VERY WELL TODAY.

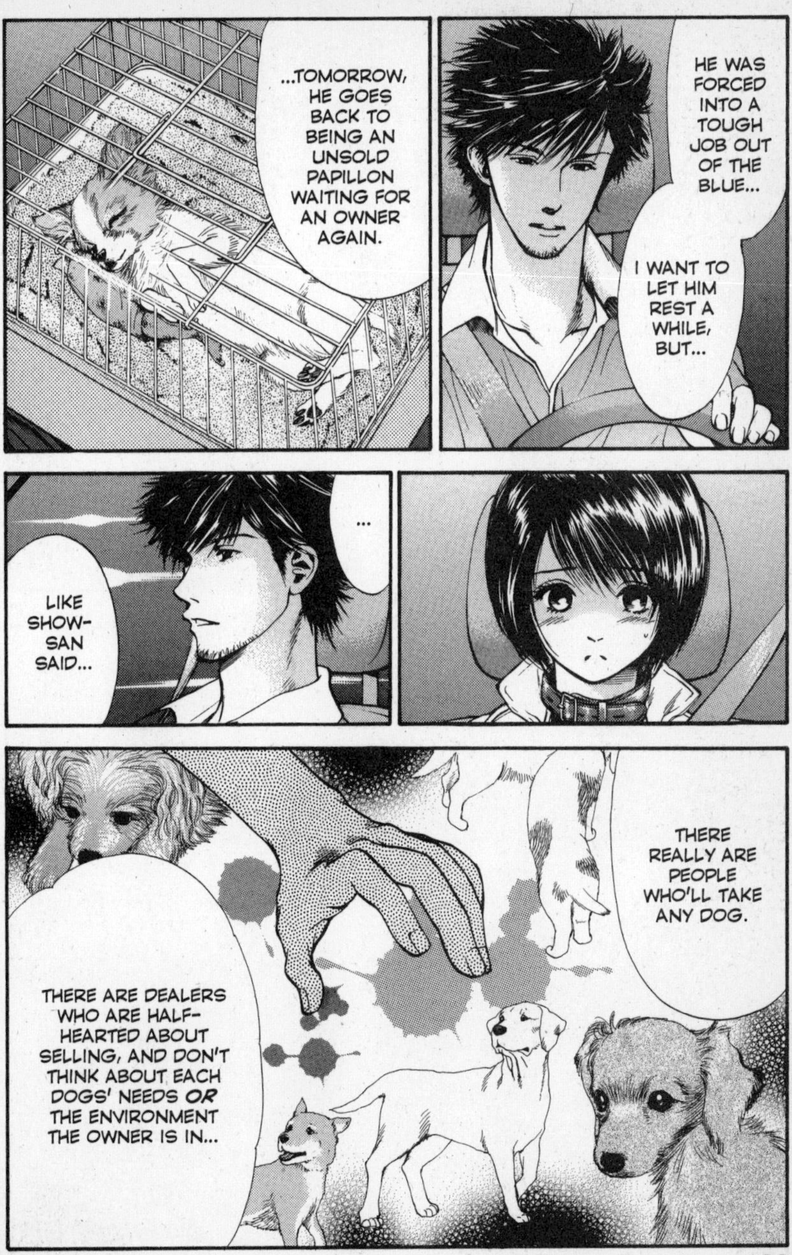
HE WAS FORCED INTO A TOUGH JOB OUT OF THE BLUE...
I WANT TO LET HIM REST A WHILE, BUT...
...TOMORROW, HE GOES BACK TO BEING AN UNSOLD PAPILLON WAITING FOR AN OWNER AGAIN.
...
LIKE SHOW-SAN SAID...
THERE REALLY ARE PEOPLE WHO'LL TAKE ANY DOG.
THERE ARE DEALERS WHO ARE HALF-HEARTED ABOUT SELLING, AND DON'T THINK ABOUT EACH DOGS' NEEDS *OR* THE ENVIRONMENT THE OWNER IS IN...

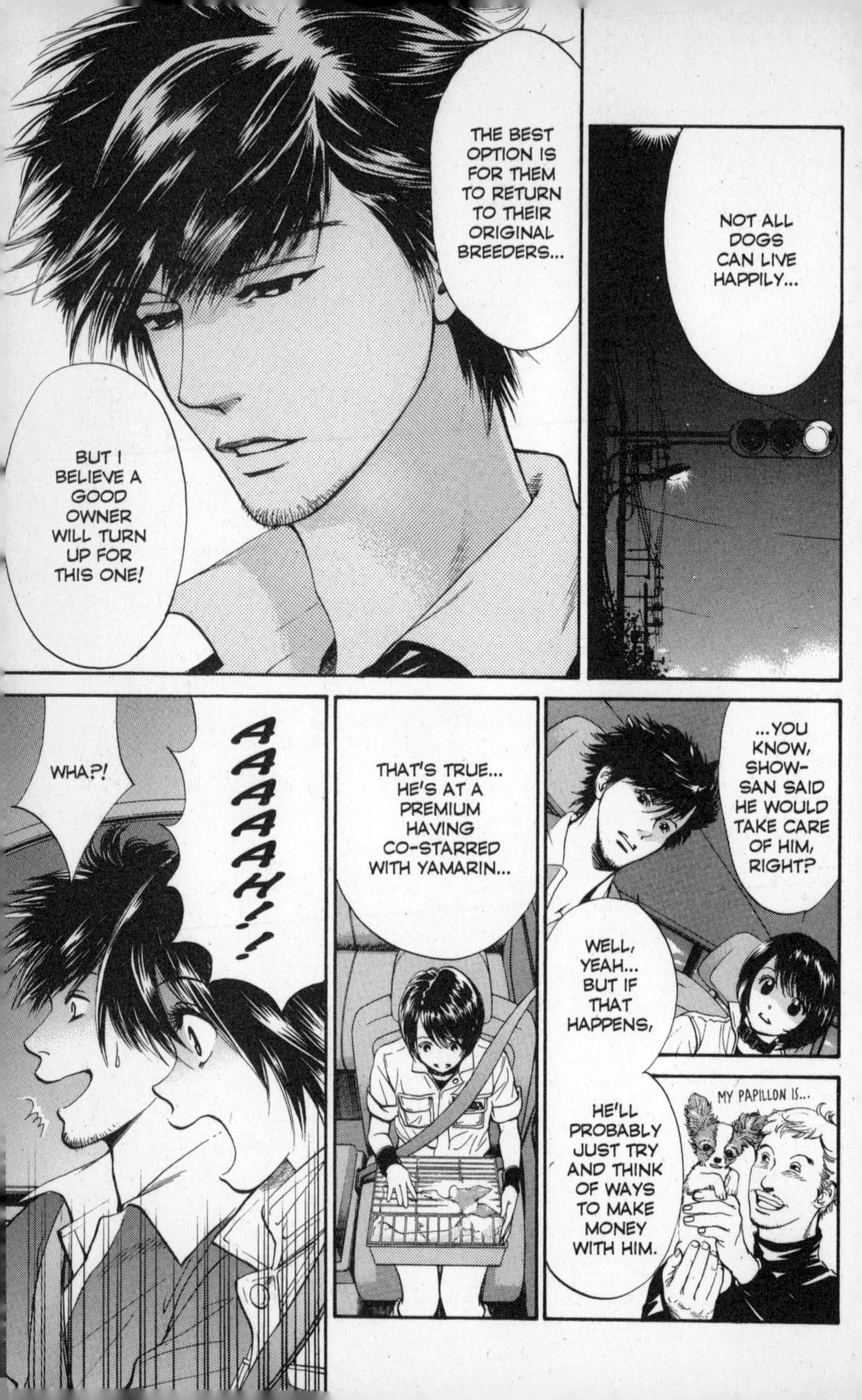
NOT ALL DOGS CAN LIVE HAPPILY...
THE BEST OPTION IS FOR THEM TO RETURN TO THEIR ORIGINAL BREEDERS...
BUT I BELIEVE A GOOD OWNER WILL TURN UP FOR THIS ONE!
...YOU KNOW, SHOW-SAN SAID HE WOULD TAKE CARE OF HIM, RIGHT?
WELL, YEAH... BUT IF THAT HAPPENS,
HE'LL PROBABLY JUST TRY AND THINK OF WAYS TO MAKE MONEY WITH HIM.
MY PAPILLON IS...
THAT'S TRUE... HE'S AT A PREMIUM HAVING CO-STARRED WITH YAMARIN...
AAAAAH!!
WHA?!

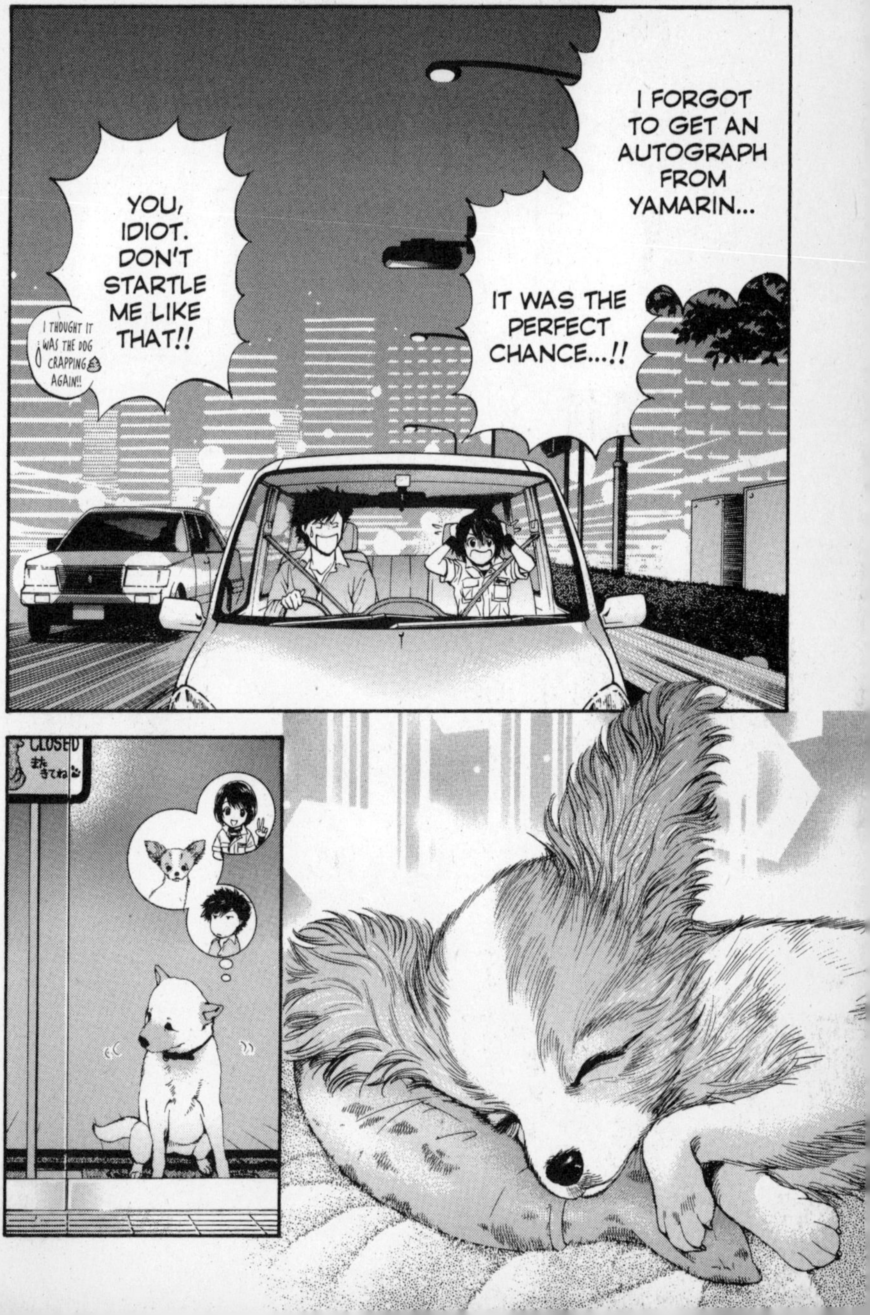
I FORGOT TO GET AN AUTOGRAPH FROM YAMARIN...
IT WAS THE PERFECT CHANCE...!!
YOU, IDIOT. DON'T STARTLE ME LIKE THAT!!
I THOUGHT IT WAS THE DOG CRAPPING AGAIN!!
CLOSED

CHAPTER 16 THE BEST "ENCOUNTER"

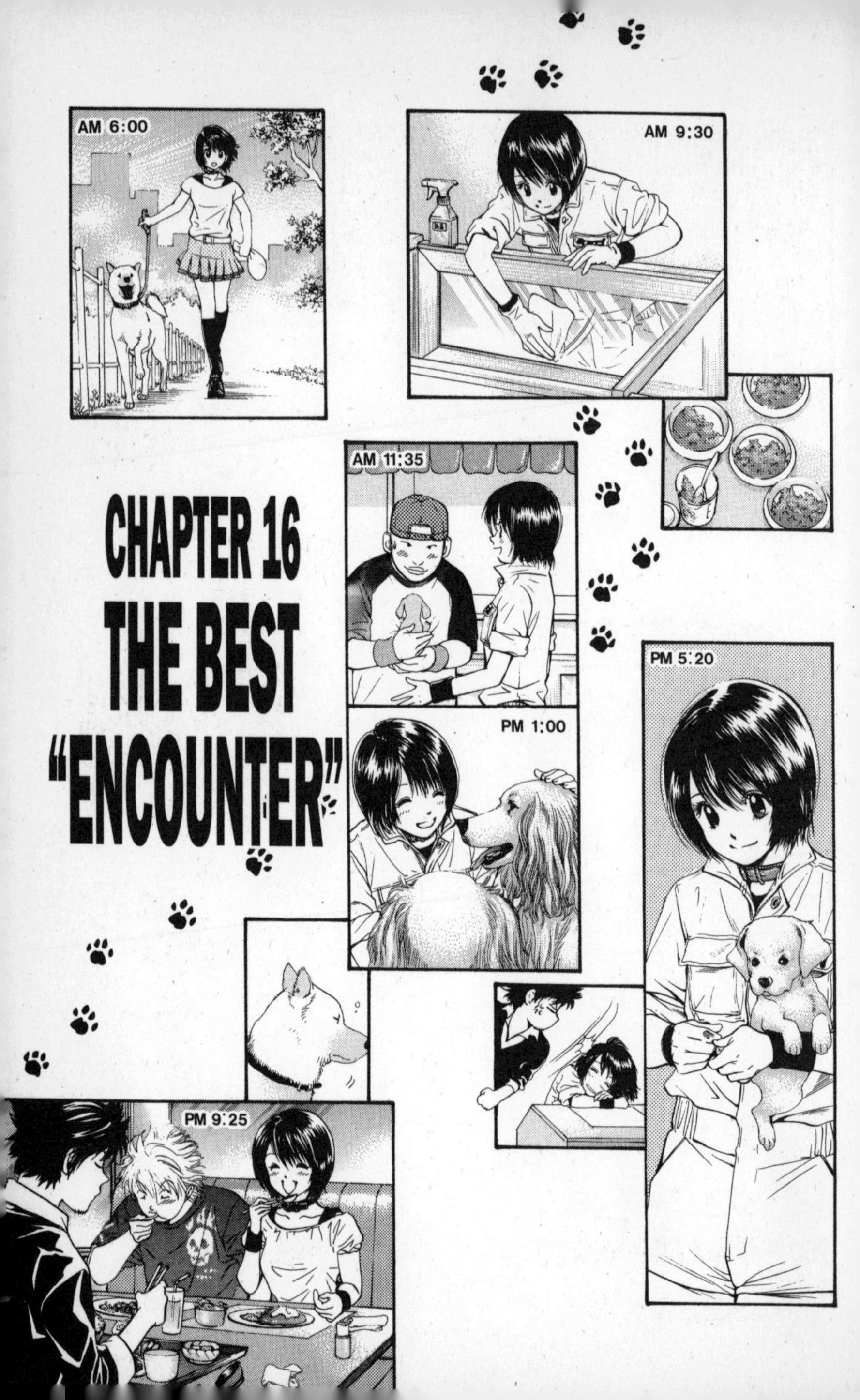
AM 9:30
AM 6:00
AM 11:35
PM 5:20
PM 1:00
PM 9:25

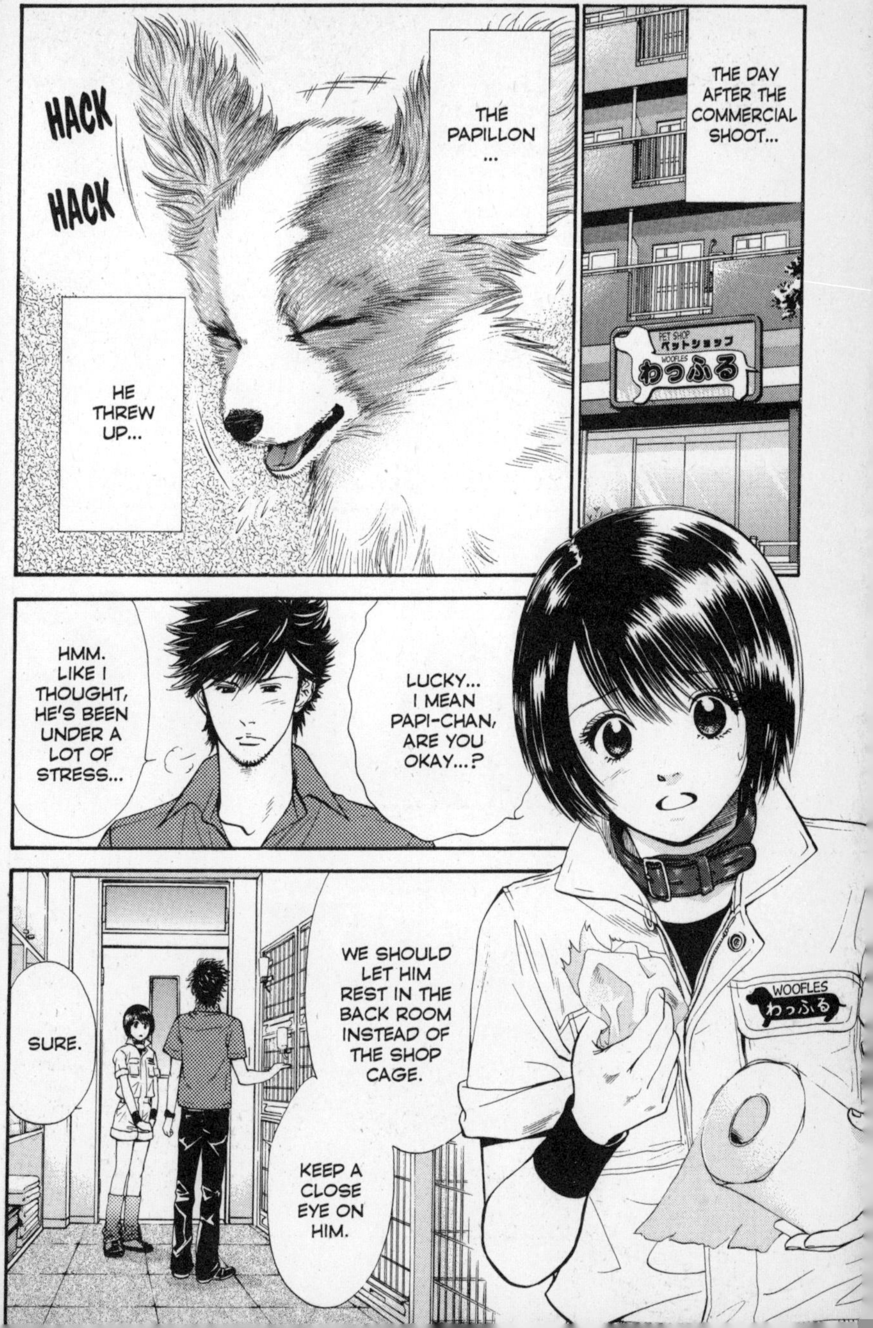
THE DAY AFTER THE COMMERCIAL SHOOT...
PET SHOP
ペットショップ
WOOFLES
わっふる
THE PAPILLON ...
HACK
HACK
HE THREW UP...
LUCKY... I MEAN PAPI-CHAN, ARE YOU OKAY...?
HMM. LIKE I THOUGHT, HE'S BEEN UNDER A LOT OF STRESS...
WOOFLES
わっふる
WE SHOULD LET HIM REST IN THE BACK ROOM INSTEAD OF THE SHOP CAGE.
KEEP A CLOSE EYE ON HIM.
SURE.

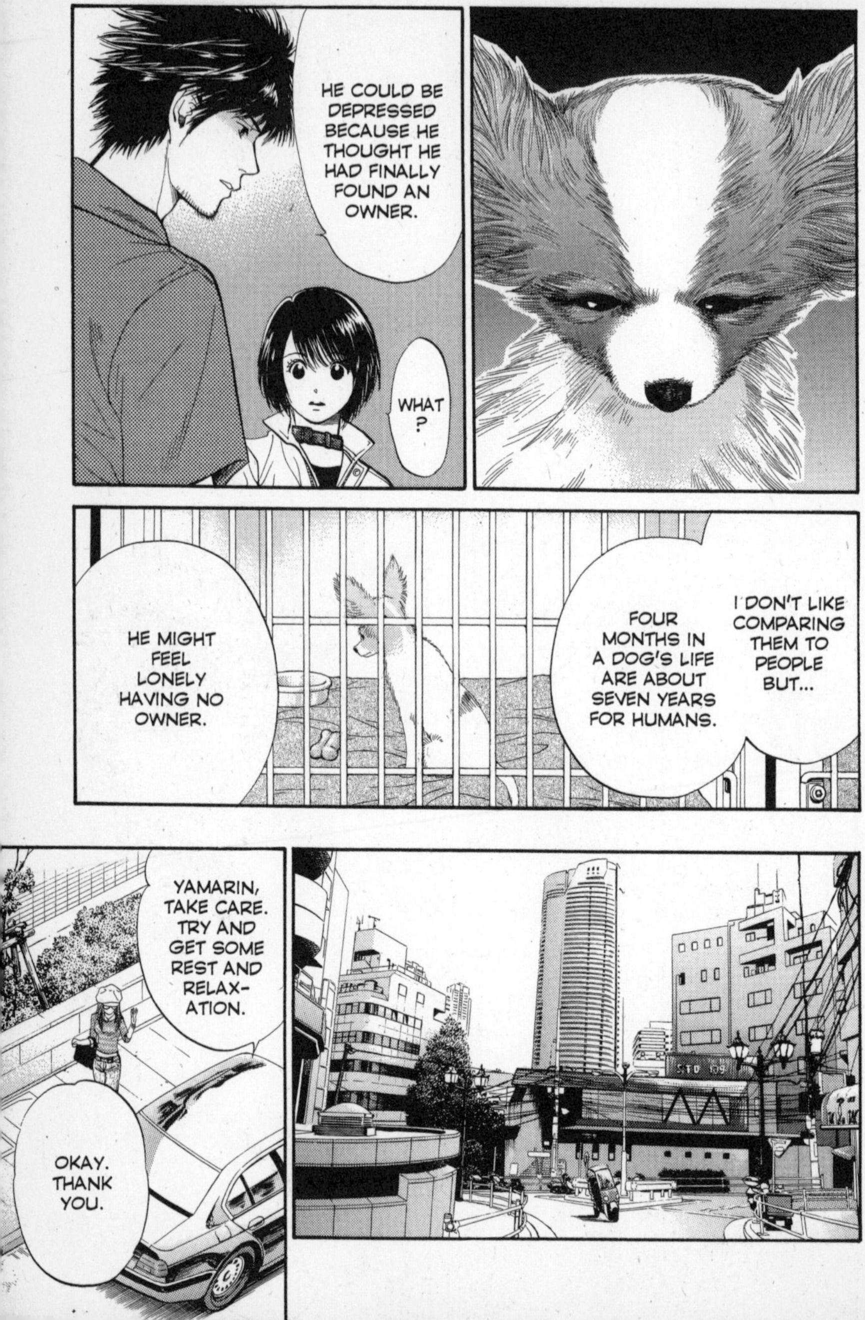
HE COULD BE DEPRESSED BECAUSE HE THOUGHT HE HAD FINALLY FOUND AN OWNER.
WHAT?
I DON'T LIKE COMPARING THEM TO PEOPLE BUT...
FOUR MONTHS IN A DOG'S LIFE ARE ABOUT SEVEN YEARS FOR HUMANS.
HE MIGHT FEEL LONELY HAVING NO OWNER.
YAMARIN, TAKE CARE. TRY AND GET SOME REST AND RELAX-ATION.
OKAY. THANK YOU.

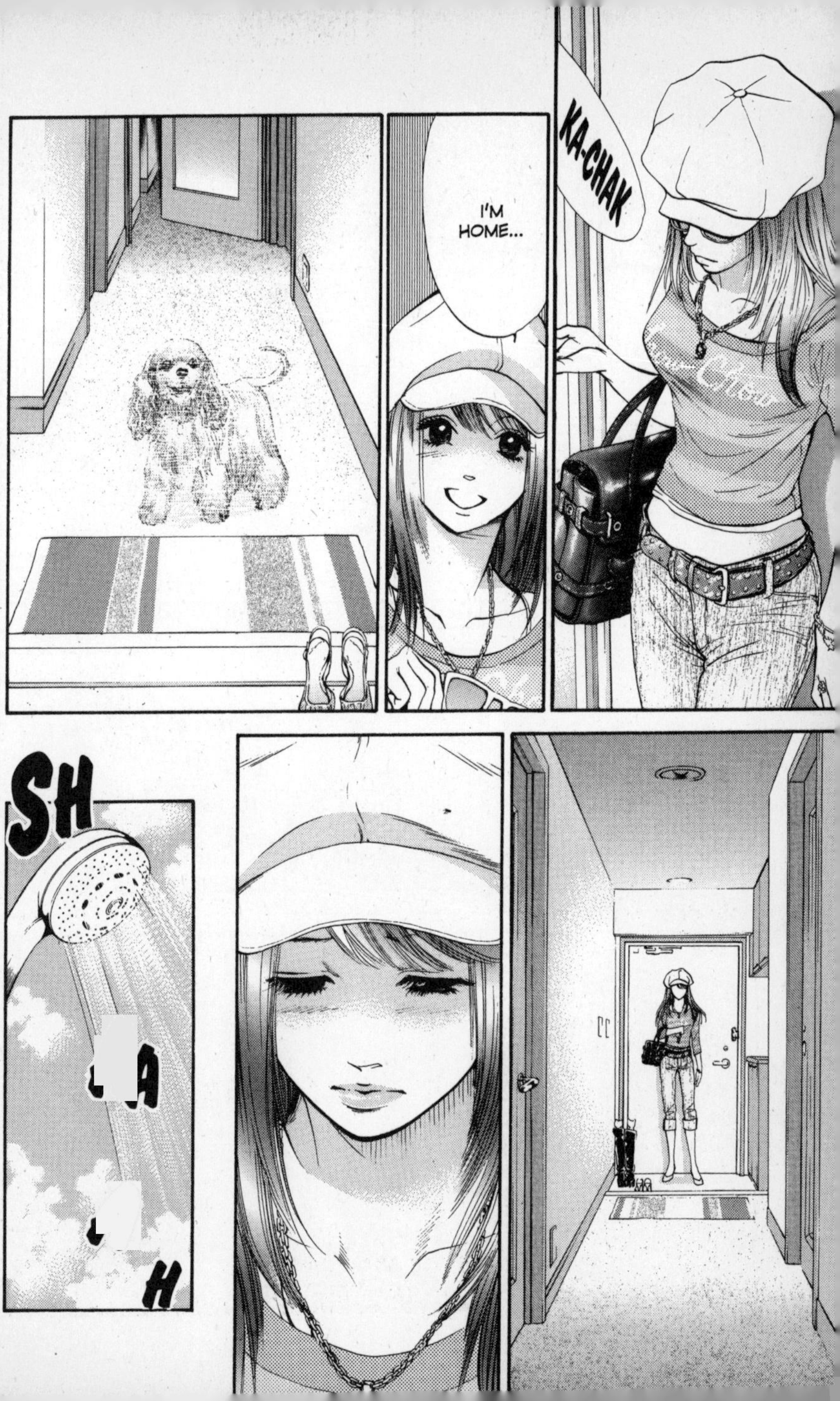
KA-CHAK
I'M HOME...
SH

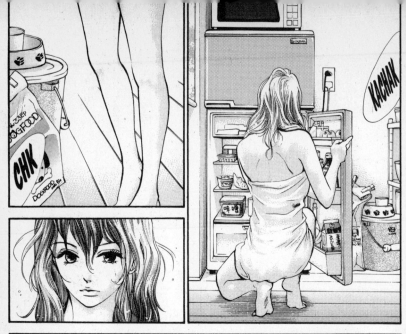

CHK

KACHAK

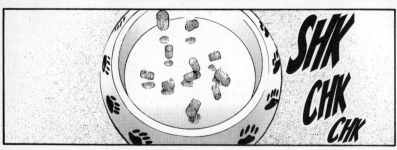

SHK
CHK
CHK

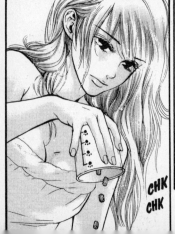

CHK
CHK

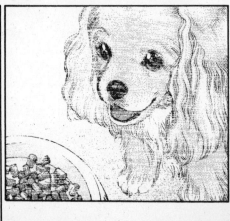

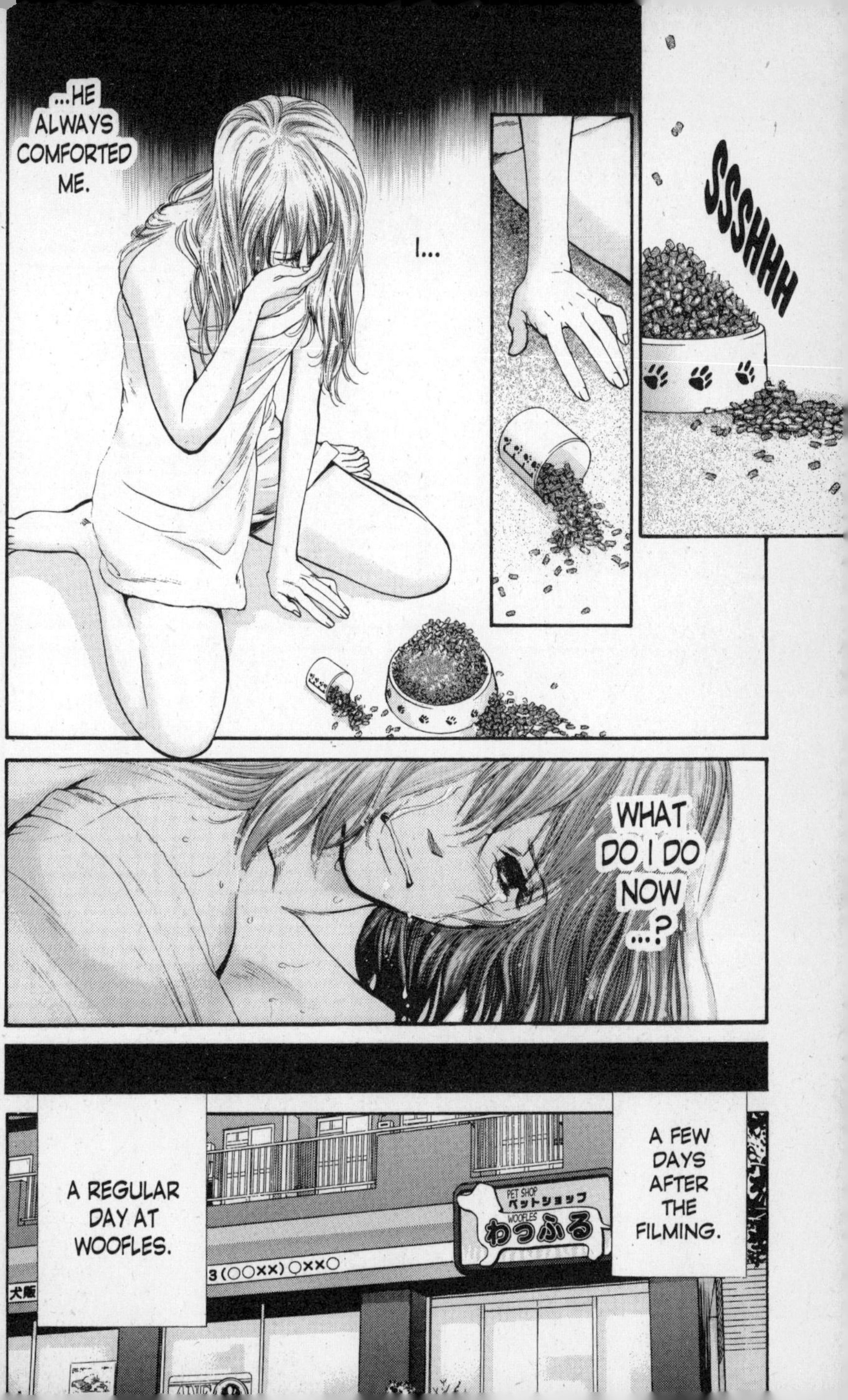
SSSHHH
...HE ALWAYS COMFORTED ME.
I...
WHAT DO I DO NOW ...?
A FEW DAYS AFTER THE FILMING.
PET SHOP
ペットショップ
WOOFLES
わっふる
3 (○○××) ○××○
犬販
A REGULAR DAY AT WOOFLES.

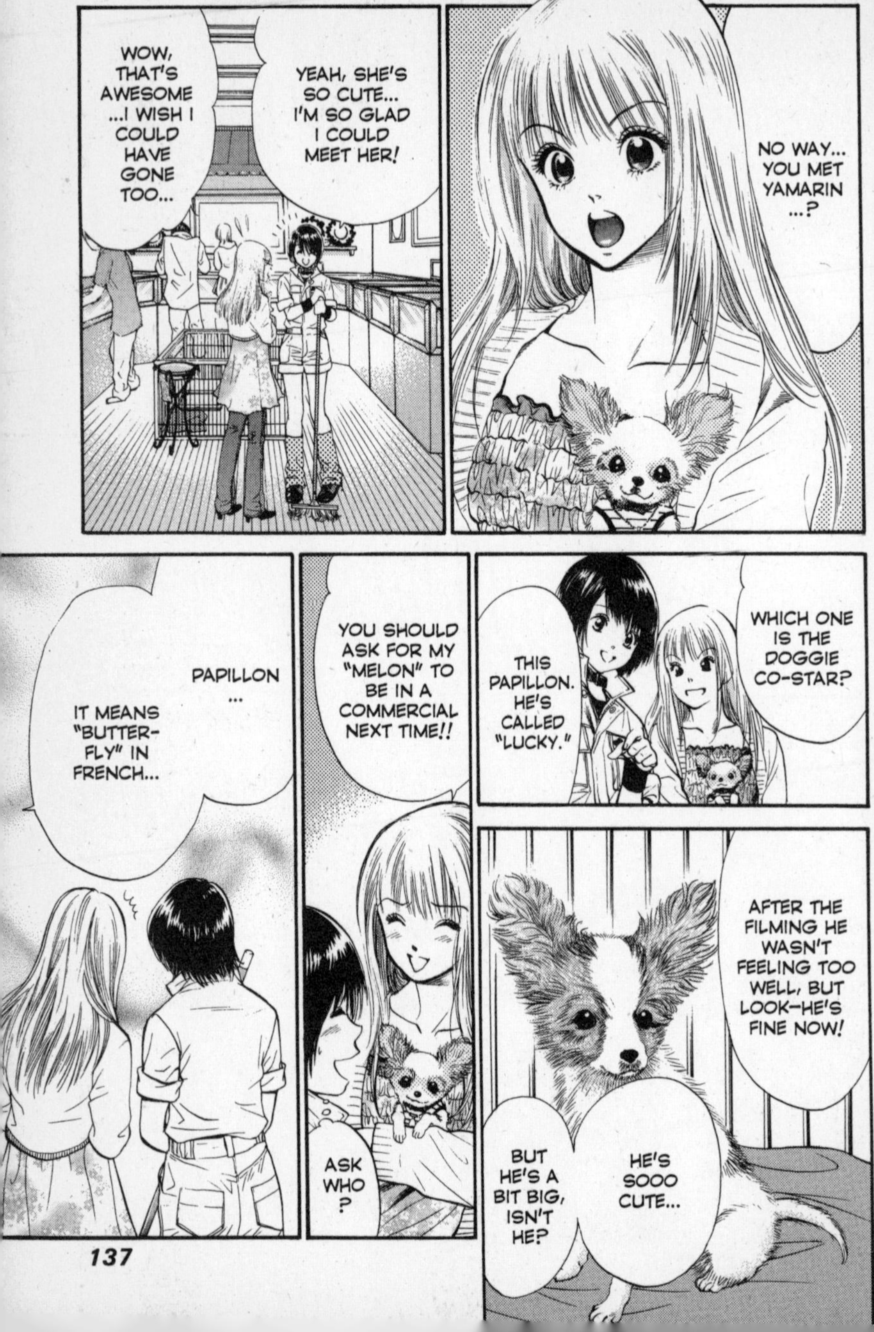
NO WAY... YOU MET YAMARIN ...?
YEAH, SHE'S SO CUTE... I'M SO GLAD I COULD MEET HER!
WOW, THAT'S AWESOME ...I WISH I COULD HAVE GONE TOO...
WHICH ONE IS THE DOGGIE CO-STAR?
THIS PAPILLON. HE'S CALLED "LUCKY."
AFTER THE FILMING HE WASN'T FEELING TOO WELL, BUT LOOK—HE'S FINE NOW!
HE'S SOOO CUTE...
BUT HE'S A BIT BIG, ISN'T HE?
YOU SHOULD ASK FOR MY "MELON" TO BE IN A COMMERCIAL NEXT TIME!!
ASK WHO?
PAPILLON ...
IT MEANS "BUTTER-FLY" IN FRENCH...

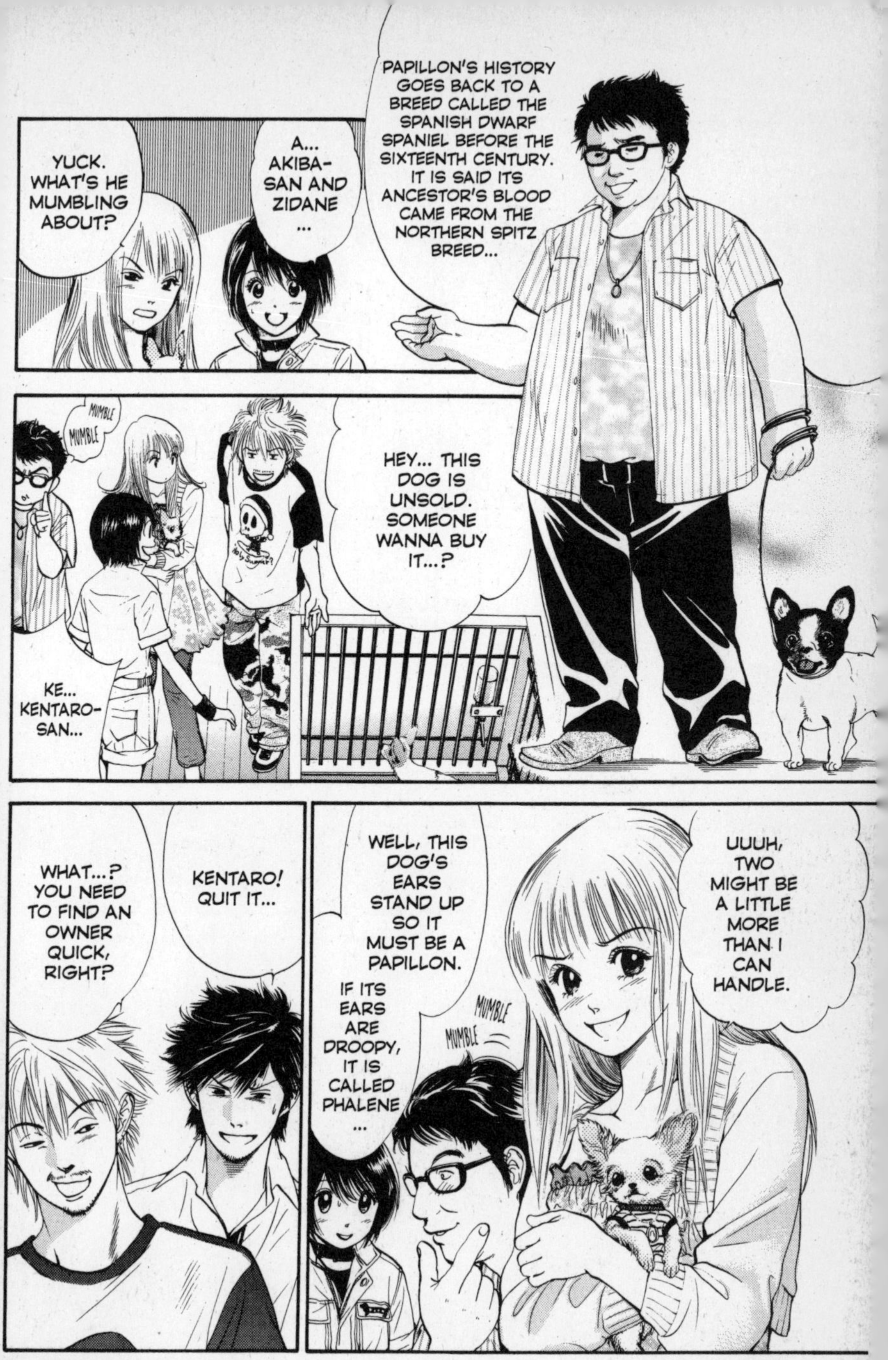
PAPILLON'S HISTORY GOES BACK TO A BREED CALLED THE SPANISH DWARF SPANIEL BEFORE THE SIXTEENTH CENTURY. IT IS SAID ITS ANCESTOR'S BLOOD CAME FROM THE NORTHERN SPITZ BREED...
A... AKIBA-SAN AND ZIDANE ...
YUCK. WHAT'S HE MUMBLING ABOUT?
HEY... THIS DOG IS UNSOLD. SOMEONE WANNA BUY IT...?
MUMBLE
MUMBLE
KE... KENTARO-SAN...
UUUH, TWO MIGHT BE A LITTLE MORE THAN I CAN HANDLE.
WELL, THIS DOG'S EARS STAND UP SO IT MUST BE A PAPILLON.
MUMBLE
MUMBLE
IF ITS EARS ARE DROOPY, IT IS CALLED PHALENE ...
KENTARO! QUIT IT...
WHAT...? YOU NEED TO FIND AN OWNER QUICK, RIGHT?

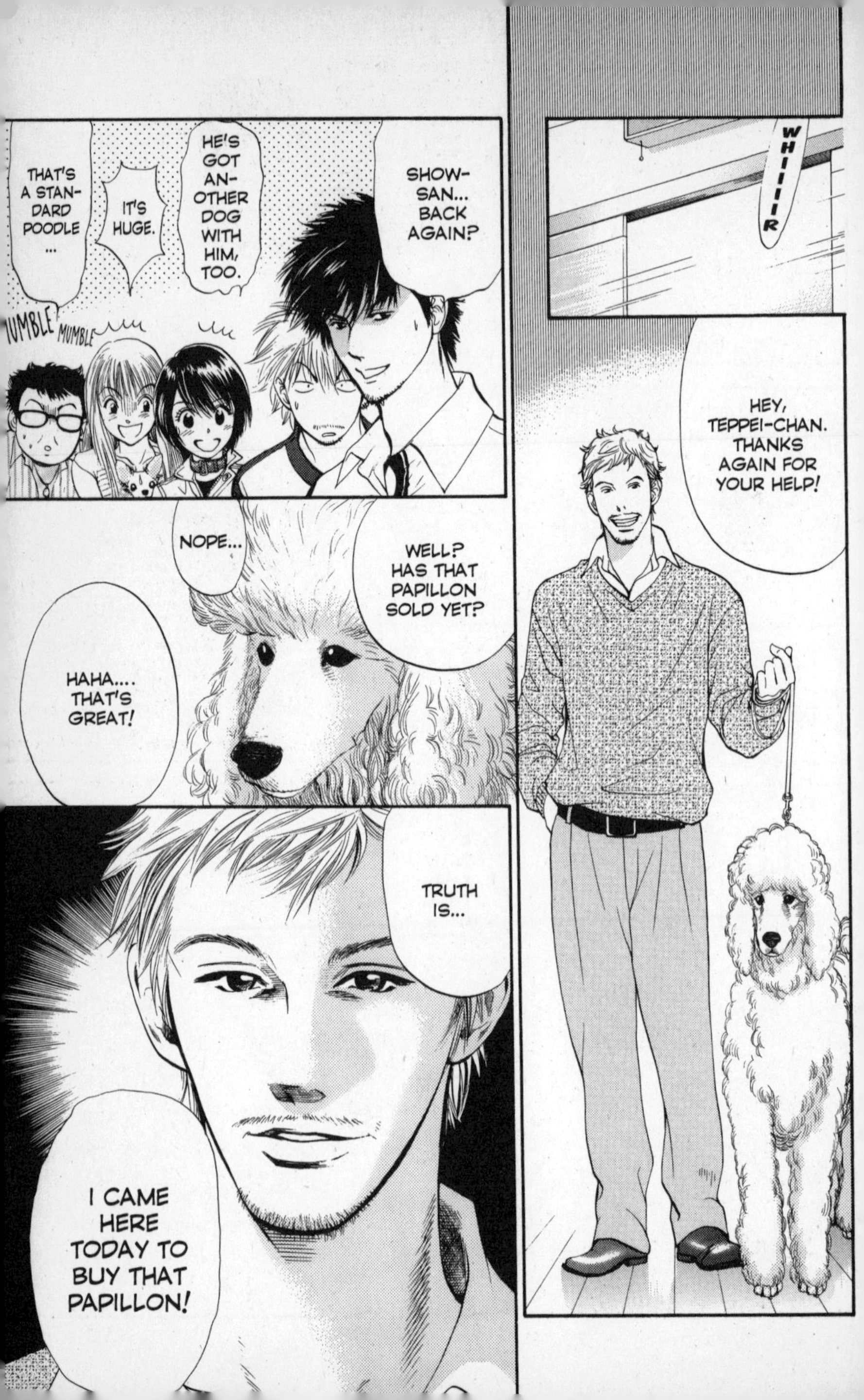
WHIIIIR
HEY, TEPPEI-CHAN. THANKS AGAIN FOR YOUR HELP!
SHOW-SAN... BACK AGAIN?
HE'S GOT AN-OTHER DOG WITH HIM, TOO.
IT'S HUGE.
THAT'S A STAN-DARD POODLE ...
MUMBLE MUMBLE
WELL? HAS THAT PAPILLON SOLD YET?
NOPE...
HAHA.... THAT'S GREAT!
TRUTH IS...
I CAME HERE TODAY TO BUY THAT PAPILLON!

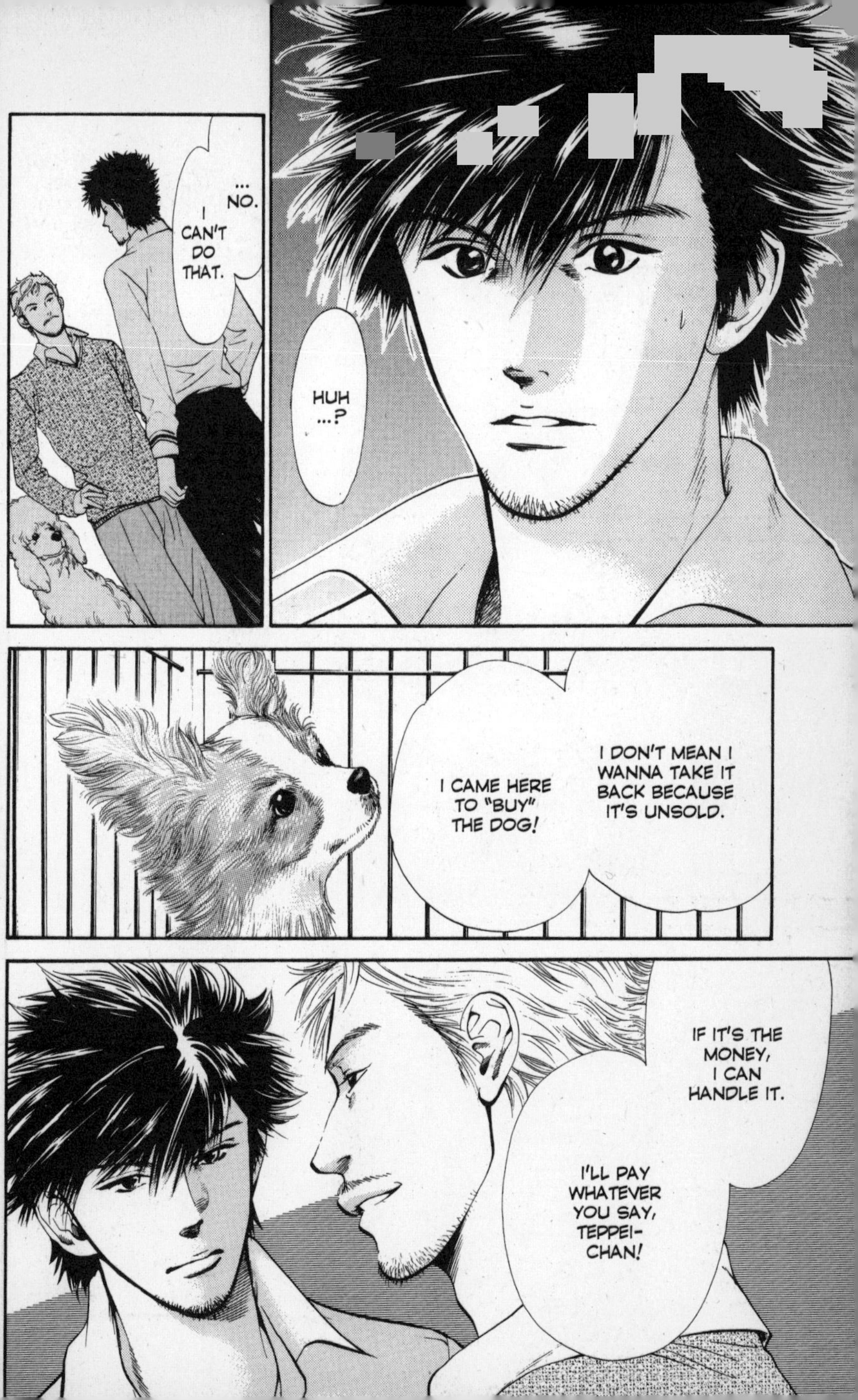
HUH ...?
... NO. I CAN'T DO THAT.
I DON'T MEAN I WANNA TAKE IT BACK BECAUSE IT'S UNSOLD.
I CAME HERE TO "BUY" THE DOG!
IF IT'S THE MONEY, I CAN HANDLE IT.
I'LL PAY WHATEVER YOU SAY, TEPPEI-CHAN!

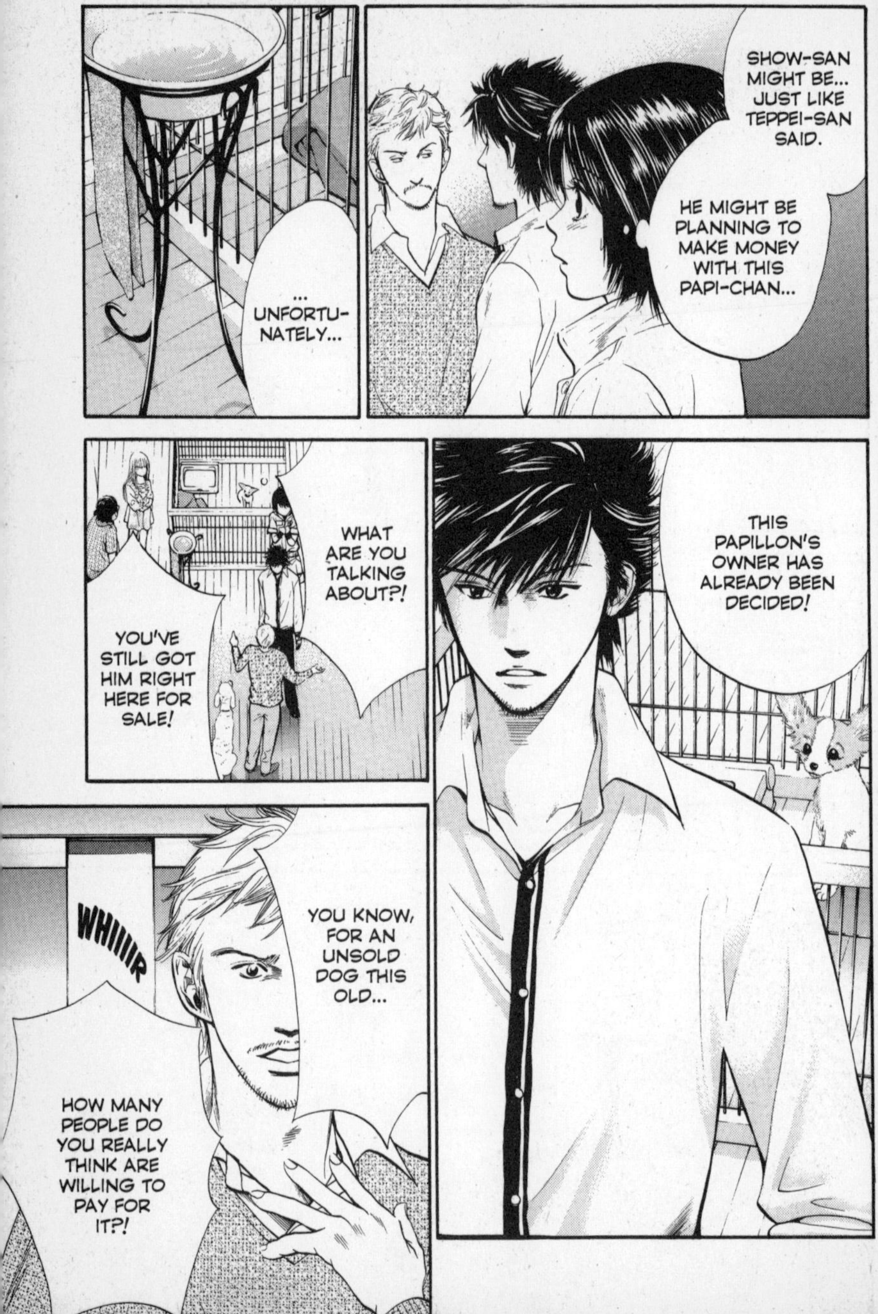
SHOW-SAN MIGHT BE... JUST LIKE TEPPEI-SAN SAID.
HE MIGHT BE PLANNING TO MAKE MONEY WITH THIS PAPI-CHAN...
...UNFORTU-NATELY...
THIS PAPILLON'S OWNER HAS ALREADY BEEN DECIDED!
WHAT ARE YOU TALKING ABOUT?!
YOU'VE STILL GOT HIM RIGHT HERE FOR SALE!
WHIIIIR
YOU KNOW, FOR AN UNSOLD DOG THIS OLD...
HOW MANY PEOPLE DO YOU REALLY THINK ARE WILLING TO PAY FOR IT?!

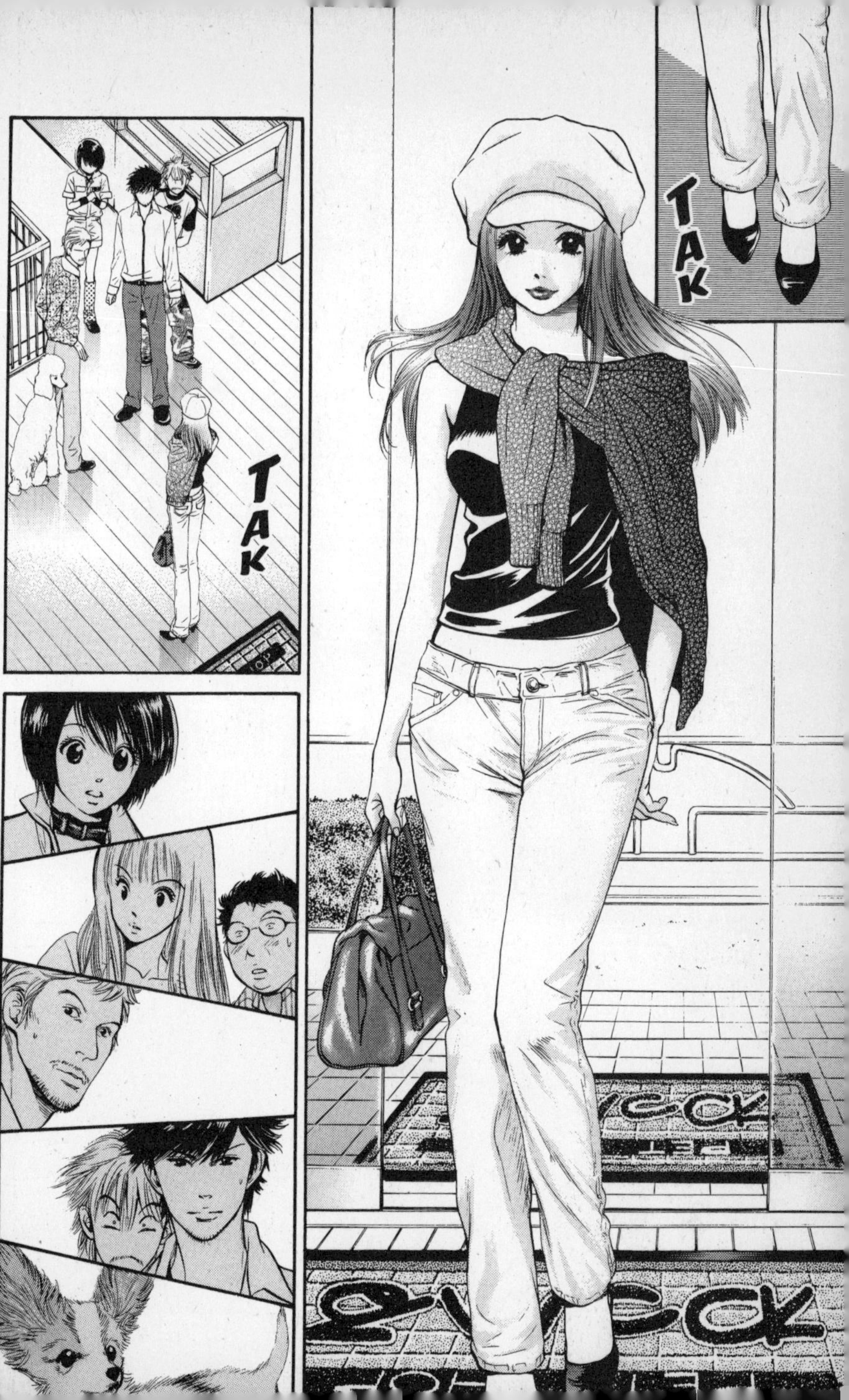
TAK
TAK

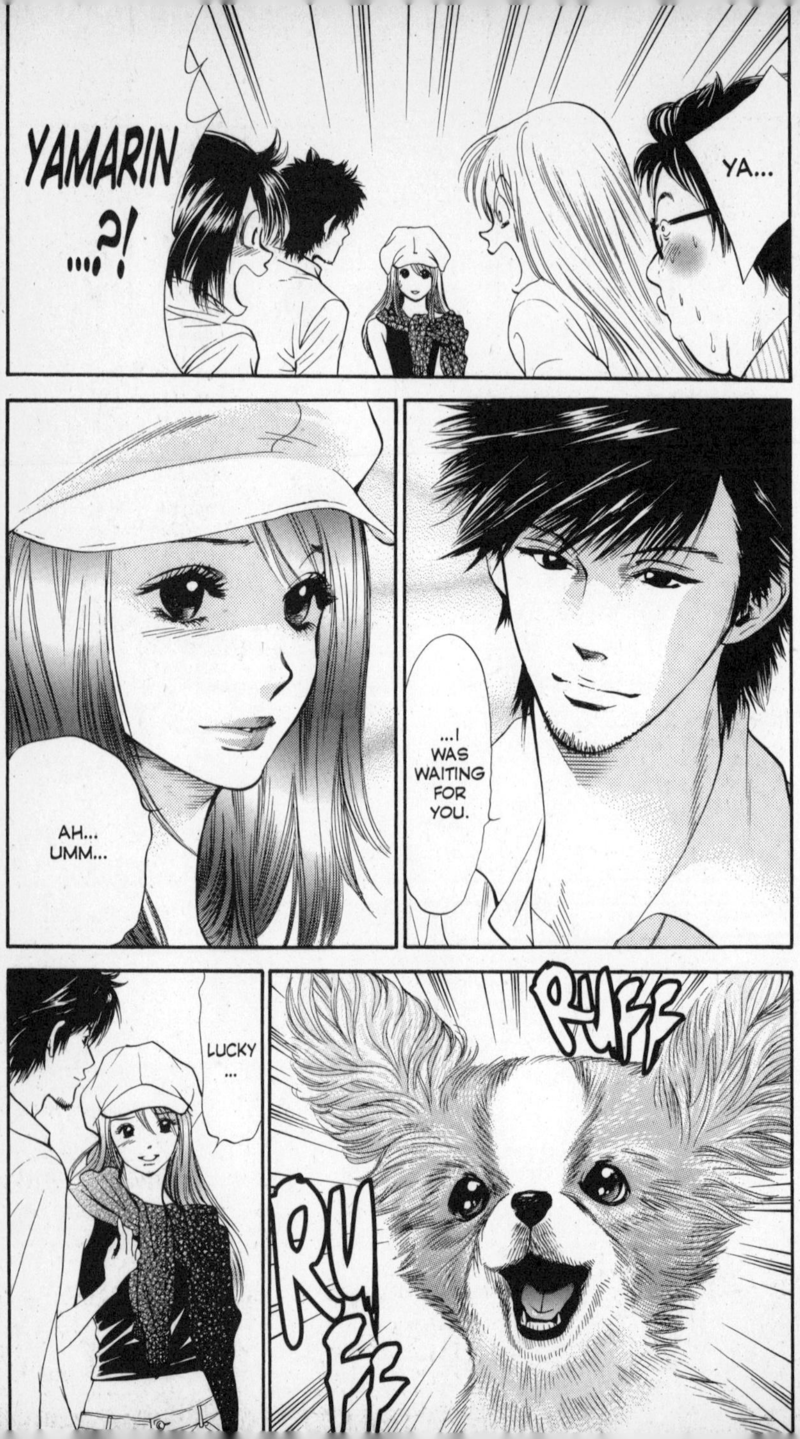
YA...
YAMARIN ...?!
...I WAS WAITING FOR YOU.
AH... UMM...
RUFF
RUFF
LUCKY ...

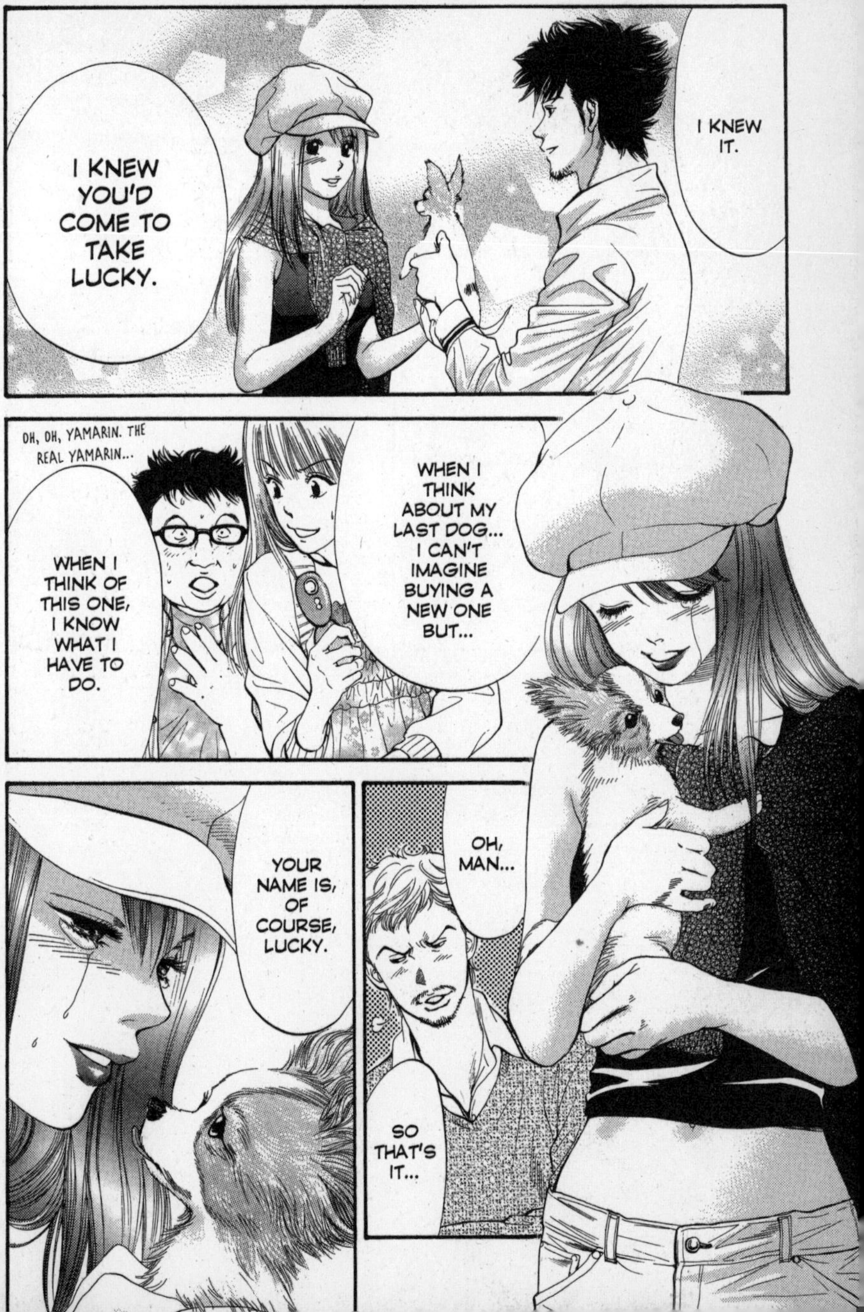
I KNEW IT.
I KNEW YOU'D COME TO TAKE LUCKY.
WHEN I THINK ABOUT MY LAST DOG... I CAN'T IMAGINE BUYING A NEW ONE BUT...
OH, OH, YAMARIN. THE REAL YAMARIN...
WHEN I THINK OF THIS ONE, I KNOW WHAT I HAVE TO DO.
OH, MAN...
SO THAT'S IT...
YOUR NAME IS, OF COURSE, LUCKY.

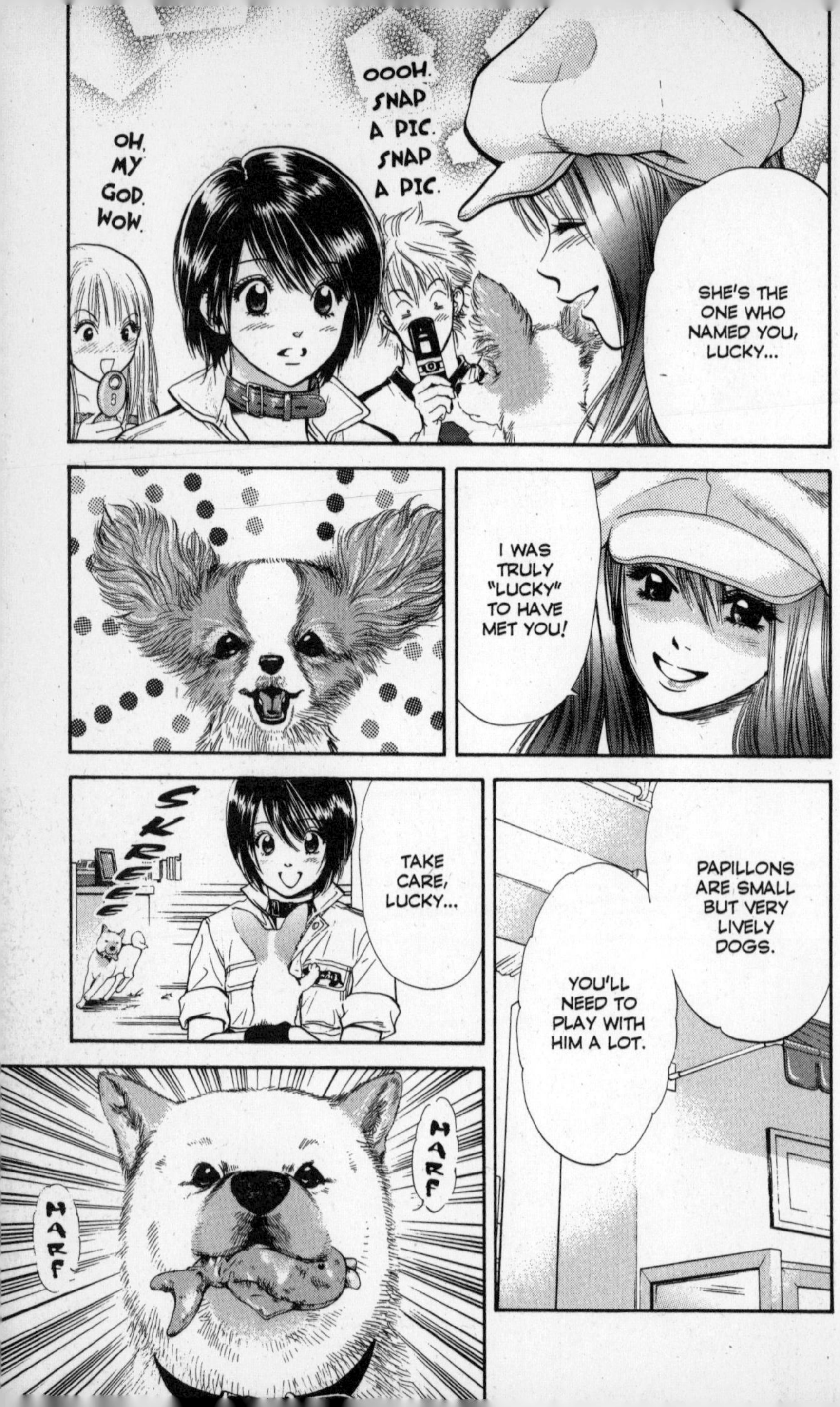
SHE'S THE ONE WHO NAMED YOU, LUCKY...
OOOH. SNAP A PIC. SNAP A PIC.
OH, MY GOD. WOW.
I WAS TRULY "LUCKY" TO HAVE MET YOU!
PAPILLONS ARE SMALL BUT VERY LIVELY DOGS.
YOU'LL NEED TO PLAY WITH HIM A LOT.
TAKE CARE, LUCKY...
SKREEEE
HARF
HARF

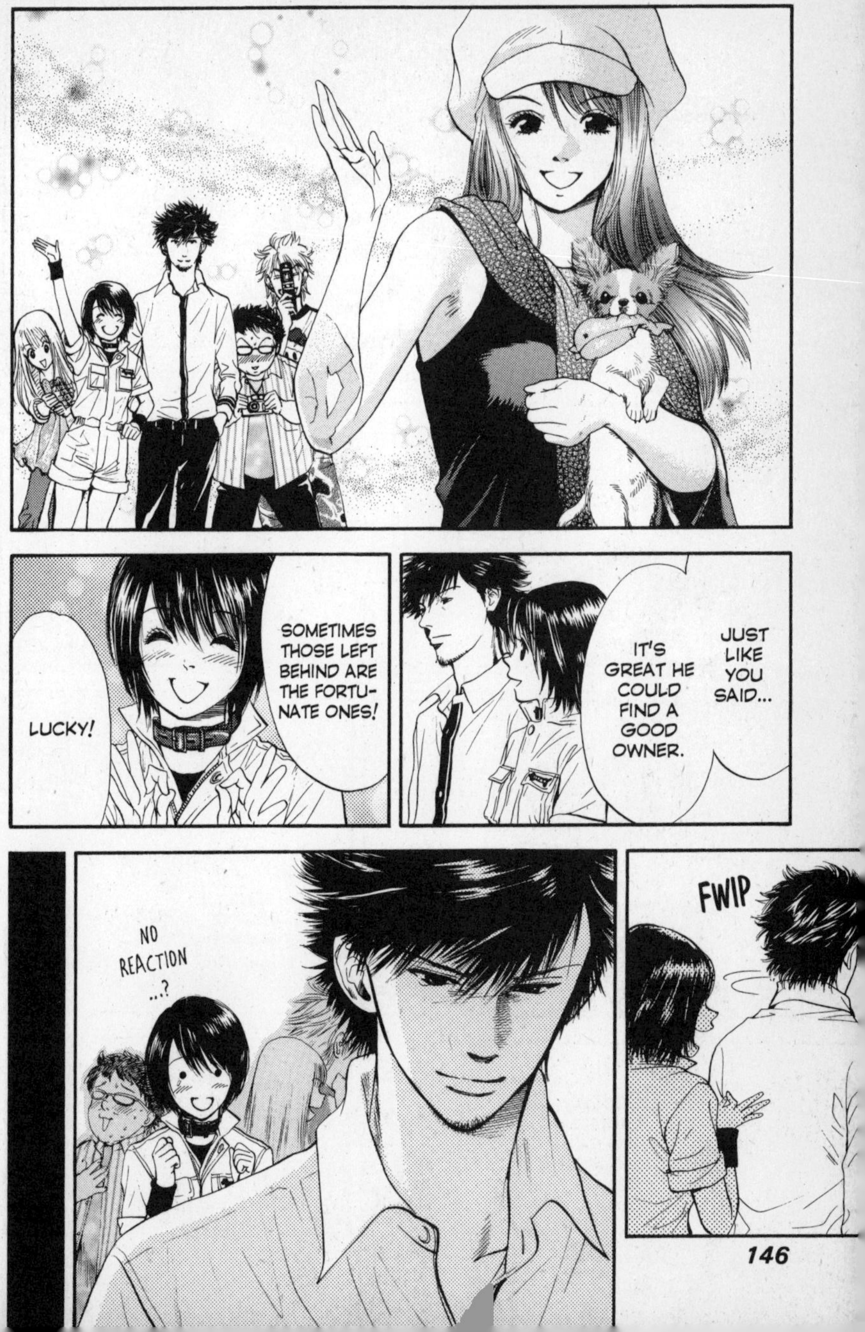
JUST LIKE YOU SAID...
IT'S GREAT HE COULD FIND A GOOD OWNER.
SOMETIMES THOSE LEFT BEHIND ARE THE FORTUNATE ONES!
LUCKY!
FWIP
NO REACTION ...?

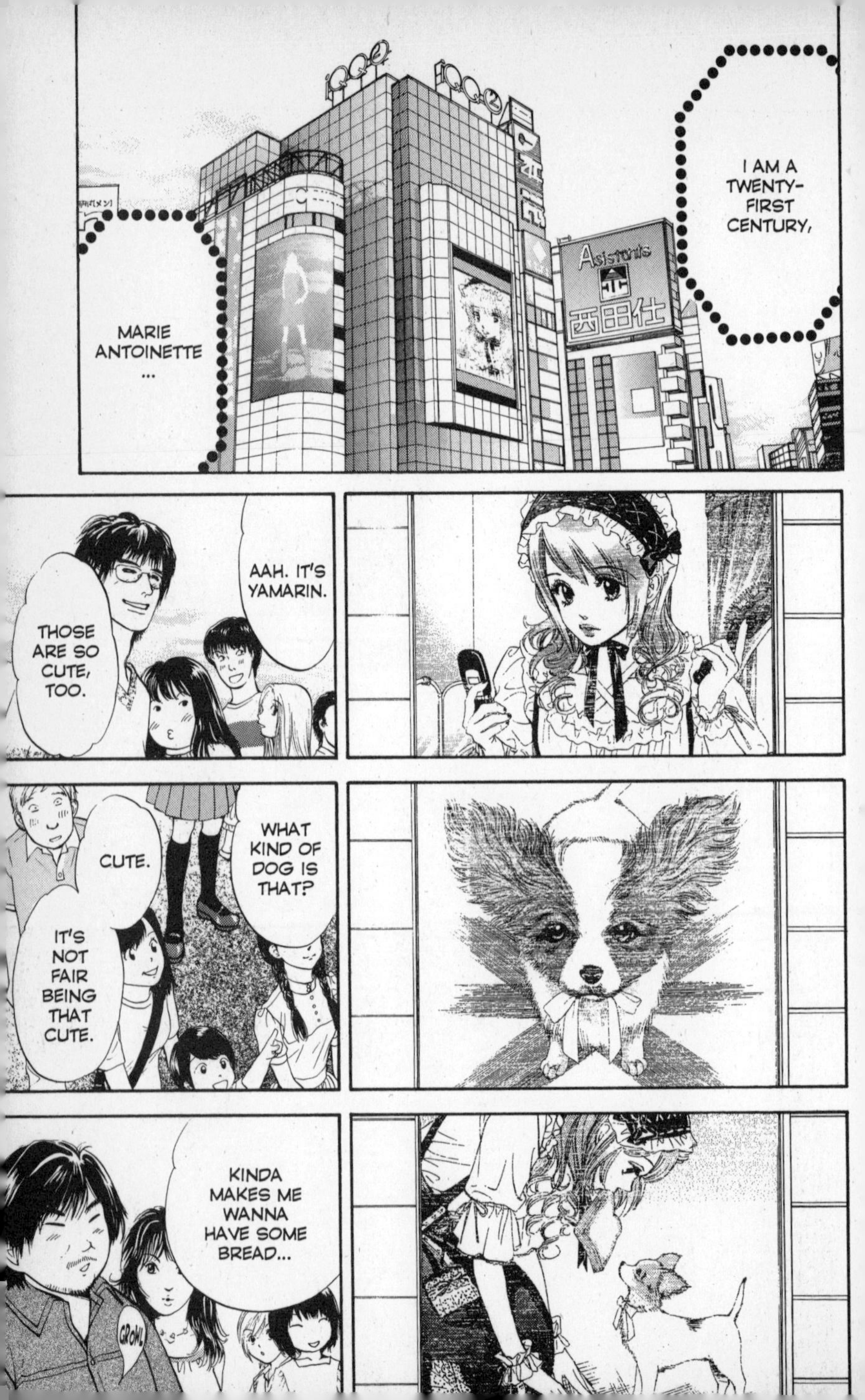
I AM A TWENTY-FIRST CENTURY,
MARIE ANTOINETTE ...
AAH. IT'S YAMARIN.
THOSE ARE SO CUTE, TOO.
WHAT KIND OF DOG IS THAT?
CUTE.
IT'S NOT FAIR BEING THAT CUTE.
KINDA MAKES ME WANNA HAVE SOME BREAD...
GROWL

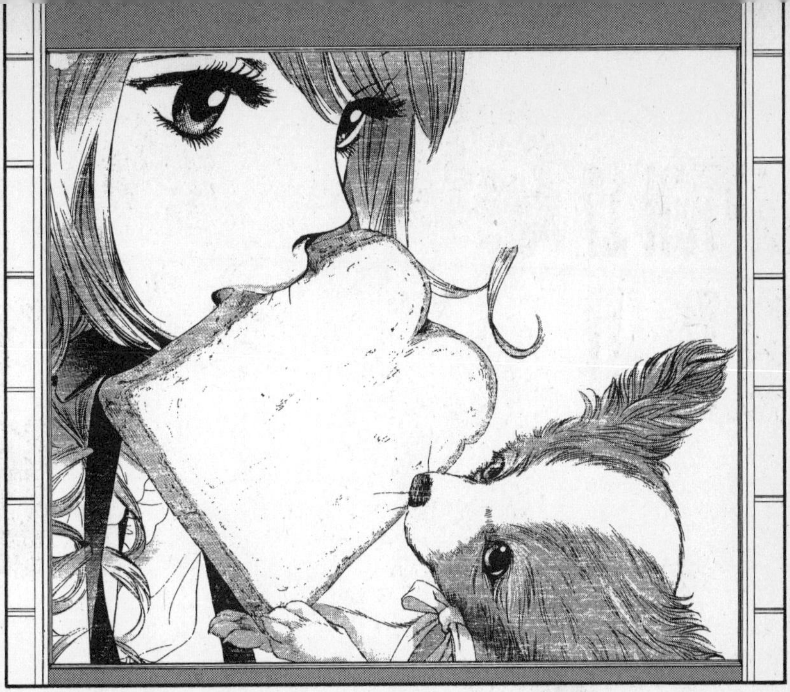

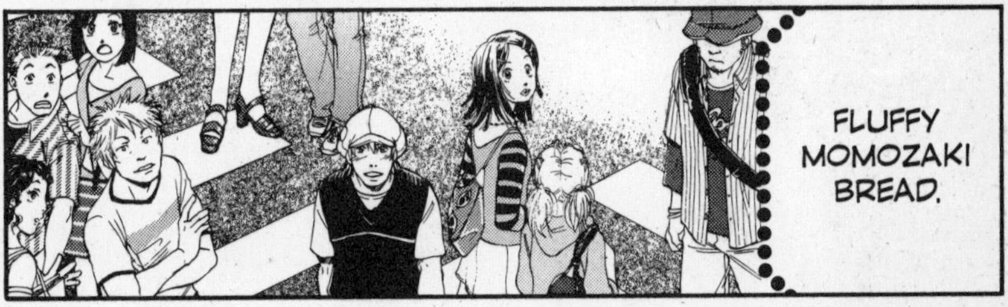
FLUFFY
MOMOZAKI
BREAD.

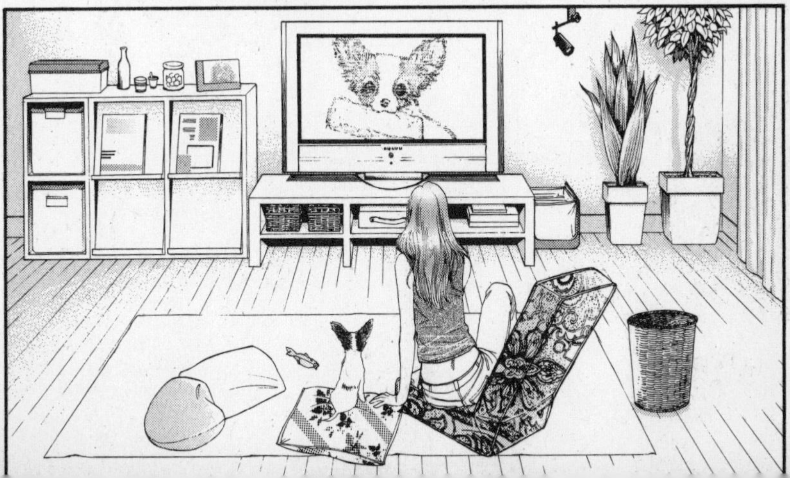

CHAPTER 17
HELP....!!

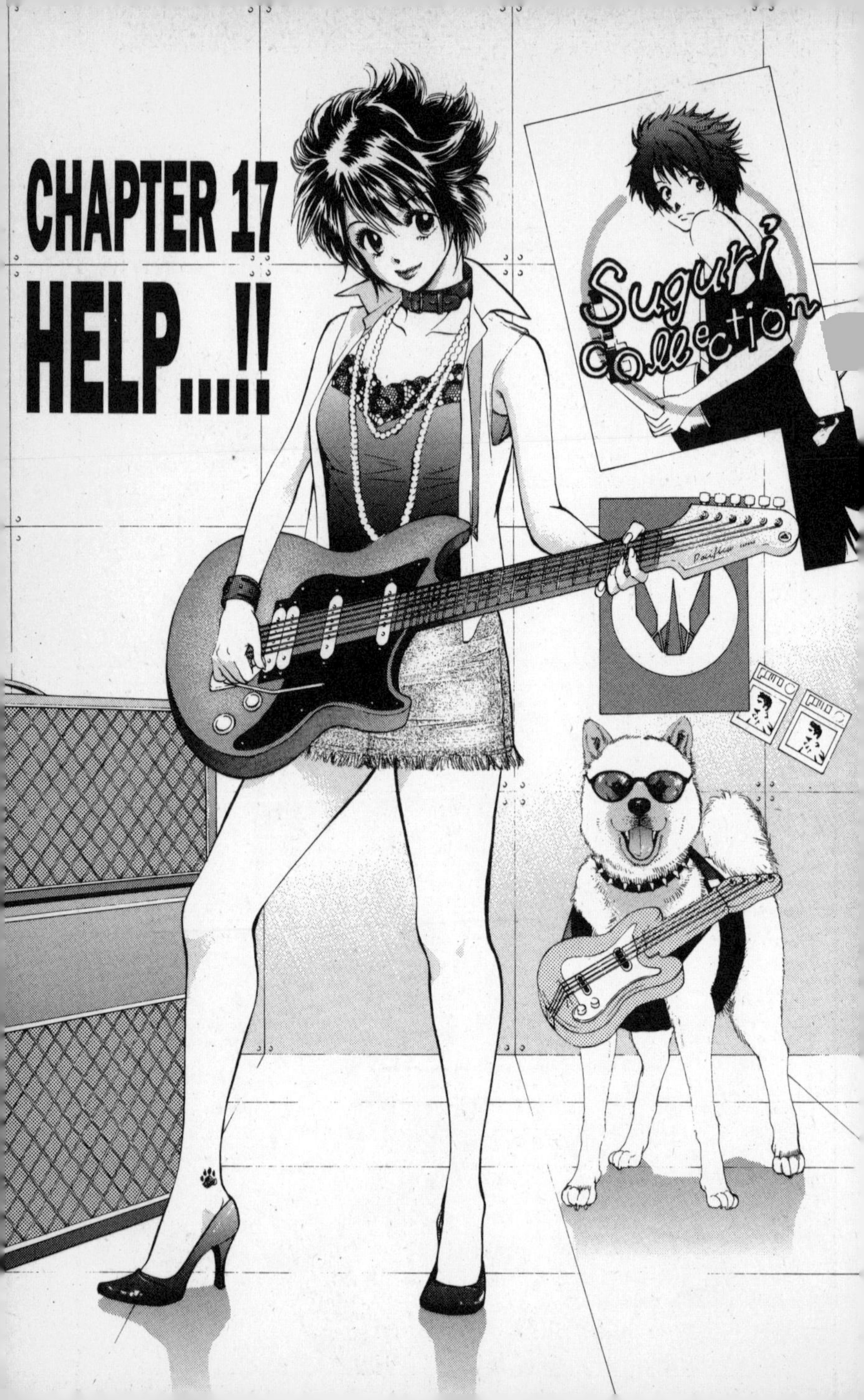
Suguri collection

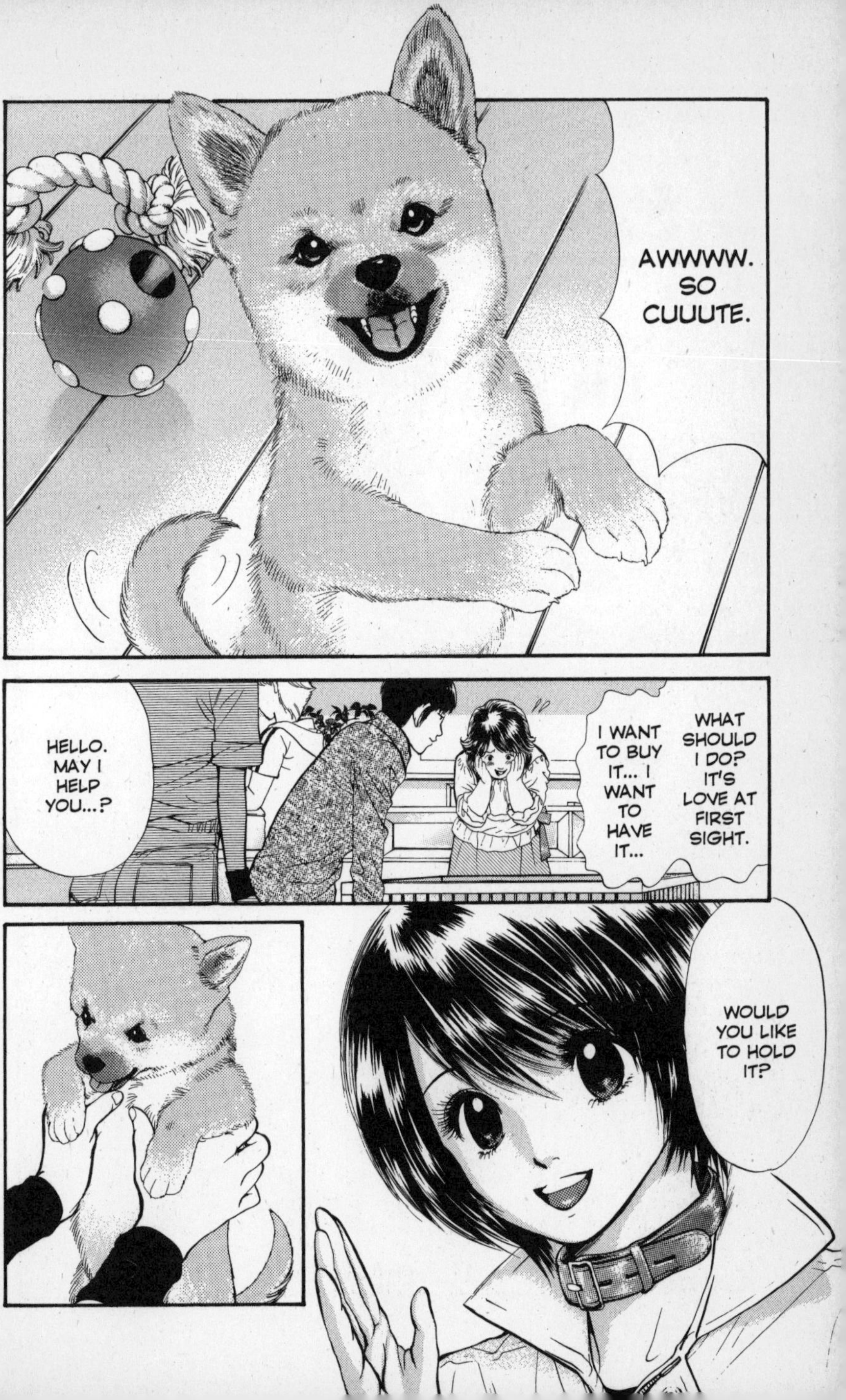
AWWWW. SO CUUUTE.
WHAT SHOULD I DO? IT'S LOVE AT FIRST SIGHT.
I WANT TO BUY IT... I WANT TO HAVE IT...
HELLO. MAY I HELP YOU...?
WOULD YOU LIKE TO HOLD IT?

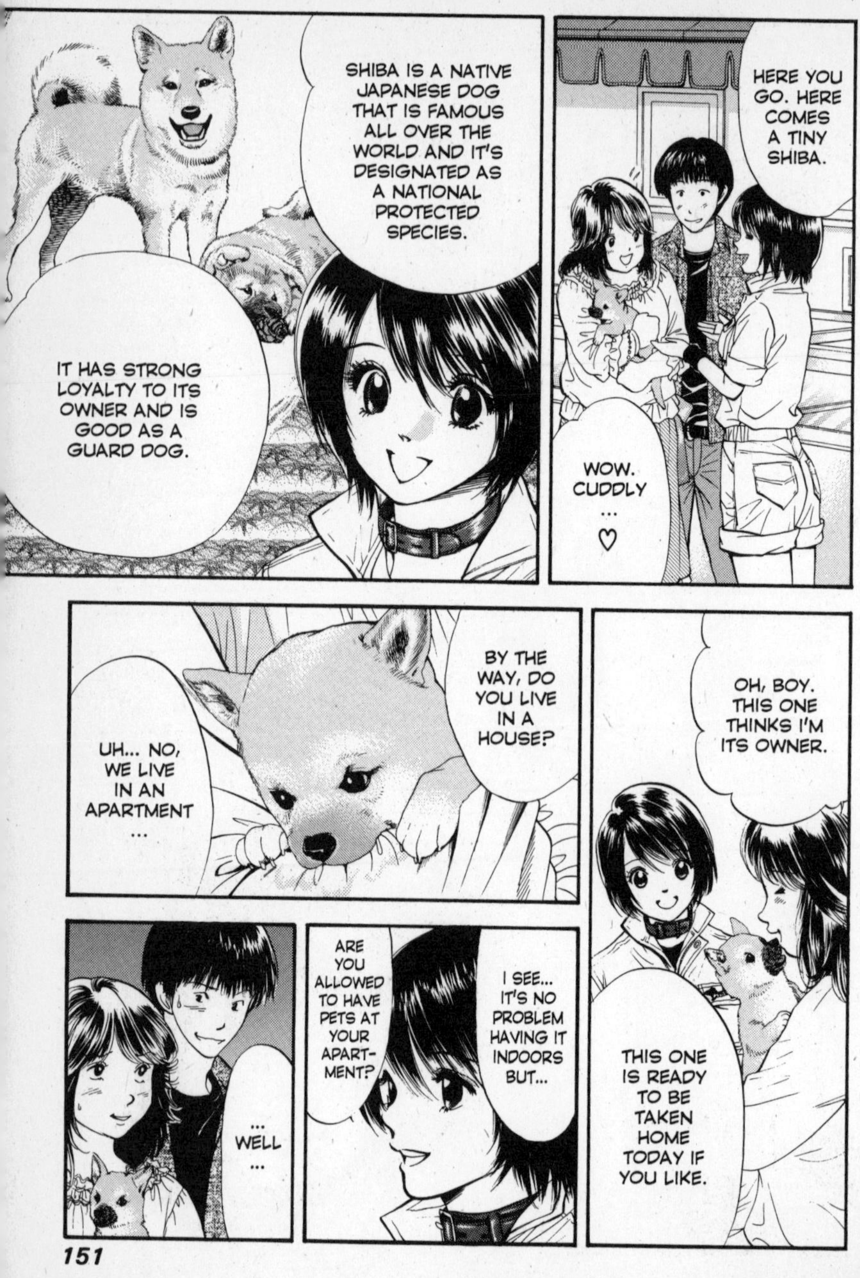
HERE YOU GO. HERE COMES A TINY SHIBA.
WOW. CUDDLY ... ♡
SHIBA IS A NATIVE JAPANESE DOG THAT IS FAMOUS ALL OVER THE WORLD AND IT'S DESIGNATED AS A NATIONAL PROTECTED SPECIES.
IT HAS STRONG LOYALTY TO ITS OWNER AND IS GOOD AS A GUARD DOG.
OH, BOY. THIS ONE THINKS I'M ITS OWNER.
THIS ONE IS READY TO BE TAKEN HOME TODAY IF YOU LIKE.
BY THE WAY, DO YOU LIVE IN A HOUSE?
UH... NO, WE LIVE IN AN APARTMENT ...
I SEE... IT'S NO PROBLEM HAVING IT INDOORS BUT...
ARE YOU ALLOWED TO HAVE PETS AT YOUR APART-MENT?
... WELL ...

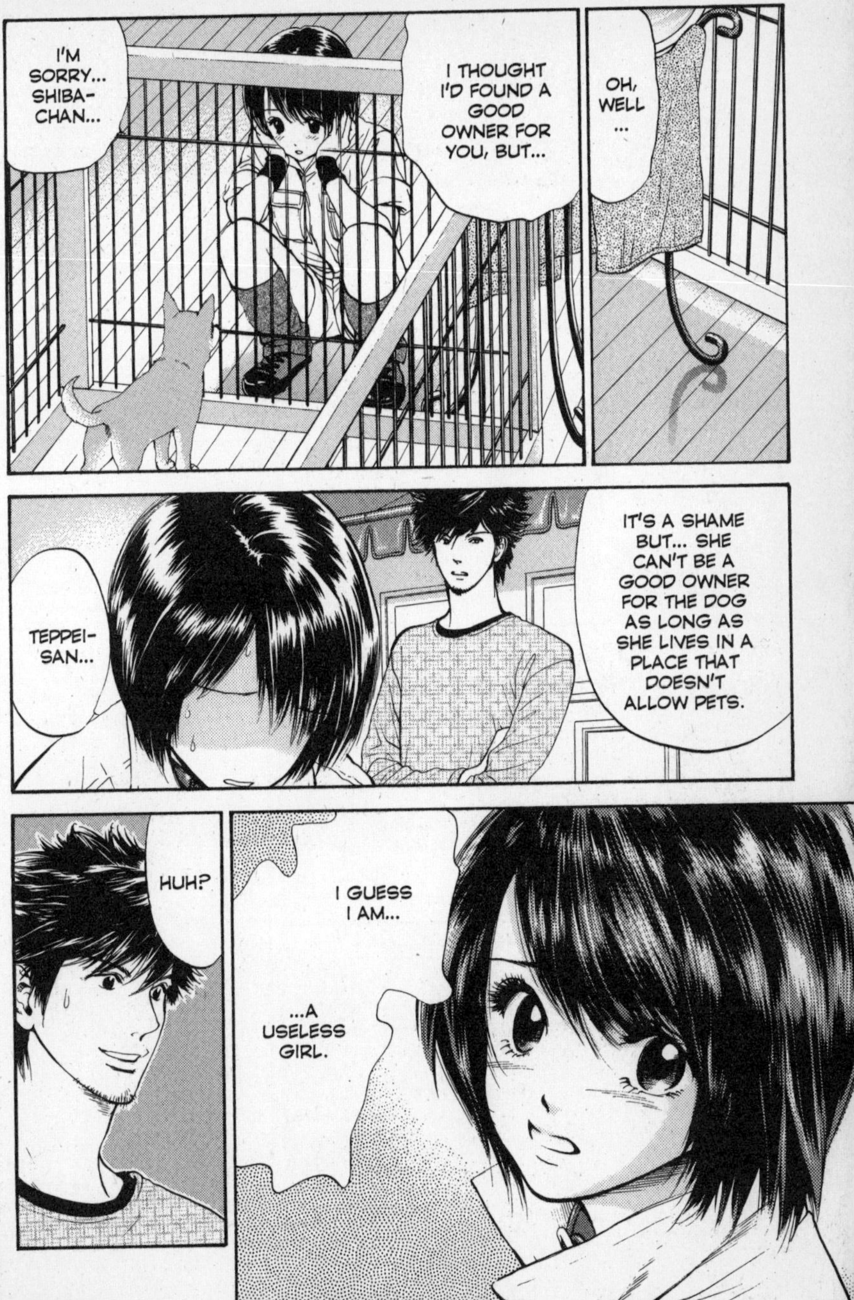
OH, WELL ...
I THOUGHT I'D FOUND A GOOD OWNER FOR YOU, BUT...
I'M SORRY... SHIBA-CHAN...
IT'S A SHAME BUT... SHE CAN'T BE A GOOD OWNER FOR THE DOG AS LONG AS SHE LIVES IN A PLACE THAT DOESN'T ALLOW PETS.
TEPPEI-SAN...
I GUESS I AM...
...A USELESS GIRL.
HUH?

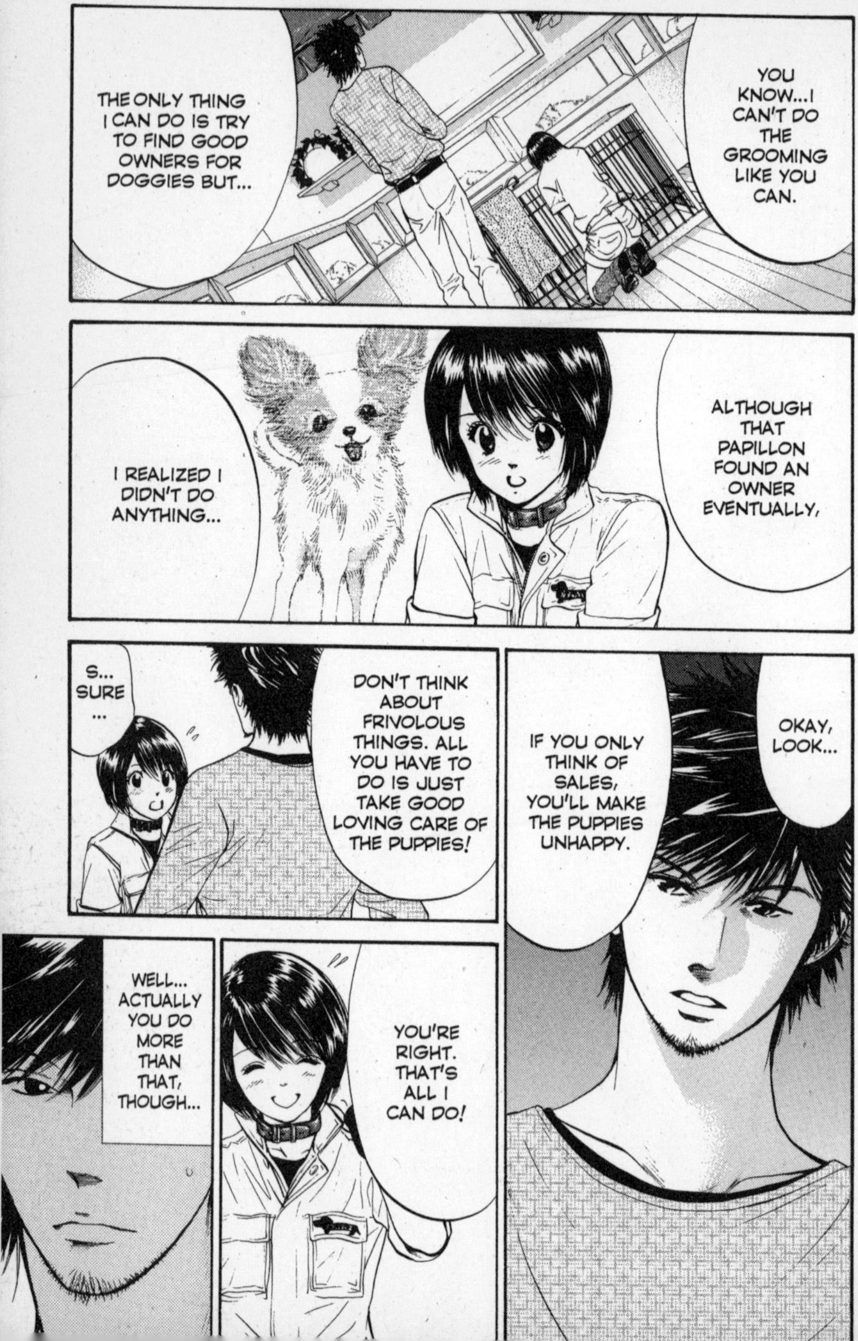
YOU KNOW...I CAN'T DO THE GROOMING LIKE YOU CAN.
THE ONLY THING I CAN DO IS TRY TO FIND GOOD OWNERS FOR DOGGIES BUT...
ALTHOUGH THAT PAPILLON FOUND AN OWNER EVENTUALLY,
I REALIZED I DIDN'T DO ANYTHING...
OKAY, LOOK...
IF YOU ONLY THINK OF SALES, YOU'LL MAKE THE PUPPIES UNHAPPY.
DON'T THINK ABOUT FRIVOLOUS THINGS. ALL YOU HAVE TO DO IS JUST TAKE GOOD LOVING CARE OF THE PUPPIES!
S... SURE ...
YOU'RE RIGHT. THAT'S ALL I CAN DO!
WELL... ACTUALLY YOU DO MORE THAN THAT, THOUGH...

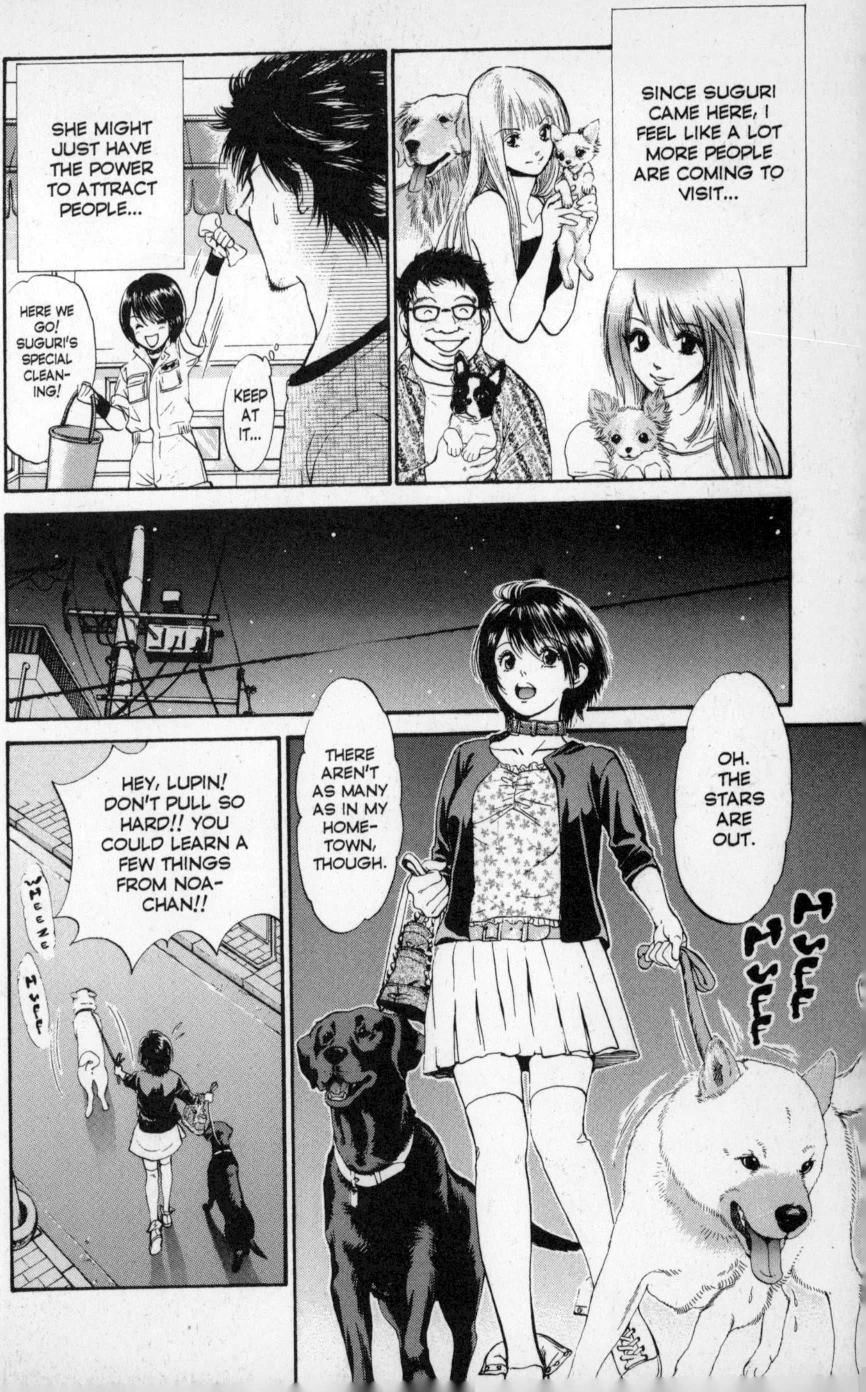
SINCE SUGURI CAME HERE, I FEEL LIKE A LOT MORE PEOPLE ARE COMING TO VISIT...
SHE MIGHT JUST HAVE THE POWER TO ATTRACT PEOPLE...
HERE WE GO! SUGURI'S SPECIAL CLEANING!
KEEP AT IT...
OH. THE STARS ARE OUT.
THERE AREN'T AS MANY AS IN MY HOME-TOWN, THOUGH.
HUFF HUFF
HEY, LUPIN! DON'T PULL SO HARD!! YOU COULD LEARN A FEW THINGS FROM NOA-CHAN!!
WHEEZE
HUFF

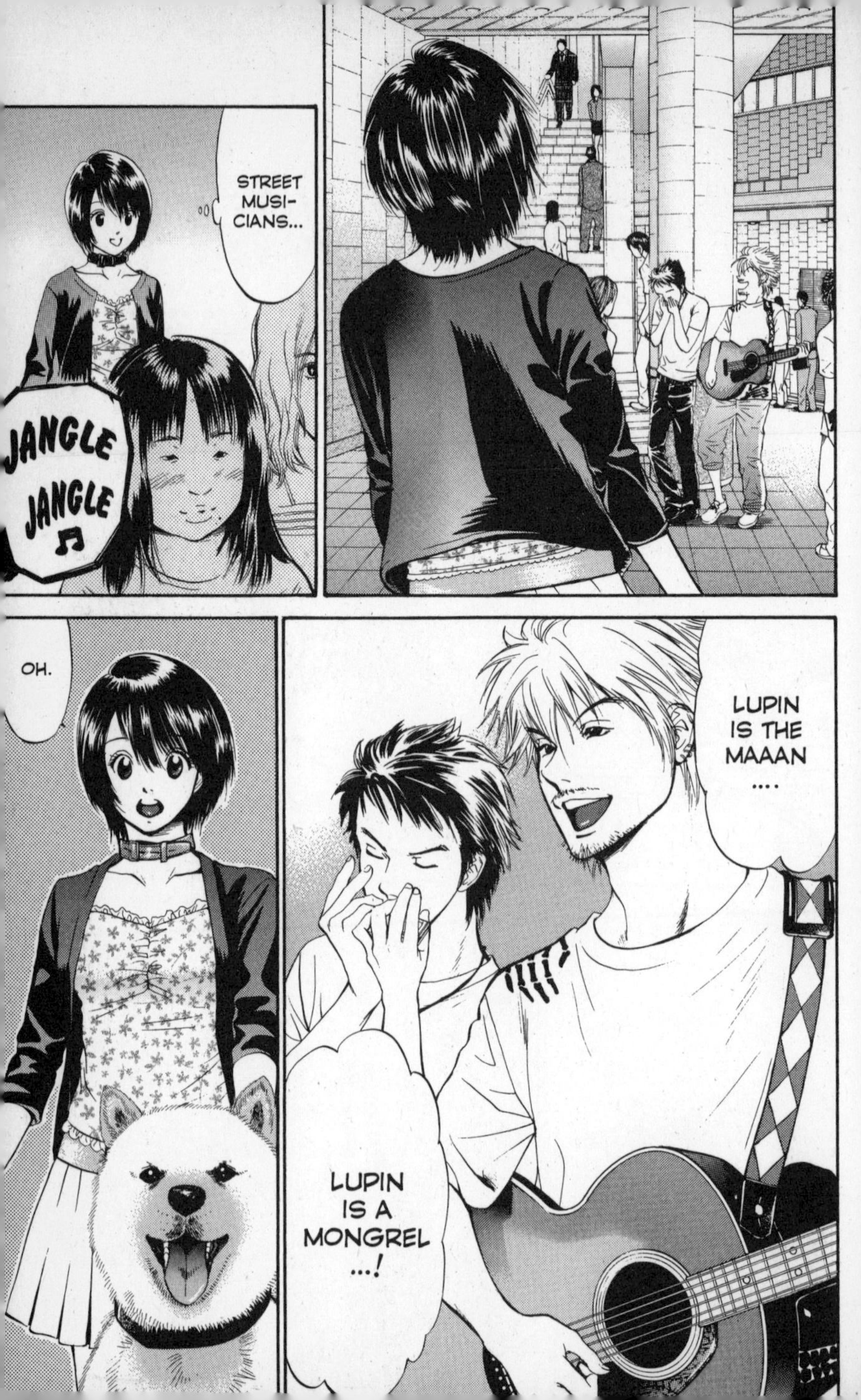
STREET MUSI-CIANS...
JANGLE JANGLE ♫
LUPIN IS THE MAAAN ....
LUPIN IS A MONGREL ...!
OH.

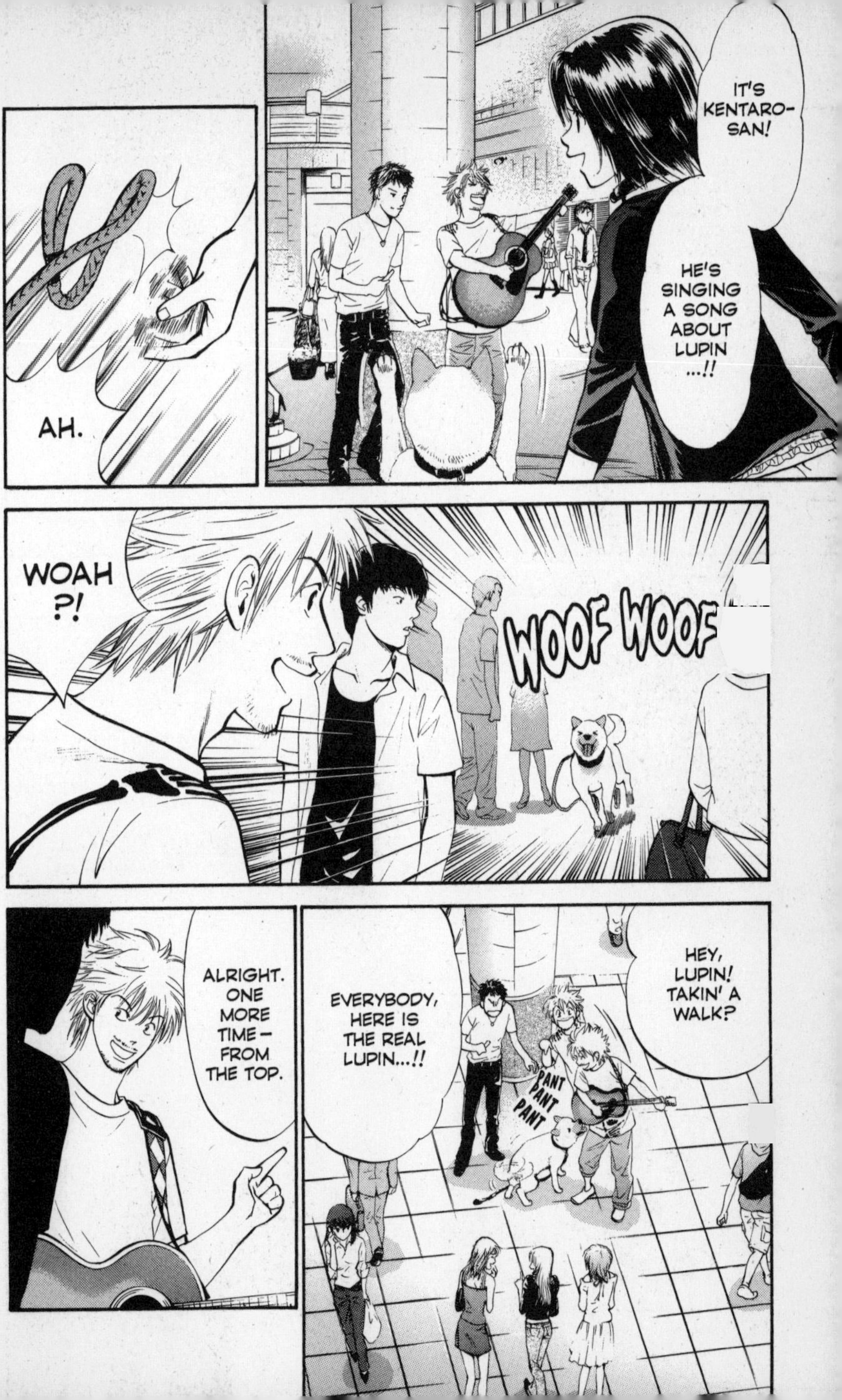
IT'S KENTARO-SAN!
HE'S SINGING A SONG ABOUT LUPIN ...!!
AH.
WOOF WOOF
WOAH ?!
HEY, LUPIN! TAKIN' A WALK?
PANT PANT PANT
EVERYBODY, HERE IS THE REAL LUPIN...!!
ALRIGHT. ONE MORE TIME— FROM THE TOP.

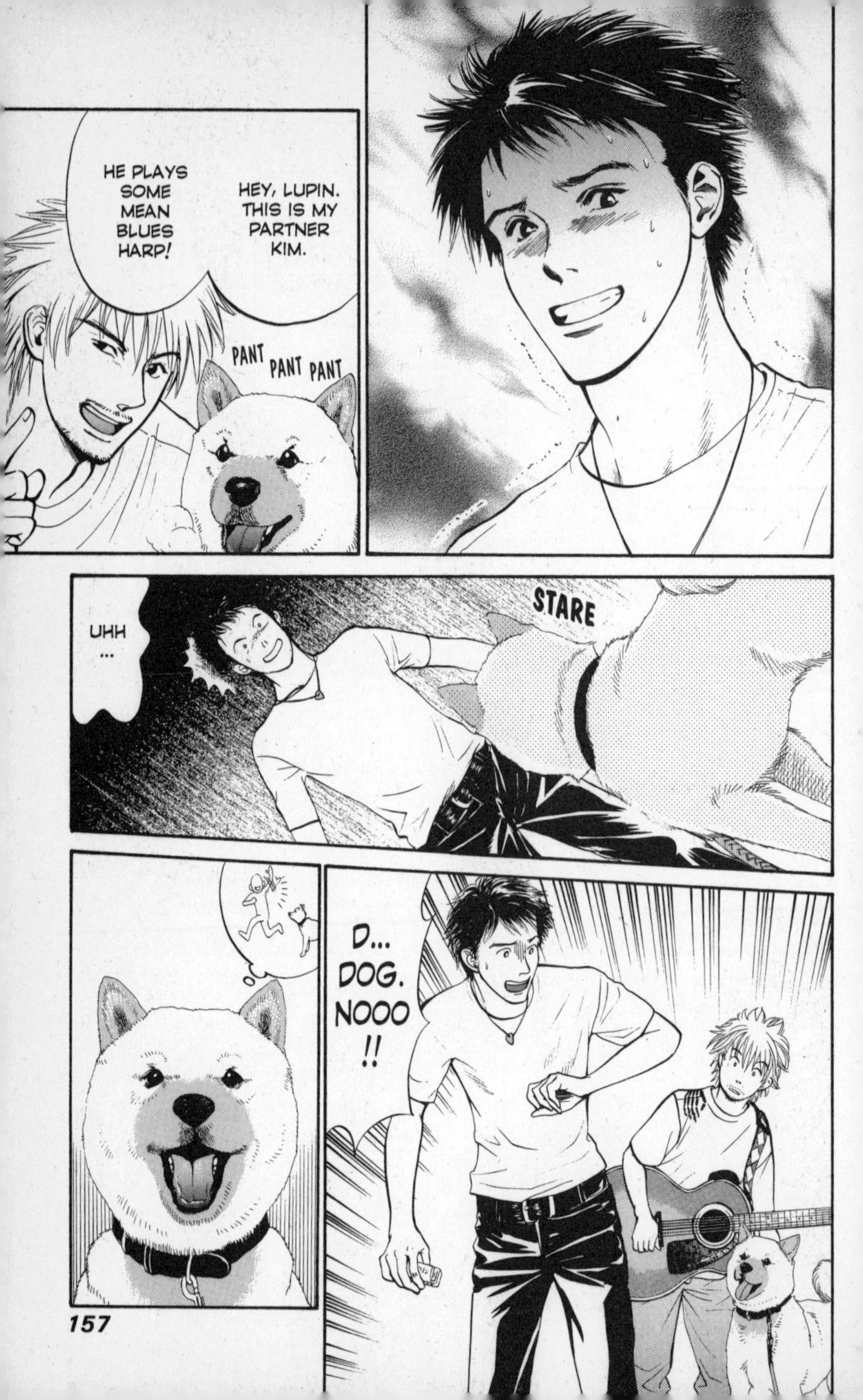
HEY, LUPIN. THIS IS MY PARTNER KIM.
HE PLAYS SOME MEAN BLUES HARP!
PANT PANT PANT
STARE
UHH ...
D... DOG. NOOO !!

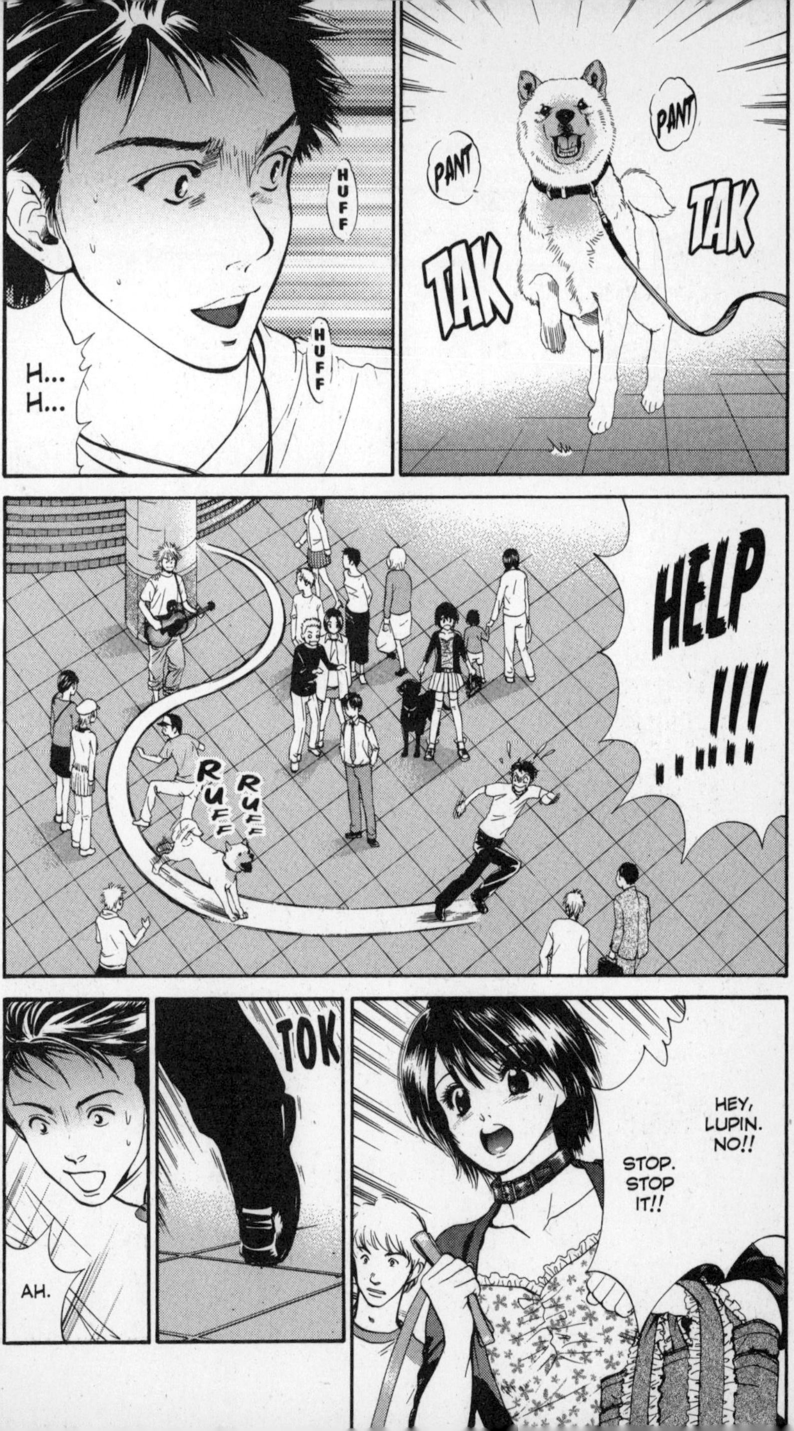
PANT
PANT
TAK
TAK
HUFF
HUFF
H...
H...
HELP ...!!!
RUFF
RUFF
HEY, LUPIN. NO!!
STOP. STOP IT!!
TOK
AH.

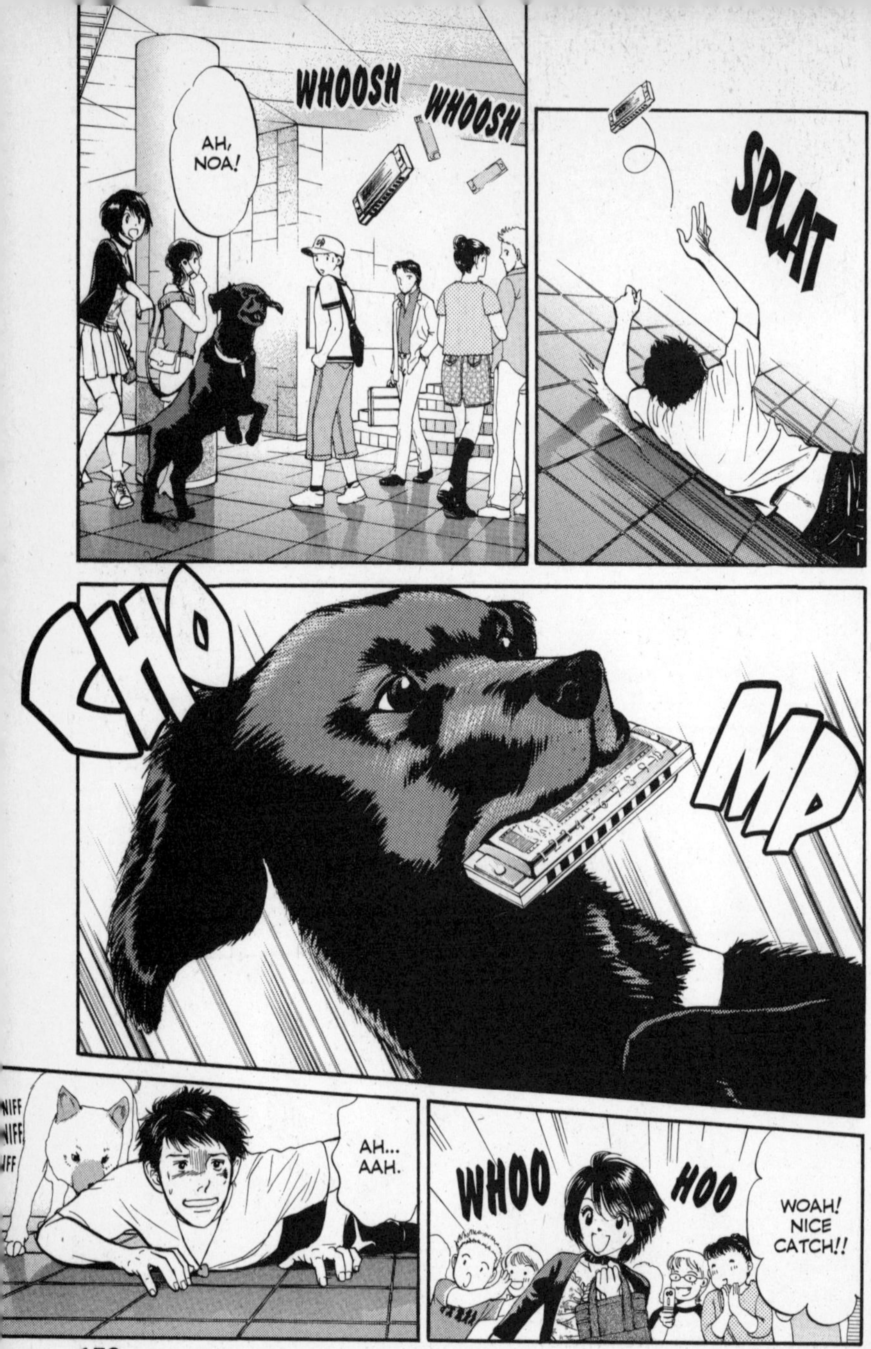
SPLAT
WHOOSH
WHOOSH
AH, NOA!
CHOMP
WHOO
HOO
WOAH! NICE CATCH!!
AH... AAH.
NIFF
NIFF
IFF

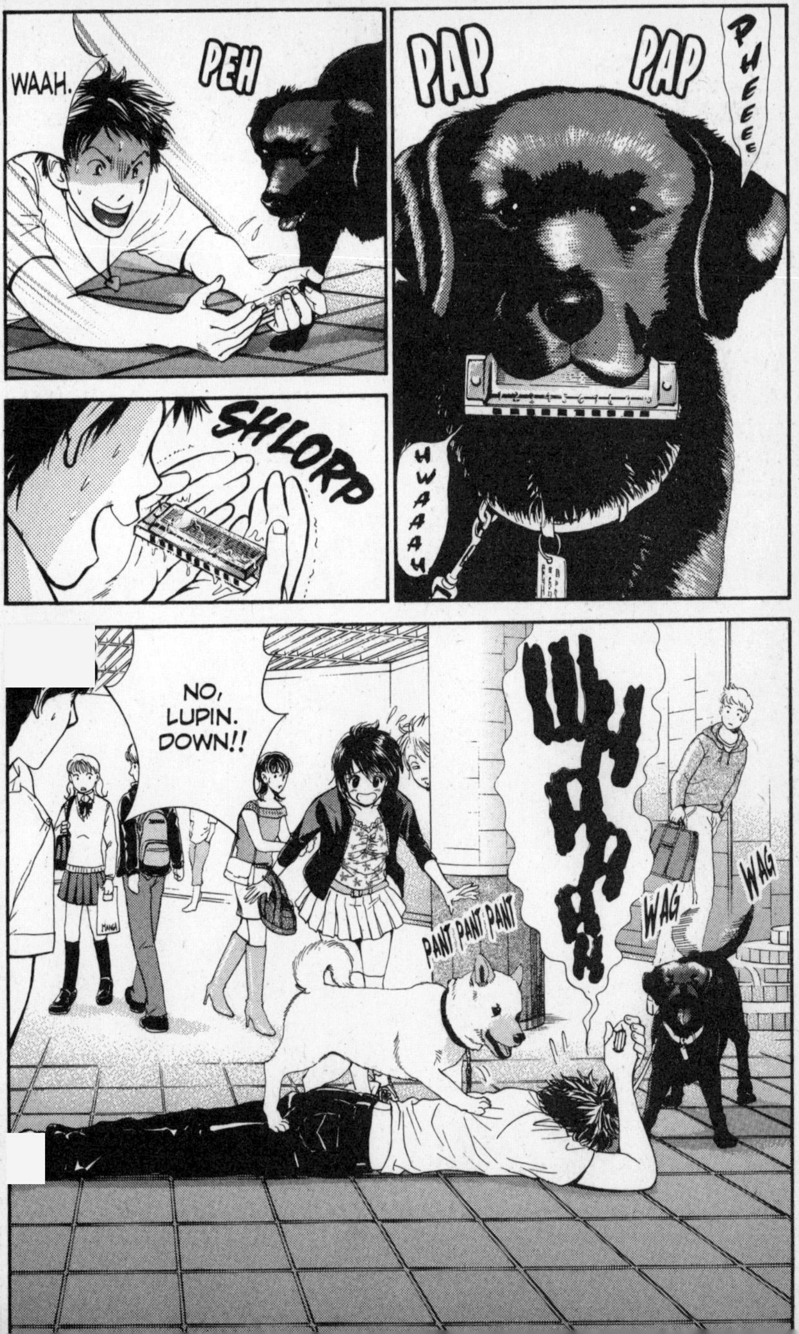
PAP
PAP
PHEEEE
HWAAAAH
PEH
WAAH.
SHLORP
WAG
WAG
WHAAH
PANT PANT PANT
NO, LUPIN. DOWN!!

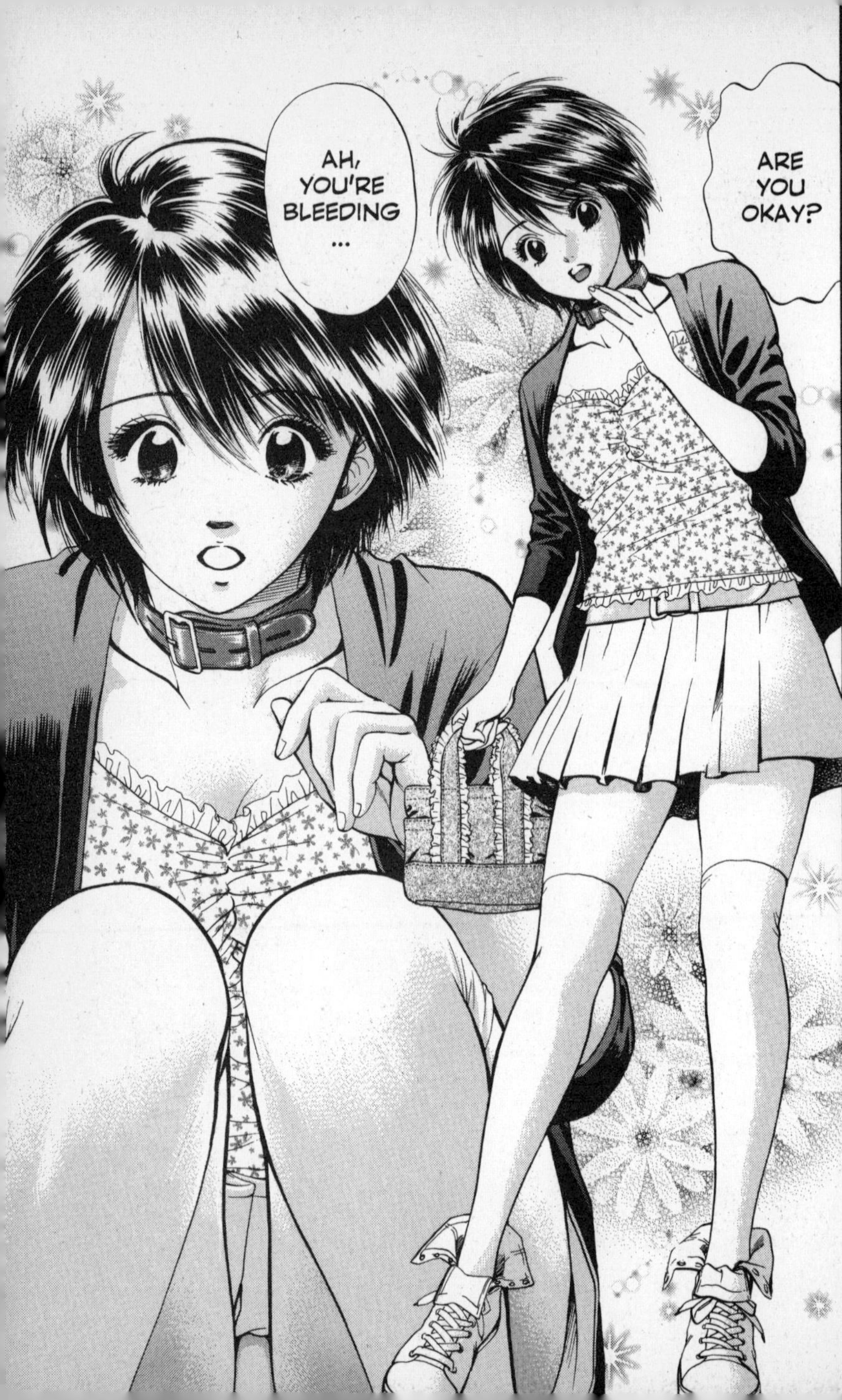
ARE YOU OKAY?
AH, YOU'RE BLEEDING ...

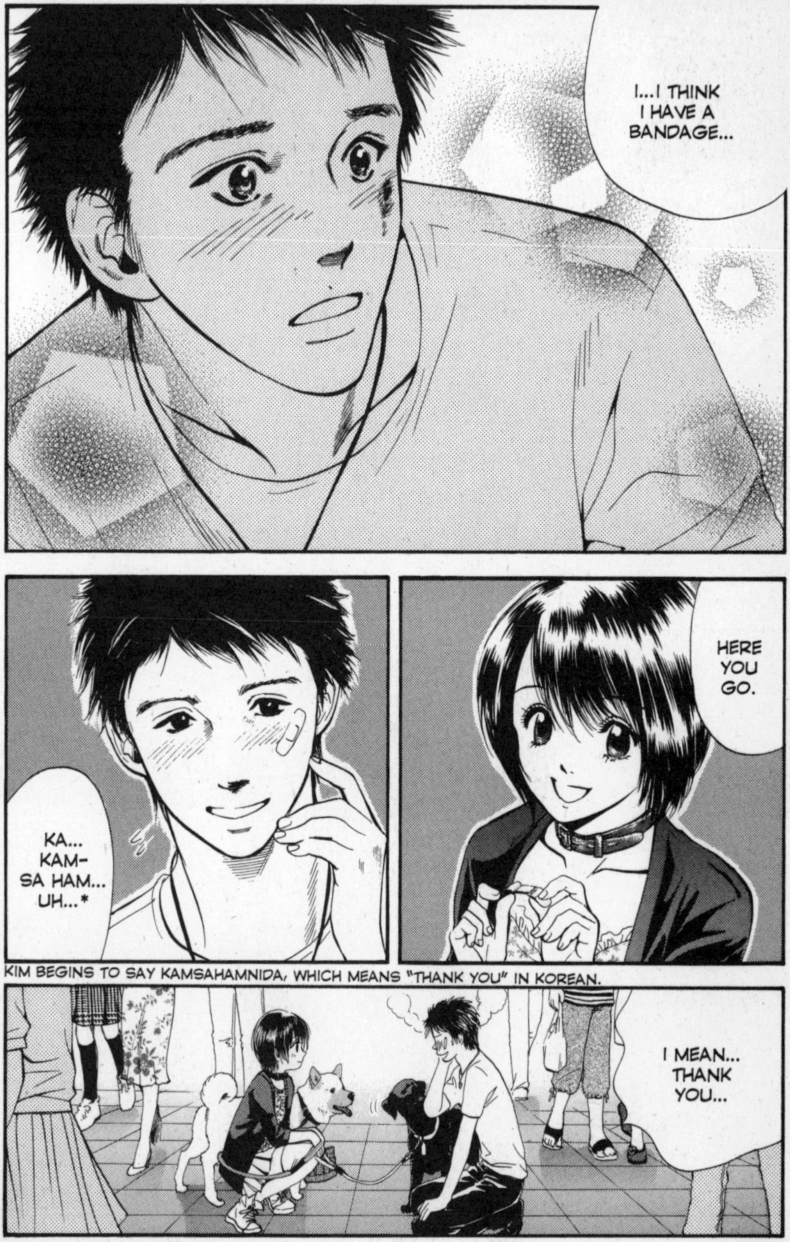

I...I THINK I HAVE A BANDAGE...
HERE YOU GO.
KA... KAM-SA HAM... UH...*
I MEAN... THANK YOU...

KIM BEGINS TO SAY KAMSAHAMNIDA, WHICH MEANS "THANK YOU" IN KOREAN.

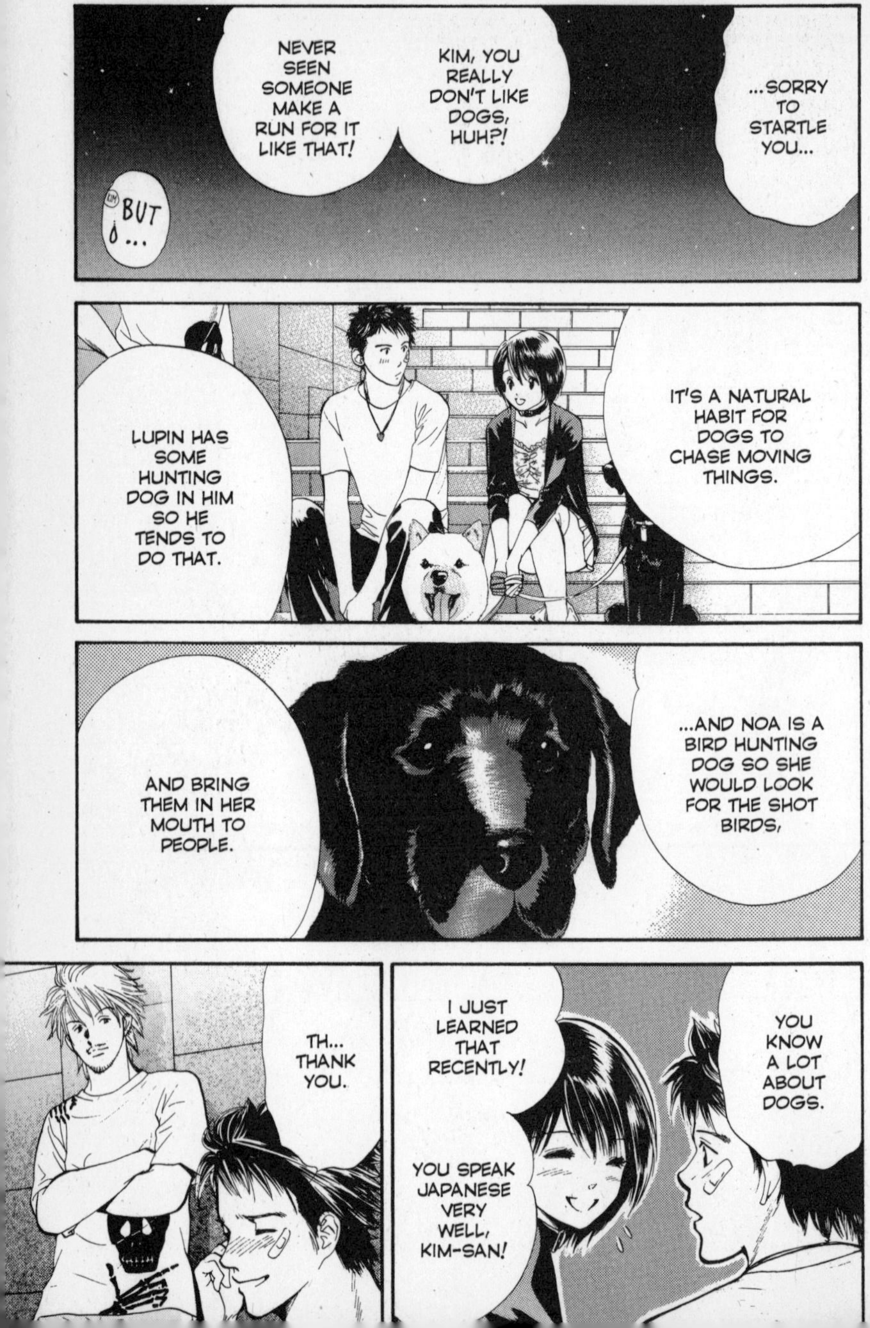
...SORRY TO STARTLE YOU...
KIM, YOU REALLY DON'T LIKE DOGS, HUH?!
NEVER SEEN SOMEONE MAKE A RUN FOR IT LIKE THAT!
KIM
BUT...
IT'S A NATURAL HABIT FOR DOGS TO CHASE MOVING THINGS.
LUPIN HAS SOME HUNTING DOG IN HIM SO HE TENDS TO DO THAT.
...AND NOA IS A BIRD HUNTING DOG SO SHE WOULD LOOK FOR THE SHOT BIRDS,
AND BRING THEM IN HER MOUTH TO PEOPLE.
YOU KNOW A LOT ABOUT DOGS.
I JUST LEARNED THAT RECENTLY!
YOU SPEAK JAPANESE VERY WELL, KIM-SAN!
TH... THANK YOU.

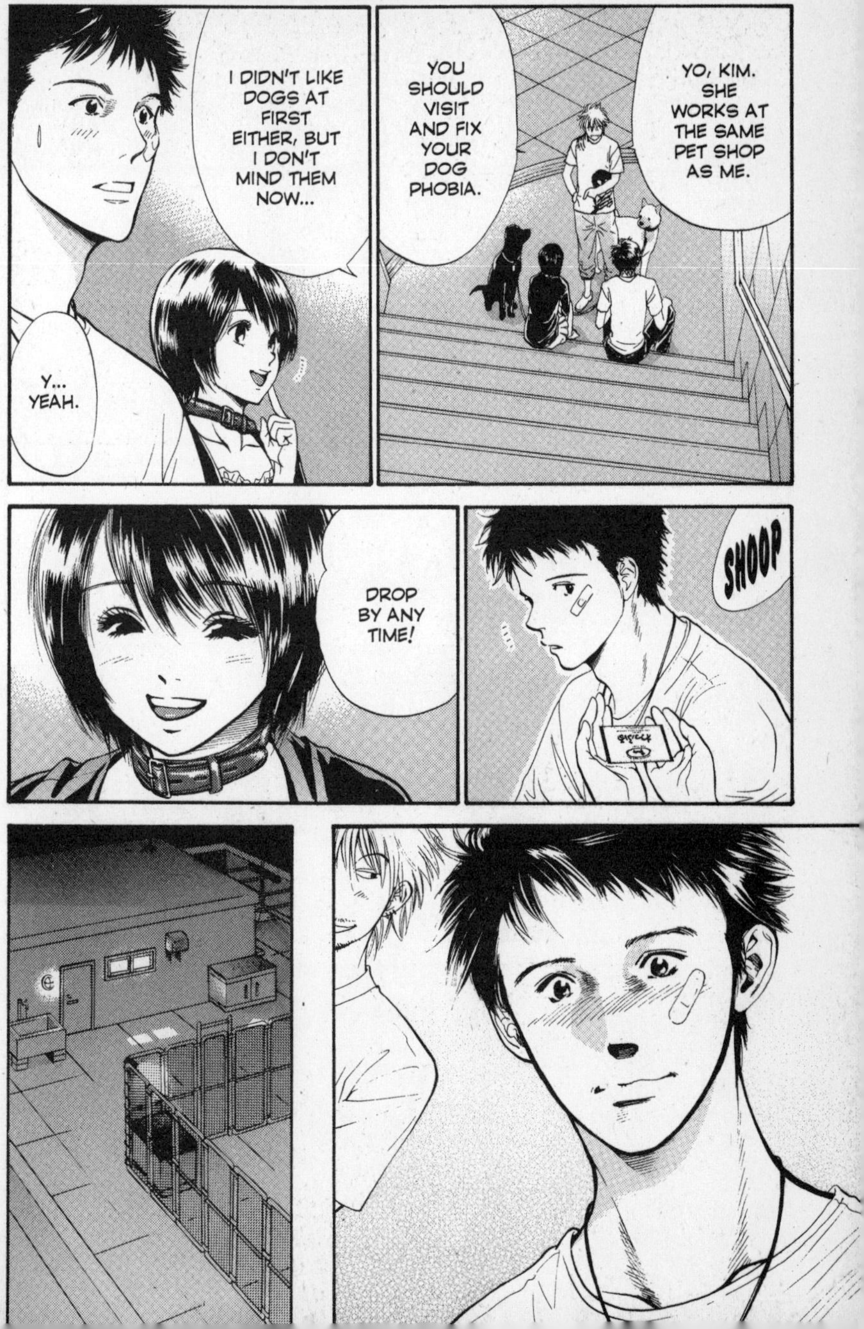
YO, KIM. SHE WORKS AT THE SAME PET SHOP AS ME.
YOU SHOULD VISIT AND FIX YOUR DOG PHOBIA.
I DIDN'T LIKE DOGS AT FIRST EITHER, BUT I DON'T MIND THEM NOW...
Y... YEAH.
SHOOP
DROP BY ANY TIME!

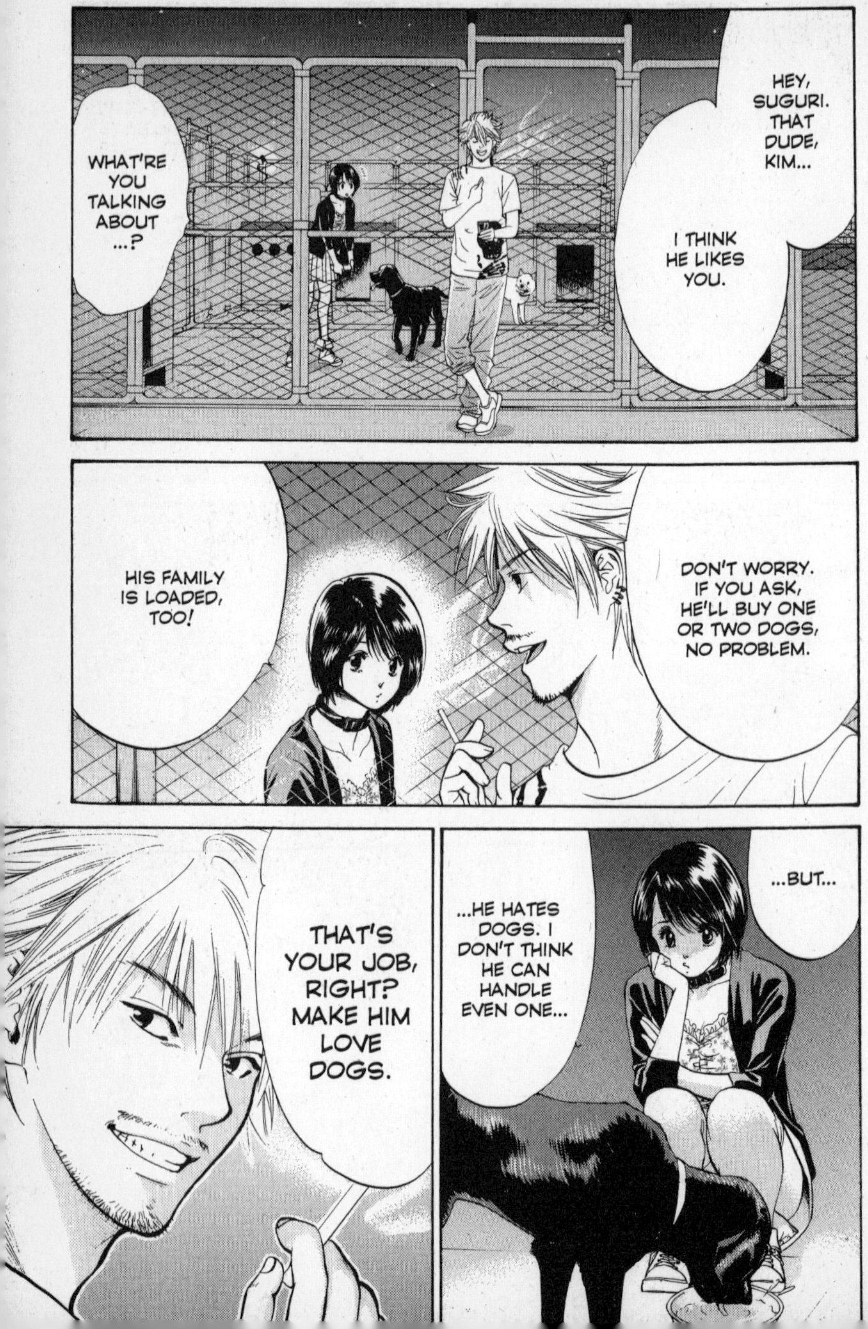
HEY, SUGURI. THAT DUDE, KIM...
I THINK HE LIKES YOU.
WHAT'RE YOU TALKING ABOUT ...?
DON'T WORRY. IF YOU ASK, HE'LL BUY ONE OR TWO DOGS, NO PROBLEM.
HIS FAMILY IS LOADED, TOO!
...BUT...
...HE HATES DOGS. I DON'T THINK HE CAN HANDLE EVEN ONE...
THAT'S YOUR JOB, RIGHT? MAKE HIM LOVE DOGS.

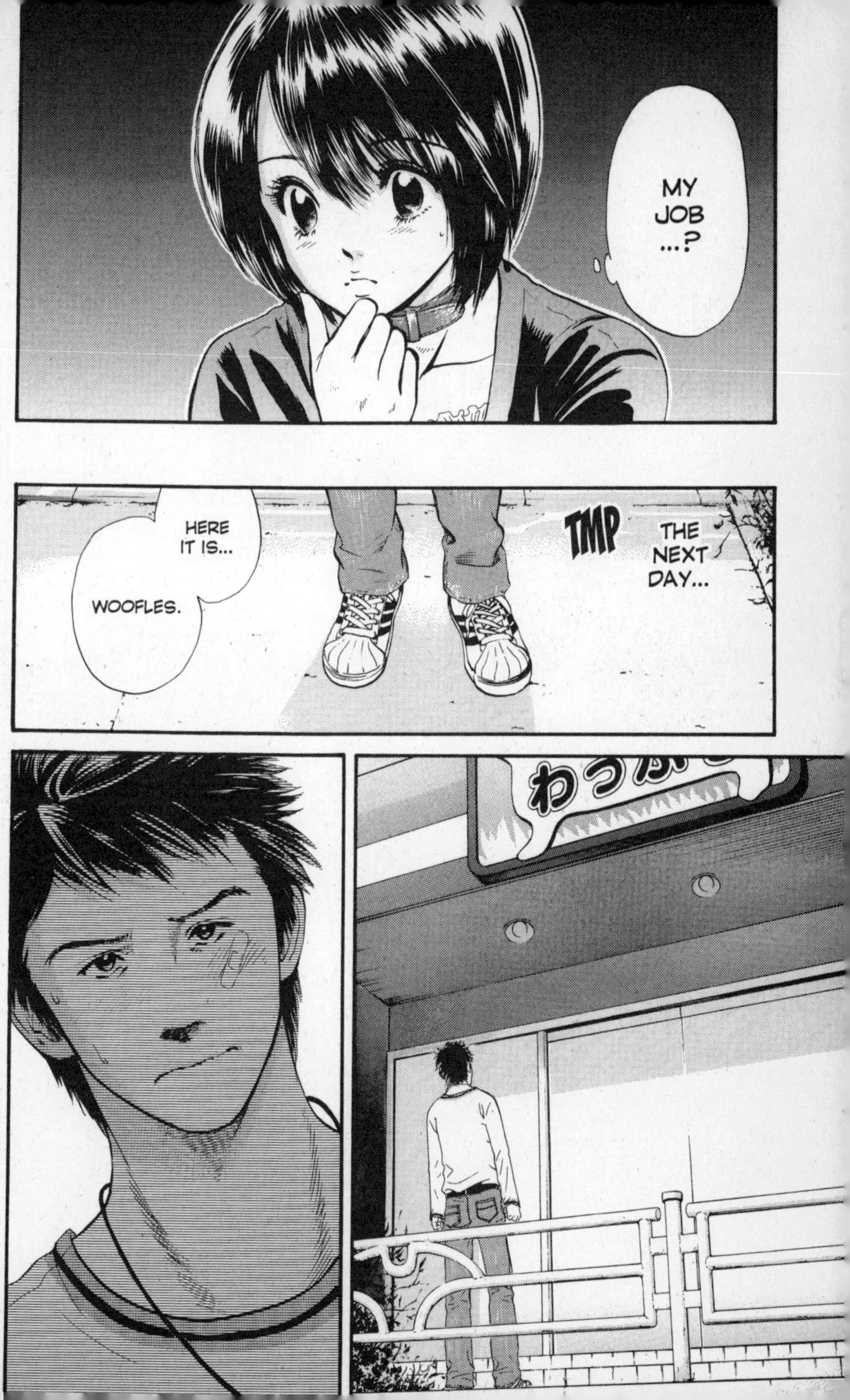
MY JOB ...?
THE NEXT DAY...
TMP
HERE IT IS...
WOOFLES.
わっふ

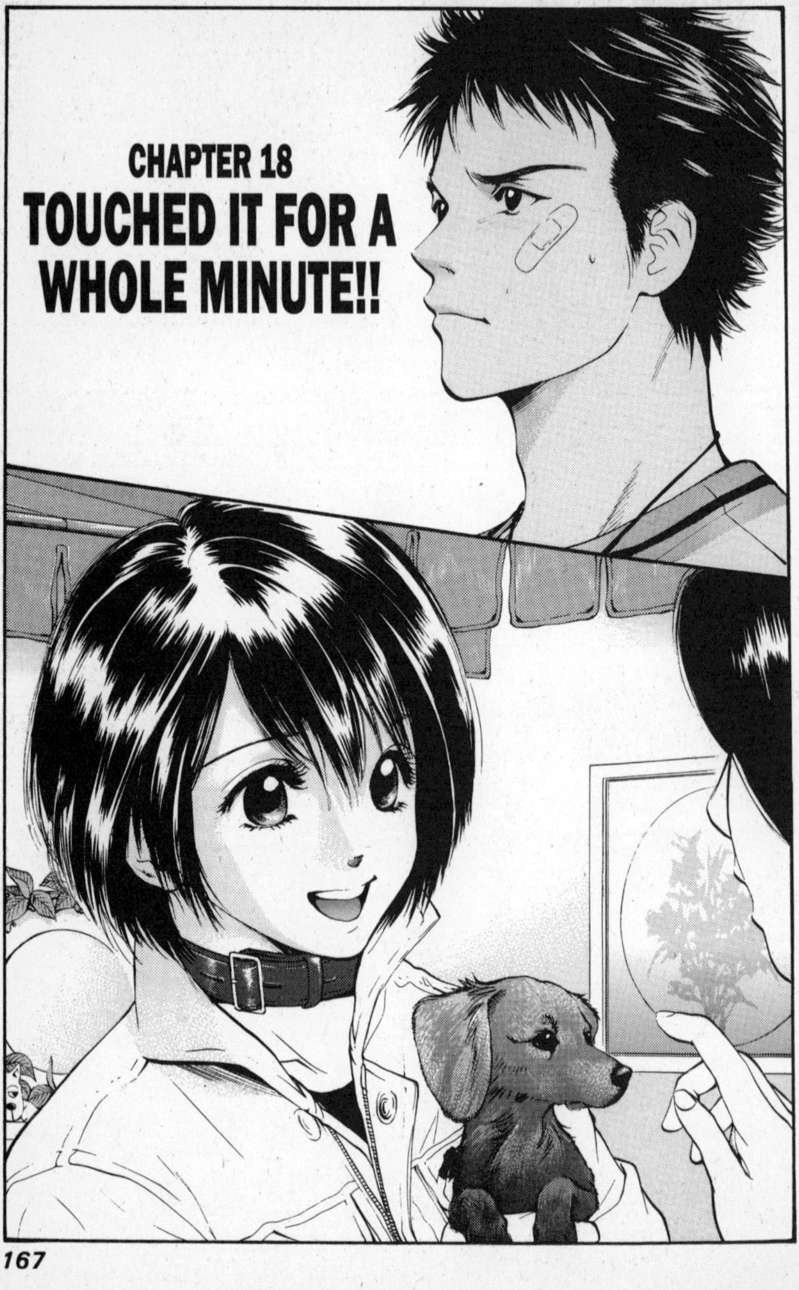
CHAPTER 18
TOUCHED IT FOR A WHOLE MINUTE!!

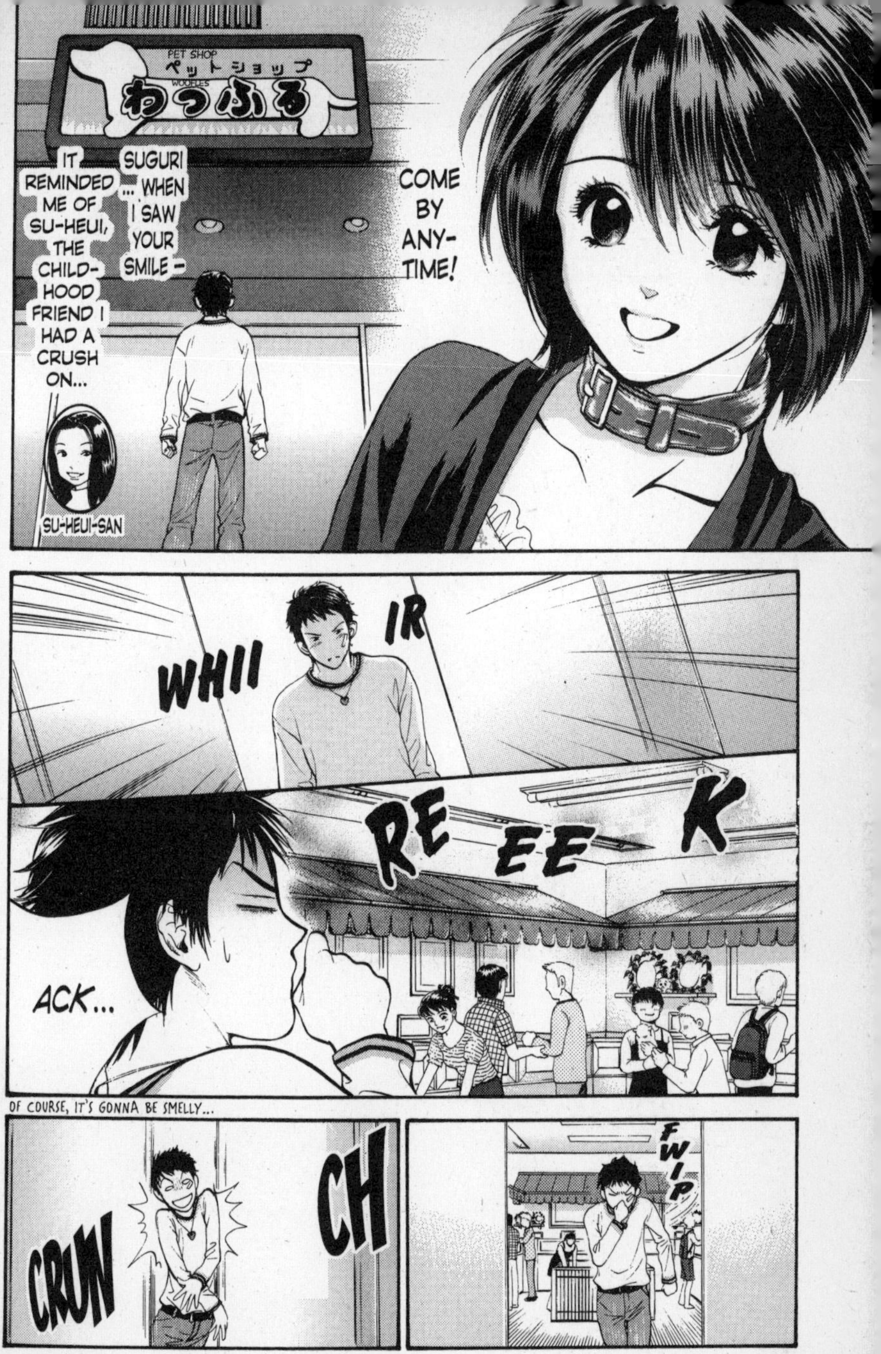
PET SHOP
ペットショップ
WOOFLES
わっふる
COME BY ANY-TIME!
SUGURI ... WHEN I SAW YOUR SMILE –
IT REMINDED ME OF SU-HEUI, THE CHILD-HOOD FRIEND I HAD A CRUSH ON...
SU-HEUI-SAN
WHIIR
REEEK
ACK...
OF COURSE, IT'S GONNA BE SMELLY...
FWIP
CRUNCH

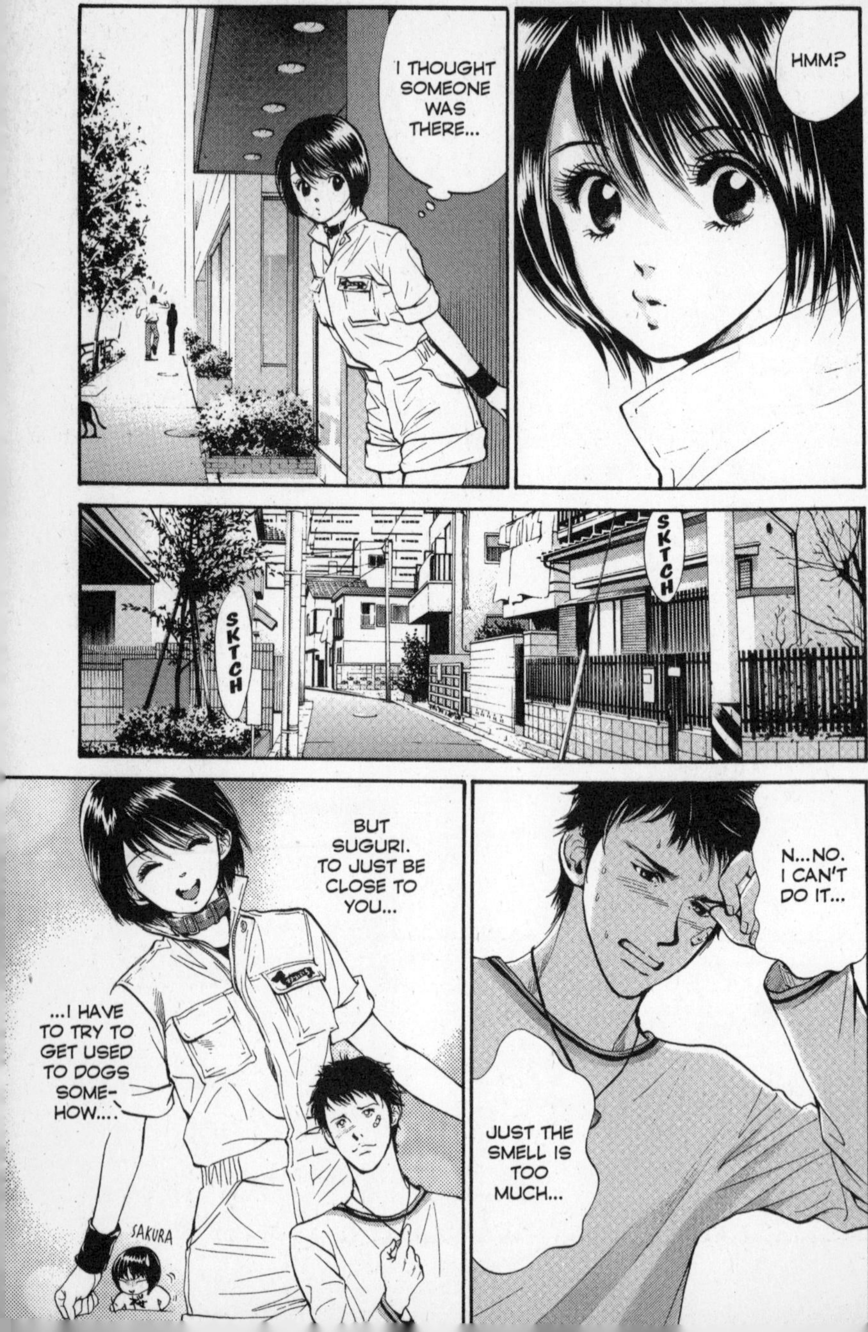
HMM?
I THOUGHT SOMEONE WAS THERE...
SKTCH
SKTCH
N...NO. I CAN'T DO IT...
JUST THE SMELL IS TOO MUCH...
BUT SUGURI. TO JUST BE CLOSE TO YOU...
...I HAVE TO TRY TO GET USED TO DOGS SOME-HOW....
SAKURA

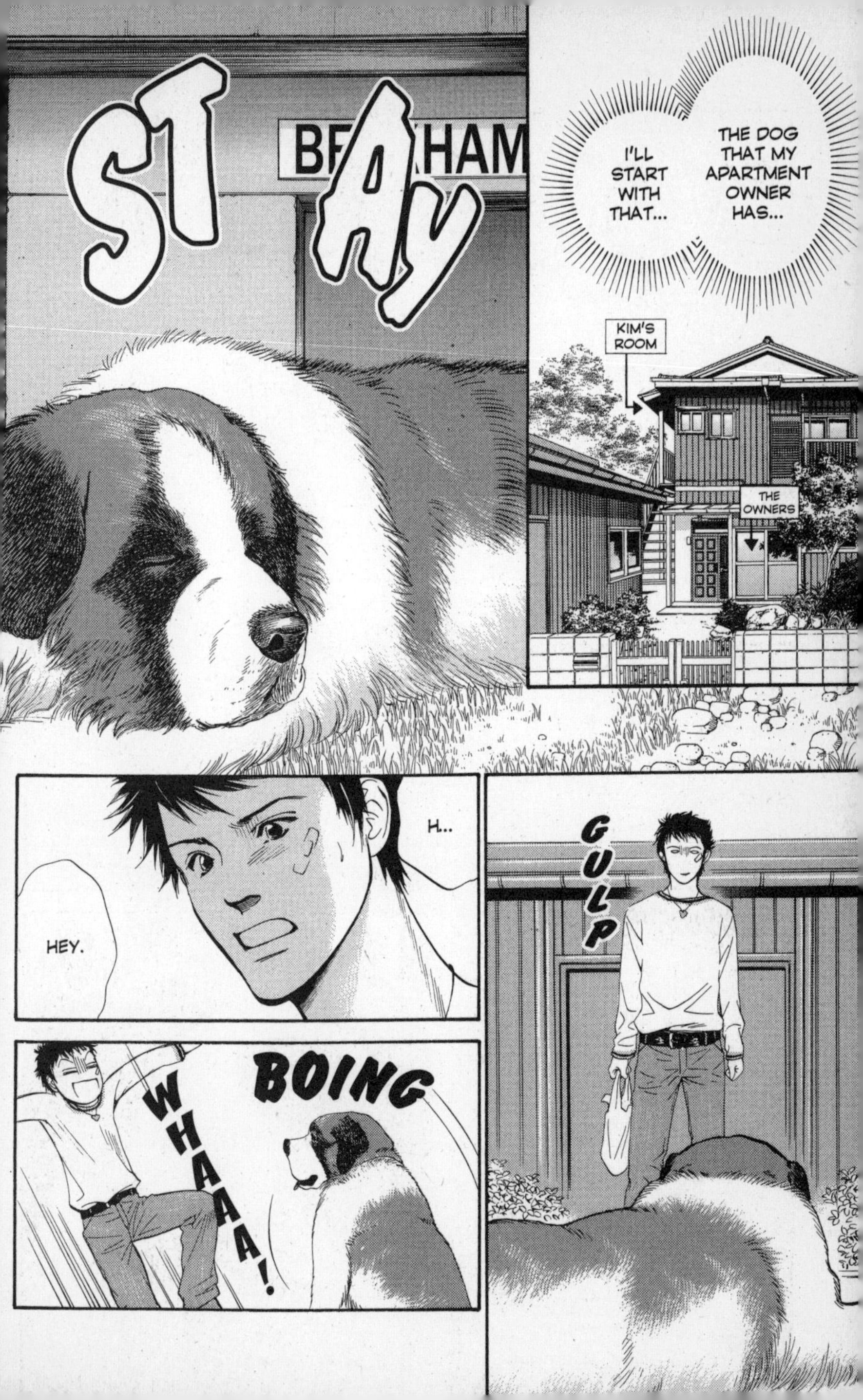
THE DOG THAT MY APARTMENT OWNER HAS...
I'LL START WITH THAT...
KIM'S ROOM
THE OWNERS
STAY
GULP
H..
HEY.
BOING
WHAAA!

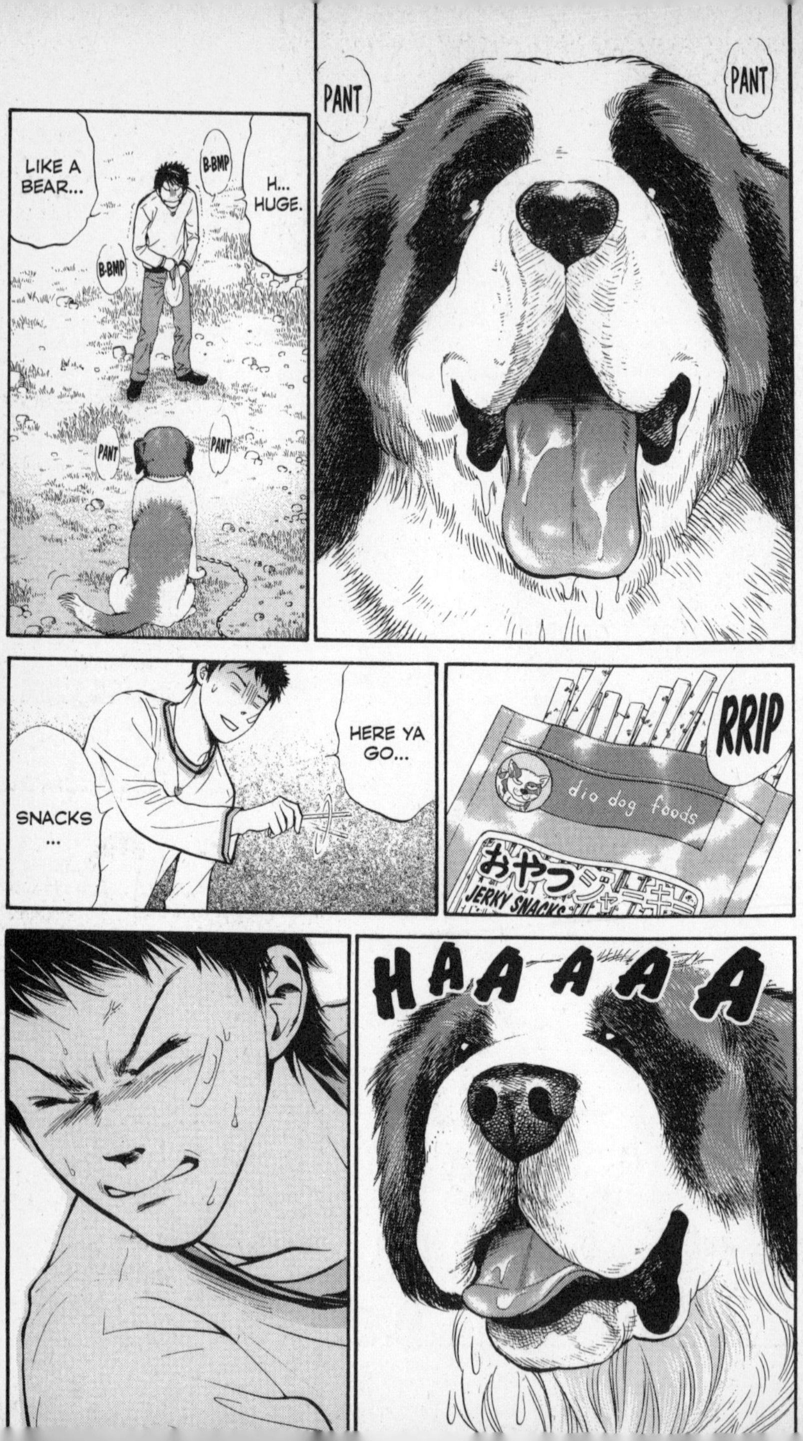
PANT
PANT
H... HUGE.
B-BMP
LIKE A BEAR...
B-BMP
PANT
PANT
RRIP
dio dog foods
おやつ
JERKY SNACKS
HERE YA GO...
SNACKS ...
HAAAAA

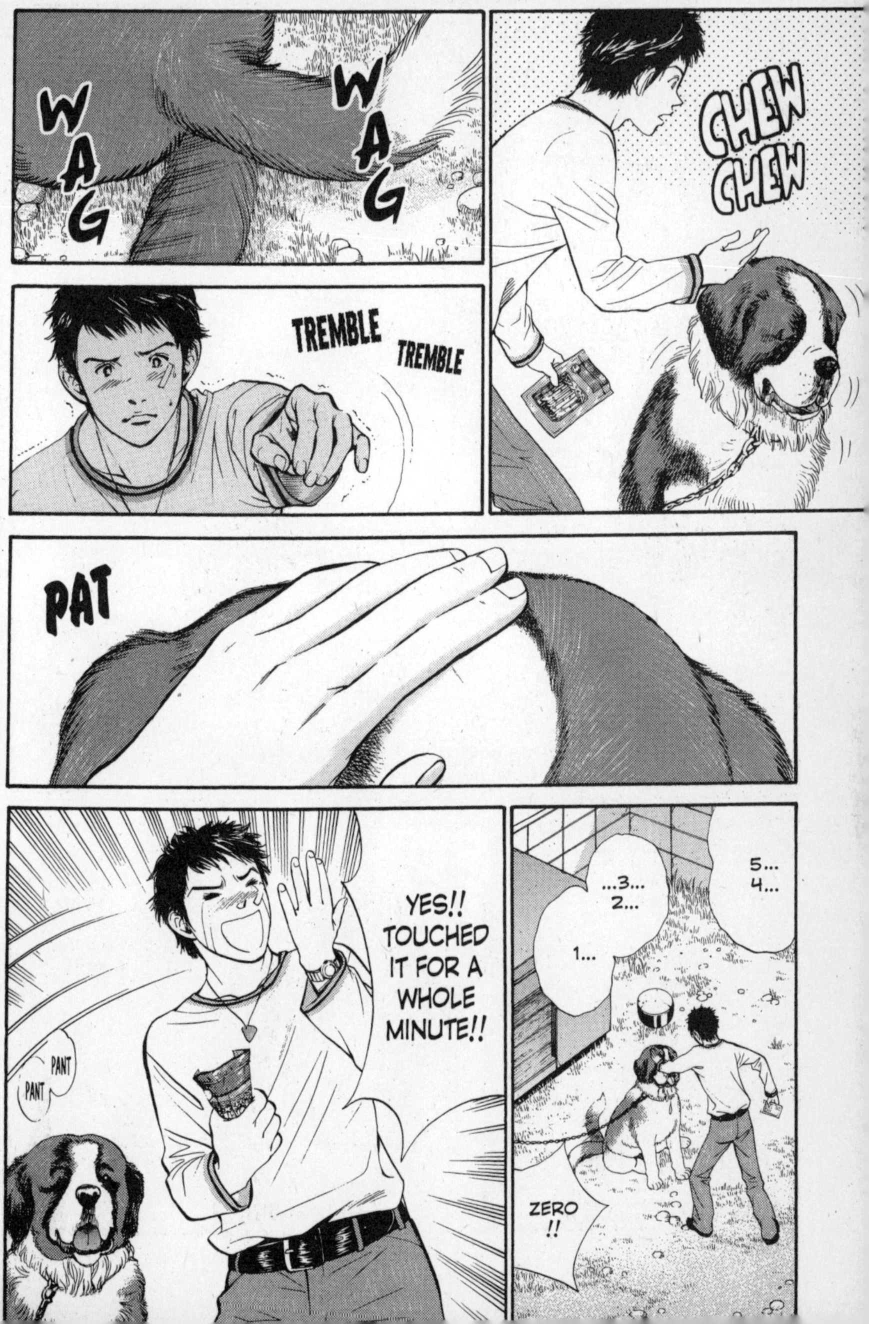
CHEW CHEW
WAG WAG
TREMBLE TREMBLE
PAT
5... 4...
...3... 2...
1...
ZERO !!
YES!! TOUCHED IT FOR A WHOLE MINUTE!!
PANT PANT

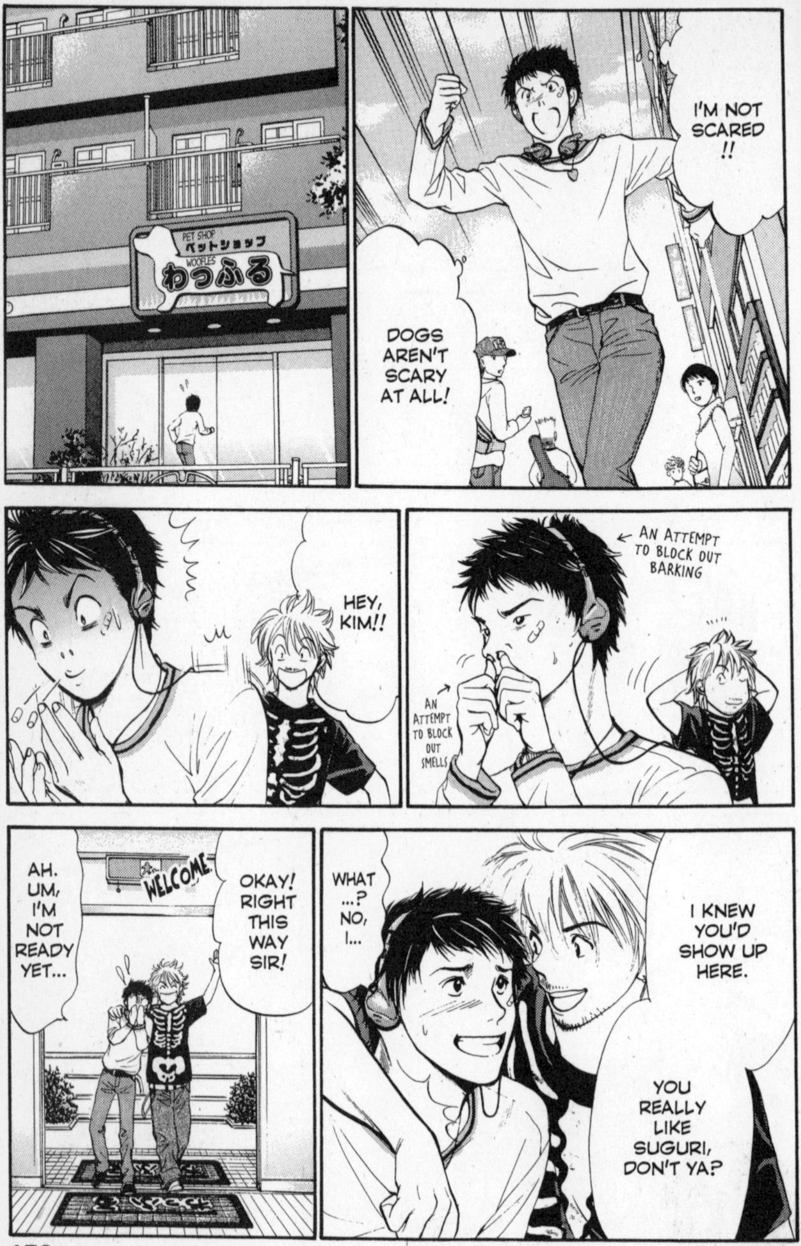
I'M NOT SCARED!!
DOGS AREN'T SCARY AT ALL!
PET SHOP
ペットショップ
WOOFLES
わっふる
AN ATTEMPT TO BLOCK OUT BARKING
AN ATTEMPT TO BLOCK OUT SMELLS
HEY, KIM!!
I KNEW YOU'D SHOW UP HERE.
WHAT...? NO, I...
YOU REALLY LIKE SUGURI, DON'T YA?
OKAY! RIGHT THIS WAY SIR!
WELCOME
AH. UM, I'M NOT READY YET...

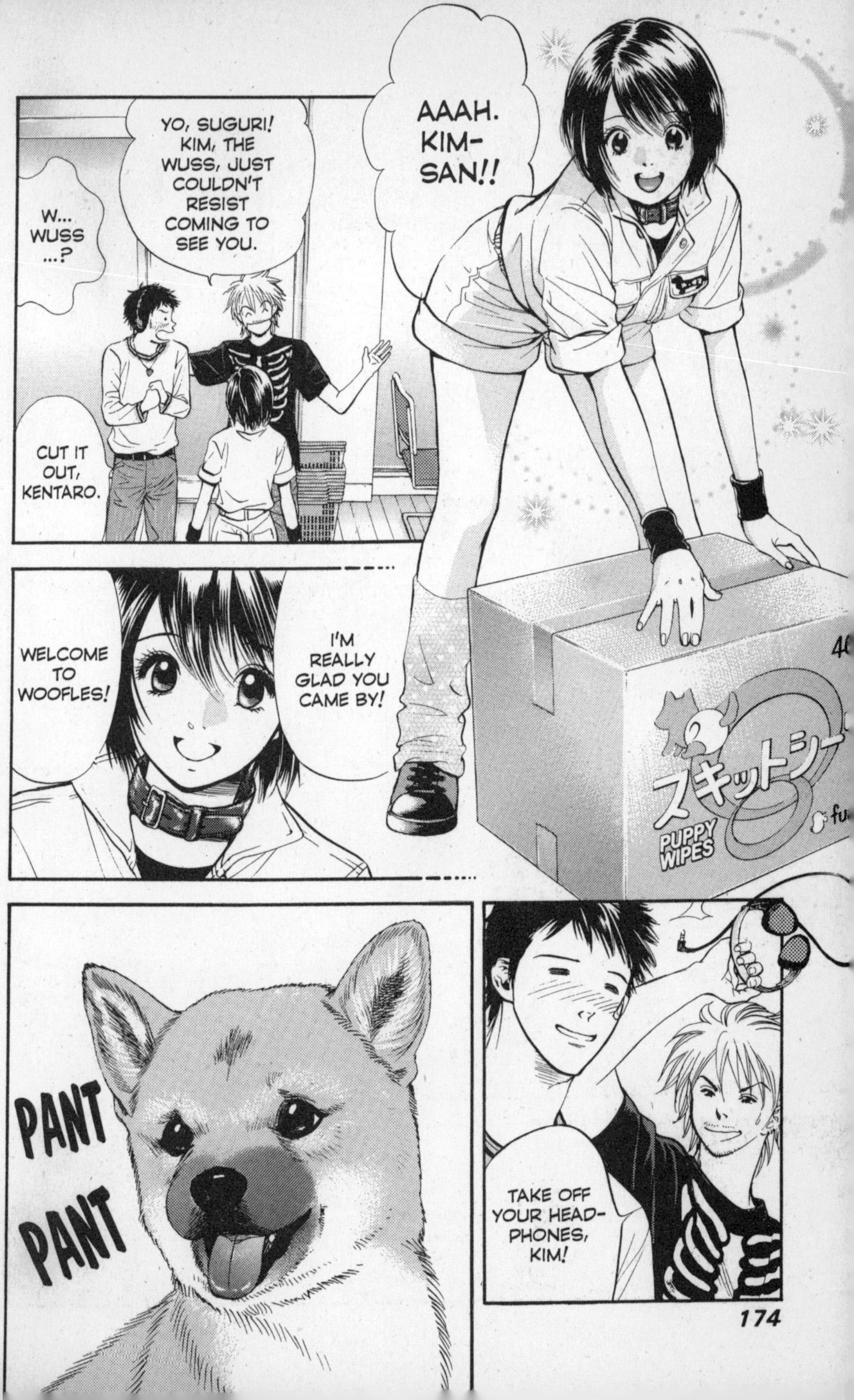
AAAH. KIM-SAN!!
スキットシー
PUPPY WIPES
YO, SUGURI! KIM, THE WUSS, JUST COULDN'T RESIST COMING TO SEE YOU.
W... WUSS ...?
CUT IT OUT, KENTARO.
I'M REALLY GLAD YOU CAME BY!
WELCOME TO WOOFLES!
TAKE OFF YOUR HEAD-PHONES, KIM!
PANT PANT

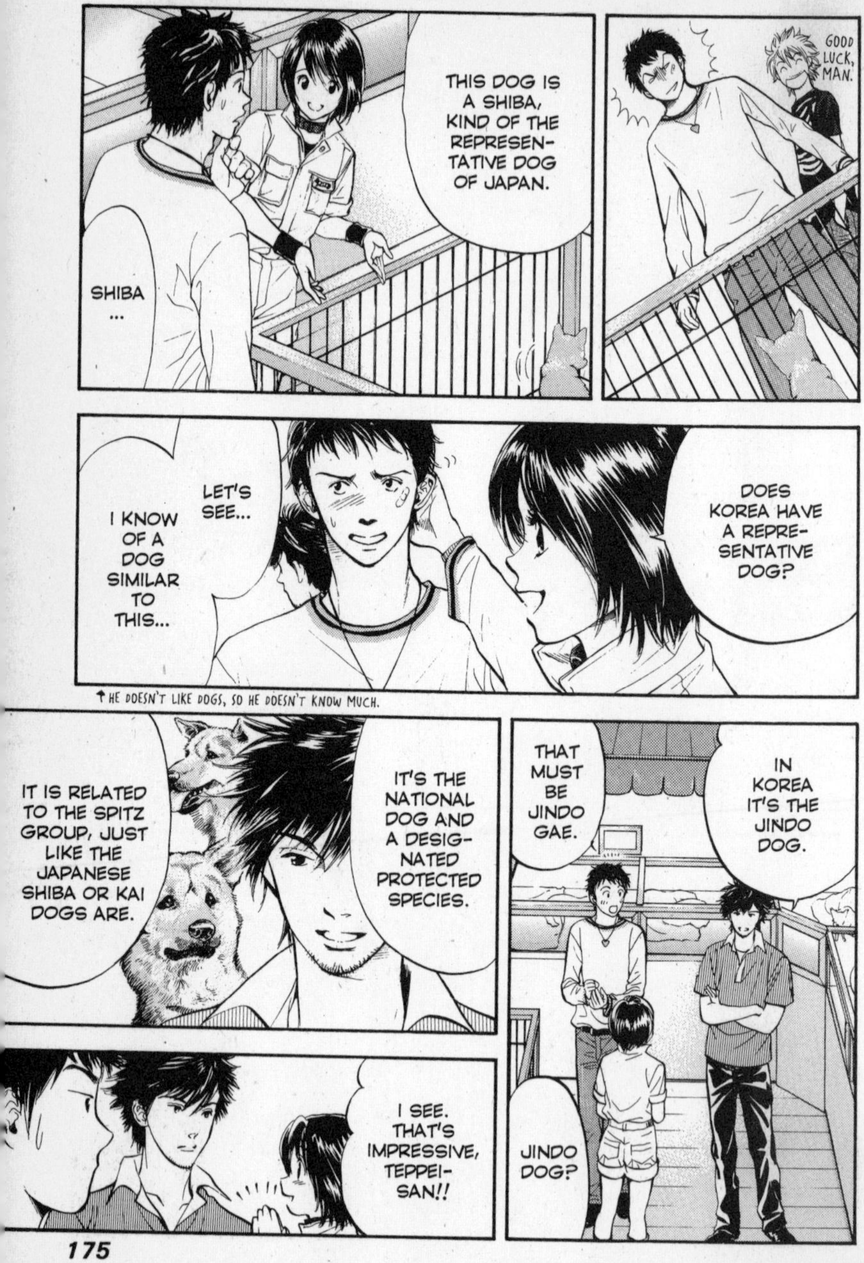
GOOD LUCK, MAN.
THIS DOG IS A SHIBA, KIND OF THE REPRESEN-TATIVE DOG OF JAPAN.
SHIBA ...
DOES KOREA HAVE A REPRE-SENTATIVE DOG?
LET'S SEE...
I KNOW OF A DOG SIMILAR TO THIS...
HE DOESN'T LIKE DOGS, SO HE DOESN'T KNOW MUCH.
IN KOREA IT'S THE JINDO DOG.
THAT MUST BE JINDO GAE.
JINDO DOG?
IT'S THE NATIONAL DOG AND A DESIG-NATED PROTECTED SPECIES.
IT IS RELATED TO THE SPITZ GROUP, JUST LIKE THE JAPANESE SHIBA OR KAI DOGS ARE.
I SEE. THAT'S IMPRESSIVE, TEPPEI-SAN!!

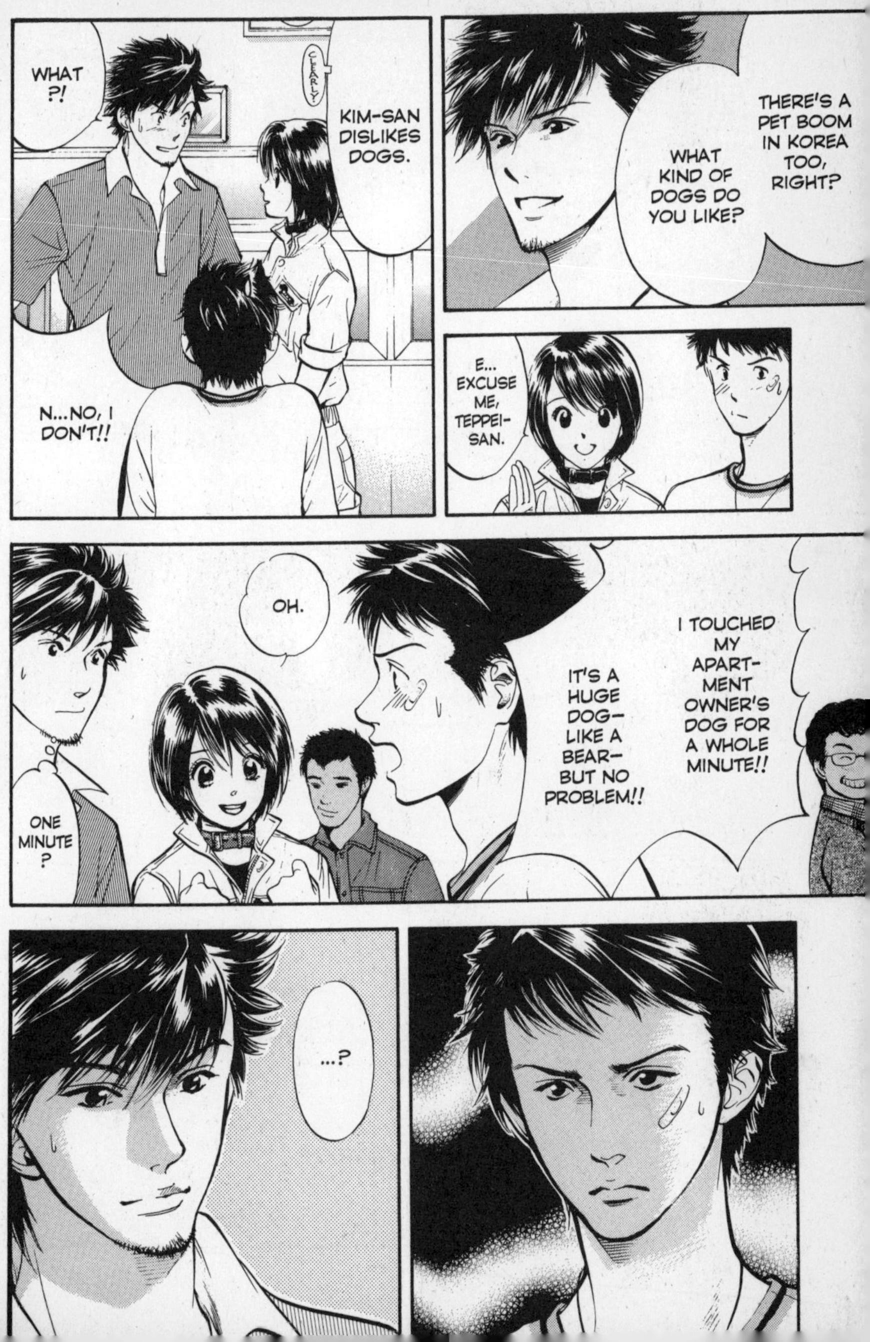
THERE'S A PET BOOM IN KOREA TOO, RIGHT?
WHAT KIND OF DOGS DO YOU LIKE?
E... EXCUSE ME, TEPPEI-SAN.
CLEARLY
KIM-SAN DISLIKES DOGS.
WHAT ?!
N...NO, I DON'T!!
I TOUCHED MY APART-MENT OWNER'S DOG FOR A WHOLE MINUTE!!
IT'S A HUGE DOG-LIKE A BEAR-BUT NO PROBLEM!!
OH.
ONE MINUTE ?
...?

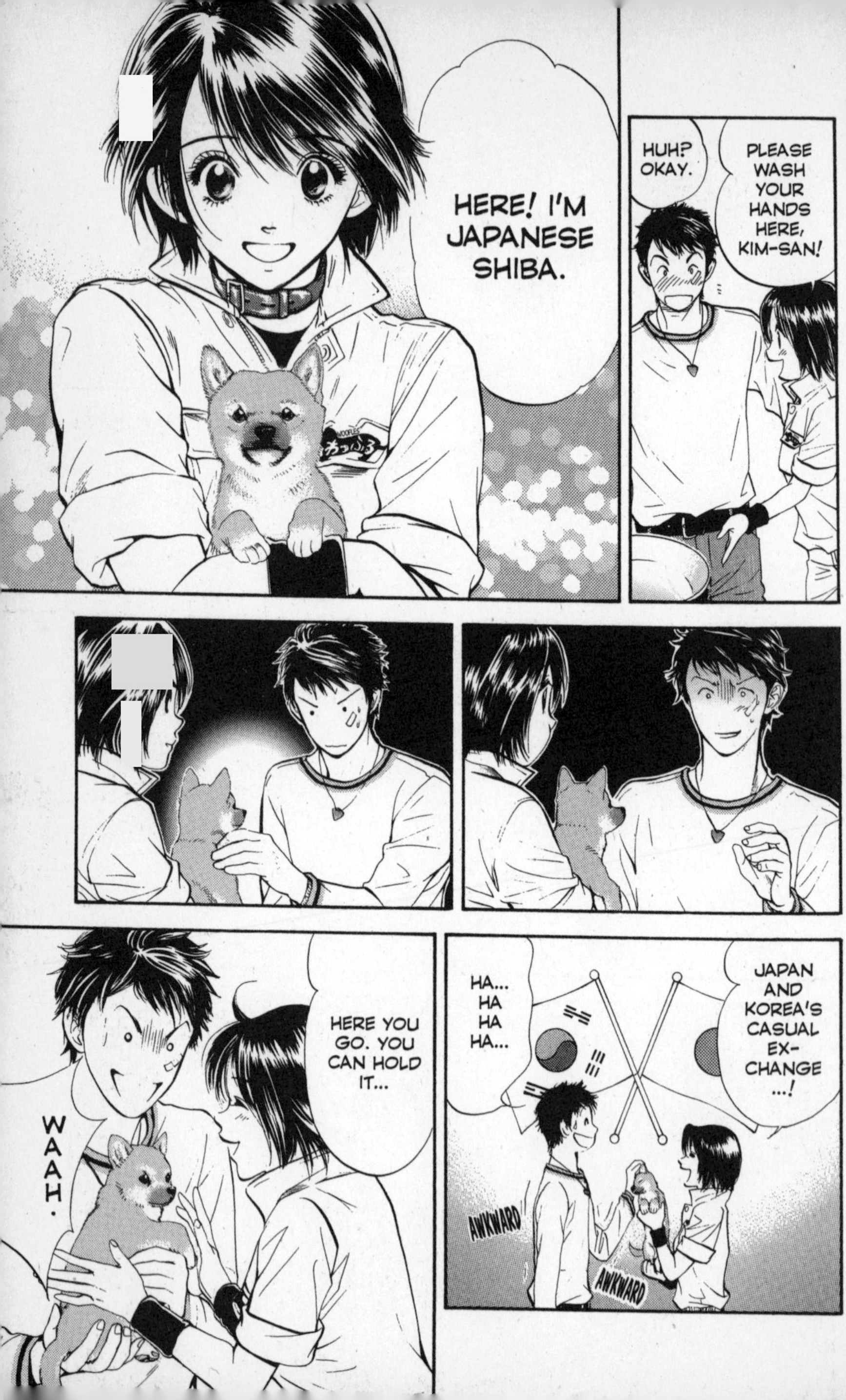
PLEASE WASH YOUR HANDS HERE, KIM-SAN!
HUH? OKAY.
HERE! I'M JAPANESE SHIBA.
JAPAN AND KOREA'S CASUAL EX-CHANGE ...!
HA... HA HA HA...
AWKWARD
AWKWARD
HERE YOU GO. YOU CAN HOLD IT...
WAAH.

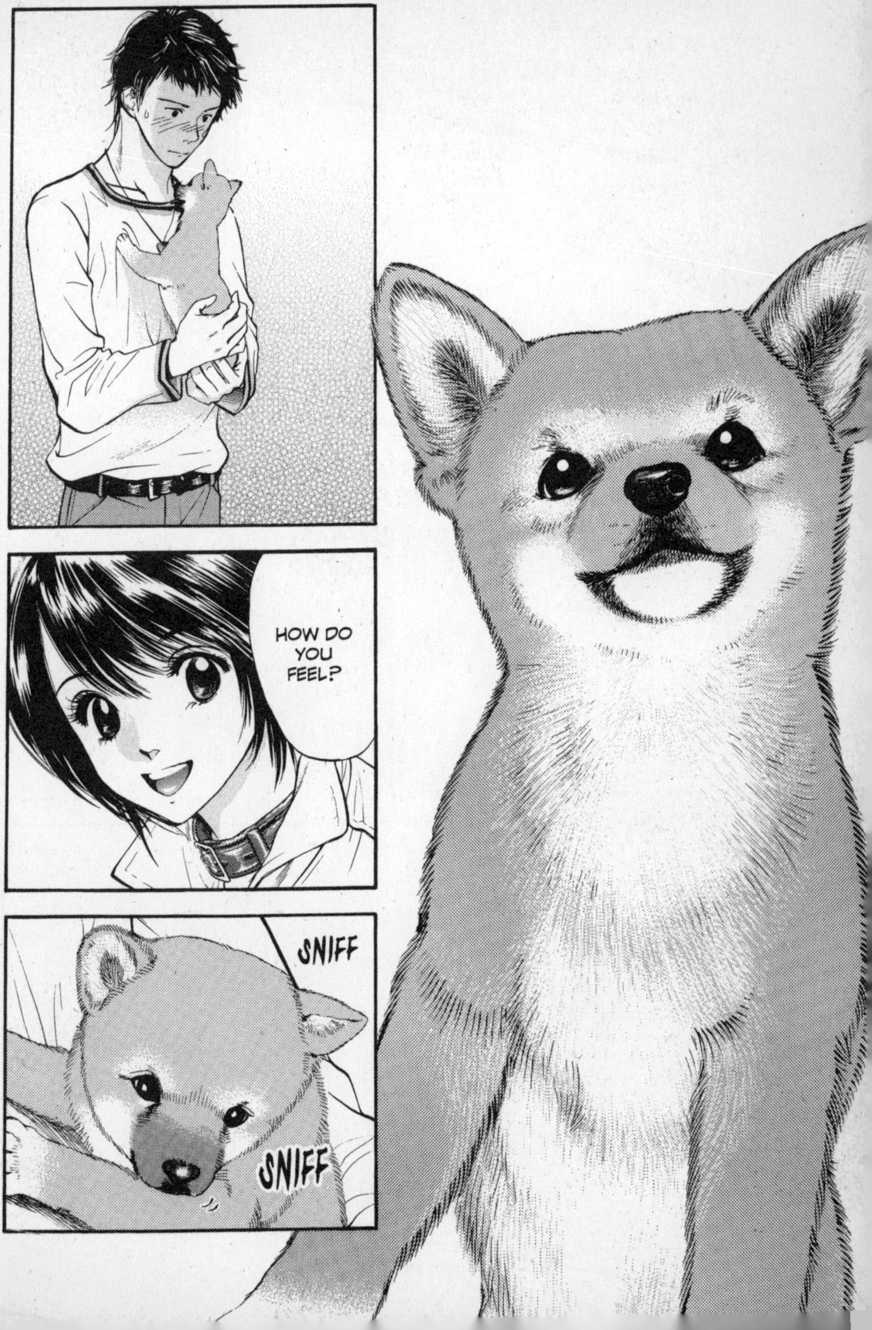
HOW DO YOU FEEL?
SNIFF
SNIFF

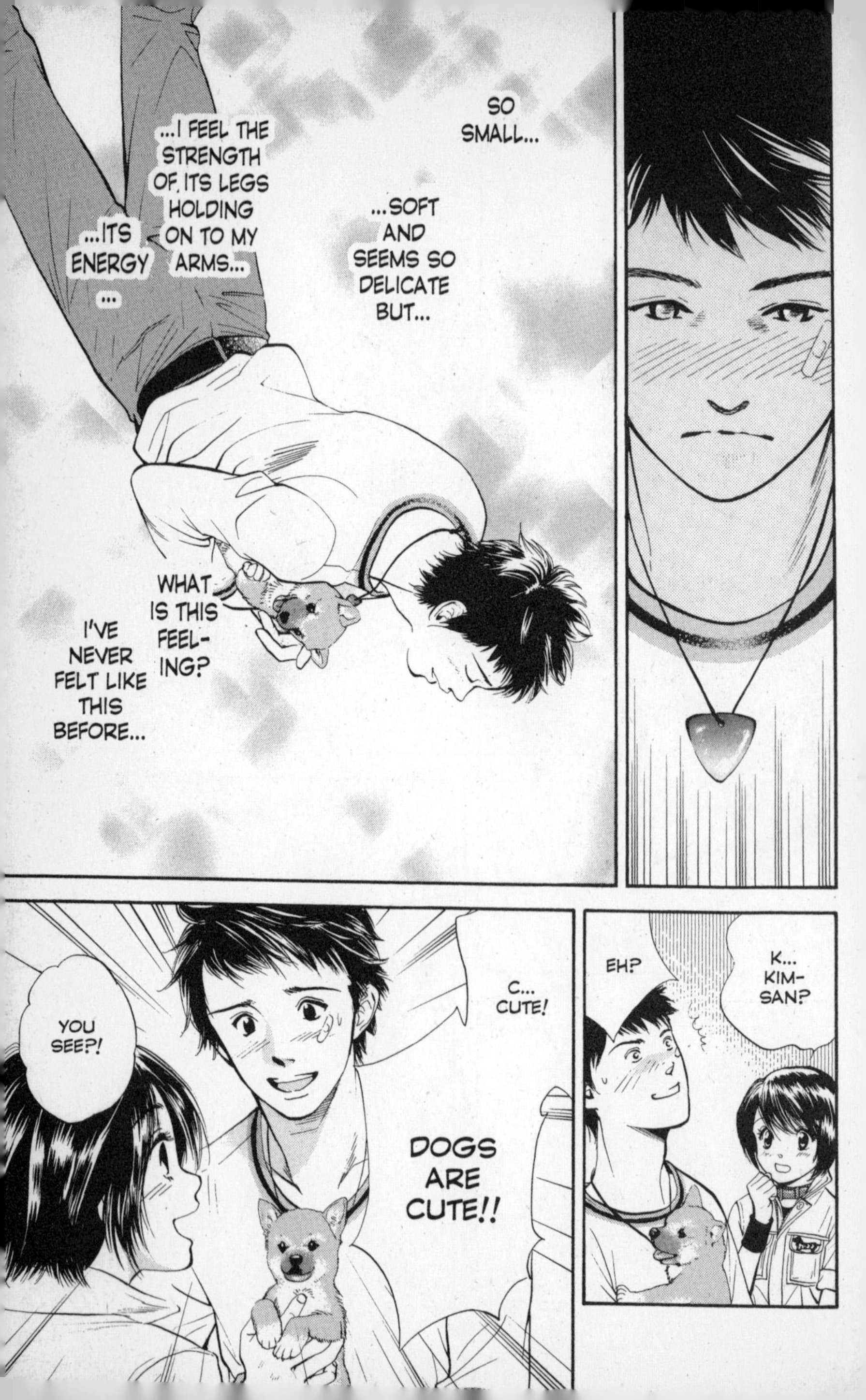
SO SMALL...
...SOFT AND SEEMS SO DELICATE BUT...
...I FEEL THE STRENGTH OF ITS LEGS HOLDING ON TO MY ARMS...
...ITS ENERGY ...
WHAT IS THIS FEEL-ING?
I'VE NEVER FELT LIKE THIS BEFORE...
K... KIM-SAN?
EH?
C... CUTE!
DOGS ARE CUTE!!
YOU SEE?!

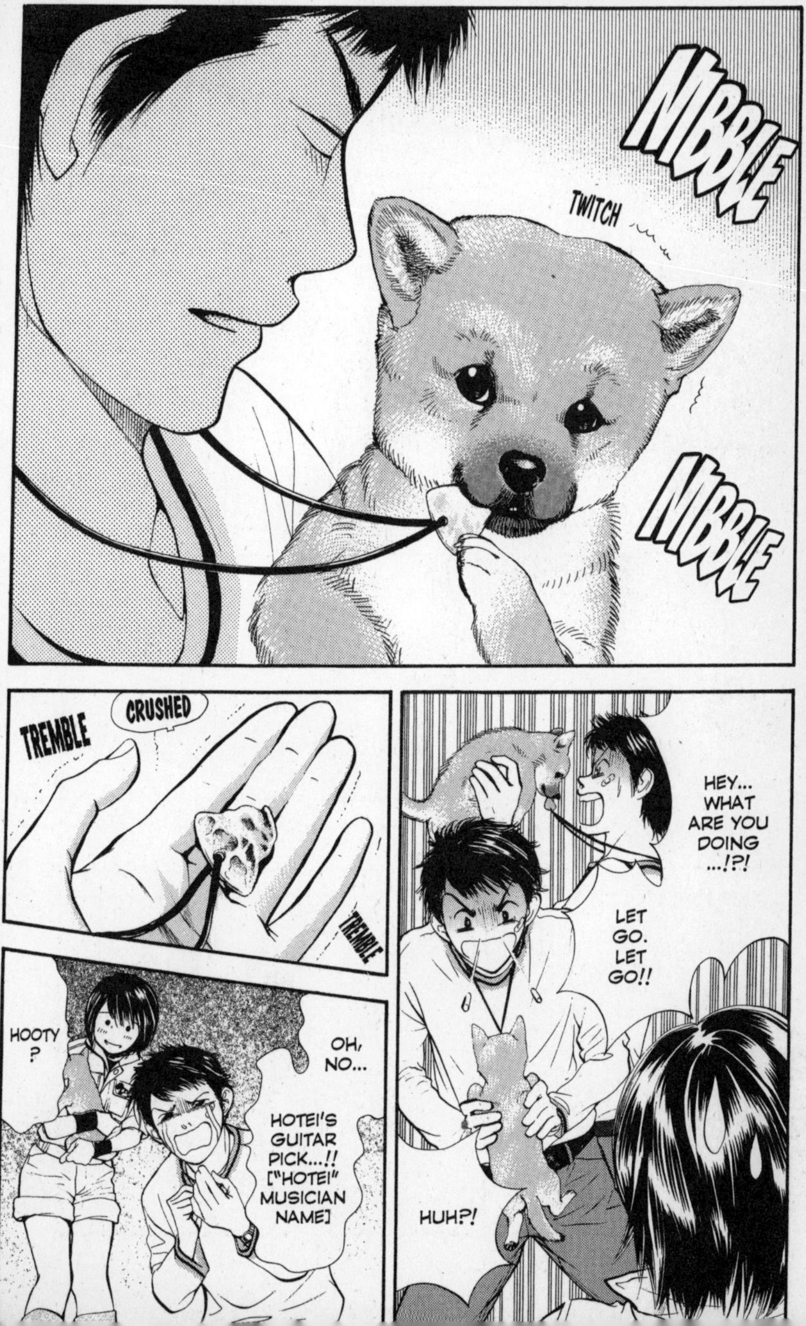
NIBBLE
TWITCH
NIBBLE
HEY... WHAT ARE YOU DOING ...!?!
LET GO. LET GO!!
HUH?!
CRUSHED
TREMBLE
TREMBLE
OH, NO...
HOTEI'S GUITAR PICK...!! ["HOTEI" MUSICIAN NAME]
HOOTY ?

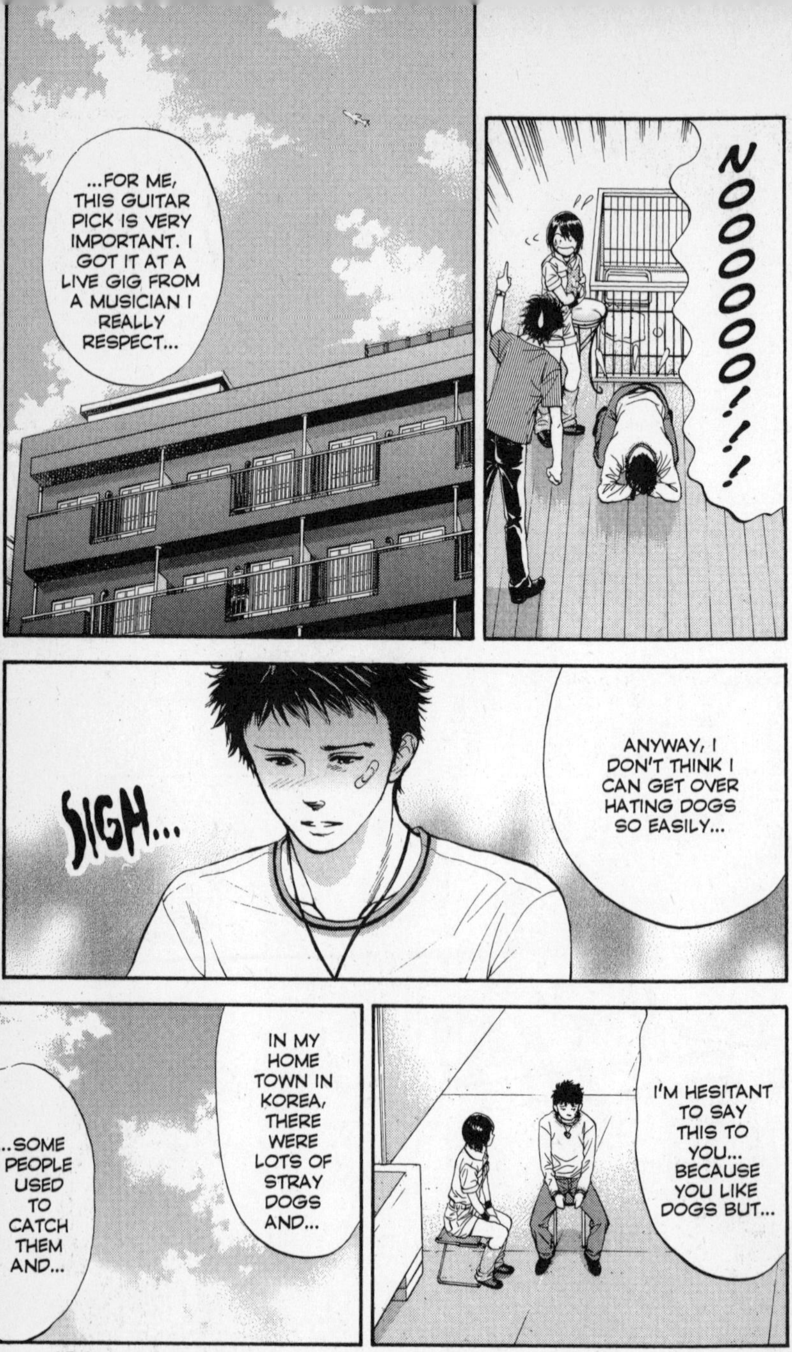
NOOOOOOO!!!
...FOR ME, THIS GUITAR PICK IS VERY IMPORTANT. I GOT IT AT A LIVE GIG FROM A MUSICIAN I REALLY RESPECT...
ANYWAY, I DON'T THINK I CAN GET OVER HATING DOGS SO EASILY...
SIGH...
I'M HESITANT TO SAY THIS TO YOU... BECAUSE YOU LIKE DOGS BUT...
IN MY HOME TOWN IN KOREA, THERE WERE LOTS OF STRAY DOGS AND...
...SOME PEOPLE USED TO CATCH THEM AND...

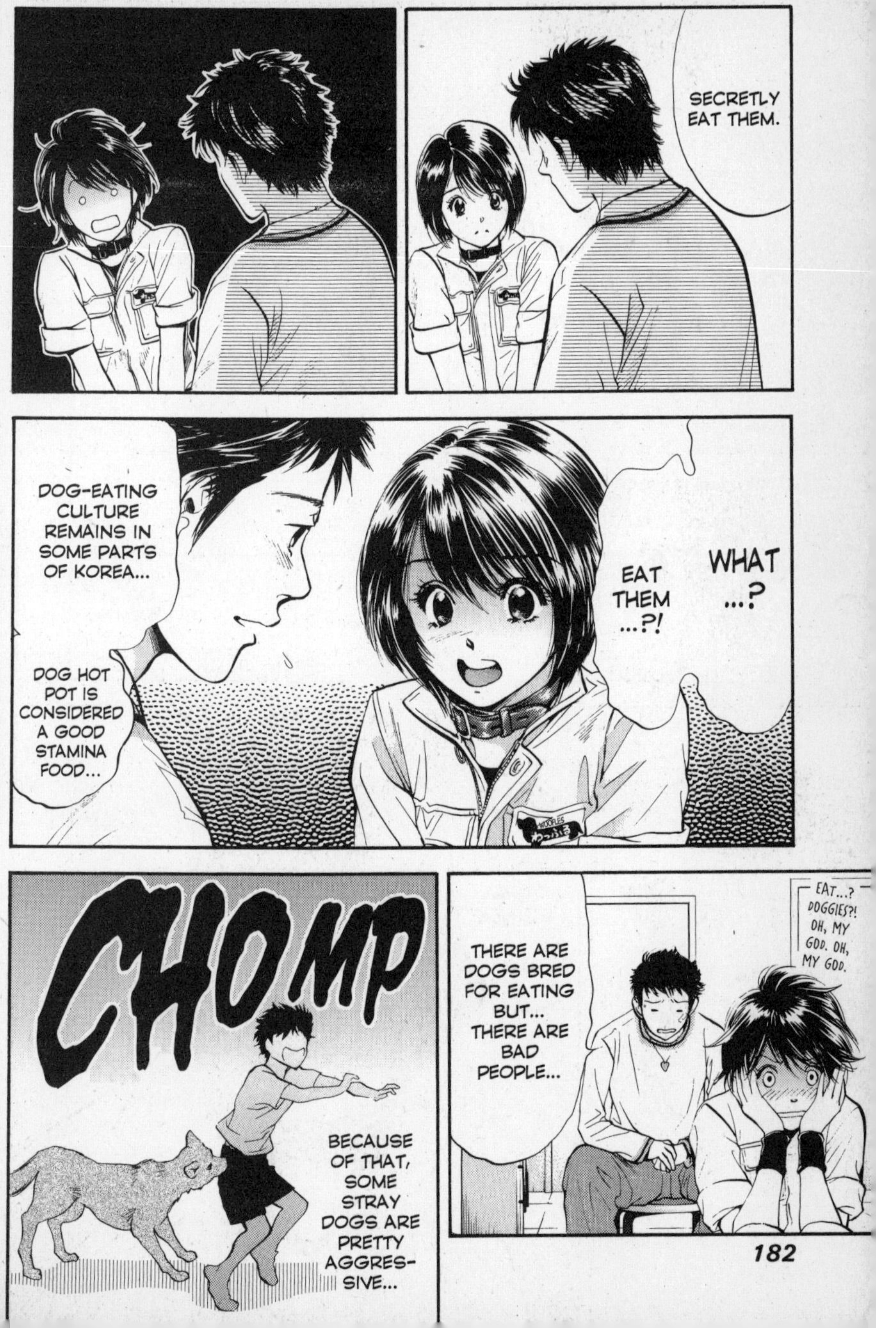
SECRETLY EAT THEM.
WHAT ...?
EAT THEM ...?!
DOG-EATING CULTURE REMAINS IN SOME PARTS OF KOREA...
DOG HOT POT IS CONSIDERED A GOOD STAMINA FOOD...
EAT...? DOGGIES?! OH, MY GOD. OH, MY GOD.
THERE ARE DOGS BRED FOR EATING BUT... THERE ARE BAD PEOPLE...
CHOMP
BECAUSE OF THAT, SOME STRAY DOGS ARE PRETTY AGGRES-SIVE...

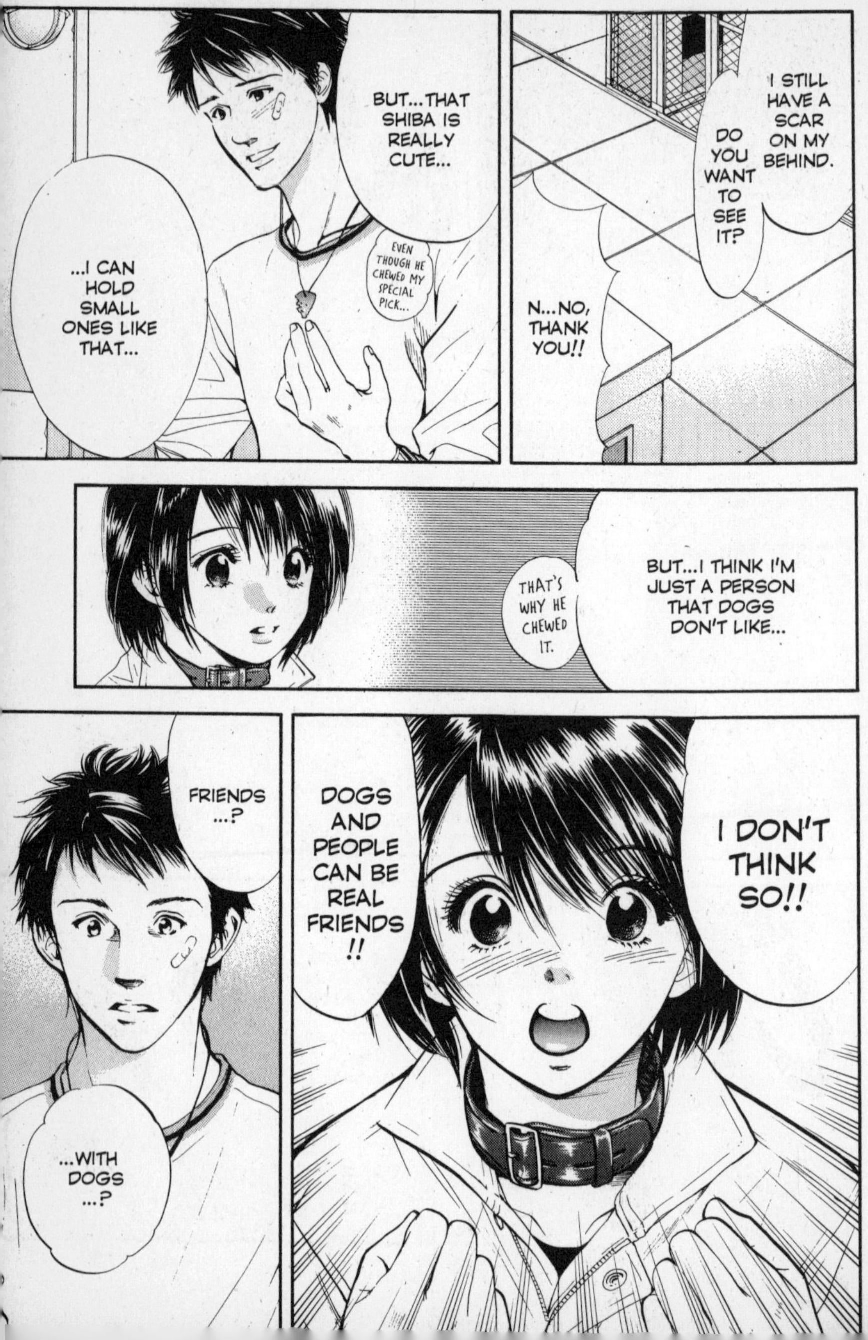
I STILL HAVE A SCAR ON MY BEHIND.
DO YOU WANT TO SEE IT?
N...NO, THANK YOU!!
BUT...THAT SHIBA IS REALLY CUTE...
EVEN THOUGH HE CHEWED MY SPECIAL PICK...
...I CAN HOLD SMALL ONES LIKE THAT...
BUT...I THINK I'M JUST A PERSON THAT DOGS DON'T LIKE...
THAT'S WHY HE CHEWED IT.
I DON'T THINK SO!!
DOGS AND PEOPLE CAN BE REAL FRIENDS!!
FRIENDS...?
...WITH DOGS...?

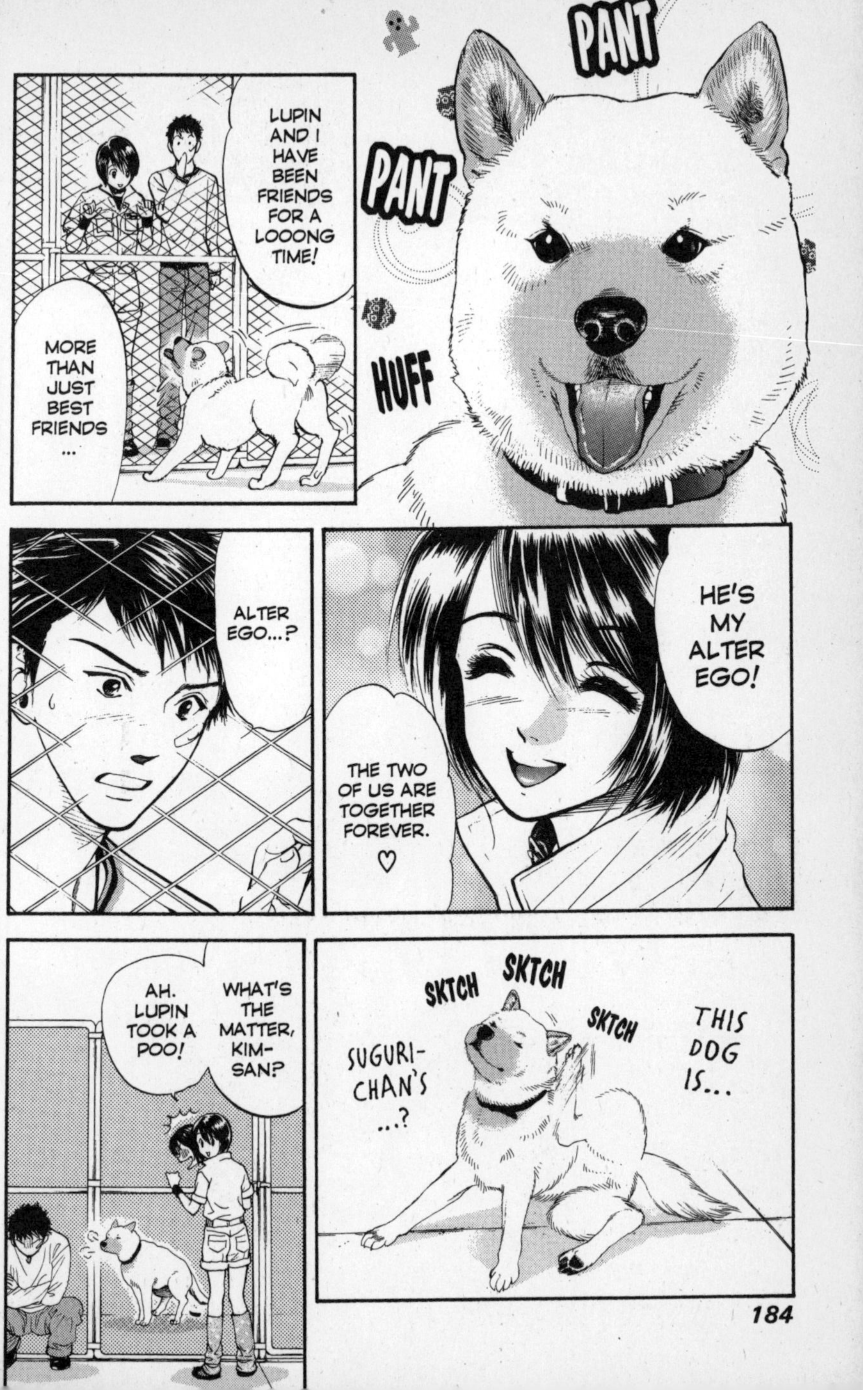
PANT
PANT
HUFF
LUPIN AND I HAVE BEEN FRIENDS FOR A LOOONG TIME!
MORE THAN JUST BEST FRIENDS ...
HE'S MY ALTER EGO!
THE TWO OF US ARE TOGETHER FOREVER. ♡
ALTER EGO...?
SKTCH
SKTCH
SKTCH
THIS DOG IS...
SUGURI-CHAN'S ...?
WHAT'S THE MATTER, KIM-SAN?
AH. LUPIN TOOK A POO!

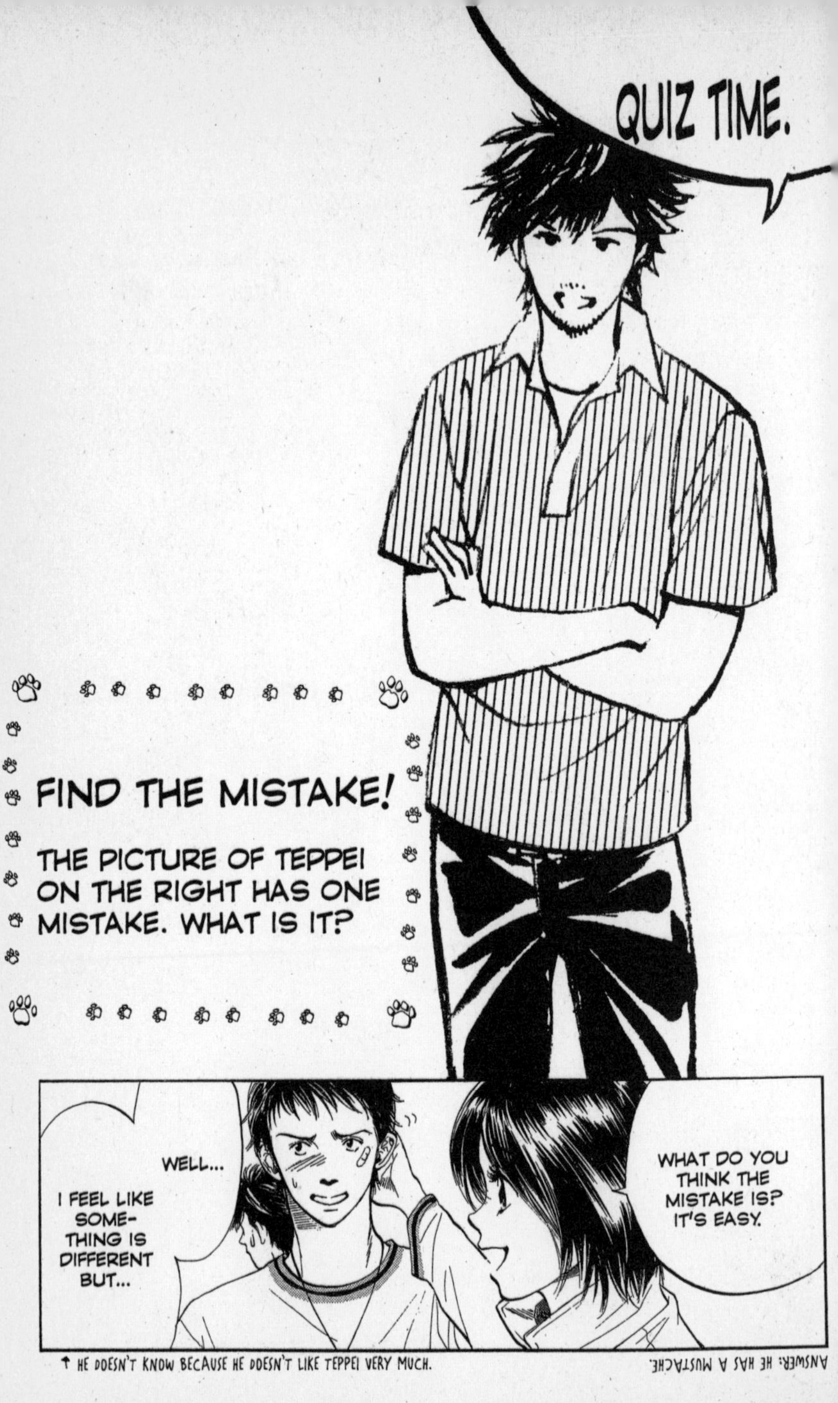
QUIZ TIME.
FIND THE MISTAKE!
THE PICTURE OF TEPPEI ON THE RIGHT HAS ONE MISTAKE. WHAT IS IT?
WHAT DO YOU THINK THE MISTAKE IS? IT'S EASY.
WELL...
I FEEL LIKE SOMETHING IS DIFFERENT BUT...

↑ HE DOESN'T KNOW BECAUSE HE DOESN'T LIKE TEPPEI VERY MUCH.

ANSWER: HE HAS A MUSTACHE.

CHAPTER 19
A GOOD OWNER, BUT...

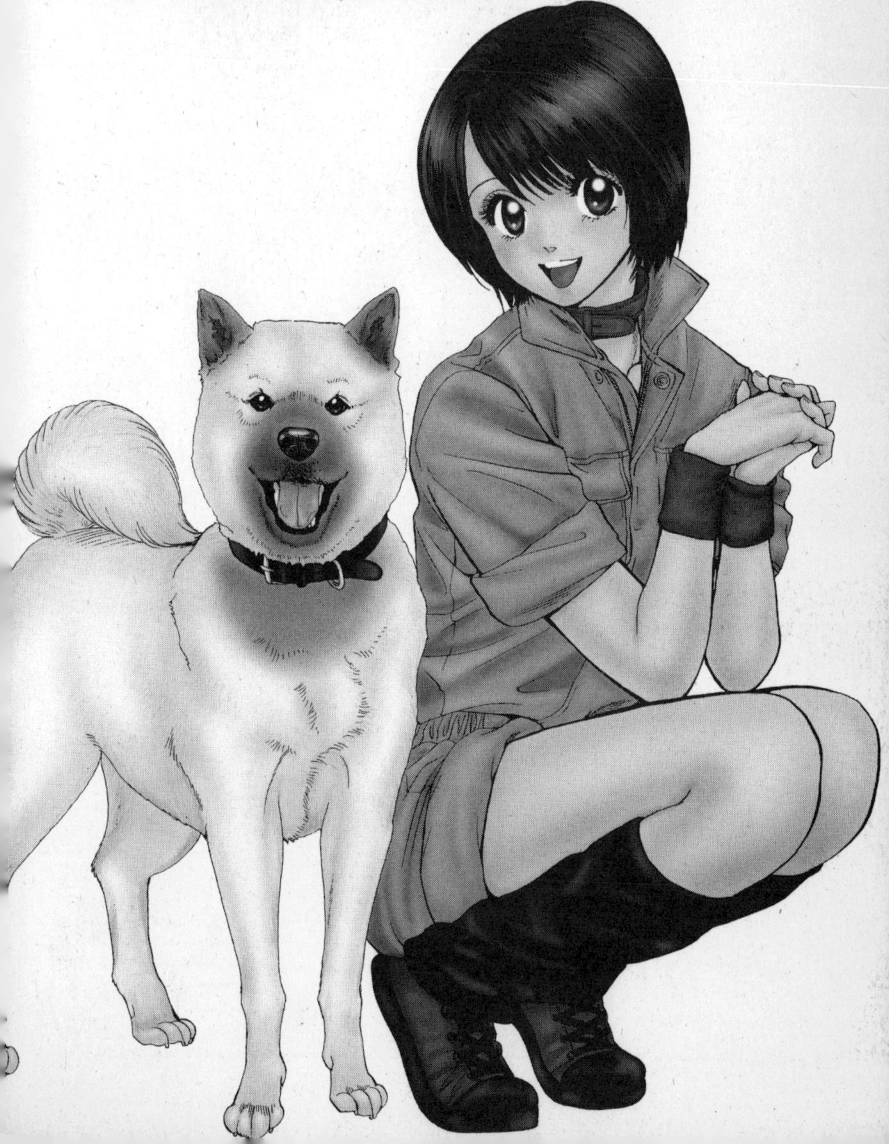

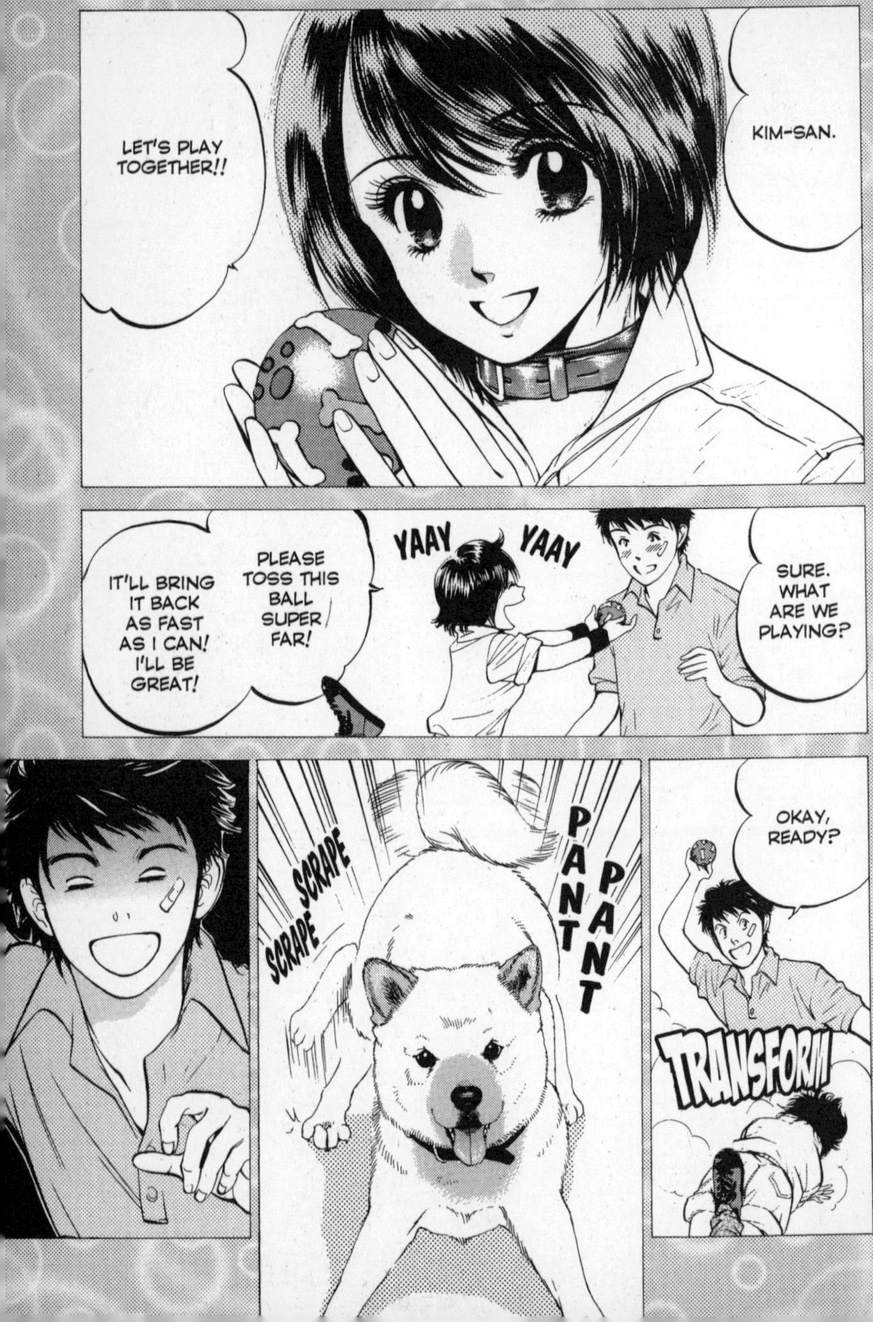

KIM-SAN.
LET'S PLAY TOGETHER!!
SURE. WHAT ARE WE PLAYING?
YAAY
YAAY
PLEASE TOSS THIS BALL SUPER FAR!
IT'LL BRING IT BACK AS FAST AS I CAN! I'LL BE GREAT!
OKAY, READY?
TRANSFORM
PANT PANT
SCRAPE SCRAPE

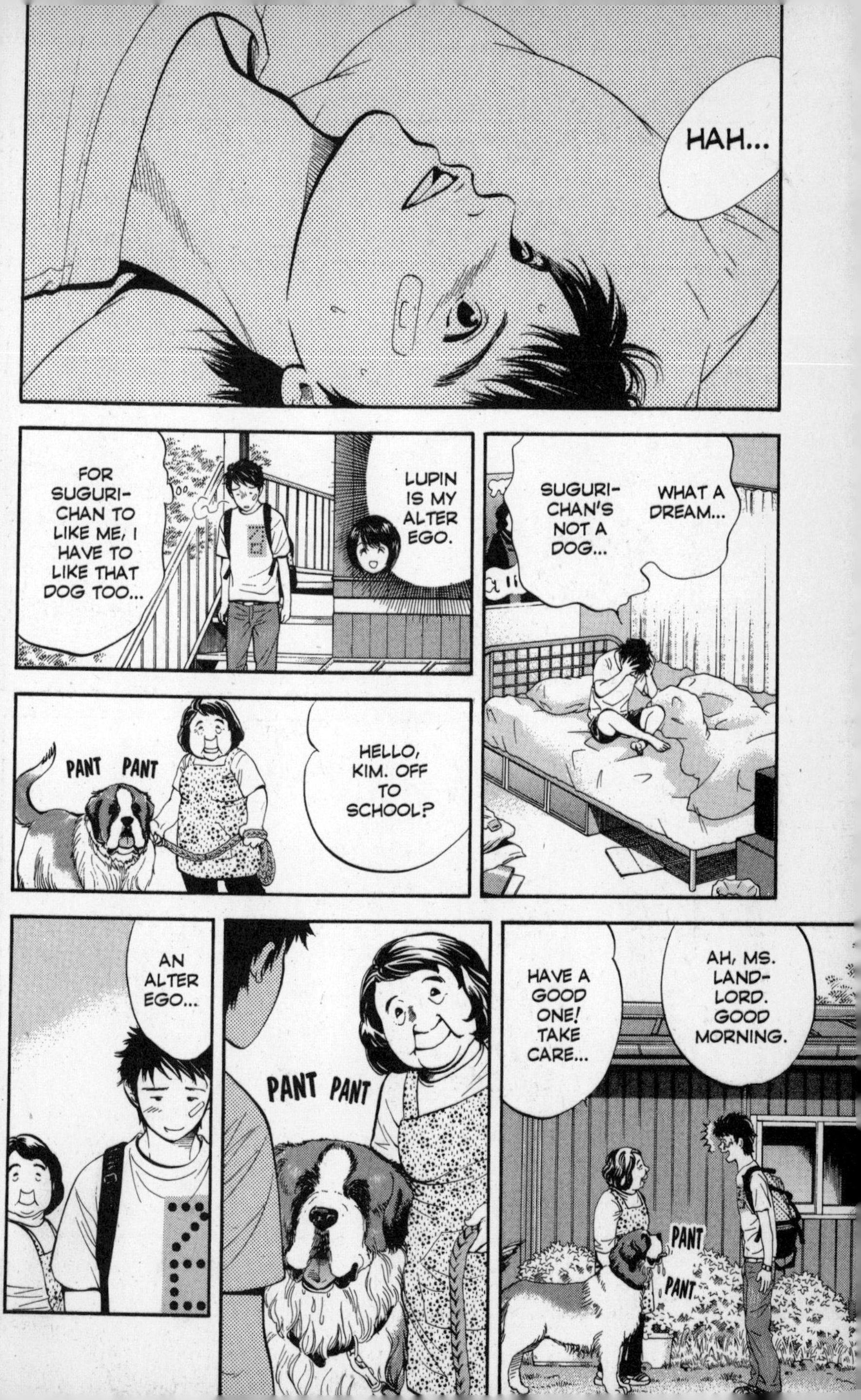
HAH...
WHAT A DREAM...
SUGURI-CHAN'S NOT A DOG...
LUPIN IS MY ALTER EGO.
FOR SUGURI-CHAN TO LIKE ME, I HAVE TO LIKE THAT DOG TOO...
HELLO, KIM. OFF TO SCHOOL?
PANT PANT
AH, MS. LAND-LORD. GOOD MORNING.
HAVE A GOOD ONE! TAKE CARE...
PANT
PANT
PANT PANT
AN ALTER EGO...

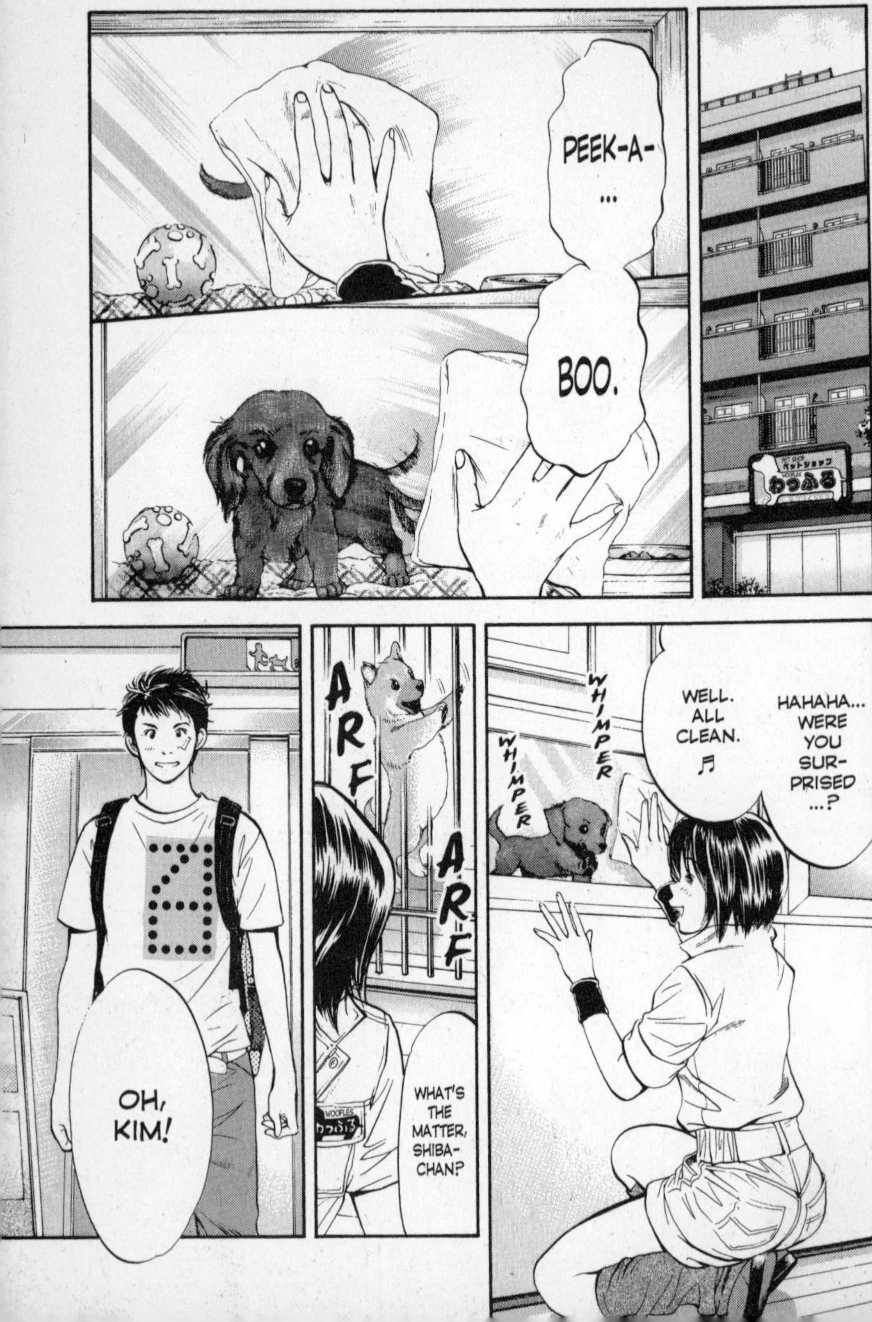
わっふる
PEEK-A-
...
BOO.
HAHAHA... WERE YOU SUR-PRISED ...?
WELL. ALL CLEAN. ♬
WHIMPER
WHIMPER
ARF
ARF
WOOFLES
わっふる
WHAT'S THE MATTER, SHIBA-CHAN?
OH, KIM!

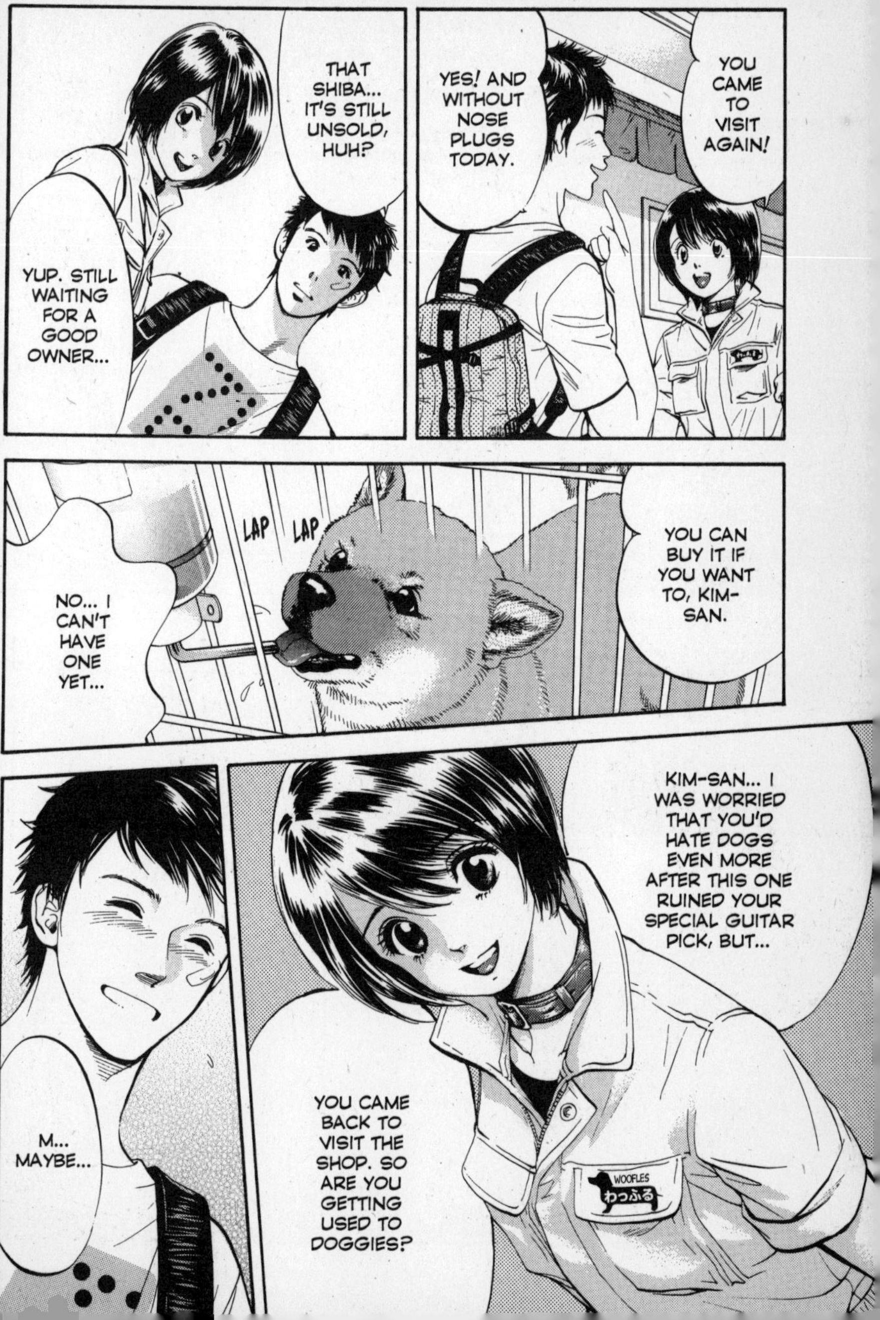
YOU CAME TO VISIT AGAIN!
YES! AND WITHOUT NOSE PLUGS TODAY.
THAT SHIBA... IT'S STILL UNSOLD, HUH?
YUP. STILL WAITING FOR A GOOD OWNER...
YOU CAN BUY IT IF YOU WANT TO, KIM-SAN.
LAP
LAP
NO... I CAN'T HAVE ONE YET...
KIM-SAN... I WAS WORRIED THAT YOU'D HATE DOGS EVEN MORE AFTER THIS ONE RUINED YOUR SPECIAL GUITAR PICK, BUT...
YOU CAME BACK TO VISIT THE SHOP. SO ARE YOU GETTING USED TO DOGGIES?
WOOFLES
わっふる
M... MAYBE...

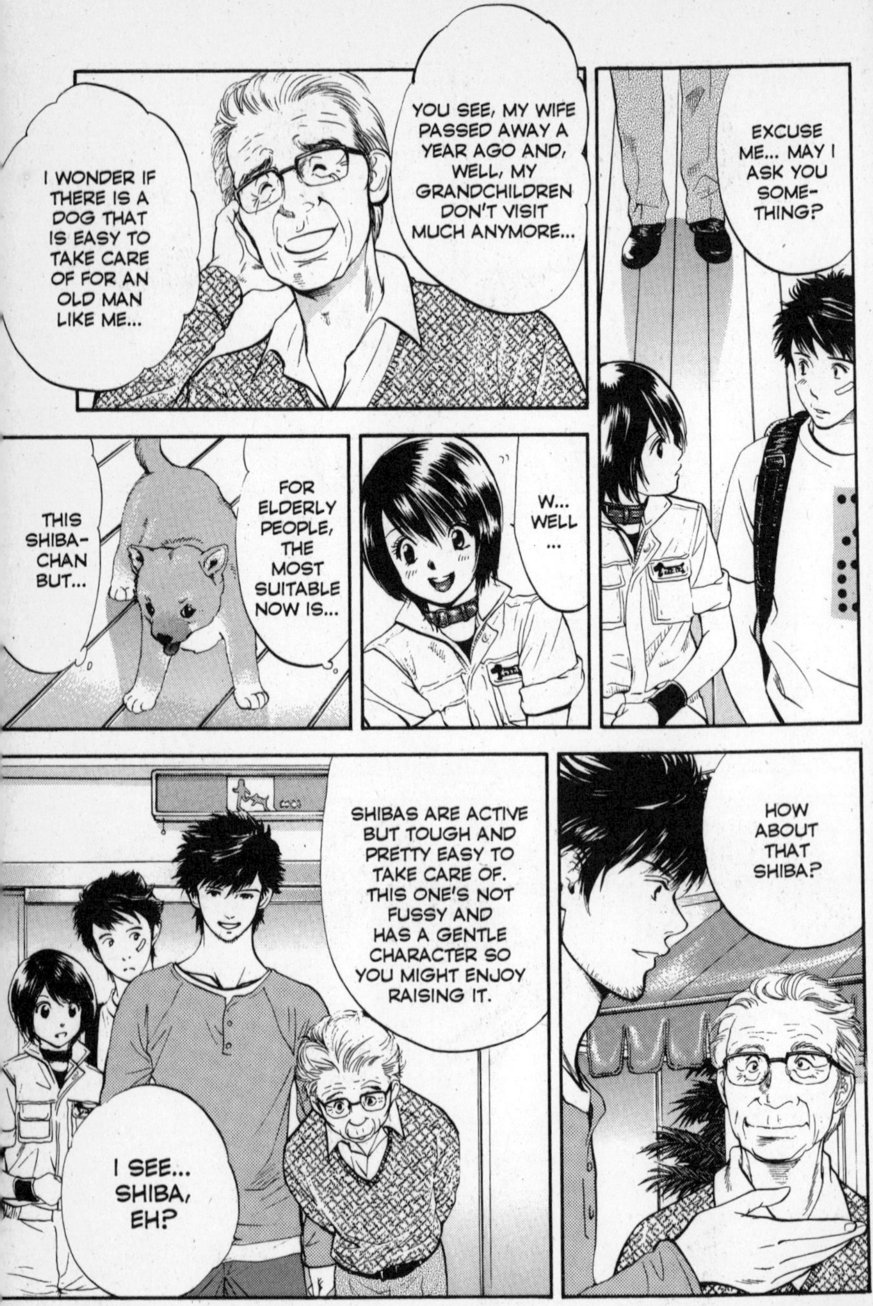
EXCUSE ME... MAY I ASK YOU SOME-THING?
YOU SEE, MY WIFE PASSED AWAY A YEAR AGO AND, WELL, MY GRANDCHILDREN DON'T VISIT MUCH ANYMORE...
I WONDER IF THERE IS A DOG THAT IS EASY TO TAKE CARE OF FOR AN OLD MAN LIKE ME...
W... WELL ...
FOR ELDERLY PEOPLE, THE MOST SUITABLE NOW IS...
THIS SHIBA-CHAN BUT...
HOW ABOUT THAT SHIBA?
SHIBAS ARE ACTIVE BUT TOUGH AND PRETTY EASY TO TAKE CARE OF. THIS ONE'S NOT FUSSY AND HAS A GENTLE CHARACTER SO YOU MIGHT ENJOY RAISING IT.
I SEE... SHIBA, EH?

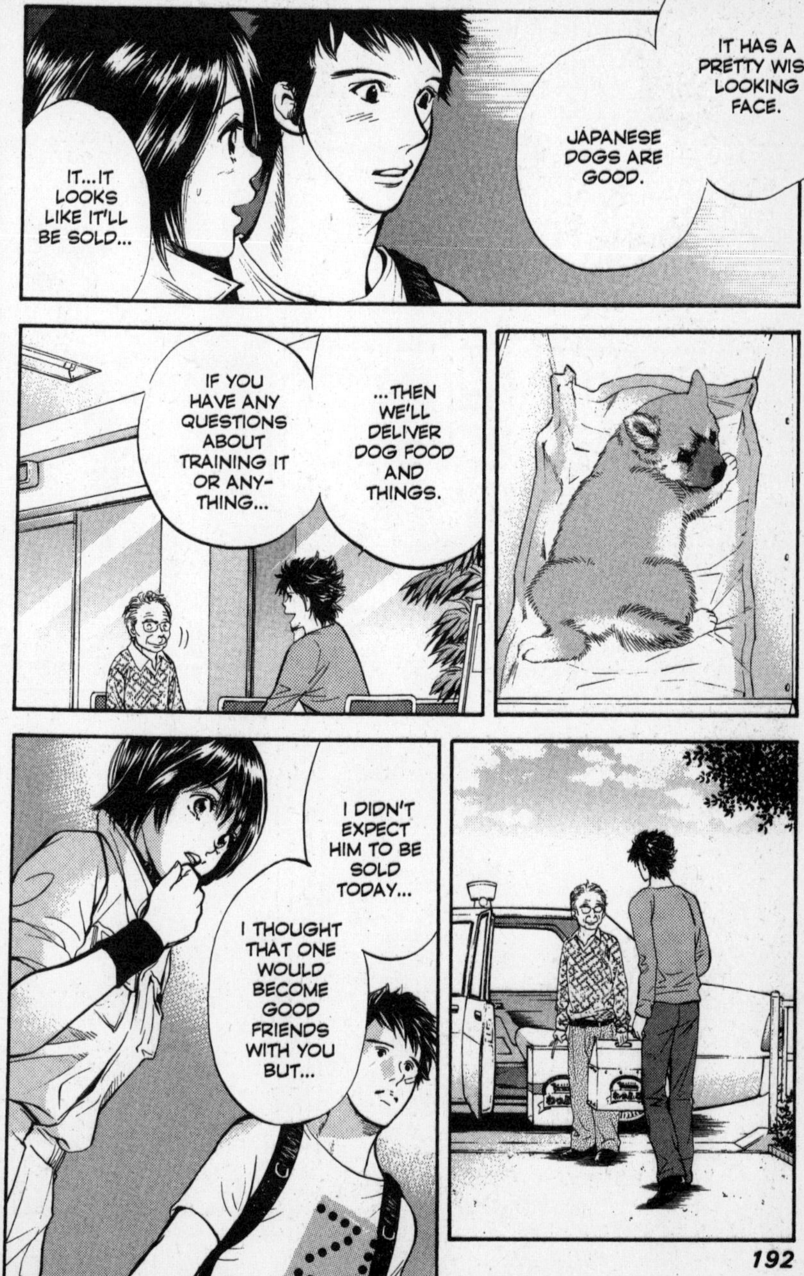
IT HAS A PRETTY WISE LOOKING FACE.
JAPANESE DOGS ARE GOOD.
IT...IT LOOKS LIKE IT'LL BE SOLD...
IF YOU HAVE ANY QUESTIONS ABOUT TRAINING IT OR ANY-THING...
...THEN WE'LL DELIVER DOG FOOD AND THINGS.
I DIDN'T EXPECT HIM TO BE SOLD TODAY...
I THOUGHT THAT ONE WOULD BECOME GOOD FRIENDS WITH YOU BUT...

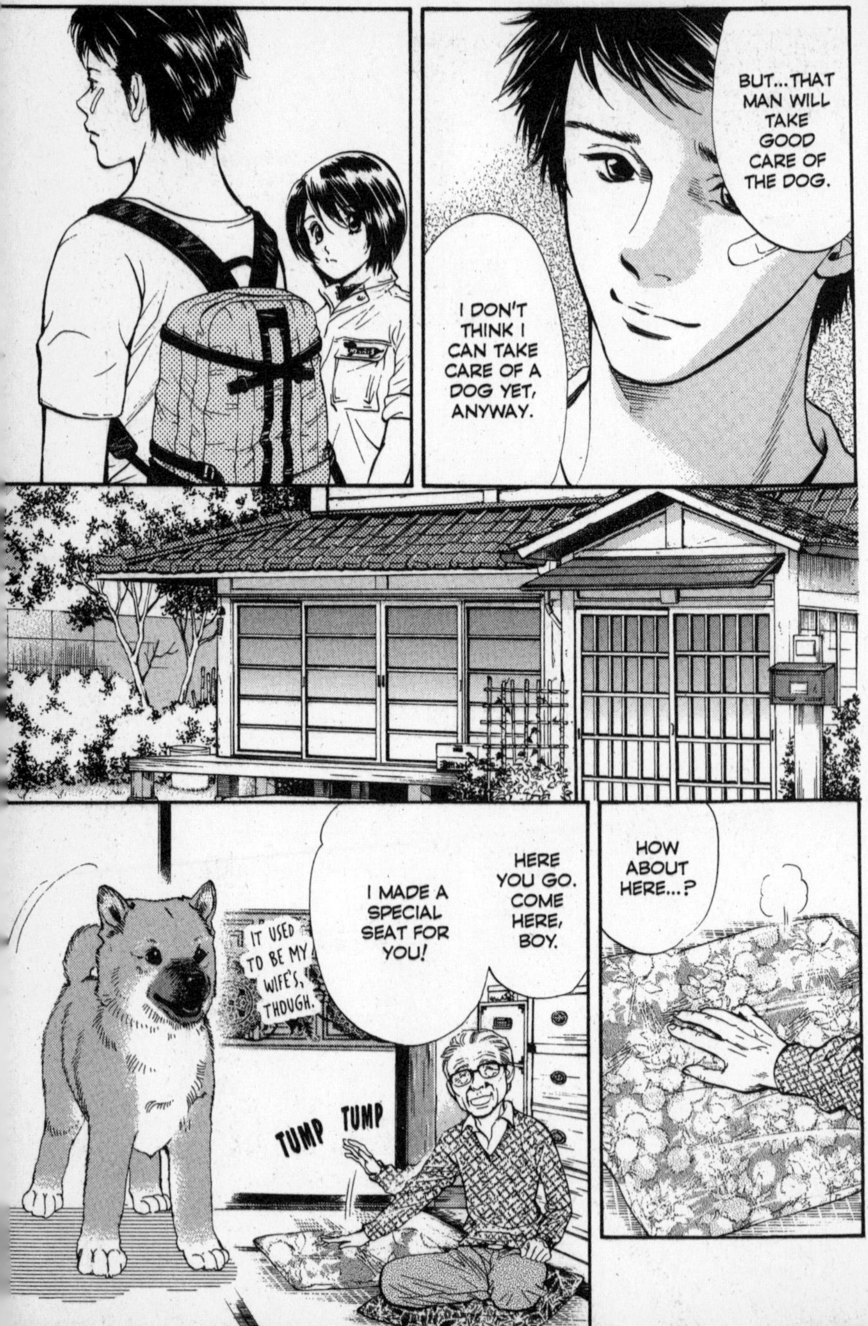
BUT...THAT MAN WILL TAKE GOOD CARE OF THE DOG.
I DON'T THINK I CAN TAKE CARE OF A DOG YET, ANYWAY.
HOW ABOUT HERE...?
HERE YOU GO. COME HERE, BOY.
I MADE A SPECIAL SEAT FOR YOU!
IT USED TO BE MY WIFE'S, THOUGH.
TUMP TUMP

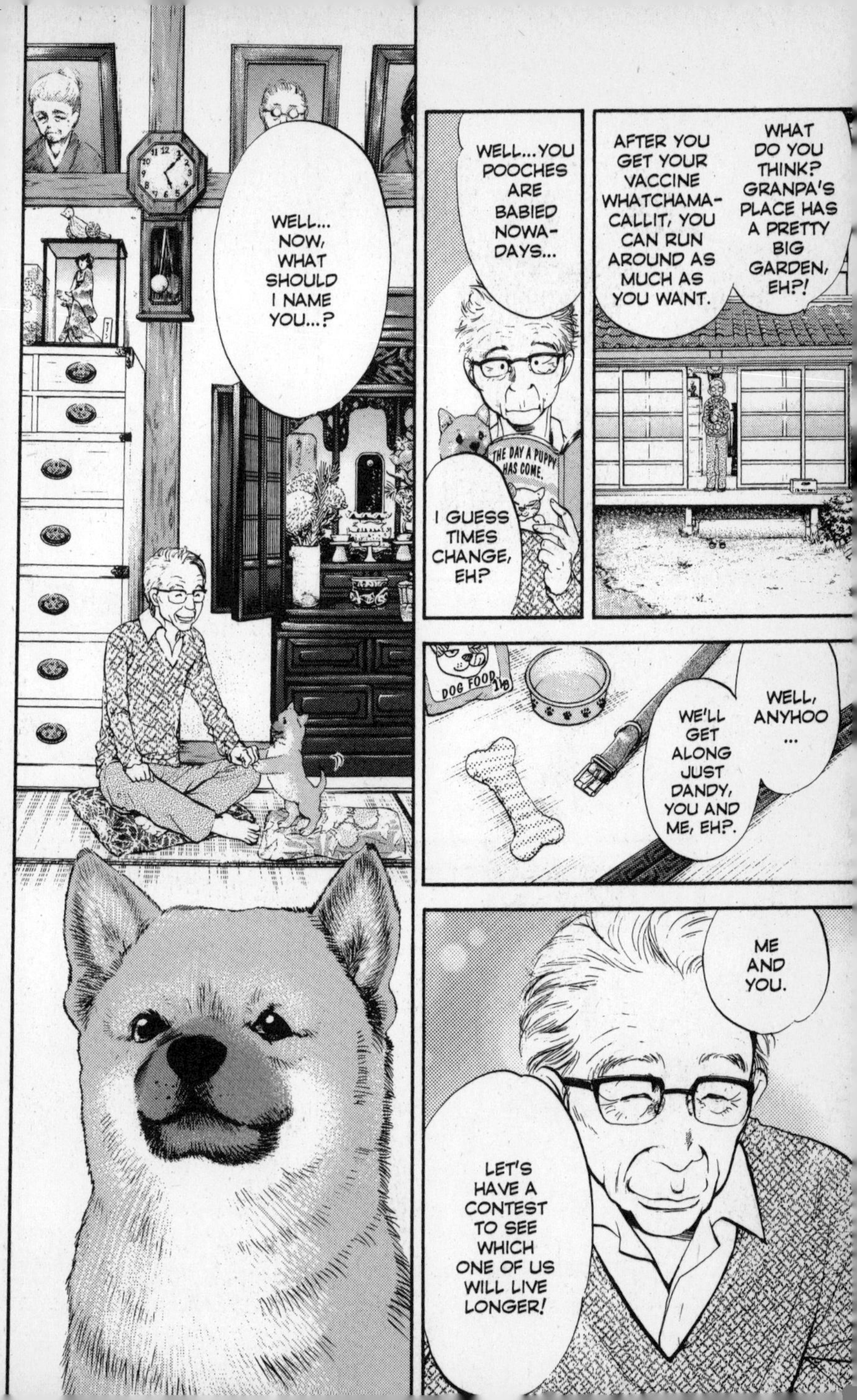
WHAT DO YOU THINK? GRANPA'S PLACE HAS A PRETTY BIG GARDEN, EH?!
AFTER YOU GET YOUR VACCINE WHATCHAMA-CALLIT, YOU CAN RUN AROUND AS MUCH AS YOU WANT.
WELL...YOU POOCHES ARE BABIED NOWA-DAYS...
THE DAY A PUPPY HAS COME.
I GUESS TIMES CHANGE, EH?
WELL, ANYHOO ...
WE'LL GET ALONG JUST DANDY, YOU AND ME, EH?.
DOG FOOD
ME AND YOU.
LET'S HAVE A CONTEST TO SEE WHICH ONE OF US WILL LIVE LONGER!
WELL... NOW, WHAT SHOULD I NAME YOU...?

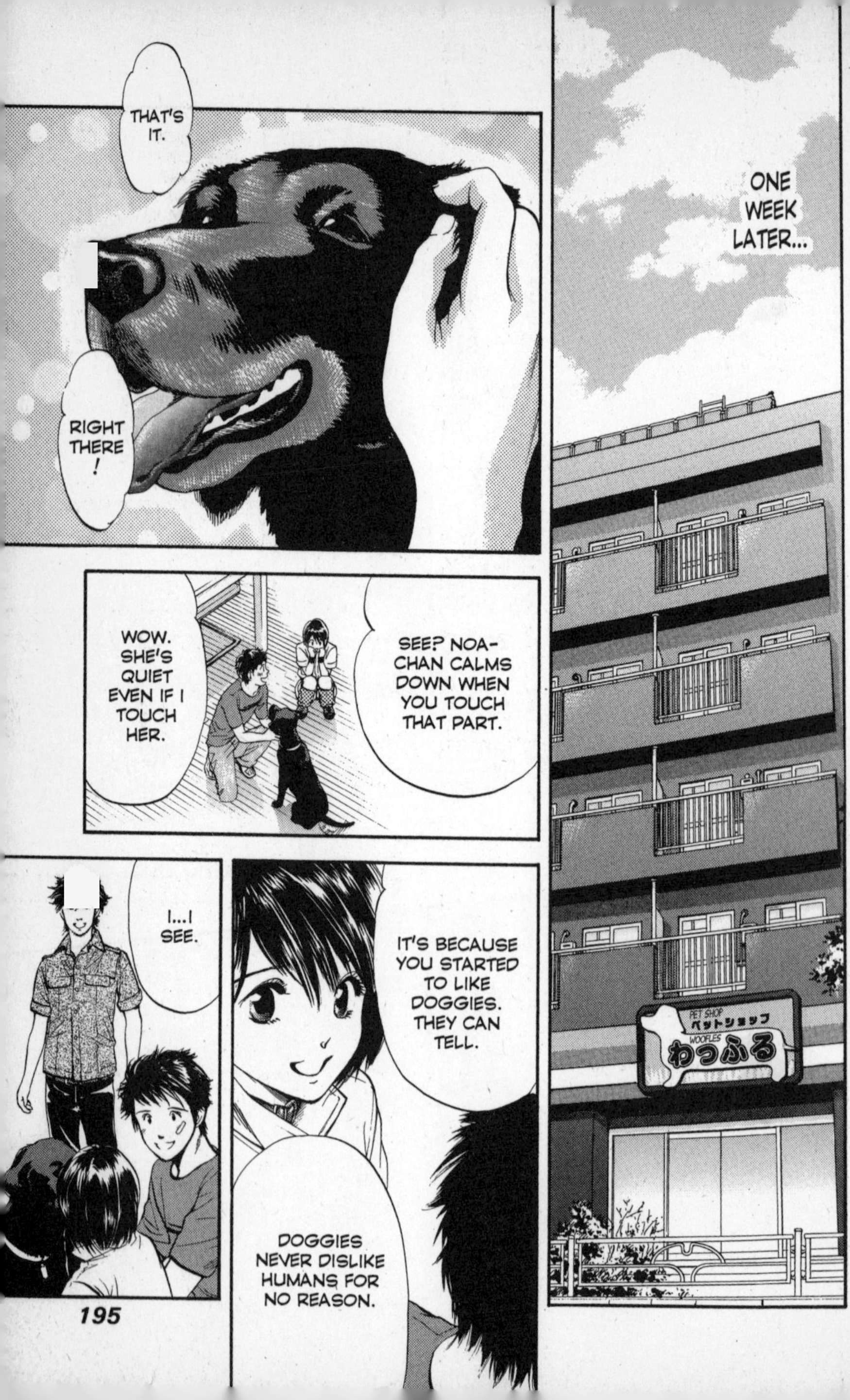
ONE WEEK LATER...
PET SHOP
ペットショップ
WOOFLES
わっふる
THAT'S IT.
RIGHT THERE!
SEE? NOA-CHAN CALMS DOWN WHEN YOU TOUCH THAT PART.
WOW. SHE'S QUIET EVEN IF I TOUCH HER.
IT'S BECAUSE YOU STARTED TO LIKE DOGGIES. THEY CAN TELL.
DOGGIES NEVER DISLIKE HUMANS FOR NO REASON.
I...I SEE.

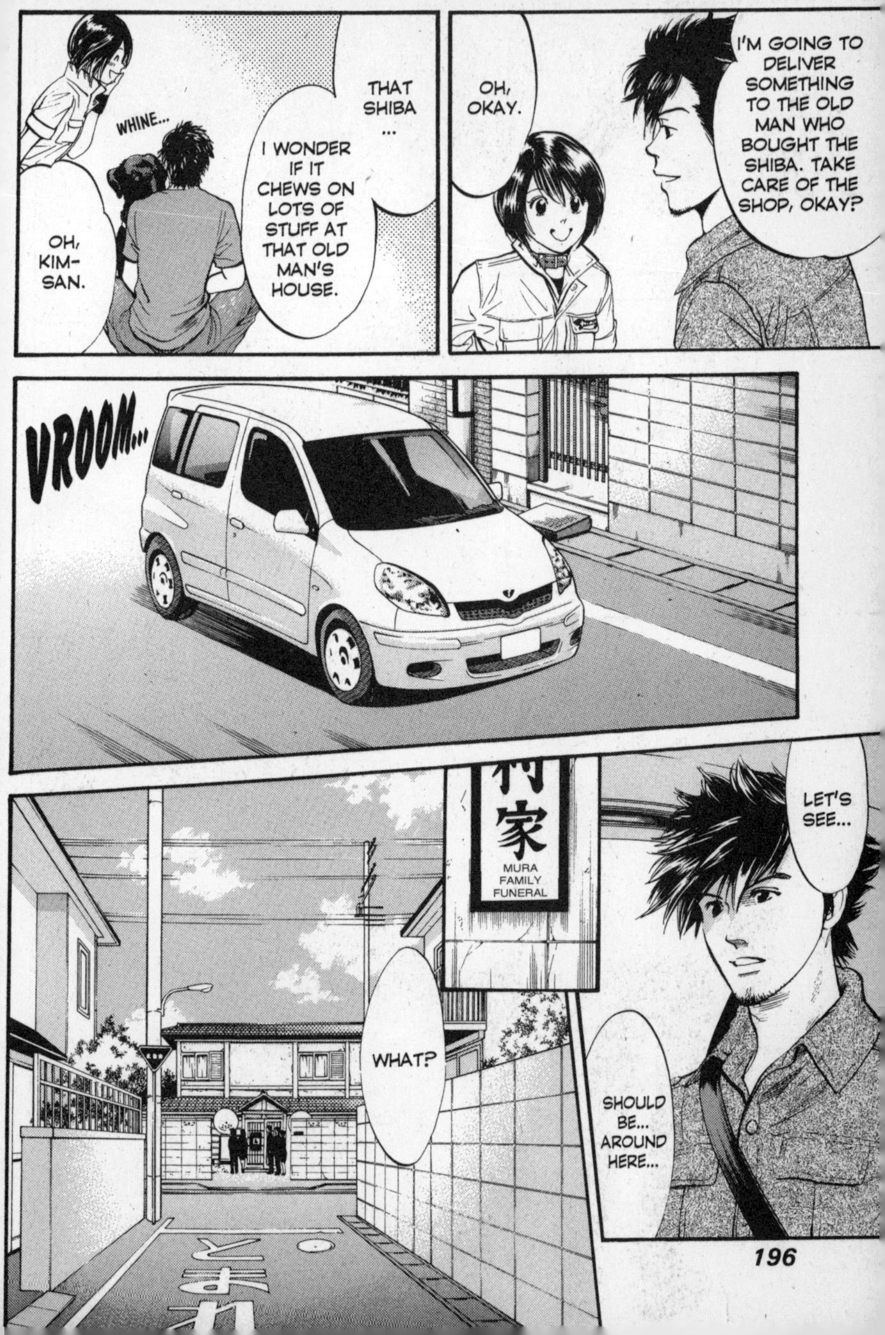
I'M GOING TO DELIVER SOMETHING TO THE OLD MAN WHO BOUGHT THE SHIBA. TAKE CARE OF THE SHOP, OKAY?
OH, OKAY.
THAT SHIBA ... I WONDER IF IT CHEWS ON LOTS OF STUFF AT THAT OLD MAN'S HOUSE.
WHINE...
OH, KIM-SAN.
VROOM...
LET'S SEE...
SHOULD BE... AROUND HERE...
家
MURA FAMILY FUNERAL
WHAT?

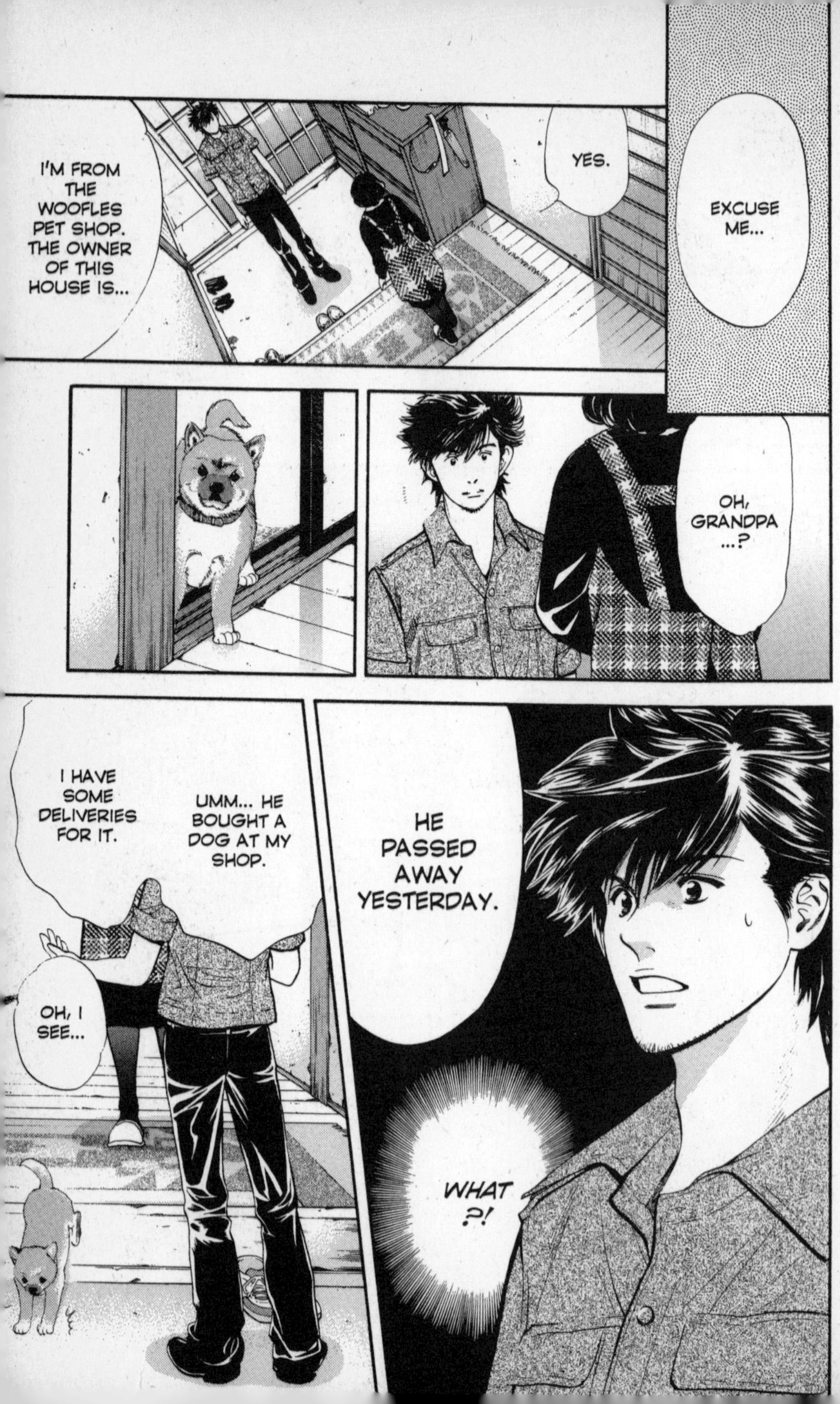

EXCUSE ME...
YES.
I'M FROM THE WOOFLES PET SHOP. THE OWNER OF THIS HOUSE IS...
OH, GRANDPA ...?
HE PASSED AWAY YESTERDAY.
WHAT ?!
UMM... HE BOUGHT A DOG AT MY SHOP.
I HAVE SOME DELIVERIES FOR IT.
OH, I SEE...

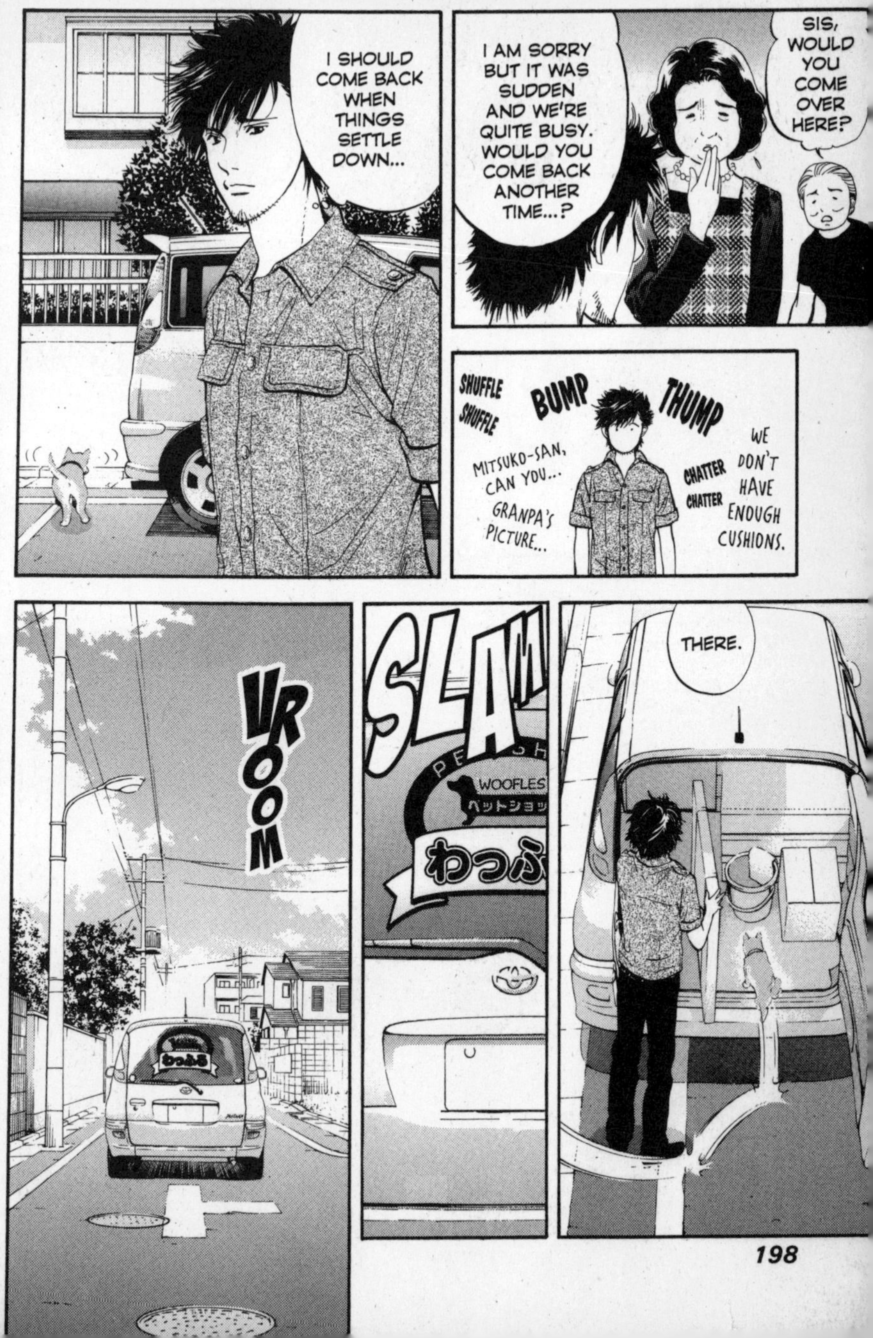
SIS, WOULD YOU COME OVER HERE?
I AM SORRY BUT IT WAS SUDDEN AND WE'RE QUITE BUSY. WOULD YOU COME BACK ANOTHER TIME...?
THUMP
WE DON'T HAVE ENOUGH CUSHIONS.
CHATTER CHATTER
BUMP
MITSUKO-SAN, CAN YOU...
GRANPA'S PICTURE...
SHUFFLE SHUFFLE
I SHOULD COME BACK WHEN THINGS SETTLE DOWN...
THERE.
SLAM
WOOFLES
ペットショッ
わっふ
VROOM

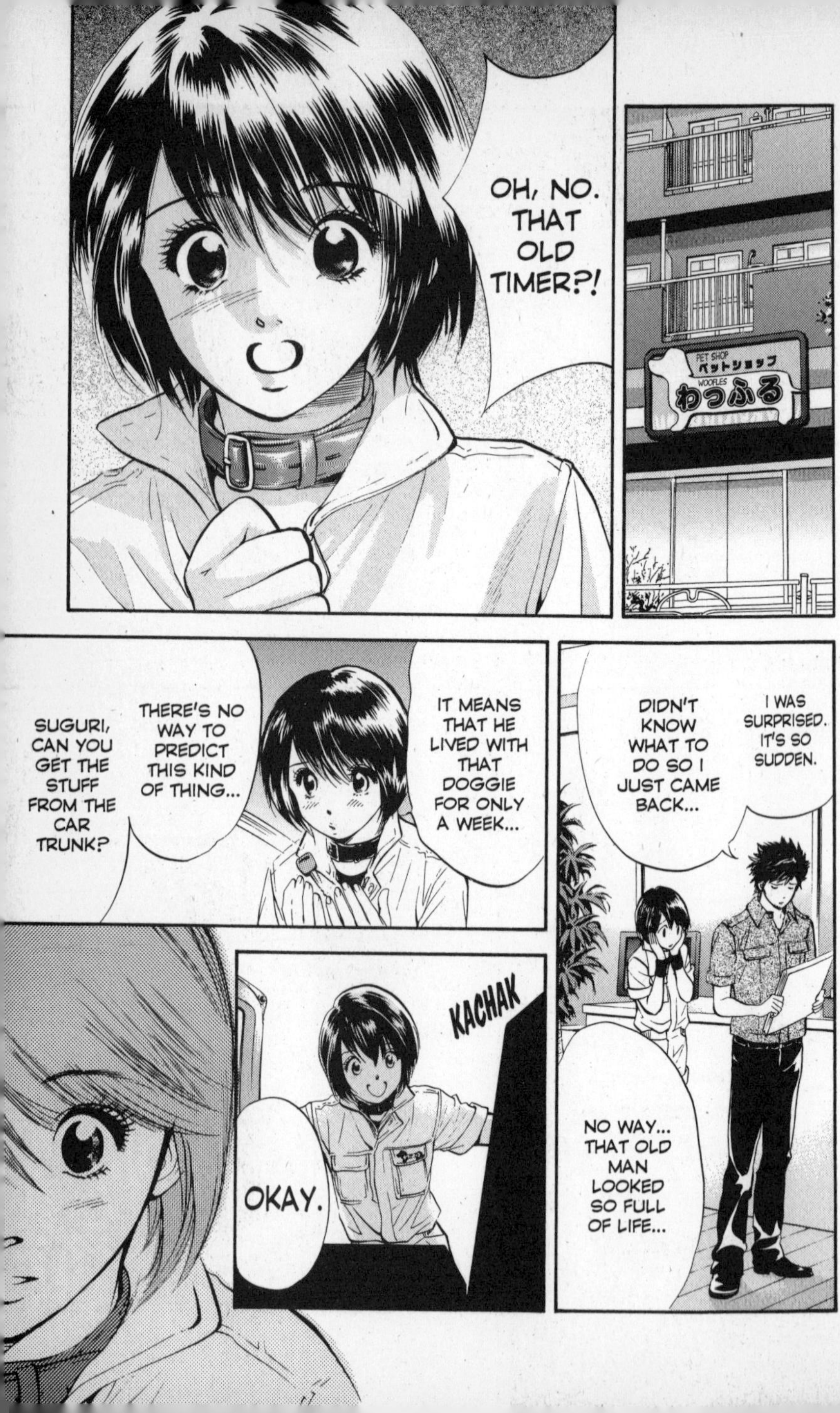
PET SHOP
ペットショップ
WOOFLES
わっふる
OH, NO. THAT OLD TIMER?!
I WAS SURPRISED. IT'S SO SUDDEN.
DIDN'T KNOW WHAT TO DO SO I JUST CAME BACK...
NO WAY... THAT OLD MAN LOOKED SO FULL OF LIFE...
IT MEANS THAT HE LIVED WITH THAT DOGGIE FOR ONLY A WEEK...
THERE'S NO WAY TO PREDICT THIS KIND OF THING...
SUGURI, CAN YOU GET THE STUFF FROM THE CAR TRUNK?
KACHAK
OKAY.

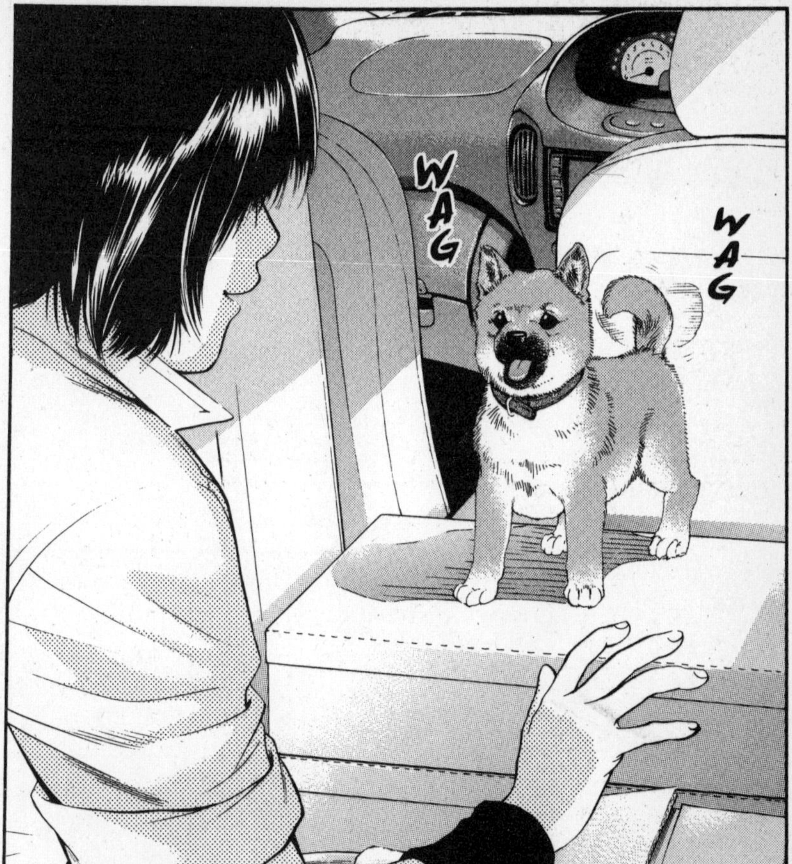
WAG
WAG
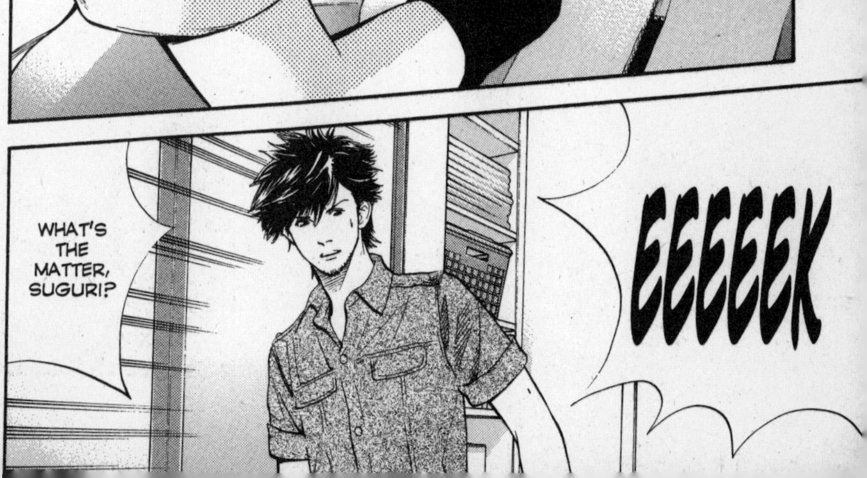
EEEEEK
WHAT'S THE MATTER, SUGURI!?

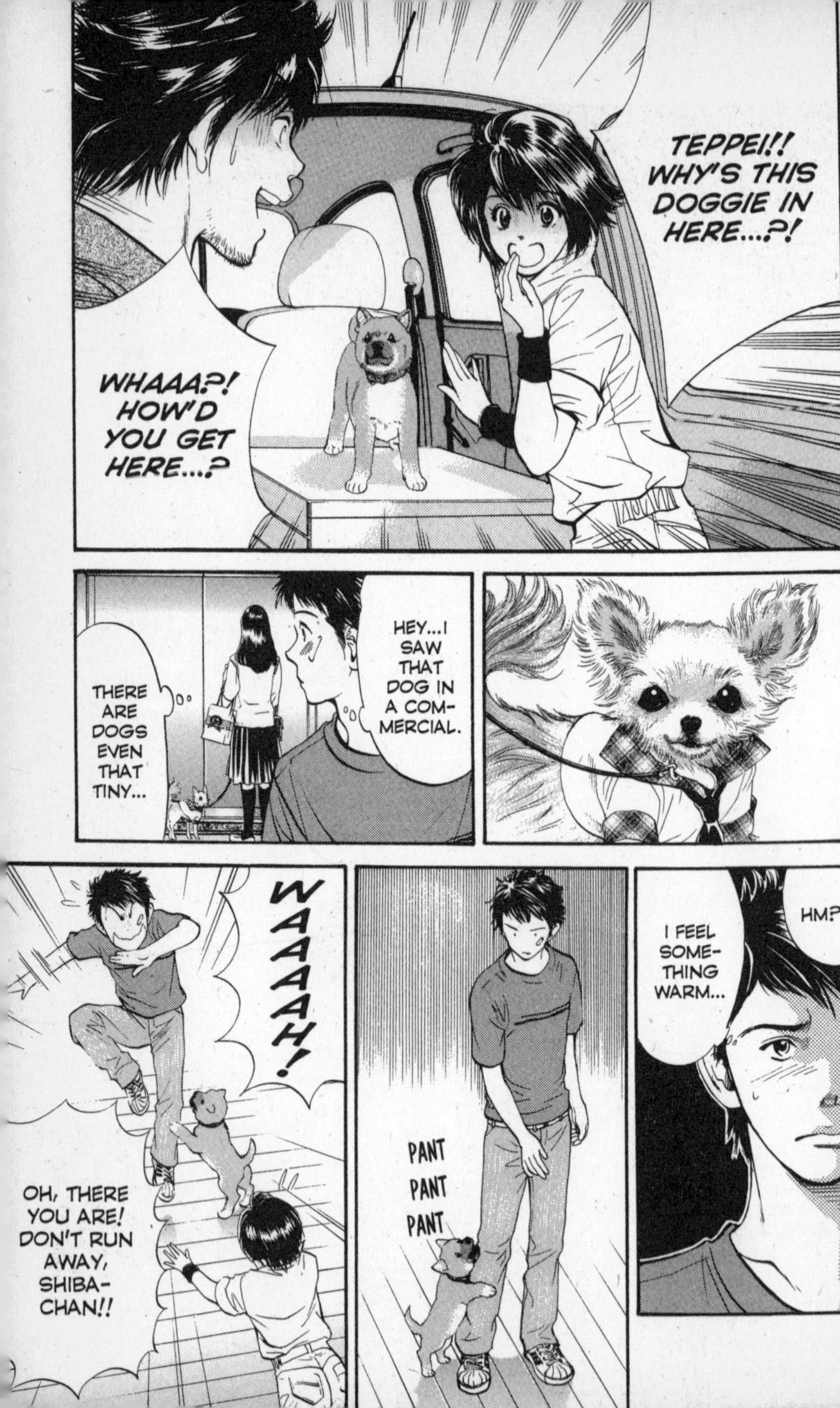
TEPPEI!! WHY'S THIS DOGGIE IN HERE...?!
WHAAA?! HOW'D YOU GET HERE...?
HEY...I SAW THAT DOG IN A COM-MERCIAL.
THERE ARE DOGS EVEN THAT TINY...
HM?
I FEEL SOME-THING WARM...
PANT PANT PANT
WAAAAAH!
OH, THERE YOU ARE! DON'T RUN AWAY, SHIBA-CHAN!!

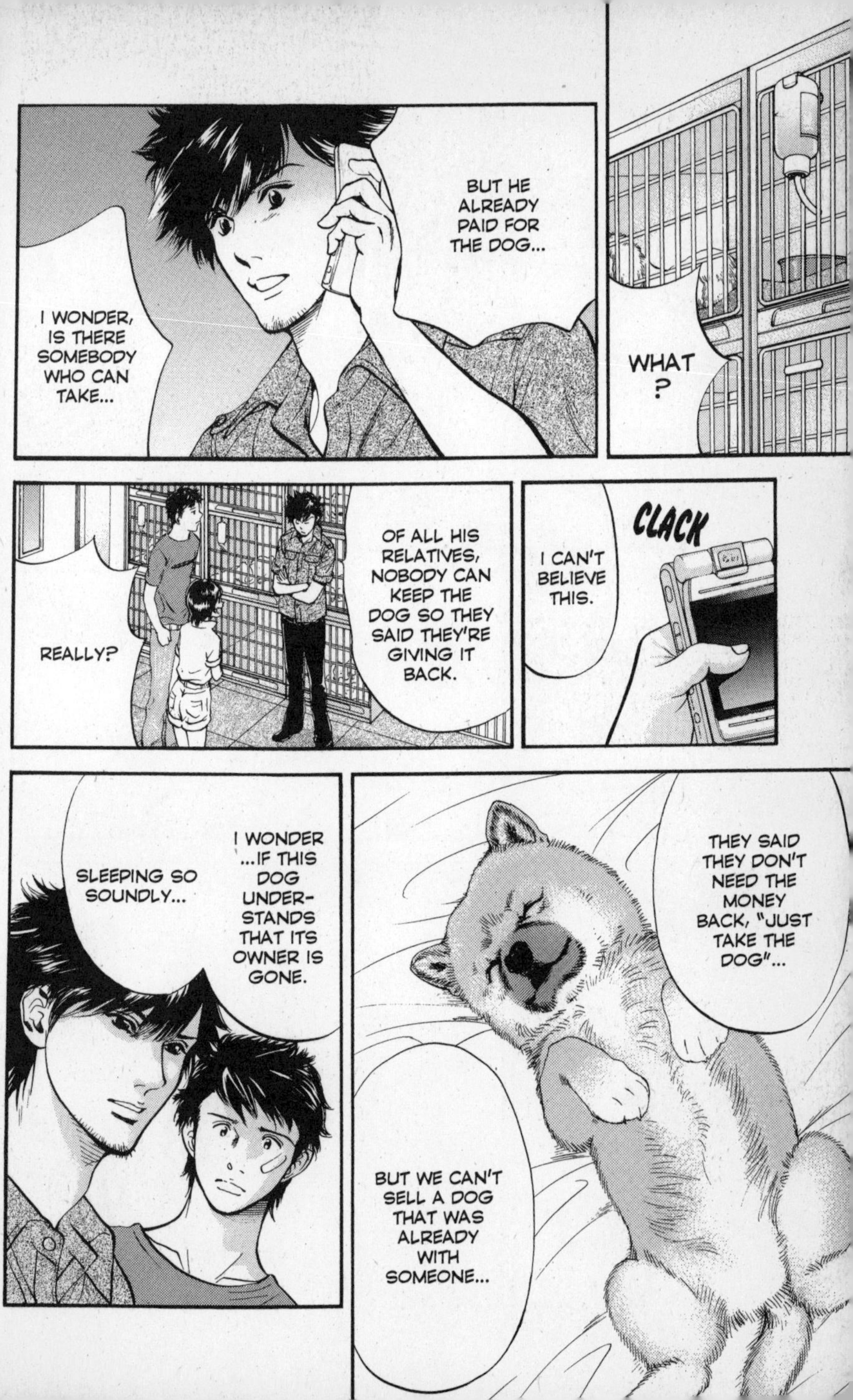
WHAT ?
BUT HE ALREADY PAID FOR THE DOG...
I WONDER, IS THERE SOMEBODY WHO CAN TAKE...
CLACK
I CAN'T BELIEVE THIS.
OF ALL HIS RELATIVES, NOBODY CAN KEEP THE DOG SO THEY SAID THEY'RE GIVING IT BACK.
REALLY?
THEY SAID THEY DON'T NEED THE MONEY BACK, "JUST TAKE THE DOG"...
BUT WE CAN'T SELL A DOG THAT WAS ALREADY WITH SOMEONE...
I WONDER ...IF THIS DOG UNDER-STANDS THAT ITS OWNER IS GONE.
SLEEPING SO SOUNDLY...

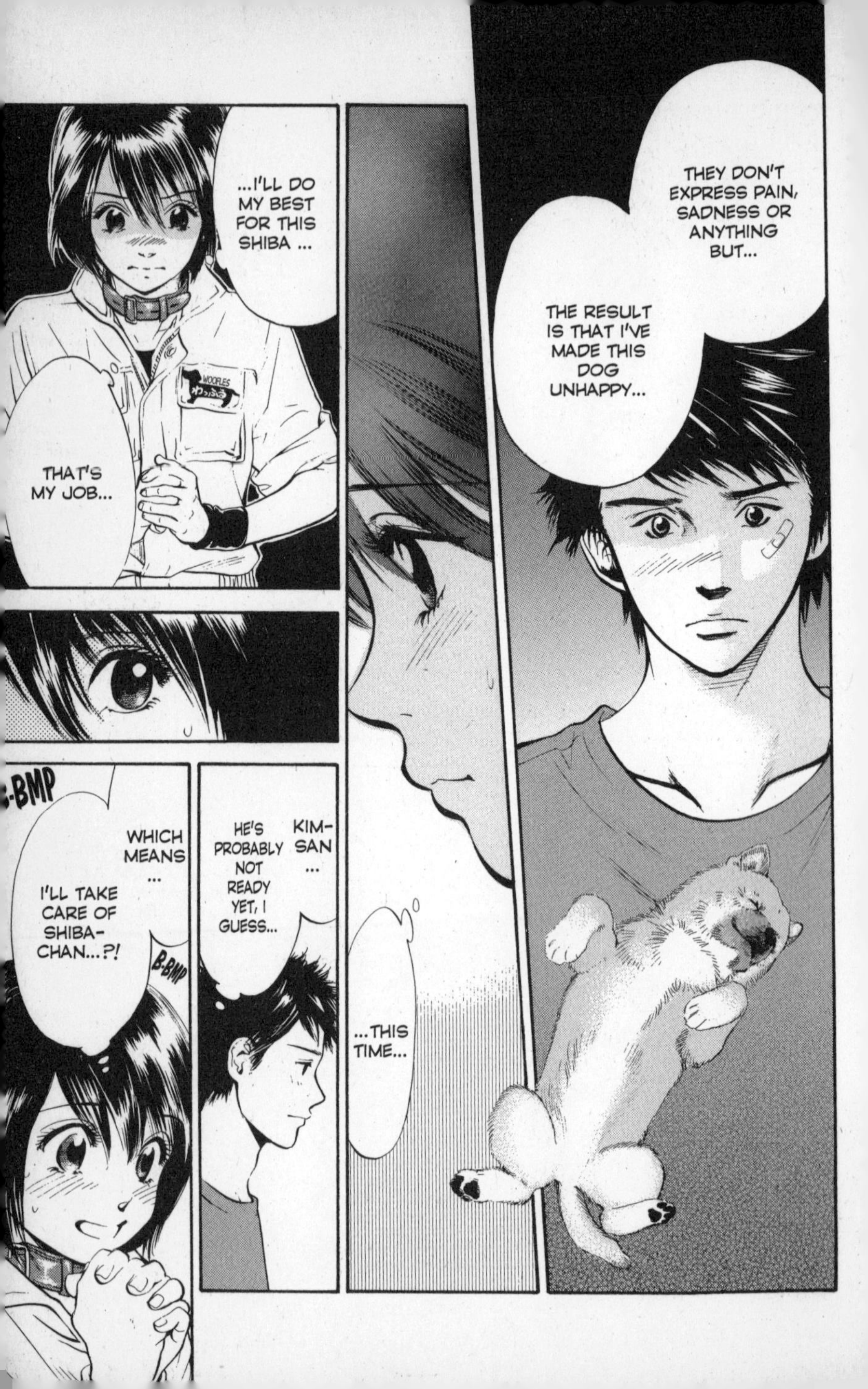
THEY DON'T EXPRESS PAIN, SADNESS OR ANYTHING BUT...
THE RESULT IS THAT I'VE MADE THIS DOG UNHAPPY...
...THIS TIME...
...I'LL DO MY BEST FOR THIS SHIBA ...
THAT'S MY JOB...
KIM-SAN ...
HE'S PROBABLY NOT READY YET, I GUESS...
B-BMP
WHICH MEANS ...
I'LL TAKE CARE OF SHIBA-CHAN...?!
B-BMP

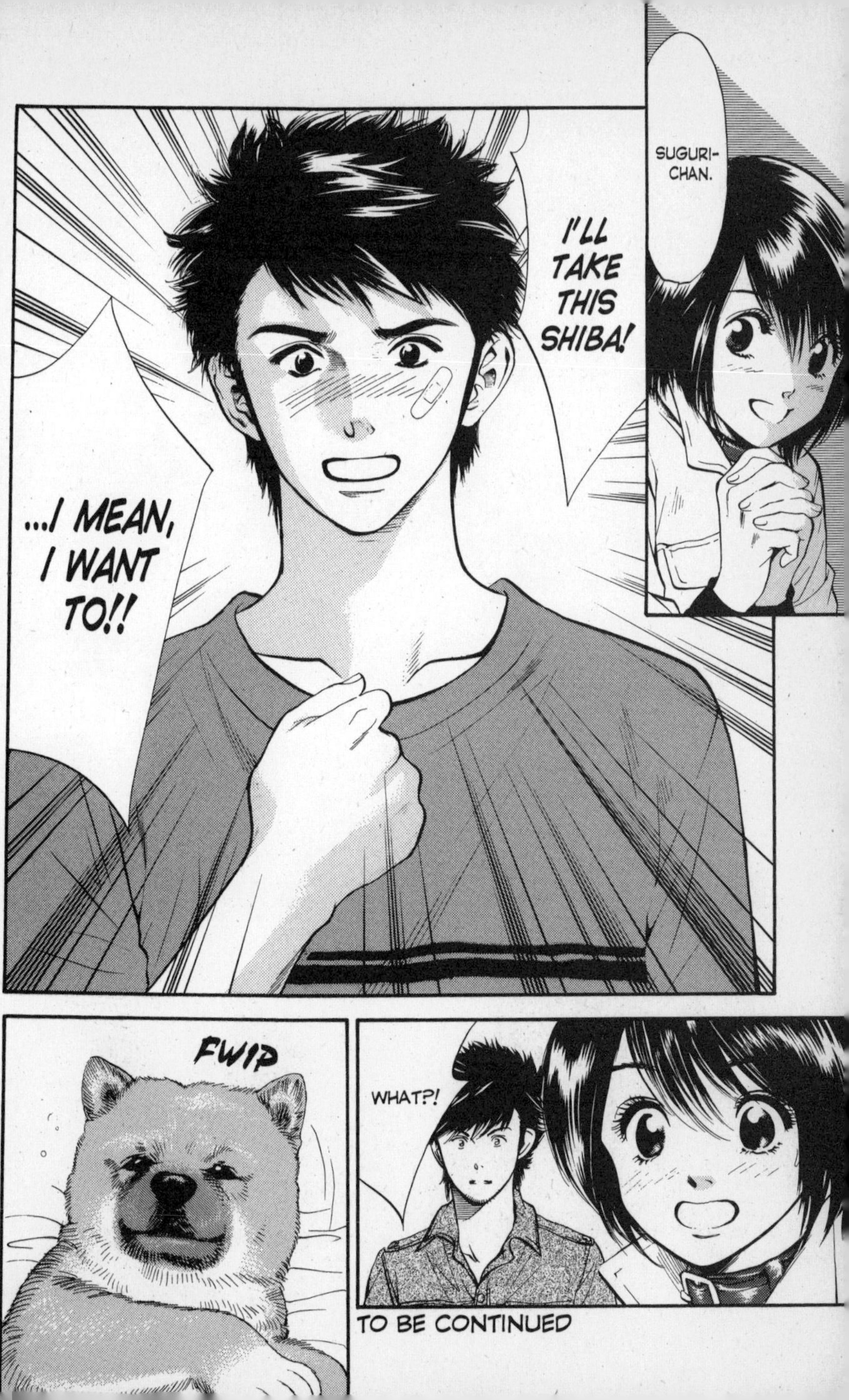
SUGURI-CHAN.
I'LL TAKE THIS SHIBA!
...I MEAN, I WANT TO!!
WHAT?!
FWIP
TO BE CONTINUED

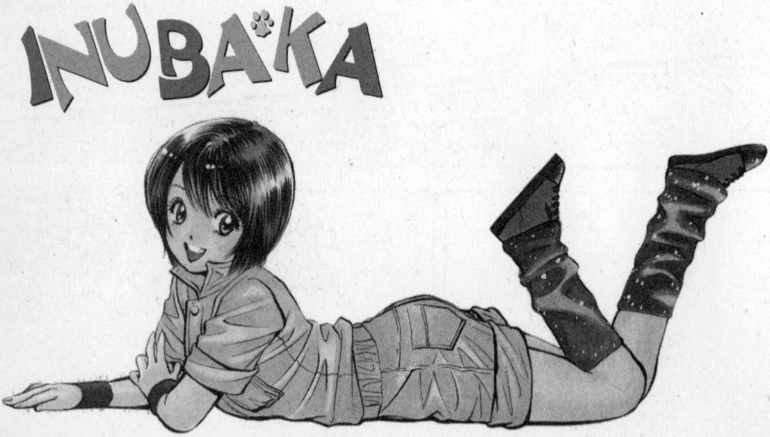
INUBAKA

INUBAKA

Everybody's Crazy for Dogs!

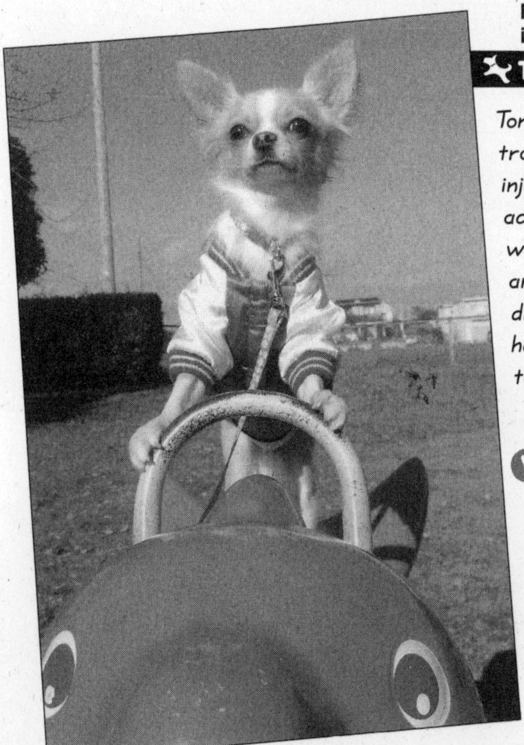

From Kawakami-san in the Tochigi prefecture:

Tono-kun (Chihuahua)

Tono-kun has lots of trouble, getting sick and injured a lot. He usually acts like a big baby, but when he fell off the bed and broke a bone he didn't make a sound until he got to the vet. Very tough. Get well soon!

Yukiya Sakura

You never know what dogs will do next... That jacket really suits him.

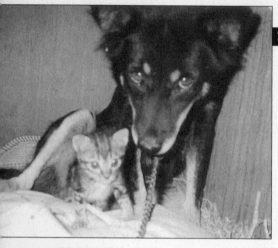

From Shimizu-san (a mother that's crazy for dogs and cats) in the Hiroshima prefecture:

🐾Ran-chan (Mixed breed)

Ran-chan came from a health care center and had lived with cats, so she sometimes acts like a cat. After taking a poo, this one kicks sand over it with its hind legs. She's a brave and gentle mom who takes in stray cats and raises them.

Yukiya Sakura Lovely spot eyebrows, aren't they?!
Mom is strong, too!! (laugh)

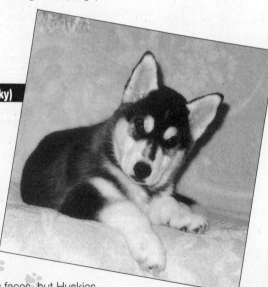

From MK-san in the Chiba prefecture:

🐾Ami-chan (Siberian Husky)

Ami-chan is a Siberian Husky who was born at my house. In spite of his strong face, he's so afraid when visitors come that he runs and hides in the bathroom!

Yukiya Sakura

They have tough-looking faces, but Huskies are nice. Take care and grow healthy!

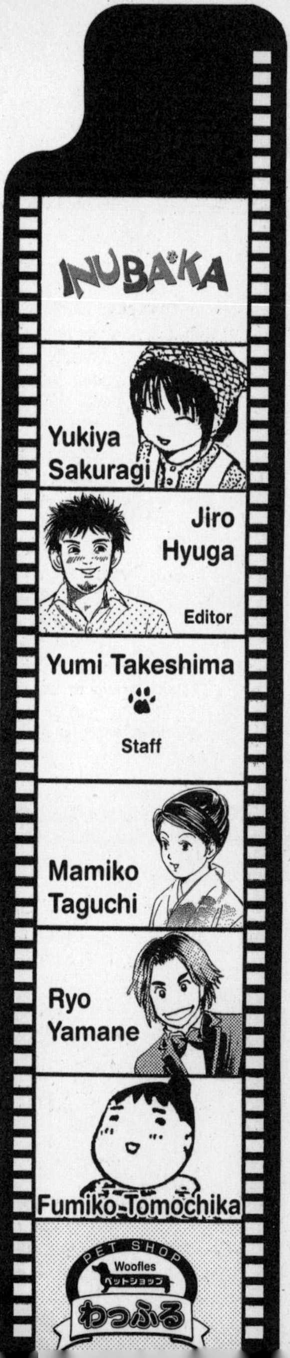
INUBA*KA
Yukiya Sakuragi
Jiro Hyuga
Editor
Yumi Takeshima
Staff
Mamiko Taguchi
Ryo Yamane
Fumiko Tomochika
PET SHOP
Woofles
ペットショップ
わっふる

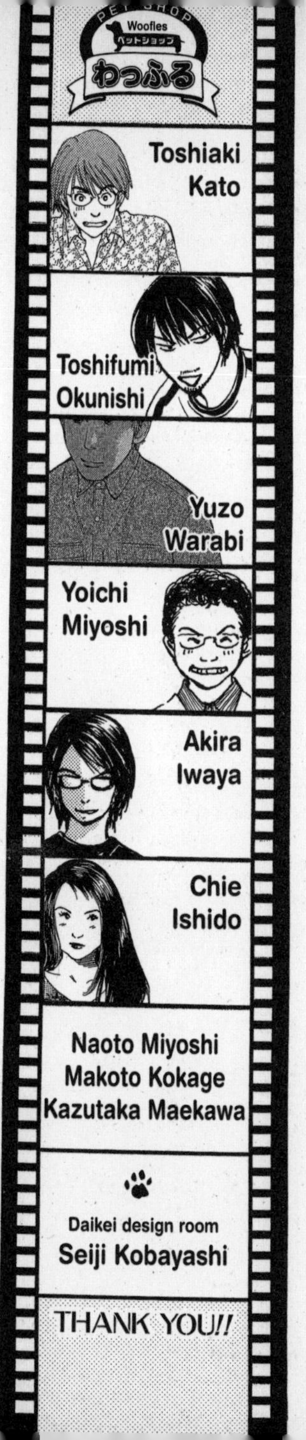
PET SHOP
Woofles
ペットショップ
わっふる
Toshiaki Kato
Toshifumi Okunishi
Yuzo Warabi
Yoichi Miyoshi
Akira Iwaya
Chie Ishido
Naoto Miyoshi
Makoto Kokage
Kazutaka Maekawa
Daikei design room
Seiji Kobayashi
THANK YOU!!

Inubaka
Crazy for Dogs
Vol. #2
VIZ Media Edition

Story and Art by
Yukiya Sakuragi

Translation/Hidemi Hachitori, Honyaku Center Inc.
English Adaptation/Ian Reid and John Werry, Honyaku Center Inc.
Touch-up Art & Lettering/Kelle Han
Cover and Interior Design/Hidemi Sahara
Editor/Ian Robertson

Managing Editor/Annette Roman
Editorial Director/Elizabeth Kawasaki
Editor in Chief/Alvin Lu
Sr. Director of Acquisitions/Rika Inouye
Sr. VP of Marketing/Liza Coppola
Exec. VP of Sales & Marketing/John Easum
Publisher/Hyoe Narita

Printed in the U.S.A.

Published by VIZ Media, LLC
P.O. Box 77010
San Francisco, CA 94107

10 9 8 7 6 5 4 3 2 1
First printing, April 2007

www.viz.com
store.viz.com

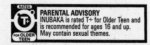

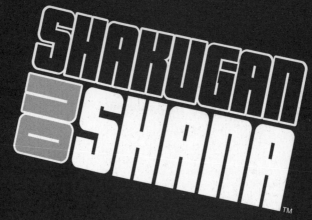
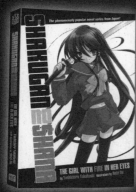
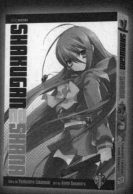

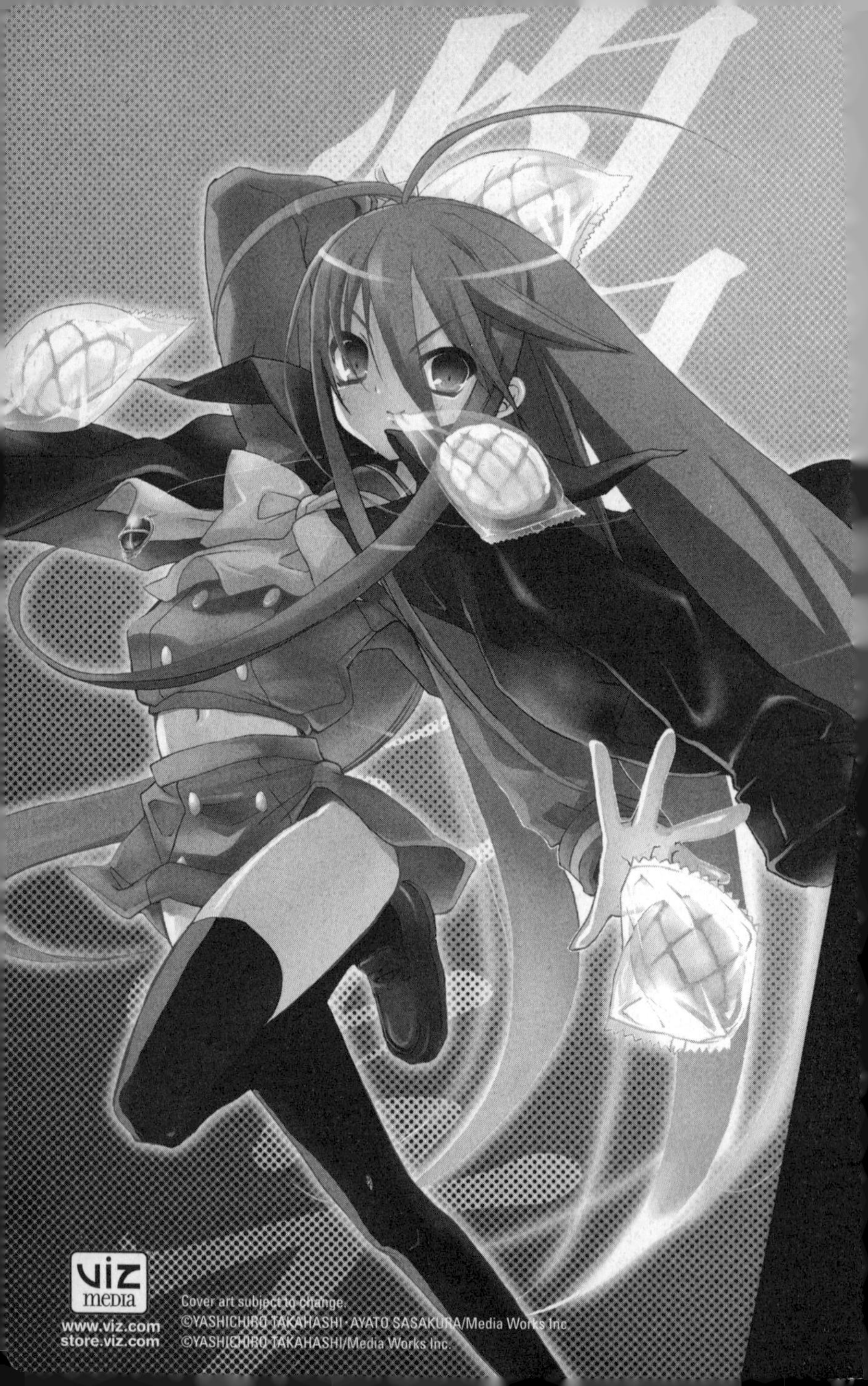

viz media
www.viz.com
store.viz.com
Cover art subject to change.
©YASHICHIRO TAKAHASHI · AYATO SASAKURA/Media Works Inc.
©YASHICHIRO TAKAHASHI/Media Works Inc.

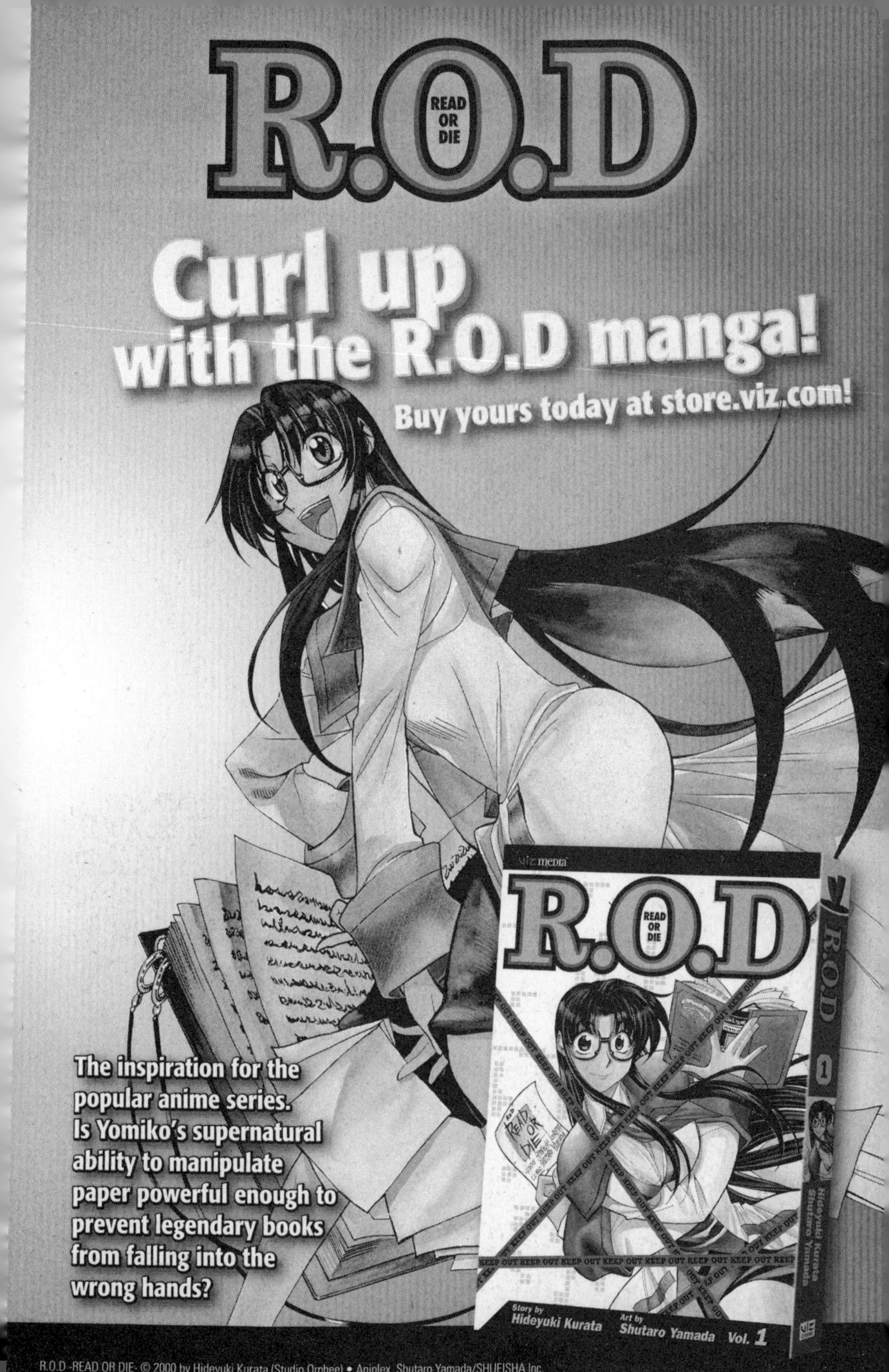

R.O.D
READ OR DIE
Curl up with the R.O.D manga!
Buy yours today at store.viz.com!
The inspiration for the popular anime series. Is Yomiko's supernatural ability to manipulate paper powerful enough to prevent legendary books from falling into the wrong hands?
viz media
R.O.D
READ OR DIE
KEEP OUT KEEP OUT KEEP OUT KEEP OUT KEEP OUT KEEP OUT
Story by Hideyuki Kurata
Art by Shutaro Yamada
Vol. 1

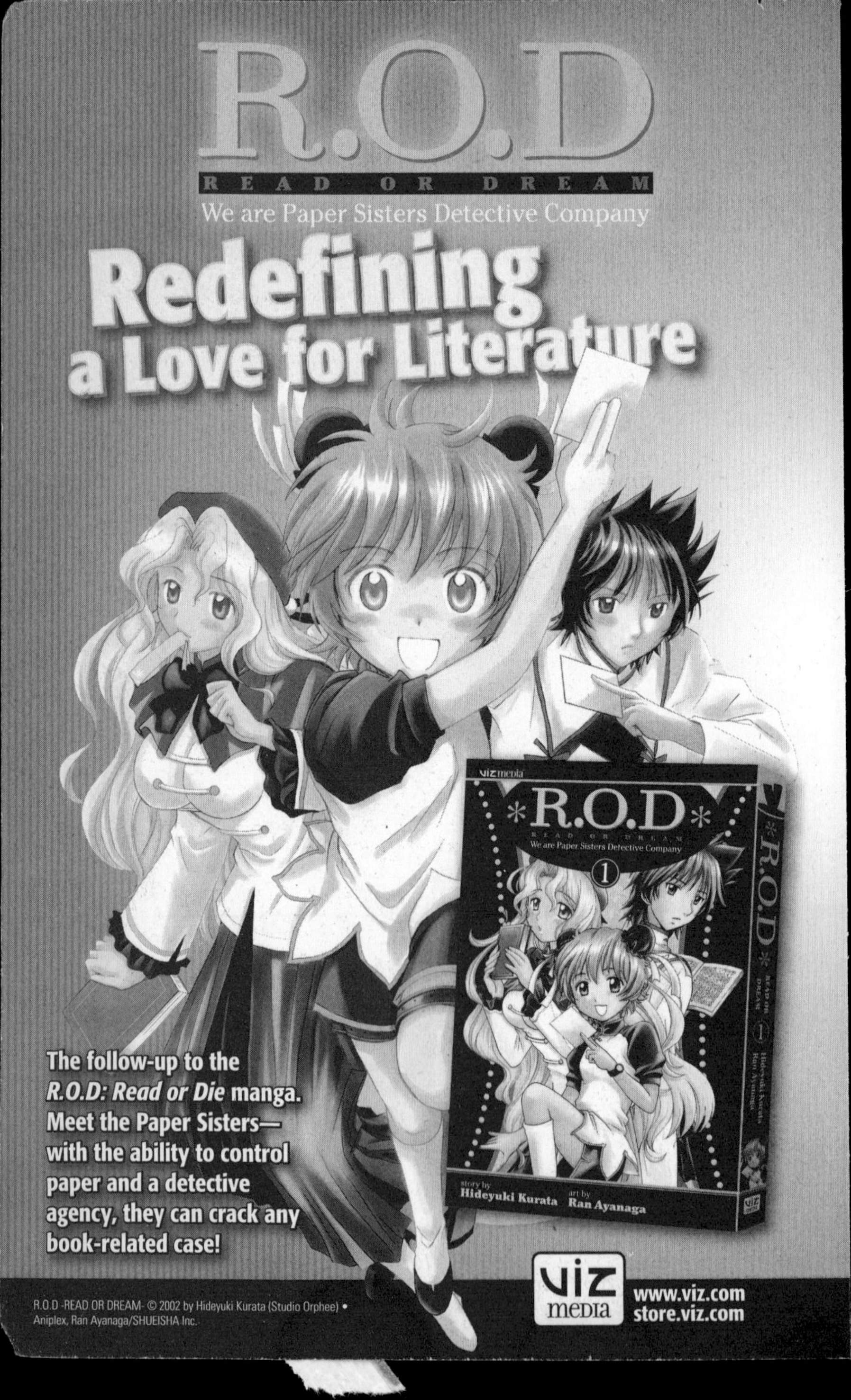
R.O.D
READ OR DREAM
We are Paper Sisters Detective Company
Redefining a Love for Literature
viz media
R.O.D
READ OR DREAM
We are Paper Sisters Detective Company
1
story by Hideyuki Kurata
art by Ran Ayanaga
The follow-up to the R.O.D: Read or Die manga. Meet the Paper Sisters—with the ability to control paper and a detective agency, they can crack any book-related case!
viz media
www.viz.com
store.viz.com
R.O.D -READ OR DREAM- © 2002 by Hideyuki Kurata (Studio Orphee) • Aniplex, Ran Ayanaga/SHUEISHA Inc.

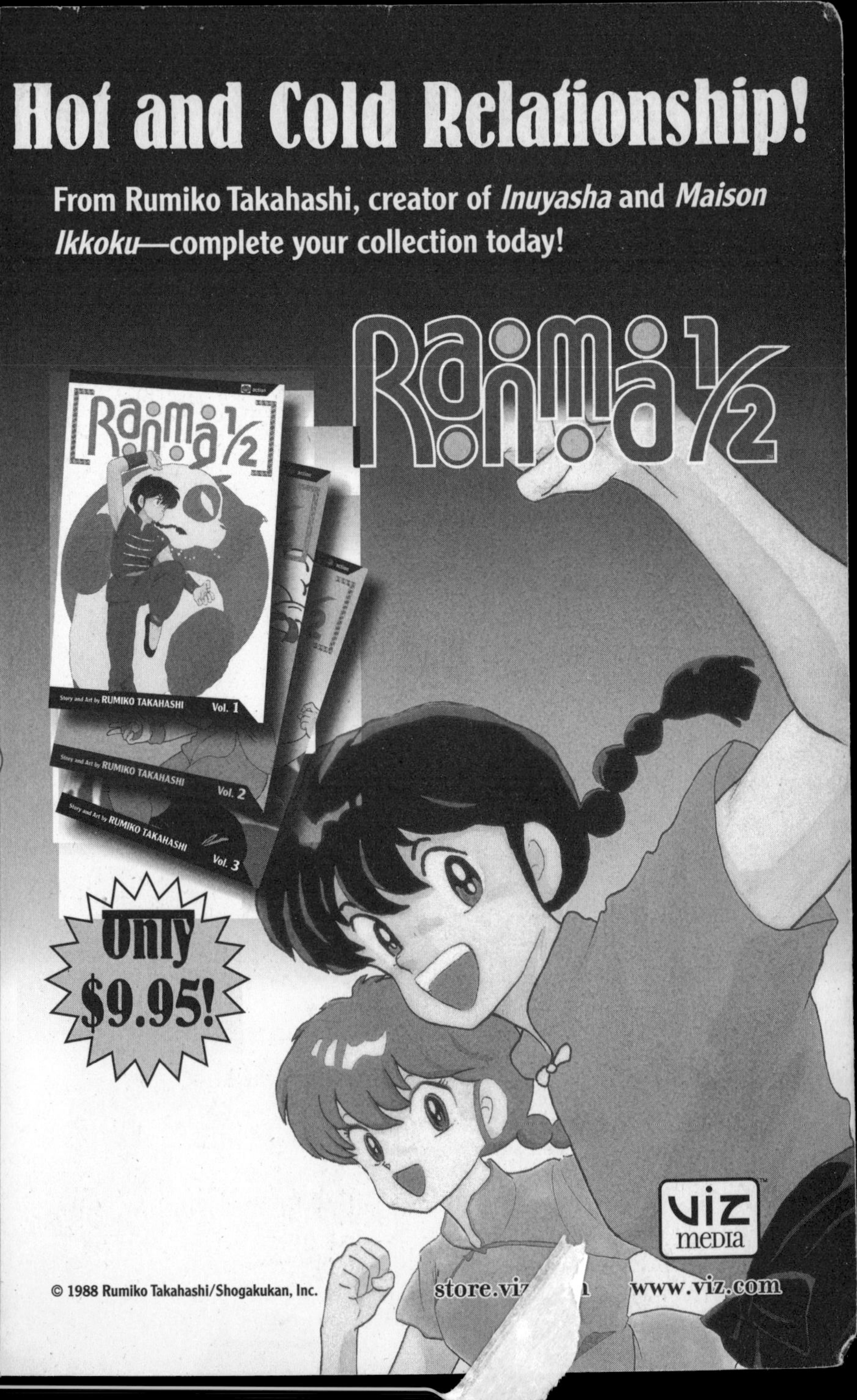
Hot and Cold Relationship!
From Rumiko Takahashi, creator of *Inuyasha* and *Maison Ikkoku*—complete your collection today!
Ranma 1/2
Ranma 1/2
Story and Art by RUMIKO TAKAHASHI Vol. 1
Story and Art by RUMIKO TAKAHASHI Vol. 2
Story and Art by RUMIKO TAKAHASHI Vol. 3
Only $9.95!
VIZ MEDIA
© 1988 Rumiko Takahashi/Shogakukan, Inc.
store.viz
www.viz.com

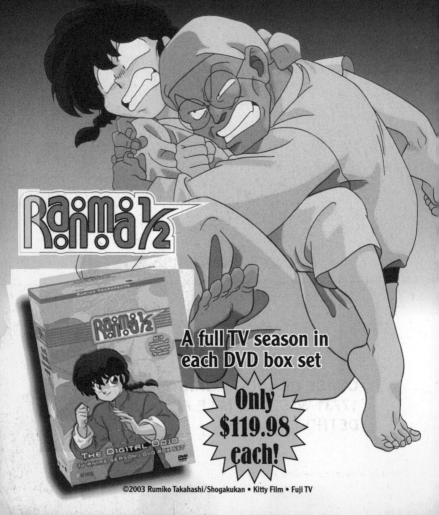

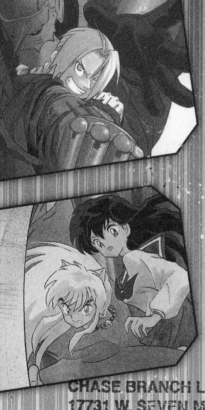

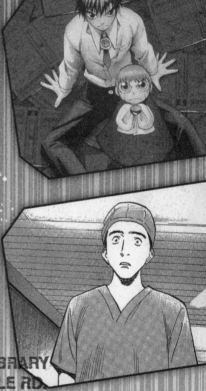

HELP US MAKE THE MANGA
YOU LOVE BETTER!

FULLMETAL ALCHEMIST © Hiromu Arakawa/SQUARE ENIX INUYASHA © 1997 Rumiko TAKAHASHI/Shogakukan Inc.
NAOKI URASAWA'S MONSTER © 1995 Naoki URASAWA Studio Nuts/Shogakukan Inc. ZATCH BELL! © 2001 Makoto RAIKU/Shogakukan Inc.